Stumps & Cranks

D0838824

Sonia Sanghani

Stumps & Cranks

An Introduction to Amputee Cycling

Meyer & Meyer Sport

Dedicated to amputees, such as Paul Jesson New Zealand, as well as the many amputees featured in this book. Truly inspirational.

British Library Cataloguing in Publication Data

A catalogue record for this book is available from the British Library

Stumps & Cranks. An Introduction to Amputee Cycling

Maidenhead: Meyer & Meyer Sport (UK) Ltd., 2016

ISBN 978-1-78255-088-4

© 2016 by Meyer & Meyer Sport (UK) Ltd.

Aachen, Auckland, Beirut, Cairo, Cape Town, Dubai, Hägendorf, Hong Kong,

Indianapolis, Manila, New Delhi, Singapore, Sydney, Tehran, Vienna

Member of the World Sport Publishers' Association (WSPA)

Manufacturing: Print Consult GmbH, München

E-Mail: info@m-m-sports.com

www.m-m-sports.com

Contents

Made of Beauty

An excerpt from *Heart on the Mountain* by leg amputee, **Philip Sheridan,**
UK, 2013. ISBN 978-1-291-61909-6. www.philip-sheridan.com/p/books.html

Made of land
Of sky
Of sun, moon and stars.

Made of wind,
Of cloud
Of mist, rain and snow.

Made of trees,
Of flowers
Of all things green.

All things
Made beautiful.

Wheel Men 2001. Watercolour by Marcy Tatge Coal Creek Canyon, Colorado.

Reproduced with the kind permission of Steve Stevens, USA, **www.goldenoldy.org**.

Coal Creek Canyon is situated in the Rocky Mountain region of Colorado, USA. The Coal Creek Canyon Park has many natural resources and habitats for wildlife. Rare, protected species, such as the Preble's meadow jumping mouse and small numbers of trout, can be found. There is also habitat for elk, bobcat, deer, and mountain lions. Plants and vegetation close to a natural water source provides food and habitat for fish and wildlife of the park as well as protects the soil from water erosion. Visit jeffco.us/parks/parks-and-trails/coal-creek-canyon-park for information on parks and trails of interest if cycling in the USA.

Introduction

Being an amputee does not necessarily mean you cannot ride a bicycle. There are various sorts of amputations (leg and arm) and lots of different bicycle solutions available so you, too, can enjoy the joy and freedom of cycling. After reading this book, you might decide to be a fair-weather leisure cyclist only. You might decide to alternate between using a car, bicycle, bus, or train on different days for different types of journeys. Or you could discover that you are far more adventurous than that, happy to go out in all kinds of weather, day or night, on a variety of different types of bicycles. Wherever your amputee cycling journey takes you, this book should, at least, help you to think about getting started.

Navigating the Book

This book is split into 14 chapters designed to focus on one specific area at a time, and you can read these in any order, depending on your needs. There is a practical section of activities at the end of each chapter for you to try. At each point, where necessary, the different aspects of each amputation (e.g., arm, leg, or combination) will be addressed so the book remains relevant to as many amputees as possible. Chapters will include information for children where applicable. We have tried to ensure a good balance between text, illustrations, and amputee experiences, and there will be plenty of suggestions as to further reading material.

Chapter 1: Why Cycle If You Are an Amputee?—Reasons for amputations and why it is felt that cycling is beneficial to amputees.

Chapter 2: About Prosthetics—Illustrates new developments in prosthetics design that enable amputees to cycle at high performance levels.

Chapter 3: Understanding Bike Parts—A familiarization of the different parts of the bike.

Chapter 4: Bike Choices—All the different cycling possibilities, such as hand cycles, recumbent, tricycles, side by sides, tandems, two-wheelers, unicycles, and more.

Chapter 5: Necessary and Useful Cycling Gear—Clothing and accessories required for different cycling journeys.

Chapter 6: Cycling Basics, Part I—Getting on, getting off, pedaling, braking, balancing, and steering.

Chapter 7: Cycling Basics, Part II—Turning corners, uphill, downhill, standing on pedals, and falling.

Chapter 8: Choosing Routes and Planning Your Journey—Navigation, route planning, safety and first aid issues, essentials to take with you and some good basic beginner's cycling routes (traffic free) around the world to try out while on vacation.

Chapter 9: Nutrition Plan—The importance of ensuring an adequate nutrient balance and sufficient calories on a daily basis to maintain a high enough energy level for cycling and other daily activities.

Chapter 10: Training Plan—The warm-up, cool-down, balance exercises, core exercises and general fitness exercises that make cycling with prosthetics easier.

Chapter 11: Basic Bike Maintenance—Basic pre-ride bike checks as well as the steps to undertake when changing a tire, repairing a flat, cleaning your bike, and when to seek out assistance from a bike repair shop.

Chapter 12: Common Injuries and Stump Care—The importance of looking after your stumps post amputation and how to deal with basic cycling and stump-related injuries (e.g., cuts, bruises, and broken bones).

Chapter 13: Expert Stuff , Part I—The things that you could do on a bike if you set your mind to it—spin cycling, indoor cycling, spin cycling in water, conquering mountains, mountain biking, cyclocross, BMX, stunt cycling.

Chapter 14: Expert Stuff, Part II—Racing, competitions, cycling in heavy traffic, setting up your own bike shop, cycling charity, cycling tour company, becoming a cycling trainer, and much more.

Chapter 1

Why Cycle If You Are an Amputee?

I am sitting here on a blustery, stormy, wet, and very windy day in the UK, reading about cycling. Why I am doing this? Just reading about it is difficult enough, let alone thinking about actually cycling for real! Especially in this weather and under these conditions—brrrrr!

The mere thought of it is bringing on a hot chocolate moment (or mulled wine for the alcohol drinkers among us) followed by a thawing out session in front of a burning log fire. Seriously, who does this type of activity on a day like this?

The answer to that is—a **lot** of people. Every day, in every city the world over, cyclists take to their bicycles. You can see young and old, men and women, city folk, and students wherever you look, going about their daily business on bicycles. The types of bicycles they use are as varied as they are—mountain bikes, road bikes, tandem bikes and fold-up bikes, bikes for commuting and bikes for fun.

As you look around, though, how often do you spot an amputee cycling? Not often, I expect!

There is no doubt that either *becoming* or being an amputee is not easy. Some amputees are born with limb problems that require amputation at a very early age while others acquire the status through medical surgery at later stages in their life. For all those who felt they were the only ones, read this and weep—at the last count, it was approximately 10 million and rising! Between 0.5 percent and 0.8 percent of global populations are amputees. The current annual rate of amputation is more than 1 million *globally*. That's nearly one every 30 seconds! If those sets of numbers don't make your eyes water, then a good dose of cycling in a brisk headwind may be the ideal challenge for you!

Map of Amputations across some areas of the World

44 in 100,000 Native American Indians annually

6,000 in Haiti Earthquake

1 in 334 Angola

3 in 100,000 Spain
6 in 100,000 Italy
31 in 100,000 Germany

1 in 631 Afghanistan
1 in 987 Iraq

3 in 100,000 Japan

Abdul Qahir, Afghanistan

I was born and live in Kabul. I am amputated below the knee on both the legs. I was 7 years old when I stepped on a mine while fetching food for my family. This incident washed all my dreams and took me to a silent side away from the community and active involvement. It not only gave me bodily injury, but my sentiments, my passion, and my zeal were also severely disrupted. I was in a desperate situation as no hope remained in my life. I had two legs, and both were taken from me. I became deprived of a very necessary and important component of my body. I was maligned and stigmatized by the behaviour of my community toward me. I felt myself in isolation and couldn't forecast what needed to be done to eradicate my problems and restart a normal life in this community.

People started to think of me as a useless and ineffective part of this society and, to speak frankly, as a burden on the community. Since my amputation, I wasn't able to attend school due to my immobility. I wasn't able to commute freely to and from school, but I attended some literacy and numeracy courses organized by Afghan Amputee Bicyclists for Rehabilitation and Recreation (AABRAR). I have a full-time job now where I work as a watchman with some foreigners inside Kabul, Afghanistan. I am able to work freely and earn a reasonable livelihood for my family. I am a permanent member of Afghanistan Paralympic Committee (APC). I am a cyclist for APC and have participated in many national and international games in Athens, Greece, as well as Cycling for Peace in Frankfurt, Germany. I have always participated as a cyclist in the Bicycle and Wheelchair race organized on 3 December (International Day of People with Disability) each year by AABRAR. In the sixth year of this event, I won!

Funny Things Happen on Bikes!

I was in a race, and I was trying something new on my bike leg. My coach says never try anything new on race day, but I ignored it that one time. I came off the bike into transition, and my foot fell off (ha, ha). I was hopping and wobbling around with my bike, trying to make it to my running legs. It was so funny for me, but everyone around was freaking out.

Rajesh Durbal, USA

Armin Köhli, Switzerland (www.tourdarmin.ch)

Armin Köhli, a double below-knee amputee, formalized his racing career by qualifying for the Sydney Olympics in 2000 where he competed against some of the cyclists mentioned in this book. His speciality is long-distance and ultra-distance touring.

Between 2001 and 2003, he cycled hundreds of kilometers in races against able-bodied cyclists. His passion for cycling, active campaigning against landmines, editing, and journalism led him to undertake further fundraising and awareness-raising tours.

In 2004, he raced the Tour d'Afrique, which involved cycling **11,720 kilometers in 99 days**. He came **third** in that tour against able-bodied cyclists. Then came three successive landmine awareness-raising tours: Geneva-Zagreb, 2005; Tour de Suisse, 2006 and Geneva-Dead Sea, 2007, followed by Pacemakers Ride Against Nuclear Weapons in 2008. Along the way, he connected with many cyclists (both able-bodied and disabled), and reports in the media of his tours have made headline news in countries affected by landmine issues. Armin has devoted tremendous zeal and enthusiasm into developing this book.

He hopes it brings as much joy and fun to those reading it as he has when he is cycling. He would highly recommend a good bike ride for any amputee to help them deal with their situation. Once you have read this book, no doubt you will agree!

→ **www.tourdafrique.com**—The foundation donates bicycles to the poorest regions in Africa and India.

→ **www.pace-makers.de**—Campaigning for a world without nuclear weapons.

Funny Things Happen on Bikes!

Preparing for training, I changed the prosthetics (one pair is almost without cosmetics). I put them on, fixed the sleeve, but it didn't feel as comfortable as usual. Something was hurting in one leg. I removed the sleeve and that leg—and discovered a dead mouse inside. Poor thing! Found its way into the leg, but no chance to get out. Too steep and no grip.

Armin Köhli, Switzerland

Why Cycle If You Are an Amputee?

Aside from trauma and war, the majority of amputations are the result of poor blood circulation (vascular disease), diabetes, smoking, and infectious diseases. Amputation can occur at any age, in any country, and, in many cases, is the result of an unpredicted event. The disabling impact of amputation is of grave concern to amputees. Typically, there is a reduced ability to enjoy an adequate quality of life in work-related activities, hobbies, and family life. Losing a limb is often associated with negative grief-like feelings, such as depression, anxiety, anger, or hopelessness. Depression occurs in 21 to 35 percent of amputees as compared to 10 to 15 percent in the general population. Social exclusion associated with disability increases the risk of depression, alcoholism, and other self-harming behaviors. Negative feelings can be counteracted by gentle, low-impact exercises such as cycling. As you focus your energy on rotating the wheels of a bicycle, mood-elevating chemicals (endorphins) such as serotonin are released into your blood stream. Serotonin release is considered to be soothing on your mind and spirit, a natural form of stress relief. Life-changing events such as amputation require you to have a positive, clear frame of mind while working out how to do activities you used to do automatically and without thinking before you became an amputee.

Cycling is often described by those who do it regularly as an exercise that gives you high levels of personal, positive energy. As you ride your bike, your heart learns to work more efficiently to improve your circulation and breathing. The sense of well-being and happiness you get from cycling helps to tackle feelings of depression. There are many different forms—mountain biking, road racing, BMX/cyclocross, and handcycling, to name just a few. For some, it will take the danger, skills, thrills, and spills of mountain biking to meet their expectations of exhilaration. Others may get the same enhancement of mood when they test themselves against the clock and leave the competition behind in a super quick race. Your mood and general energy levels will be affected to differing degrees, depending on the type of cycling you do and the goals you set yourself to achieve while cycling.

Every amputee (of any age) is an individual; some require big challenges and others small challenges. Some are adventurers and innovators, others are not. Testing the limits of possibility has long been the driving force of adventurers and explorers. These elements are visible among many of the examples of real amputees portrayed throughout this book.

Just because you may have lost a limb (or three) does not mean you are not allowed to cycle, can't cycle, or dare not cycle. On the contrary, losing a limb gives you more reason than ever to cycle. The need to develop balance, coordination, and flexibility that cycling facilitates is the same (if not slightly greater) for amputees following limb loss as for the general population.

Cycling in all its forms and disciplines is a highly subjective, personal experience. It is inevitably a social activity that encourages and facilitates the development of strong, close friendships. If you do not like the thought of cycling alone, consider joining a cycling group or club. You might meet lots of different people, and many cycling possibilities become available to you. You could decide to share those enjoyable cycling moments with family, friends, or as a couple. Just using a bicycle for the daily commute in a big, anonymous city will introduce you to other cyclists by default. Eventually, you may like to try pedaling along alone in search of those guilty moments of pleasurable solitude.

Dan Sheret, USA

When I was contacted about contributing to this book, I at first balked at the notion. Life had again changed so much for me that I really did not feel I had much to contribute. The author posed the question of where were all the people today that set so many goals just a few years back. I had to think about that and realized that she was really asking a deeper question about the nature and progression of the stages of change surrounding amputation.

While still unproven, I have a theory that when amputation or other major trauma occurs, the body undergoes a biochemical change. One can liken the change to a prolonged fight or flight response within the body. This could be a reason why one sees so many rising up again and not only return to everyday life after amputation but, as was my case, taking a physical activity to the extreme. To say that an individual is simply overcompensating just does not answer the question.

I was a happy fat little furniture maker going about my life, and the next thing I know I am an amputee, solo riding across the American deserts in July and loving it. I liken my story to the character, Forest Gump. After a great loss, he would run back and forth across a continent for years until one day he just stopped. He was done. As odd and uninformative as it is, that really is about it. Perhaps this biochemical switch turns off, I don't know, but one day you are simply finished with endurance cycling, and you move on. But in the meantime, it can be a time filled with grand adventures, so enjoy it.

I believe it is this fundamental shift in attitude and awareness that has led to the success of so many barriers being broken by those in the sport of amputee cycling. In 2003, I was told on many occasions that what I was trying to do I could not because of my disability. They were right. As long as I accepted my limitation, then I could not do so. My cycling was a way for me to understand my limitation was of my own making and that of the social norm. I, however, decided to go beyond the accepted boundaries and feel whole again. It was a very important part of my life and a great personal achievement at the time. One has lots of time to reflect while cycling, and my time led me to the understanding that once I no longer viewed myself as disabled, I somehow moved beyond the label of being an amputee.

I once held great pride in my being an amputee and achieving all I had done. Today, a decade later, I rarely think of myself in those terms. Perhaps I have achieved the Seven Stages of Grief (according to Elizabeth Kübler-Ross) in terms of my limb loss. Whatever the reason, much of the world of a professional endurance cyclist is behind me. Today,

I am pleased with having returned to school and to teach at a local college. I care for rare and endangered carnivorous plants. I commute 12 miles to work each day by bike and, yes, my right leg never grew back. But in its place is a richness I don't think I would trade for its return. Cycling brought me full circle, and while I am not the same as when I started, I am pretty happy with the results!

An article featuring Dan Sheret and his work can be found at
→ **www.starnewsonline.com/article/20130610/articles/130619970**.

Why Cycle If You Are an Amputee?

Not everyone cycles because it is cheap, quick, easy, helps the environment or keeps them physically healthy. Fundamentally, a lot of cyclists say they cycle simply because *they enjoy it.* They enjoy the freedom, the exhilaration, the tests of courage and endurance, and, most of all, the feeling of well-being and pride that a good bike ride provides. Such pleasurable feelings enhance the cycling experience considerably, making it easier to integrate it as an activity into your existing lifestyle.

Mobility and transportation issues take on greater significance if you are an amputee (especially lower limb). For all the reasons you know or have been told about why you shouldn't cycle, when you ask other amputee cyclists why they ride their bikes, they will cite as many reasons why you should. A bicycle (or its many variations) enables better mobility so you can go outdoors, come into close contact with nature and simply relish the feeling of being alive. Spectacular scenery, fresh air and enchanting wildlife are always an added bonus to every journey of discovery you undertake on a bicycle or its many variations, even in, or close to, a busy city!

If you are not a cyclist (or have never been a cyclist), it can all seem rather perplexing and difficult to understand. To top it all, being a fairly new amputee may make you inclined to put cycling rather low down on your priorities of dealing with the profound psychological effects of undergoing limb amputation. Immersing yourself in the broader elements of cycling, such as experiencing its history and development from a museum visit, attending a display of cycling art or getting involved in festivals or sports events organized by cycling communities, can help you catch that all-important, if as yet elusive, cycling bug! For some it may even require a holiday to a cycle-friendly town or city in countries such as Denmark or Japan to work out how to join in the fun of it all. You will soon discover that leisure cycling is a form of exercise that doesn't involve a high level of skill. It doesn't have to be expensive to do, and it may help you come to terms with your amputation, lose excess weight, and simply feel better.

For children with amputations, cycling should be an integral daily activity as it enables them to be more independent and confident as individuals. Being able to find their way safely to and from school (either with their friends or on their own) encourages children to think and learn about the place they live in for themselves. Involving children with amputation in general childhood activities with other non-amputee children allows them to learn to enjoy each other's company as equals. It is important for your child's social development not to isolate them from others because of your concerns about their disability. The world can cope with it, and so can you!

Different forms of cycling are worth trying as an amputee, and you may interchange between them to various degrees as you progress. The more you cycle, the easier it becomes. Muscles in your body adapt as you become fitter and stronger. You will start to feel better and be able to do more on an everyday basis. This will increase your levels of happiness and satisfaction with your situation, and you will *want* to keep cycling on a more regular basis.

Dory Selinger, USA (www.doryselinger.com)

The wheels of the bike whirl at a dizzying pace. The blur that is Dory Selinger hurtling toward another medal beguiles the crystal-clear memory of what got him there in the first place. It was a typical morning ride with his teammates in 1993 when a car from nowhere slammed into them all, killing his friend, mangling his leg, and placing him in a coma for seven days. Life changed in an instant, but not just in the physical sense, for Selinger. Through the grief and heartache of a lost teammate, through the pain and struggle of an agonizing rehabilitation, one constant, singular focus helped Selinger persevere: the bike.

It was a love for cycling that rescued him from despair, inspired him to regain his strength, and drove him to become something even greater than himself. Selinger is one of America's best-known Paralympic cyclists.

He has claimed repeated national titles in track and road racing and time trial competitions in the Disabled Division at the U.S. Cycling Championships. He has won victories at the 1998 and 2002 World Championships and 1999 and 2001 European Championships. He started this off with winning the gold at the 1996 Paralympic Games in Atlanta, Georgia. He holds two world records as well as every U.S. velodrome record for cyclists in his classification.

→   Re-produced with kind permission by Dory Selinger **www.doryselinger.com**

Funny Things Happen on Bikes

My friend and I went out on a trail near Cwmavon, and time was flying. It had been a bit of a hot day, so we thought we would go out later in the afternoon. When we started, it was a lot later than we thought it was, and we actually came back in darkness. The last half hour of the trail was pitch black—thank god my friend had a head flashlight so we could find our way back, but we totally mistimed that one altogether! What you tend to find is that when you are in forestry trails, once the sun goes down, everything goes dark very quickly due to the density of the trees and shrubbery, so, yes, that was a bit of an experience as well coming out of there in the dark with just one head light between us!   *Jon Pini, UK*

Why Cycle If You Are an Amputee?

The best people to explain in words and actions are the amputees *of all ages* who cycle on lots of different forms of bicycles on a regular basis. In their own words, throughout this book, they will be explaining to you why it is they cycle, how they started and learned, what they find helps them, and lots more. Some of the amputees featured here you may have heard of through their competitive cycling achievements at national or international level, and some may be new to you. They are all, in fact, extraordinary, everyday individuals with immense passion, commitment, and vision. Enjoy reading, and, most of all, enjoy this miniature glimpse into the world of amputee cycling. It really is full of the most amazing and inspiring people you could ever hope to meet!

If you have *never* cycled before (or not considered it before), reading this book may just be the motivation you need to try it out for yourself. You might catch yourself wondering what it would be like to be one of those hyper-cool urban messengers whizzing around the city. Or a high-level racer setting a personal and world best record for others to aspire to, perhaps? Or even find yourself dreaming about cycling around the world on a penny farthing or handcycle. The possibilities are truly endless and achievable with the right attitude and support in place.

As this book seeks to encompass as many possibilities that cycling can bring you either directly or indirectly, here is an article that shows the achievements which many would consider impossible are, in fact, possible. It highlights how innovative and experimental cycling is as a flexible method of transportation. In the 1980s, sports cyclist, Yvon Le Caer, proved it was possible to cycle across the English Channel. No one has attempted to break that record to date, and no amputee has admitted to have tried it out yet, but there is always the future. Enjoy being totally amazed at what you are about to read!

AquaCycle Across the Channel, Sure! (www.yvonlecaer.com)

Yvon Le Caer was a world-class competition cyclist before he embarked on his ocean-going exploits. His speed records for human powered watercraft still stand more than twenty years later. An innovative watercraft which would merge bicycle and marine technologies: that was the ambition of champion racing cyclist Yvon le Caer. His "AquaCycle" was years in development, and he had already crossed the Gulf Stream between the Bahamas and Florida on a prototype when he decided to test his latest model on the difficult waters between France and England. This was a second attempt—his first, in 1983, ended in disaster when his own escort vessel sliced 4 feet off the front of his craft, all in the middle of the night of his 22nd wedding anniversary! Wiser and better equipped, and, on the eve of his 50th birthday, Yvon was determined and motivated like never before.

In May 1985, Yvon had just tested a brand new propulsion system, with frame and rudder apparatus, finally achieving the right level of sea craft efficiency. The totally independent gear-driven propeller system (with "pushing" and "pulling" mode options), complete with crank arms and pedals, could be replaced at sea with very little loss of time. For crossing the Channel in 1985, Yvon opted for the "pulling" mode—propeller upstream of the flow on the forward side of the "outdrive."

"Operation English Channel" would take Yvon from Cherbourg to Poole in September 1985. Although swimmers stroke across the 21-mile-wide Strait of Dover, Yvon Le Caer's chosen route lies 180 miles west of the Strait.

The 75-mile-wide body of water lying between Cherbourg at the tip of the Peninsula of Normandy and Poole on the Dorset coast of England features strong currents, busy shipping lanes, unpredictable weather and turbulent, cold, and foggy waters. Extreme tidal ranges also create constantly shifting high velocity tidal currents.

His earlier career in competitive cycling was an essential part of his preparation. In the early 80s, he was still riding an average of 15,000 miles a year, and during the few months preceding the 1985 crossing, it was not unusual for him to ride 60 to 70 miles on the road in the morning, then AquaCycle for 2 or 3 hours in the afternoon.

Finally, on September 9, 1985, despite hostile conditions, Yvon left Cherbourg at dusk, with his escort vessel, support personnel and a French TV crew onboard. He "pedalled" all night, across shipping lanes and through a sharp broadside chop. Due to tidal currents, it was a rather long 92-mile meandering path with constant course adjustments. After a moonless and cold night (48 °Fahrenheit), the morning brought dense fog, hampering navigation during the final hours. Adverse tidal currents when approaching the Solent meant he lost some time. Still Yvon never gave up, he reached Poole harbour entrance by late morning, 10 September, 16 hours, 42 minutes after leaving Cherbourg. In resolutely confronting the elements, he had, against all odds, gained the last word.

"It required a great deal of effort, coordination and planning," says Yvon. "In such adverse conditions, it is essential to have a good escort vessel. In this regard, my wife Andrea, and all navigators and technicians onboard as well, did a fine job; so did the French Marine Nationale (Cross-Jobourg) and the British Coast Guard who kept a vigilant watch all along, alerting continuously all passing ships of our position and movement at sea."

"I read once that: 'Doing what you want is achievable, if you set realistic goals and follow through,' a saying so true, in my case. I came out of the starting gate like a bullet (sort of), leaving Cherbourg for Poole at dusk. The rest is history. At last, I made it through, in a time that will be most likely broken someday, but still stands for now, more than two decades later."

Esneider Muñoz Marín, Colombia

I have a transtibial distal amputation that occurred 11 years ago. I didn't cycle before the amputation. There's not a specific route for cyclists to ride or practice. In some cases, the roads have separate space for cycling. In the roads where there are no separate spaces, we train with vehicular traffic. It's difficult to cycle in traffic in Colombia due to the high incidents of

cycling accidents, but it's just a minor issue compared to the passion that we feel for this sport. I remember a time in Denmark when I was training on the highway. The culture is one where they are very respectful to cyclists on the road, and a lot of people admire this sport. It felt very peaceful, even when it was a cold day. It was very comfortable and pleasant on my bike. I had the feeling that the environment had less pollution. You don't feel insecure on the streets, in traffic, or with the people.

Funny Things Happen on Bikes!

We had a fun time once when we were on Subachoque-Cundimarca, and we had a friend who has cerebral palsy training with us. We were descending at great speed, and there was a closed turn in which my friend lost control and fell from his bike. When the paramedics arrived, one was very concerned. She said my friend was convulsing without knowing that his movements were exaggerated due to his condition.

This made us laugh, because she really wanted him to "get better" without knowing what else to do. Finally we told her the reason of his unintentional movements. It was very funny to see how she was calmed after that scary moment!

Esneider Muñoz Marín, Colombia

Still not sure you'd like to try cycling to see if it helps you deal with your amputation and daily living activities? Then consider this Zen proverb:

A Zen teacher saw five of his students returning from the market, riding their bicycles. When they arrived at the monastery and had dismounted, the teacher asked the students, "Why are you riding your bicycles?"

The first student replied, "The bicycle is carrying the sack of potatoes. I am glad that I do not have to carry them on my back!" The teacher praised the first student, "You are a smart boy! When you grow old, you will not walk hunched over like I do."

The second student replied, "I love to watch the trees and fields pass by as I roll down the path!" The teacher commended the second student, "Your eyes are open, and you see the world."

The third student replied, "When I ride my bicycle, I am content to chant nam myoho renge kyo." The teacher gave praise to the third student, "Your mind will roll with the ease of a newly trued wheel."

The fourth student replied, "Riding my bicycle, I live in harmony with all sentient beings." The teacher was pleased and said to the fourth student, "You are riding on the golden path of non-harming."

The fifth student replied, "I ride my bicycle to ride my bicycle." The teacher sat at the feet of the fifth student and said, "Ahh...I am your student!"

There are many ways to interpret proverbs, and you will devise your own interpretation as you read it. In its simplest form, the reasons to ride a bicycle are:

1. Healthy, safe transportation (don't want to get physically hurt or damage important areas of the body carrying heavy items)
2. Observation and attentiveness (admiring the natural beauty around)
3. Contentment, stress relief, ease of mind (meditation, calming thoughts)
4. Peaceful living (avoiding harm to others and to the environment)
5. Pleasure (riding in order to enjoy riding a bicycle)

Have you ever considered why it is *exactly* that you don't cycle? Is there just one reason in your particular case or is it a combination of reasons? Are these reasons not to cycle new and recently developed or long standing, possibly even outdated ones? Are they still sufficiently valid to hold on to or is it now time to leave them behind and become a part of the amazing revolution embracing amputee cycling around the world today?

The Transtheoretical Model of Behavioural Change developed by Prochaska and DiClemente is worth considering if you want some help in working out those reasons. There are six different stages: pre-contemplation, contemplation, preparation, action, maintenance, and termination. Take a look at it and see if you find it useful for working out why cycling is beneficial if you are an amputee.

→ **www.prochange.com/transtheoretical-model-of-behavior-change**

Further Reading

1. Why Cycle?: www.bikehub.co.uk/featured-articles/why-cycle
2. Amputee Bicycling: www.oandp.com/articles/2005-01_10.asp
3. Factors Causing Disability: www.un.org/esa/socdev/enable/dispaperdes2.htm
4. Peak Oil Theory: en.wikipedia.org/wiki/Peak_oil
5. Landmine Monitor: www.the-monitor.org

Things to Try for Yourself

1. Visit a bicycle or transportation museum.
2. Investigate current public transport options (capacity/routes/timetables) in your area. Is it practical for you to use, what needs to change, and who are you going to let know?
3. Get to know some amputees who cycle (there are plenty on Facebook, Twitter, and in this book).
4. Try to find the nearest cycling club or disabled cycling group in your area through the disability sports network.
5. Make a note of how many times you use your car and work out how many of those journeys could easily be done by bike or public transportation.

Did you know?

1. 60 percent of local cyclists in Shanghai, China, pedal to work every day. The city has 9,430,000 bicycles.
2. It is thought that globally around 3,000 amputees *do cycle* for leisure and general exercise.
3. In Germany, 9 percent of all trips are made by bicycle.
4. More than 40 million children under 5 years old were overweight in 2011.
5. In Denmark, 18 percent of all trips are made by bike, and 1 mile (1.6 km) is cycled on average.
6. Globally, more than 350 million people of all ages suffer from depression. It is the leading cause of disability worldwide.
7. Diabetes complications such as foot ulcers are the cause of 40 to 60 percent of amputations in Europe, 25 percent in Italy and Japan, and 90 percent in North American Indians.
8. In Britain, 55 percent of journeys under 5 miles (8 km) and 40 percent of journeys less than 2 miles (8.2 km) are by car or van.
9. According to the Arbor Day Foundation, "a mature leafy tree produces as much oxygen in a season as 10 people inhale in a year."
10. The term *runner's high* refers to the feelings of boundless energy, elation, and high spirits experienced after prolonged intense exercise.

Joe Beimfohr, USA

I'm a bilateral amputee. I was injured in Iraq on July 5, 2005, when my patrol walked into an improvised explosive device (IED) that was buried in the ground. I cycled as a kid but stopped as I got older. I was active in soccer during middle and high school; most places I grew up were within walking distance. I started handcycling in 2008. My very first race was the 2008 New York City (NYC) Marathon. For new amputees, attend either an adaptive sports camp or clinic and try different types of bikes. Your level of injury will determine what bike you can ride, but the bikes are so advanced these days that no one model is faster than another. It still all comes down to the rider!

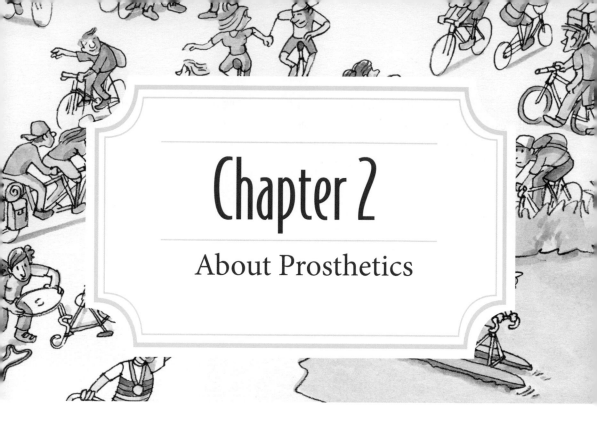

Chapter 2

About Prosthetics

Prosthetic device is the term used to describe arm or leg replacements that enable amputees to remain functionally independent throughout their lives. Globally, there is huge demand for these devices. The World Health Organization estimates that in Latin America, Africa, and Asia combined over 30 million people require prosthetic limbs, braces, or other devices. Future services are predicted to exceed $3 billion for amputee patients in the USA alone. Children may require new limbs every 6 to 12 months to accommodate their growth rate, whereas adult limbs generally last 3 to 5 years. Over a young amputee's lifetime, up to 20 sets of limbs may be required.

The human leg is made up of bones, joints, muscles, nerves, and blood vessels. These allow the leg to be used for walking, running, jumping, swimming, kneeling, and other general activities. The human arm is made up of bones, joints, muscles, nerves, and blood vessels. These allow the arm and hand to be used for grasping, holding, carrying, writing, washing, cleaning, throwing, swimming, and other activities of daily life.

The most difficult forms of amputation are shoulder and hip. These areas have many vital joints and bones that support the body during movement. Damage to these areas causes significant immobility and loss of function. The higher up the amputation, the more artificial components are needed which increases the financial cost of the limb.

Each element of joint, bone, muscle, or other tissue removed and replaced by an artificial limb results in more loss of function, impairment, and increased energy requirements during limb use. If there is a lack of muscle, the stump becomes bony. This increases the amount of friction experienced during prosthesis use.

Healing of the wound without complications of the scar area is the ultimate aim of the immediate post-amputation phase. Good levels of blood flow to the remaining limb area are vital for wound healing to occur. Appropriate wound dressing improves the chances of good wound healing without infection.

Prosthetic limbs are normally fitted between one to six months following amputation. Waiting longer reduces the chance of it being accepted and used for daily activities. Amputated skin has to be mobilized and desensitized to keep the stump pliable and accustomed to the friction of wearing prosthesis. Scar tissue must be completely healed before mobilization or desensitization is undertaken. These techniques involve deep massaging the bony areas of the stump and moving different texture fabrics over the skin. This must be done gradually without irritating, breaking, or infecting the stump skin.

Habib Jan, Afghanistan

I have been an amputee for almost 21 years. I used to be an official employee in our district before my amputation. One day I was on my way to the office when suddenly I heard an explosion. It was a roadside bomb. After the explosion, I was unconscious for almost 24 hours. When I opened my eyes, I was in the hospital, and later on, I was told I had lost my right leg. It was 1992. I did not cycle before my amputation; I used to walk to work. But since I have been an amputee, I have been cycling. I always ride a bike which has two wheels and is made in China. I don't have any adaptations on the bike.

Funny Things Happen on Bikes

One day, I had my two sons and daughter with me on my bike. I wanted to take them to a picnic very far from my home. On the way, I saw some wonderful sights, such as people on the roadside busy in their fields; the safe, calm route; the interesting and romantic sounds of the birds in the trees; and the soft and clean water we had in a spring along the way. We really enjoyed that journey. It is worth mentioning that my spouse was very angry with me because we arrived back so late that night!

Habib Jan, Afghanistan

Hoang Thi Lan, Vietnam

I was born and grew up in the west of Dông Hói, Vietnam. After graduating high school, I got a job at a small sugar mill. I had a work accident and lost my left arm. I was only 19, full of the dreams and hopes of a teenager. I lived in suffering and despair.

Many times I planned to commit suicide, but all the care and love from my family and the people in my community helped me to rise up and overcome the trauma and complex feelings. I realized that I had to take care of myself and find a job that was suitable for my situation. There weren't many jobs suitable for people with a disability; therefore, I decided to start a small vegetable business at a local market.

As you know, vegetables wither easily. With the long distance to the market, they would not stay fresh if I carried them and walked to the market. Therefore, I decided I need to learn to ride a bicycle.

I had experienced cycling before I had the accident, but since then, I possessed the fear that I couldn't handle something difficult like that. I tried to remember how to ride a bicycle, the feeling of balancing the bicycle, and how the feet work on the pedals. I remembered it all, and my family supported me by sharing their feelings about a cycle ride. The day that I rode the bicycle again, I didn't have as much difficulty as I imagined.

The emotion was different from before as I still could handle everything. I was so happy that I overcame my fear.

And since I could ride a bicycle, I could carry 45 to 110 pounds (20-50 kg) of fresh vegetables to the local market so much faster than walking. I want to send a message to other people with disability: What I can do, you can do better. Be confident, my friends.

Funny Things Happen on Bikes

My friend, Geoff, had a habit of leaving his parking brake on when he started a race. One time he rode 6 miles before he realized it was on. So now, whether he's at a race or not, before we start racing, I always say out loud to everyone, "Take off your parking brake Geoff!"
Joe Beimfohr, USA

About Prosthetics

Once a device has been measured and fitted, the amputee is shown how to put it on and take it off. Prosthesis users are shown how to clean the socket area of the device daily and undertake basic maintenance checks, such as looking for defects, scratches, loose screws, or weak rivets. This should be done on a weekly basis. The device should be kept free of dirt, sand, and other debris.

Initially a treatment plan is drawn up for an intermittent wearing schedule to prevent skin breakdown. Prosthesis use is gradually increased until worn on a regular basis. Many amputees aim to wear their limbs all day, every day, with as much functionality as possible. The more complex the requirements, the more technology goes into manufacture, resulting in an expensive limb.

During the first year or so, if the amputee uses the prosthesis regularly, there will be a reduction in stump volume and a change in the overall shape of the stump. This will affect the closeness of fit. New sockets or adaptations have to be made at this stage. It may take some years for a stable stump size to be reached. Any change in body weight (increase or decrease)

Rust inside the prosthetics following the Tour d'Afrique!

may also affect the fit and ease of use of the limb. Components usually come with a manufacturer's warranty from 12 months to 3 years. Most amputees will choose to keep specific components that they are satisfied with longer than the official warranty period. However, the older the component, the higher the risk of mechanical failure, so it is worthwhile to change parts regularly.

Prosthetics Parts

There are common and specific parts to a prosthesis, depending on individual need. There are lots of user-specific components which are not covered in this section. Further reading suggestions are provided at the end of the chapter.

The common parts are referred to as:

A. The socket—The amputee's limb fits into this part.
B. A soft liner—This is typically situated within the interior of the socket.
C. The pylon—This is a metal or carbon fiber rod that provides the structural support.
D. Foam and covers—The pylons are sometimes enclosed by a cover that is shaped and colored to match the recipient's skin tone. The cover is usually made from a foam-like material.
E. Suspension system—This keeps the limb attached to the body.
F. Prosthetic socks—These are used to achieve a snug fit inside the prosthetic.
G. Sleeves—These are used to keep the prosthesis in place, especially on suction sockets.

Specific components include:

1. Elbow joint
2. Knee joint
3. Foot
4. Hand
5. Cables

Common Prosthetic Parts

A. Sockets protect the stump area where the most force is felt by the user. The better the fit, the better the control, and the less irritation or damage to the stump skin or tissues.

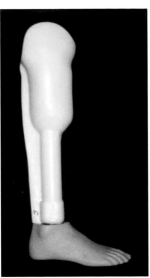

B. Liners are made of flexible, cushioning material, such as silicone, polyurethane or coplymer. In developing countries, rubber from tires has been used. They require the amputee to wear a thick sock next to the skin. The aim is to protect the stump skin from chaffing and movement while wearing the prosthetic. Silicone liners are used with the lock and pin prosthesis. Polyurethane liners are used for bony, scarred tissue and work best on vacuum or suction prosthesis. Copolymer can be used in both types of prostheses. The liners are anatomically shaped, and some have antibacterial additives or soothing gels, such as Aloe Vera, incorporated into them.

Heat causes amputated skin to sweat and break down, leading to infection. Efficient regulation of heat and sweat may enable higher activity levels. Increased sweating during cycling also loosens the fit of the limb to the stump and can result in it falling off. Using a liner that has exposed silicone on it causes it to stick to the sleeve. This increased grip reduces the risk of the limb falling off due to sweating.

The pushing and pulling effect that results from prosthetics use causes shear forces to break down skin in vulnerable areas, such as the knees and ends of the stump. The GlideWear patch is a new development to absorb the motion that would normally be transferred to the skin. Another option under development is the socket-cooling sleeve. It uses a water bottle sized canister of liquid carbon dioxide (CO_2) to keep the skin cool during exercise.

From the Amputees

Armin Köhli, Switzerland

I don't use a pin at the bottom, so the liner is not connected to the shaft. I fix it just through the sleeve. Indeed, I had two races where one leg fell off; so we had to think about fixing it better, and we ended up with the sleeves and the liners partially without fabric.

That's the crucial bit. These are taken on and off in the same way as normal liners, and it's almost 100 percent safe. You couldn't tear it away!

→ The liners and their sleeves are produced by Wagner Polymertechnik in Germany: **www.wpt-gmbh.de**.

Esneider Muñoz Marín, Columbia

Formerly, the government health system offered me the prosthesis in order to improve my well-being, but it was not suitable for cycling.

Nowadays, the International Olympic and Paralympic Committee and Coldeportes have given me suitable prosthesis to cycle and perform.

The Kenyan Cycling Team

Ibrahim Wafulah has lost a leg—the right one to be exact. In a car accident some years ago, his leg was amputated, and he doesn't have a replacement. A cheap prosthetic doesn't work well for him. He doesn't have any health insurance to pay for a good prosthetic leg; neither does he have enough money to buy it. Even if he did, good prosthetics are not manufactured in Kenya, he said. He hoped one day to buy one from Korea. Even then, Ibrahim Wafulah accompanied the Tour d'Afrique in Kenya over the tarmac roads on an old mountain bike with 3x7 gearing. He has been training for many years on his bike.

One day, he wants to qualify for the world championships or the Paralympics, but that is still a long way off. There aren't any bike races in Kenya for disabled people, so how can he measure himself internationally? The Kenyan Paralympic Committee could select him, but places are limited and very in demand. Who would reward a Kenyan athlete if Swiss, Slovak, and numerous other more influential nations strive regularly for these places? And finally, who should pay?

Ibrahim always trained alone, occasionally taking part in able-bodied races, until he met Douglas Sidalo. Douglas became blind after falling victim to the bombings against the US Embassy in Nairobi in 1998. Despite this, Douglas rides a tandem with different pilots. He has become quite famous and has already been invited to international races. The one-legged man and the tandem often train together. Douglas also accompanied the Tour d'Afrique in Kenya. Sometimes, the tour now resembles a disabled cycling race.

During the last 40 kilometers (25 miles) to Nairobi, we had other companions. Cyclists from the Kenyan national team took us through town. The pace was comfortable, and one could chat easily. There are around 20 bike races in Kenya per year, Singh told me. Approximately 50 cyclists have their own racing bikes, and of those, 20 are really strong, able to keep up with the African and international racers. One of them had qualified for the world championships the year before last. But for races in Kenya, the field consists of more than 50 riders. Many start with Chinese-made single-gear bikes. It's not easy to get enough distance from them, says Singh. He rides a nice, average Bianchi bike that costs around 3,000 Swiss Francs. He bought it in England, and has difficulties maintaining it properly. There are bike shops in Nairobi, but they only offer cheap, low-quality stock.

Singh worked for a safari travel firm in Arusha, Tanzania, and earned a good wage. But then came the Gulf War 2003, and the tourists stayed away. He lost his job and now has a lot of time to train. But he can't really motivate himself for it so much now.

Written by Armin Köhli, 25 March 2004

→ Excerpt from the Tour d'Afrique; translated from **www.tourdarmin.ch**

Common Prosthetic Parts

C. Pylons are made from bamboo, wood, or plastics in developing countries. Metals and carbon fiber are used more widely in developed countries. A bike frame can be used in developing countries to form an adjustable prosthesis which is useful for children as they grow and develop.

D. Foam and covers tend to be found mainly in general use prostheses for cosmetic purposes. Limbs with foam and covering are designed to be as close to the amputee's skin tone as possible for ease of presentation in social settings. They do not have a role to play in performance cycling limbs as the foam and cover adds bulk and weight which is something cyclists wish to reduce rather than increase when competing.

E. Suspension systems are required for the stump to remain fixed in the socket. These come in several different forms. The main ones are harness systems, straps, belts, vacuum, pin, and lock. Vacuum systems require the stump to fit snugly. This creates an air lock. The vacuum may be assisted by pump or valve suction.

In the pin and lock suspension system, the liner has a pin attached which fits into a lock at the bottom of the socket. A push button system is used to detach the pin.

The type of suspension required for arm amputees consists of straps and harnesses. They are either in a figure-eight or chest strap.

For leg amputees, additional suspension can be provided with a silesian bandage, which is a light belt that fits across the pelvic area and waist.

From the Amputees

Jon Pini, UK

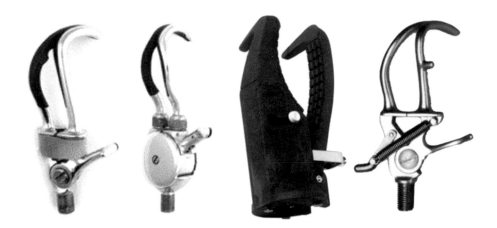

I used to have an artificial arm that had a lot of straps to hold everything on. I used to find it quite cumbersome to put on, and it used to get in the way, particularly in hot weather. Eventually, I started using my arm to give me that extra balance. It was a simple arm with a steep, long hand which is a hand in a fixed hook position, and I just used it to rest on the handle bars. And that is all I've done ever since, throughout the generation of different types of arms I've had.

Habib Jan, Afghanistan

I have a prosthetic limb instead of my right leg for cycling, and that helps and supports me in riding my bicycle. Initially, I was using crutches for daily walking. In 1994, I heard of an organization, ICRC (International Committee of the Red Cross), providing Afghan amputees with plastic legs, so I also went there. After taking my leg size, they gave me a leg within one week.

Jim Bush, UK

The prosthetic leg is a fairly standard National Health Service (NHS) composite leg, with a polyurethane socket (which I had a plaster cast created for), an aluminium shin tube, and a plastic foot. The most complicated bit is the Total Knee (knee unit), now manufactured and distributed by Össur. Compared to expensive bits of gear with microprocessors like the Otto Bock C-Leg, it's quite cheap. It doesn't do much that's complicated, but it does bend enough for cycling and has better durability than most alternatives. I use the same leg for everything (cycling, standing, walking, and sitting), and I wear the leg for approximately 18 hours a day, from when I get up to when I go to bed, except that I take the leg off to go swimming.

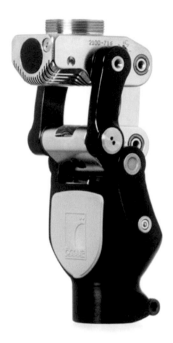

I do have a spare leg, which is basically the same as the main one, except that the socket doesn't fit as well, and the knee unit isn't as good. I think I currently have the high-activity Total Knee unit with a special back linkage which I am testing for Össur and the NHS. Basically, cycling is the exercise and sport which kills off knee units fastest. I cycle approximately 6,000 miles per year, and if you assume a pedaling speed (=cadence) of 80 rpm and a speed of 10 mph, that means you get the knee to bend and straighten (6000 / 10) x 80 x 60 = 2.9 million times per year. There is oil in the Total Knee unit, which keeps heating up when you cycle and eventually needs replacing. If you cycle as often as I do (every day), you get to the servicing interval and oil changing sooner.

Common Prosthetic Parts

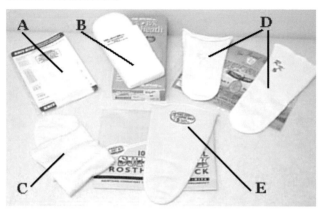

F. **Prosthetic socks** are available in different thickness. The number and thickness of socks used will vary based on the activity, humidity, and other factors. Socks can be made from wool, cotton, or synthetic fibers. Lycra is used for prosthetic sock manufacturing to help control volume changes. Wool combined with manmade fibers improves the strength and resilience of the sock. Some socks have antibacterial additives in them to reduce odor and bacteria or fungus.

Gel socks are good for cushion and pressure distribution. Half socks can be worn with full socks over them to add extra cushioning to the lower part of the stump without increasing the pressure nearer the knee. The sock should be applied smoothly to the limb so there are no wrinkles, otherwise the skin will become red and sore, and cuts will appear around the wrinkle area. It is recommended that socks should be changed on a daily basis, and rotating socks keeps their fibers more resilient.

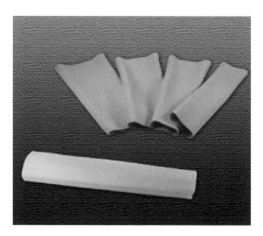

G. **Sleeves** are used for vacuum and suction systems to form an airtight seal at the top of the socket. This keeps it in place while in use. Sleeves are made of elastic materials, but they tend to tear or stretch quite easily if the amputee uses them regularly. This reduces their ability to seal the prosthesis effectively. They come in various forms; some have shaped knee areas, and some are covered with material.

Specific Prosthetic Components

1. Above elbow prostheses require an elbow joint. The most common method is using a lock that can be operated without using the other hand to press the button. The action required is for the amputee to move the chest, shoulder, or other muscles in the body slightly. The elbow unit is positioned to allow rotation as naturally as possible. Adjustable coil springs assist elbow flexion.

2. Above-knee amputees require a functional knee joint. The original method of providing a "knee" was to increase the level of friction by use of a brake or lock. The knee is a single axis, and stability is provided by ensuring this axis is behind the hip and ankle axes. The need for an adjustable knee joint has led to the development of a computer-controlled knee that automatically adapts to an amputee's walking style.

Microprocessors and sensors continuously measure the angles and forces of the walk and use this data to change the stiffness of the knee. The method of knee stiffening can be produced by the use of fluid containing metal particles. Sending a magnetic signal through the fluid thickens it and causes the required stiffness.

Automatic knee brakes are activated on heel contact with the ground. New developments in above-knee prosthetics have enabled a design that coordinates the motion between ankle and knee action to improve the gait and stability of above-knee amputees.

An option for above-knee amputees is that of osseointegration in which titanium rods are implanted into existing bone tissue. The concept was discovered by Professor Per-Ingvar Brånemark (1950s) and is used for dental and hearing aid applications. The main disadvantage is the infection risk. The first two years of follow-up require intensive monitoring to ensure the acceptance and functionality of the implant.

From the Amputees

Jon Pini, UK

For above-knee amputees, the longer the stump above the knee, the better the lever and control they have to push that prosthetic knee to get force through the pedals. Very high transfemoral amputees may find this more difficult, as the shorter the residual limb, the shorter the lever and, therefore, the less the control they have to push the knee. It is better to have more surface area to put that force through so you have less pressure on the stump. The higher up the limb the amputation is, more energy is required to do daily activities, such as walking and cycling. There are some above-knee amputees who BMX, and for those, the socket has to be altered. For above-knee amputees using an old socket, cutting areas away around the top of the socket gives them more freedom around the saddle. How the leg stays on can be a lot more difficult. Some use suction systems, some lock and pin, and some harness and belts. Harness and belt systems can be more difficult as you get a lot more movement between the belts, the socket, and the residual limb, so for the best control, you would be looking at either suction or a pin and liner system.

Specific Prosthetic Components

1. Feet were originally made from hardwood such as maple. The main functions are shock absorption, weight transfer during the walking process, stability, and accommodation to uneven surfaces. Ankle motion was simulated by the use of compressible material in the heel section of the foot. Movement around the foot can be single axle, multi-axle, or energy storing.

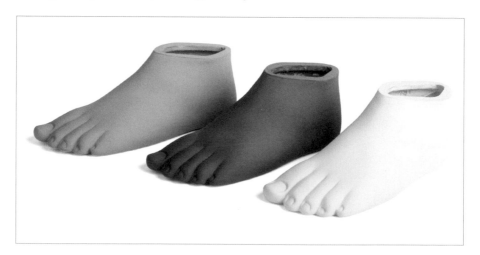

2. Hooks have been in use for many centuries as a substitute for hand function. These had limited functionality, and a more modern version is now available that is pincer like and can be open or closed as the user requires. This new development brings much of the functionality together into one system. Prior to this, arm amputees were given different hands for different functions.

3. Cables and motors have enabled the development of body-powered prosthetics. The way the dominant shoulder, chest, or arm is moved sends signals through the cable to control the prosthetic device. Motors are switch control or button control and either operated through the opposite shoulder or by using muscles in the stump. Different sequences of switch control result in different movements of the hand or arm.

For the future, the development of 3D printing technologies might enable the production of better functional limbs. It is a form of manufacturing that can make a three-dimensional object of different shapes from a digital model.

From the Amputees

Jon Pini, UK

For below-knee amputees with a socket set up in the normal way, when you are in full flexion, it always digs into the back of the knee or into the hamstrings. So we cut that down by about half an inch to give the knee clearance. If you have a short stump, you have to look at different ways to maintain that purchase within the socket, so consider a suction socket with a suspension sleeve. You could cut the back down and have a valve in the socket. The repetitive motion may cause the suspension sleeve to wear out quickly. If that gets a hole in it, then you lose suspension pretty quickly, so you might need spares. They could also try a lock and pin system to see if that works any better.

Sometimes we have to set up the legs in a different alignment with a bit more flexion in them. Limbs are normally set up for standing and walking as the main activities. When you are cycling, you are in a different posture and want to get past that 90-degree flex position, so the socket has to be set up at a different angle than when you are walking. Not a huge amount; again, it depends on the person, the length of the stump, and how much muscle power and coordination they have got.

Mark Ormrod, UK

I took a kayak hand which is a big rubber lump with a belt-type mechanism that clips the arm onto the bike, and I secured it on there with lots of zip ties and duct tape. It has a quick release mechanism. It simply clips off, so the hand part stays on the bike, and my arm can come away whenever I want to stop riding. It wasn't difficult to adapt. The hardest part about it was that when my arm was inside my socket, I had a sleeve which was designed for a below-knee amputee, so it was very stretchy. Every time my arm was pumping around the socket and the flexible sock were "pistoning," it was causing a vacuum effect and creating massive blisters on the end of my arm stump.

Robert Bailey, USA

This was taken at the Challenged Athletes Foundation Para-Triathlon Camp in Pensacola Beach, Florida. I met some wonderful challenged athletes and coaches. I ran my first triathlon. Next week, I will be at the University of Central Oklahoma for the Endeavor Games. It is a major competition of challenged athletes. I will be in at least one cycling time trial and the triathlon.

The cycling feet were made from the foot bed of a mountain shoe. Everything else was cut away. It was mounted so the cleat fits directly under the pylon (pipe). One of the problems with riding with a regular prosthetic foot and cycling shoe is the cleat is under the ball of the foot. The whole leg wants to rock back and forth. You can't "mash." This foot allows me to apply power straight down. The only change I had to make to the bike was to shift the saddle forward about 2 centimeters. I can walk pretty well with them—within reason. I do plan on using them at RAGBRAI this year.

Pain

Pain is usually due to poor fit, resulting in pressure sores, friction, or skin pulling (tractioning). Pressure sores affect all areas of the shin bone and the knee. Above-knee amputees experience pressure pain in the groin area and in the thigh bone.

Friction occurs when the prosthesis pistons up and down loosely. Padding the area between the liner and prosthesis with prosthetic socks of different thickness may help reduce friction issues.

Traction pain can have two causes. If the stump does not touch the bottom of the socket or if the limb is wider at the bottom than at the top (in the shape of a bulb), then this type of pain can occur. It affects the soft tissue around the bone and can be fixed either by padding the inside of the socket or drilling a hole in the socket and pulling the sock through the hole to help the soft tissue farther into the socket.

Wheelchair Use

For amputees with severe levels of amputation, or following a loss of confidence in their ability to walk or balance effectively, wheelchair use may be the most practical option. While the overall aim for amputees is to reduce wheelchair use to a minimum, some find it more comfortable to alternate between wheelchair and prostheses use. Attempting wheelchair use without additional psychological support can lead to depression, physical de-conditioning, and weight gain. In most societies, wheelchair use for mobility is extremely difficult and restrictive without assistance. It is an area of work that amputees could help support through campaigns, lobbying, or general awareness raising and feedback to local decision makers and town planners.

Prosthetics Adaptations for Cycling

Lower-limb amputations are mainly below knee or above the knee. Keeping the knee joint is beneficial as it enables the amputee to undertake normal activities such as cycling. In above-knee amputees, the loss of the knee joint makes it more difficult to undertake normal activities, such as walking or cycling. The amputee should be able to lift the leg over the seat post of a two-wheeler, for example, in order to get onto a bike. The foot angle set for stability during walking may cause the heel or toe to hit the cranks and chains. A slight adjustment in this angle makes the foot more suitable for cycling but reduces the amputee's ability to walk safely. Once you are fully conversant with your prosthetic leg(s), ask the prosthetist to show you how to adjust the toe angle slightly to help you cycle or walk better.

The backs of prosthetic legs usually have to be cut a few millimeters to allow enough flexion at the knee to rotate the pedals. This could result in less support of the leg during standing and walking, so safety and performance issues might require compromises. The loss of an ankle joint makes it difficult to use the same efficient technique for pedaling as non-amputees, but this does not stop you from being able to cycle. For more performance-related cycling, specialist prostheses are often designed. In some cases, amputees choose to ride without prostheses, and in other cases, they ride with prostheses that have particular knee flexion capabilities.

From the Amputees

Mirsad Tokić, Croatia

In Croatia, I have very good rights about prosthetics: every year a new socket and every three years a complete new prosthesis with an expensive carbon foot. Everything for free with some money limits (Health Ministry can't buy me a very expensive foot). My prosthesis has a silicone liner. The problem with this was sweating and bruising of skin behind the knee while pedaling. Every time I turned the pedal, the edge of the prosthesis pushed the liner against my skin. So I took an old prosthesis, made some changes in critical places, and now I have a cycling prosthesis and another one for daily use.

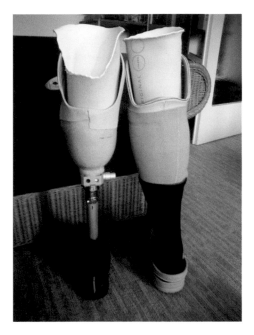

Take a close look at the photos. You will notice the upper edge of the prostheses in the yellow slipper is higher and the liner is regular. That leg is for walking and daily use. You can't bend the knee over 90 degrees. The other one with the bike shoe has the liner cut at the back and is perhaps half an inch lower. It is not good for anything else except for pedaling. It allows me to bend the knee over the magic limit of 90 degrees which is crucial for cycling.

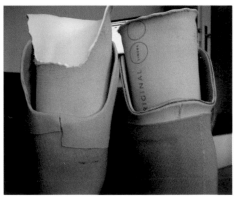

Prosthetics Adaptations for Cycling

Upper-limb amputations are mainly below elbow or above elbow. In below-elbow amputees, thumb or partial hand amputations can present problems with grasping and holding things, such as a bicycle handlebar, gear, or brake lever. Missing hands and wrist areas can make gear changing, braking, and holding on to the handlebars an issue. The hand should be designed so that it can rest on the handlebars with the arm at a comfortable angle.

From the Amputees

Sara Tretola, Switzerland

A Swiss orthopedist made two special carbon arm extensions for me.

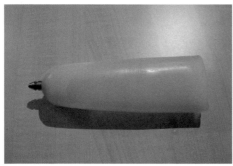

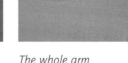

Liner   The whole arm

Will Craig, USA

After I lost my arm, I started to road bike. I was able to use my standard prosthesis and hook and run both brake cables off one lever. I grasped the bar with my hook right at the brake hood. This would allow my hook to rotate around the bar and rock side to side to allow me to turn. I could even pull up on the bars to some degree to hop potholes or railway crossings. The brake hood would keep the hook from sliding off the bars. I could unlock my elbow to extend it for climbing or flex it for descending. As my riding became stronger, the elbow started to fail on me, and eventually I had to bolt it at one angle. This setup would still work for the casual rider, although there may be some challenges with the newer shifting systems that are now integrated with the brake lever. A mountain bike shifter may have to be mounted on the bars for the front derailleur.

The real challenge came when I started riding off-road. The standard hook would not stay on the bars when I pulled up. I initially used a rubber ski hand slid over the end of the bar. This would allow the hand to rotate around the bar and gave some shock absorption. No release was possible from the bars, so I had to rely on the socket sliding off my shoulder. Not a recommended technique these days with the improved socket suspension systems. After this hand broke, I used a regular hook tied to the bars and made sure to ride with a friend to untie me.

As my riding progressed, the elbow and forearm became the weak point with almost weekly catastrophic failures. Eventually I had a suspension forearm built  *and a releasable hand after collaborating with some engineering students. The hand was activated by a cable hooked into my harness so I could manually release it. This presented some of its own challenges. Sometimes when I hung off the back of the bike, the harness would tense up and release the hand. Other times a crash would happen too quickly, and I did not have time to think about releasing.*

→ **www.prostheticarm.com/page3.html**

Prosthetics Adaptations for Cycling

In above-elbow amputees, the lack of elbow joint to assist in shock absorption when cycling over variable surfaces can make it more difficult. Factors that impact the use of prosthetic arms for cycling are the weight and the suspension system.

While the arm device may be acceptable for short cycling journeys, undertaking prolonged, endurance, or performance cycling may be easier without arm prostheses.

As the type of cycling undertaken (e.g., mountain biking, endurance, or long-distance touring) becomes more difficult, the arm or leg has to be fixed firmly in position by locking mechanisms. Some amputees find it more comfortable to cycle without prosthetics. This requires higher levels of balance while cycling but can be done with practice.

The following photos are examples of the experimentation in prosthetics design that enable amputees to remain fully active in the cycling arena at performance level.

Össur leg

The cycling legs are able to clip in and out of pedals using commercial clip-ins integrated with the prosthesis. It can be difficult to walk on a bespoke cycling prosthesis that is lightened or aero-formed as it won't have a conventional prosthetic foot. But you can walk on it satisfactorily with care as a single below-knee amputee to get to and from your bike.

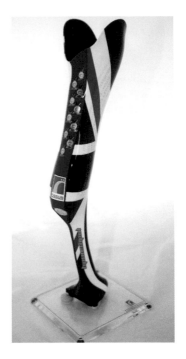

If the prosthesis is for competition, it is important to optimize for lightness or aerodynamics—anything that gives you advantage or minimizes disadvantage. If it is for domestic or recreational cycling then it might be a case of making minor modifications to a normal walking prosthesis.

Prosthesis options are being continually developed and improved based on the experiences and feedback of elite amputee cyclists in the various cycling disciplines.

From the Amputees

Dan Sheret, USA

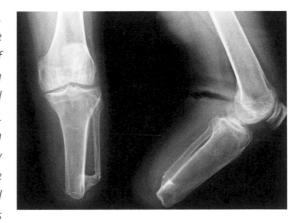

Technology has, without a doubt, played a major role in the advancement of the abilities of those with limb loss. In my own case, it was the medical advancement of the ERTL amputation procedure that, from the beginning, gave me many distinct advantages over those with a traditional guillotine-styled amputation. Its key advantage is the ability to end weight bearing and the reduction of volume change for the amputee. In a nutshell, the residual limb is designed and engineered for the use of prosthesis, not the other way around. New socket designs, feet, knees, and suspension systems all give

the user greater freedom to move beyond their amputation. But technology is only part of the equation.

I have trained many above-knee (AK) amputee cyclists, and my advice is the same to them, with a few modifications. AK riders need to work both with their prosthetics provider and their bike shop to create a system that works best. Many AK riders will, first of all, choose to use a recumbent bike to overcome socket and suspension issues. Others will have a socket custom made with the trim lines reduced to allow the user to comfortably ride an upright bike. Ideally, take your prosthetics person to your bike shop and have him watch you being fitted for a bike. This will give him a better understanding of the seat needs you will have. Take your time with this process as comfort for AK riders will determine the success and enjoyment of the sport.

Since I am no longer representing any prosthetic manufacturer, I get to tell you the real secret of prosthetics and cycling. You do not need anything special! Use an older, slightly loose socket. Since cycling is low impact, the considerations you have with walking are not the same as for biking. All you need to be concerned with is that the suspension is still fine, and you will not pull out of your socket when pedaling. For years I have used my first foot, a Campbell-Childs foot, $250.00 USD for cycling.

The foot is just fine to walk in, and I don't have to worry about breaking it or getting it covered in mud.

AKs can consider the old Mach Knee you have sitting in a closet, keeping your moisture-sensitive electronic knee for your regular use. Of course, if you are so inclined and have the resources, by all means have a specialized cycling leg made—one can never have enough legs! I am sure there are tons of other details that could be said, but time proved to me that you really need very little to succeed with cycling and limb loss. The key ingredient is not equipment or money, but rather it is the inherent drive to overcome one's limitations.

Today, I just have one leg. I use an Össur Sealin Liner and a Rush Foot, nothing extraordinary. Over the years, I have worn just about everything and have found that, for me, the simplest is best and most reliable.

Mark Inglis, New Zealand

One of my biggest frustrations is trying to get amputees to understand that you can do 99 percent of everything on your standard leg. It is only when you want to do that very last 1 percent that a specific limb brings any benefits, so lesson number 1—just try it!

You do need to ensure that the foot is correctly placed on the pedal—just like a real foot—so use a toe clip and as soon as you can, learn to use a set of mountain bike (MTB) pedals. They work differently from road cycling pedals and are easier for the prosthesis to clip out of. Currently, I mountain bike with either my FlexFeet walking legs in an MTB shoe or, recently, to lighten things up, I have converted an old set of FlexFeet to riding legs.

For the 2000 Sydney Olympics, I designed and had made a very specific set of road–track cycling legs that gave me a 13-degree toe down foot aspect coupled with very thin carbon and kevlar blades for the least air friction. They are the ones in the cycling images.

For 99 percent of my riding, I just use my FlexFeet. The leg developments I have done have all been just an engineer and myself; we are not constrained by traditional limb design thinking which allows us to explore totally new ideas. A lot don't work, but some do, for very specific situations. In New Zealand, you are normally allowed one limb or set of limbs at any one time through our government schemes. Sports legs and the like need to be self-funded.

Nathan Smith, New Zealand

I spent the first few years adapting my walking leg to cycling, making sure I had a knee with the maximum amount of flexion. I have a long stump, so a pin and lock socket meant my knee position was too far forward on the bike. I tried the suction socket, but when I really tried to pull on the pedals in a sprint or a tough climb, the leg would end up bouncing along the road. I've settled for a lanyard attachment which keeps the knee in a more natural position and never comes loose. I make sure that the top of my sockets are severely cut away so that there is no rubbing on the saddle or rubbing on the top of my stump where the thigh meets the hip. There was a bit of trial and error over the first couple of years and many blisters.

Once I made the New Zealand team, we made a cycling-specific leg which is impossible to walk on for very long. It is a very tight, cut-away carbon socket with a pin and lock attachment. The pin pokes through the socket into a carbon "pocket" which fits between the hinges of the knee unit. The knee unit is just a free hinge. There is no foot. An aluminium tube attaches the knee unit to a stainless steel plate which the pedal cleat is screwed to. Since I've had a bike-specific leg, the issues have been fairly minimal.

When I was converting the walking leg, I'd wear out the knee units in less than six months. Unless it's just adding a bit of oil or trimming the shank length or replacing a broken lanyard, the prosthetists sort it out. I have never cycled with a knee unit which enables me to cycle out of the saddle.

Robert Bailey, USA

Jay Tew of Hanger Clinic Baton Rouge is my prosthetist, as well as my friend. If your prosthetist is in it for the money, run. You need a "leg man" who will do everything he can to make great prosthetics. Jay made me a set just for cycling. Walking legs just don't work. They do not bend enough. You have to cut the back—the bar—of the socket down. Over three years, my legs changed, and so did I.

I dropped my weight down to 190 pounds (86 kg). My diabetes was under control. My prosthetics changed, too.

Every time I lost 20 pounds (9 kg), he had to make a new set. Soon I didn't even use my walking legs. I just wore my cycling sockets all of the time. When I rode the trike, I would switch to non-flex feet with cycling shoes. When I walked, I wore my FlexFeet. Before I rode, I would loosen the Allen screws and straighten the feet. When I walked, I would angle them out a bit. One of the difficulties of cycling as an amputee is everything has to be adjusted manually. An able-bodied cyclist, someone with original equipment, just jumps on and rides.

Steve Middleton, Canada

The prosthetic knee needs to have a flexion of at least 120 degrees. This will enable the knee to bend enough to complete the pedal cycle. A few amazing amputees actually prefer to cycle without wearing a prosthetic leg—again, trial and error and personal preference!

New prosthetic knees are now available to assist above-knee amputees to stand up and pedal, but it is difficult, and one must be very proficient at cycling. They are expensive and not normally covered by healthcare policies.

→ Advice from Orthotics and Prosthetics Information **www.oandp.com/oandp-l/ message.asp?frmMessageId=05174C26-8DFE-466C-B2F0-433526BC32C7**

For AK prosthesis, especially, I always need an almost straight alignment of the foot, as well as a swing-only type knee. That was very efficient for cycling, but not at all optimal in terms of gait dynamics. On that leg, I have found it extremely useful to use the Ferrier Coupler, so I am able to quickly and easily switch out of my everyday component to my cycling setup, without having to go through the hassle of taking off the socket. While it does add weight, it certainly makes my life much easier, so I can quickly change components for various activities.

For $5,000 to $7,000 USD, a patient can get a serviceable below-knee prosthesis that allows the user to stand and walk on level ground. By contrast, a US$10,000 device will allow the person to become a "community walker," able to go up and down stairs and to traverse uneven terrain.

A prosthetic leg in the US$12,000 to US$15,000 price range will facilitate running and functioning at a level nearly indistinguishable from someone with two legs.

Devices priced at US$15,000 or more may contain polycentric mechanical knees, swing-phase control, stance control and other advanced mechanical or hydraulic systems.

Computer– assisted devices start in the US$20,000 to US$30,000 range. These take readings in milliseconds, adjusting for degree and speed of swing. Above–the–knee amputees can walk with a C–Leg without having to think about every step they take.

Upper–extremity amputees can buy a nonfunctional cosmetic hand for US$3,000 to US$5,000 that "just fills a sleeve". It allows getting by in public without being noticed.

US$10,000 will buy a trans–radial upper–extremity prosthesis that is a functional "split hook" device for below–the–elbow amputees.

Cosmetically realistic myoelectric hands that open and close may cost US$20,000 to US$30,000 or more. These contain processors that tell how much pressure the amputee putting on a held object and whether it is hot or cold.

A neuroprosthetic arm (i-Limb, DEKA, Utah Arm3) may cost as much as US$100,000.

→ Examples of prices of prosthetic limbs in 2012 and 13: **www.nist.gov/tip/wp/ pswp/upload/239_limb_prosthetics_services_devices.pdf page 11**

From Bike to Limb

Bike parts can be used to make limbs. The seat post becomes the leg (pylon)—rubber from the tires combined with some wood make the foot and rear wheel supports make the socket. Foam and wooden discs support and reduce pressure areas on the stump.

Further Reading

1. Lusardi, Jorge, and Nielsen. 2012. *Orthotics and Prosthetics in Rehabilitation, 3rd Edition* (Philadelphia, PA: Elsevier).
2. Children's Healthcare of Atlanta. Available at: www.choa.org/Childrens-Hospital-Services/Orthopaedics/Programs-Services/Orthotics-and-Prosthetics
3. Strait, Erin. 2006. *Prosthetics in Developing Countries*. Available at: www.oandp.org/publications/resident/pdf/DevelopingCountries.pdf
4. *Parenting Magazine*. Available at: www.amputee-coalition.org/expectations/components.html
5. Peelle, Lydia. 2008. "Phantom Pain," from *Reasons for and Advantages of Breathing* (New York City, New York: Harper Perennial). The text highlights many of the thoughts, emotions, and experiences of new amputees. Available at: http://www.fiftytwostories.com/?p=548#more-548

Things to Try for Yourself

1. Visit a prosthetics museum or look for displays of prosthetics in war museums.
2. Practice putting on and taking off your prosthetics, get used to sock changing, and familiarize yourself with stumps shrinking.
3. Ask other amputees which types of sockets they have tried and which ones they find useful and why.
4. Develop a good relationship between you and your prosthetist so they can understand your requirements easier.
5. Take a close look at your prosthesis: what is it made from and how best to look after it? Do you want to check out the properties of each component used and suggest or consider other alternatives?

Did You Know?

1. In the 1930s, a prosthetist went to an amputee's house to measure his stump. Using those measurements he would carve and sand a block of wood, then glue leather on to make the prosthesis.

2. The wood used for prosthesis comes from yellow poplar, willow, basswood, and balsa. Maple and hickory are hardwoods used in the manufacture of feet.

3. The materials used during the American Civil War were wood, rawhide, and glue. Each limb cost between $75 and $100.

4. Phantom pain was first documented in 1551 by a French military surgeon, Ambroise Paré. The term *phantom limb* was coined in 1871 by American neurologist, Silas Weir Mitchell.

5. The ERTL amputation technique is a particular surgical method used for below-knee amputation. It was developed in 1920 and named after the Hungarian professor, Janos Ertl, Sr.

6. In January 2010, a large magnitude earthquake (scale 7) caused 6,000 amputees overnight in Haiti.

7. World War II socket developments included the patellar tendon bearing (PTB) prosthesis for below-knee amputees and the quadrilateral socket for above-knee amputees.

8. 46,500 tons of carbon fiber was consumed globally in 2013. Important producers are North America (30%), Europe (24%), and Japan (20%).

9. Upper-limb prostheses have two components: the crane and the terminal device. The terminal device acts as the hand. It can be a hook- or lyre-shaped three jaw chuck.

10. Children require a new lower-limb prosthesis annually up to the age of 5, biannually from 5 to 12, and then one every three or four years until age 21.

John Thraves, UK

I have been a right below-knee amputee since June 2010. I am 70-plus years young! I cycled a lot before the amputation and run a social cycling unit called Purbeck Freewheelers, which is part of the Dorset Cyclists' Network. Small modifications (standing aids) enable me to mount and dismount the recumbent trike. I do not cycle without prosthetics. My riding now is  *purely for leisure and shopping. I have always cycled, but on two wheels, so getting the electric trike is the first. I achieved the National Instructor award with bikeability plus the disability module. I am an ambassador for the charity Limbcare.*

After consultation with friends in the US and in Europe, I have come up with a list of benefits for cycling using electric bikes. I must point out that this is not a definitive list, and you may have one or two of your own additions.

1. *Commuting. Getting to work not out of breath and leaving a pool of perspiration behind.*
2. *Recreation. Enjoyment of cycling both for getting to work and leisure trips.*
3. *Exercise. You still have to pedal to get the electric assist to work.*
4. *Transportation. Saving money in transportation costs, particularly car.*
5. *Fun. It is fun and brings back the joy of cycling.*
6. *Opportunities. It provides opportunities for elderly cyclists and young children with disabilities.*
7. *Enabling. People with injuries or disabilities achieve independence and confidence.*

Chapter 3

Understanding Bike Parts

Bicycles of all varieties are quite simple in design. While two-wheelers, tricycles, recumbents, and handcycles all look different, they have common features that can be recognized easily as well as other parts specific to their design features. It is useful to become familiar with different bike parts and the effect they have on enjoying cycling whether you intend to undertake your own bike maintenance or not. It may seem daunting at first, especially if you are not mechanically minded, but eventually it will become second nature to consider these aspects, especially when investing in a new bicycle.

The main parts you are likely to find in one form or another are:

A. Frame
B. Saddle
C. Pedals
D. Wheels
E. Tires
F. Gears
G. Handlebars and steering
H. Brakes

It obviously gets more complicated than that and is worth learning about as you get more involved in cycling. There's really nothing stopping you from building your own personalized version once you know what it's all about.

A. Frame

The frame has to support the rider, turn pedal force into forward motion, and steer. The shape of the frame depends on whether it is a two-wheeler or other variety. The more common shapes are diamond, step through and cantilever.

Familiar materials used today include cast iron, alloys of steel, aluminium, titanium, carbon, glass, aramide, magnesium, and scandium. The frame material is chosen based on its strength, elasticity, and weight. Steel and titanium will not break despite wear. Aluminium is more likely to wear, crack, or break if used in a careless manner. Carbon frames are extremely light and fail only on impact.

An innovative East Asian concept is to use bamboo as frame material. Bamboo has excellent tensile strength and flexibility which allows it to be moulded easily using arborosculpture. An example of this is the Ajiro designed by Alexander Vittouris.

Wooden frames made of lighter materials are also available. A prototype of a low cost cardboard bicycle frame made from recyclable and renewable materials has been developed by Izhar Gafni and can be seen at:

→ www.dezeen.com/2012/11/12/cardboard-bicycle-by-izhar-gafni/

B. Saddle

A bicycle saddle is where the rider sits as they cycle. In two-wheelers and tricycles, it is attached to a metal seat post which is adjustable. The basic saddle consists of a shell, padding, cover, and rails.

Saddles come in three main categories:

Comfort   Sport   Race

Racing saddles are the most aerodynamic: narrower and harder than saddles made for comfort and leisure rides. Women's saddles tend to be wider than men's due to the fact that a woman's pelvis is a different size and shape to a man's. Many saddles (for male and female) now come with a cut-out area or low-density foam section in the center to take pressure off the pubic bone. Some men's saddles (especially ultra-distance racers) have the "nosepiece" of the saddle cut off to ease pressure on the sitting area.

An alternative to a saddle is a seat such as the banana seat (popular on wheelie bikes) or the recumbent seat. These can be made from mesh, plywood, carbon fiber, hard plastic, aluminium, fiber glass, or fabric.

From the Amputees

Steve Middleton, Canada

A comfortable seat is crucial. A narrow seat is recommended for leg amputees, allowing accommodation of the socket and eliminating interference of the socket to seat (causing chaffing and discomfort). One helpful tip is to turn the seat a slight degree away from the prosthetic socket.

C. Pedals

On most bikes, apart from the handcycle, the pedal is the place where the rider places their foot. Pedaling causes the bike to move. Usual materials for pedals are nylon, carbon reinforced plastic, and polycarbonate, and lightweight pedals can be made from magnesium. Aluminium and magnesium are used for mountain biking pedals as they provide better grip in the wet or mud.

On a handcycle, there are hand levers (sometimes called handlebars, handgrips, or crank handles) instead of pedals. These are mounted on the front of the handcycle and are turned either in the same direction by both hands or alternately in a manner similar to foot pedals.

Pedals come as flat platform, quill, clipless, or magnetic. For better control over the pedal and to improve efficiency, systems such as toe clips or foot basket and straps can be added to flat pedals. A cleat is a metal or plastic attachment on the cyclist's shoe that slots into the pedal. Quill pedals with clips are not to be used for mountain biking because it is too difficult to release the foot in time. Fixed foot attachment systems are best tried once the cyclist is well practiced on the bike as they can cause difficulties when starting and stopping. Cages are not recommended for prosthetic feet as they are more likely to get stuck in them.

From the Amputees

Armin Köhli, Switzerland

Older systems have a kind of a small basket on the pedal that covers the front of your foot. This you can use with your regular shoes. But it's not that easy to get your feet out if you have to stop quickly and unexpectedly. I use clipless pedals that fix the foot on the pedal. You need to get used to it and might fall while trying. But it will give you great relief after, as your feet will stick to the pedals. Shimano has a system called SPD which makes it easy to walk despite the cleats. They also have multifunctional pedals that you can use with or without fixing. The pedals clip in themselves, if you find the right position. That's the problem with the SPD system: The cleats are so small that it's difficult to find where they should clip in (with prosthetic legs).

I use a different system, LOOK pedals, for the road bike. They have much bigger cleats, so it's much easier to find the correct position for clipping in. The disadvantage is that it's much more difficult to walk with such big cleats. So for mountain biking and touring, I prefer the SPD system.

Mirsad Tokić, Croatia

I have to lock up my foot with the SPD system (special shoes with special pedals). It is much better.

Being able to keep prosthetic feet on pedals and having an adequate toe position are of importance for leg amputees cycling with prosthetics.

As beginners, leg amputees may find the thought of clipless pedals and the associated fall risk a bit daunting. Starting with alternatives, such as magnetic pedals, dual-sided pedals, and cleats for the non-amputated side only, are just some of the suggestions you will find on Internet forums contributed to by avid cyclists, both able-bodied and amputees.

Once experienced and comfortable, the Shimano Pedalling System SPD clip-in pedal might be a good option.

To limit the chance of a fall because of a trapped foot on the pedal, reduce the toe angle and try a BMX style pedal. An alternative is the Crank Brothers pedal and cleat system or egg beater pedal system.

Pedal Adaptations for Above-Knee Amputees

For above-knee amputees who want to ride a two-wheeler using just their dominant leg and no prosthetic, a cuff or sleeve can be attached to the top tube to hold the stump in place. It is fixed at an angle that is comfortable for the rider and helps provide the support if they want to pedal standing up.

Alternatively, an above-knee amputee may find it more comfortable to cycle without cuffs or prosthetics; however, circulation in and around the residual limb should be closely monitored to ensure no swelling occurs.

From the Amputees

The following pedal and crank suggestions are from Joe Sapere, founder of Amputees Across America, to improve mobility, comfort, and safety of the riders. Joe has many years of experience both as an amputee and cyclist. His invaluable words of wisdom are readily available on his website, www.amputeesacrossamerica.com, along with lots of information on bike rides he has completed to date.

To overcome issues of heel strike by the prosthetic leg, a pedal extension may be required.

Leg amputees may find standing on pedals easier with the use of Rotor Crank and Q-Rings which virtually eliminate the dead spot at the top of the stroke. These work on recumbents and trikes to increase the power transmitted to the pedals.

For single-leg amputees, it may be worth using a shorter crank on the prosthetic side as compared to the good side. Below-knee amputees could try using a BMX pedal with trainers on to keep the leg in place on the pedal before attempting clipless pedals.

D. Wheels

Bicycle wheels consist of a hub, spokes, and rim. The bike tire is mounted on the wheel rim. Rims can be designed to hold tires that are glued on or tires that are tubeless. They can be hollow, single, double, or triple walled. Optimizing rim aerodynamics is crucial for bike performance.

Spokes hold the wheel in shape, helping it to absorb shock. If there are fewer spokes, the bike can be more aerodynamic but requires a heavier metal for the rim. There are usually 28, 32, or 36 spokes on two-wheelers. Tandems require more spokes (up to 48) to help the wheel take the weight of the extra person.

The wheel must be adjusted laterally, vertically, and from left to right to ensure even wear across the surface area. This is known as *truing* and is best done by a bike repair expert or after some training. If spokes are loose, the wheel becomes easily damaged or out of shape.

The heavier the wheel, the harder to accelerate and brake. Variations of wheels include the disk wheel, spoke wheel, combination bladed spokes wheel, and carbon fiber wheels. Images of these are available on the Internet.

Wheels usually come in different sizes depending on the bicycle: 26 inches, 28 inches, 29 inches, or 20 inches. Wheel and tire sizes should match; put too small a tire on too big a wheel or too wide a tire on too thin a wheel rim will not work well. Recumbent wheels can be of any size, and the front wheel is usually smaller than the rear. This overcomes the problem of heel strike which happens when doing tight turns.

Kiera Roche, UK

I was involved in a road traffic accident at the age of 31 in 2001, becoming an above-knee amputee. Having been an active person, I wanted to get fit and feel normal again. In 2004, I agreed to be filmed for a television program, learning to cycle to take part in the 54-mile London to Brighton bike ride. Having a goal to work toward helped keep me focused and motivated. I took part in the bike ride and found it exhausting, but invigorating. Being on a bike gave me a sense of freedom I thought I had lost. I had the bug and decided I wanted to do something more challenging, so I signed up for a week-long charity bike ride in Egypt, cycling along the river Nile and through the Valley of the Kings. This has to be one of my favorite experiences. The weather was beautiful, and the scenery was monumental.

Next I came up with the idea for a team of amputees to cycle from Lands End to John o' Groats, visiting limb centers en route to inspire other amputees. We cycled 60-plus miles a day for 21 days, not the shortest route, but it was an experience I will never forget. Some days were incredibly grueling, while others were a sheer delight. It was incredibly rewarding seeing a team of amputees achieve something amazing, so we decided to launch a one-day bike ride for amputees, including a cycling clinic to teach amputees how to cycle using a prosthesis. This was a great success and led to the concept of the Amputee Games, which we launched in 2008 and features a cycling clinic. I have since cycled from London to Paris and around London at night to raise funds for amputee charities and to encourage other amputees to take up cycling.

Funny Things Happen on a Bike

We have some steep hills around here in the Purbecks, and I was determined to cycle up Creech Hill. I managed to get three-quarters of the way up on the ICE Adventure Trike. I lost all energy, stopped, and tried to dismount. The prosthetic foot could not accommodate the incline, pitched me to one side, and I fell into the ditch nearby with the trike on top of me. I was rescued by a passing motorist and my fellow riders, but I could not stand on the road, it was too steep!   *John Thraves, UK*

E. Tires

Today, most tires contain inner tubes that hold air pressure. These are made out of butyl rubber or latex. Inner tubes slowly lose pressure over time. Butyl rubber inner tubes are better at holding air pressure. The invention of tubeless tires in the early 20th century enabled lower tire pressure to be used. This reduced flat and pinched tubes due to high pressures. Some tires attach to the rim by a slotting-in mechanism and an airtight inner tube which is then filled with air. Most tires come in a variety of outer tread surface pattern suited for the cycling conditions. *Tread* is the term used to describe the part of the tire that comes in contact with the ground. It can be double-layered in the middle and single-layered on the edges. Tread patterns are designed along a spectrum of smooth, slick, or knobby. Smooth tread tires are more suitable for roads that are in a good state of repair.

They offer low rolling resistance to take the strain out of town riding while also giving sure-footed grip in all weather conditions.

Slick tires tend to be used for road and track racing. Designed for super stiff and smooth BMX tracks, the low and smooth tread pattern with tread blocks in optimal density provides adhesion and fine control.

Knobby tread tires are more suitable for poor or off-road conditions. The knobby tread comes in different sizes to suit the type of off road cycling, such as mountain biking or cyclocross.

The tread knobs are not too high but give good bite on most surfaces and fast corners. They also have good self-cleaning properties to ensure the tread does not clog, and they give great braking stability in all descents in cross-country racing.

Knobby tread tires are primarily for rough terrains, freerides, and endurance rides. These rides require the maximum use of their robustness, shape, and zooming of the individual tread pattern to provide safe grip in downhills while overcoming terrain obstacles.

The direction of the tread can affect which way the tire is supposed to be mounted. It can also affect whether the tire should be on the front wheel or the back wheel. The tread patterns are circular in profile so the tire can roll even when turning. For winter conditions (e.g., snow or ice), tires can have metal studs in the treads of knobby tires, and fatter (balloon) tires can also be used. For better visibility at night or when cycling in bad weather, reflective strips placed on the sides of the tires help others to see cyclists more easily.

Tires should be inflated to their recommended pressure rating. This is stamped on the side of the tire. Air pressure is measured in bar (pound force) or in psi (pressure per square inch) which is the pressure relative to atmospheric pressure at sea level. The recommended tire pressure comes as a lower and upper limit or range.

Having lower pressures in the tires gives more grip to the road surface. This makes the ride more comfortable. Higher tire pressure makes cycling quicker and reduces the chance of punctures. Tyres can also be inflated with carbon dioxide or helium, but these lose pressure quite quickly. They should only be used for emergency repairs.

F. Gears

Gears used to be single or fixed in the early days. Now most bikes come with multiple gears. Fixed-gear or single-speed bicycles are mainly used for children's bikes and some adult bikes. It is trendy among urban cyclists and cycle messengers to use fixed-gear bikes.

Gears are invaluable for cyclists to make uphill, downhill, or flat surface cycling easier. The more varied the terrain, the more gears are necessary. There are various methods of measuring the gearing; the main one is known as the gear ratio. This is measured by the relative sizes of the crank set, chain rings, and sprockets. If one turn of the cranks turns the sprocket four times, then the gear ratio is 4:1; this gear is big and gives speed. If it turns the sprocket once, then the gear ratio is 1:1; this gear is low and allows for climbing up hills slowly.

The main purpose of gears is to maintain a smooth pedaling action between 60 to 100 rotations of the pedal per minute (RPM) along various road conditions and surfaces. In lower gears, the cyclist has to pedal faster but with less force. In higher gears, the cyclist has to use more force to move the bike faster. Bicycles can come with gears in just the rear wheel or in both front and rear wheels.

There are two main types of gear change mechanisms: derailleurs and hub gears. There are plenty of resources available on the Internet or in books explaining the differences between these mechanisms for those with a more advanced level of interest in gearing. Hub gears form the internal gearing mechanism; they are hidden within either the wheel hub, crank set, or bottom bracket.

Mark Inglis, New Zealand www.markinglis.co.nz

I have always loved cycling—that passion culminating in a silver medal on the track in the Sydney 2000 Paralympic Games. Never one to slow down, using my science and winemaking, I developed a range of performance sports foods which became for a while the sports food of choice for serious athletes in New Zealand.

Life is, for me, all about participation. I've always felt it's no use being just a voyeur in life, as we are all here to make a difference. The concept of challenge and personal excellence is an integral part of my life, responsible on many levels for how I have turned what many people would think of as stumbling blocks to the stepping stones of life.

Recently, I have struck out in new directions, inspiring people to excel through presentations to corporate, school, and community groups. The more we can use the lessons we have learned through pushing the limits the better—both in our businesses and in our personal lives. There are a lot of people in our world today that need our support to really achieve their own potential in life.

Mark's books about his many adventures are available to order from his website.

Gears can be changed either by pressing a lever or twist shift action. The original lever system worked by friction and required the cyclist to guess how much to push or pull a lever in order to change gear. This was difficult to get right simply by experience and judgement. Improvements led to indexed gear levers that click when the gear is reached, letting the cyclist know it has been changed correctly. The lever could be finger operated or thumb operated, depending on which side of the handlebar you mounted it on. Another option involves twisting a barrel (twist shift) on the handlebar. The gear is changed by turning the dial by using a thumb, finger, or both. Levers can be different lengths, farther away or closer together on the handlebars. Integrated dual control brake levers and twist shifters are now available for arm amputees who require controls on one particular side of the bike.

G. Handlebars and Steering

Bicycle handlebars are in different positions, depending on the type of bike. On two-wheelers and tricycles, the handlebars are at the front of the bike above the front wheel. They form the main steering mechanism and support for the rider's weight.

Brake levers, bells, and gear levers are usually mounted on the handlebars.

There are many different handlebar designs. Racing handlebars are termed drop, pursuit, and triathlon. They enable the cyclist to assume the most aerodynamic position possible while racing and allow hand and body positions to be changed during long rides.

Mountain bike and BMX handlebars have to be strong enough to withstand crashes and provide fine control for moving over obstacles.

Wider handlebars allow better control at slower speeds; narrower handlebars allow better control at faster speeds. Tape or grips are put on handlebars to provide cushioning and comfort and help with grip in wet or cold weather or on uneven roads. Tape can be made from polyurethane, cork, rubber, plastic padding, cotton, or leather. Once it is wound around the handlebar it can be held in place with bar ends. Grips are made from soft plastic, foam, gel, or leather. Grips are anatomically shaped to fit the natural curve of your hand.

Steering for recumbent bikes comes as over seat, under seat, or center seat. For handcycles, the steering is usually over seat.

Suspension and Shock Absorption

Certain parts of the bike cushion the rider from uneven surfaces and ensure at least one wheel is in contact with the ground. This is especially important when dealing with potholes and loose stones. The main areas of suspension are the front, rear, saddle, stem, and wheel hub. Full suspension bikes have front and rear suspension whereas rigid bikes have no suspension. Riders can only achieve suspension by standing in the saddle and using their knees. Hardtail mountain bikes have only front suspension. Suspension systems in bike forks use a spring and damper mechanism. The spring is in one arm of the fork, and the damper is in the other arm. The damper consists of oil passing through small holes.

From the Amputees

Sara Tretola, Switzerland

Adapter on steering   *Ball clips onto an adapter on the bike*

I have a brake system called two brake. It links the front brake cable to the rear brake cable. When I operate the brake lever with the left hand, both front and rear brakes act at the same time. I also have an electric Shimano gear system which I have mounted on the left-hand side of the bike.

H. Brakes

Brakes are designed to allow the cyclist to stop the bike. The very early braking systems (spoon and duck brakes) led to a back pedaling brake mechanism used on bikes for disabled people. These are often seen on handbikes and tricycles. Brakes mounted on the front wheel tend to stop the bike more quickly than those mounted on the back wheel. Most bikes come with brakes on all wheels, depending on whether the bike is a two-wheeler or tricycle, for example. The components for braking systems are levers or pads, cables, hoses or rods, and calliper or drum. Road bikes use calliper brakes which are placed over the wheel frame and have two arms that squeeze either side of the wheel rim. They are mostly found on bikes where the tires are quite slim. They are side pull, center pull, or dual pivot systems. Dual pivot brakes do not brake well if the wheel is not trued correctly. U-brakes are a modern version of center pull calliper brakes and are the current standard on freestyle BMX frames and forks.

Cantilever brakes are often seen on mountain bikes as they work better with wider tires. V-brakes are a side pull version of cantilever brakes. They are regarded as a direct pull or linear pull system. They are more suited to mountain bikes with suspension systems.

The three main forms of braking systems in use today are rim, disc, and drum. Rim brakes are lightweight, easy to maintain, and perform better in good weather than in wet weather. They require regular maintenance and replacement when worn.

Disc brakes are metal discs attached to the wheel hub. They are good in all weather conditions as there is less build-up of mud or dirt in the mechanism. They are better for wide tires. Disc brakes can be mechanical or hydraulic. Mechanical versions use cables to attach the brake to the lever. They are inexpensive, low maintenance, and lightweight. Hydraulic disc brakes require two liquids: a mineral oil and a glycol ether brake fluid.

Drum brakes are also good for wet, muddy, or dirty conditions as the braking system is in the wheel hub. Coaster brakes are a type of drum brake also known as the back pedal brake, the foot brake, the contra, or the torpedo. When pedaling backward, the clutch is forced between two brake shoes that press against a brake mantle or into a split collar that expands against the brake mantle. Coaster brakes require little maintenance apart from regular grease. They are good for use in rain and snow as the braking system is internal. They are fitted to the rear wheel and can cause wheel skid. The front wheel should also have a suitable braking system applied to it if using coaster brakes.

It is customary to place the front brake lever on the left in countries that drive on the right side, and vice versa, because the hand on the side nearer the center of the road is more commonly used for hand signals, and the rear brake cannot pitch the cyclist forward. Track bikes do not have brakes. The only way to slow down is to lock the pedals and force a skid or pedal backward. Some BMX bikes do not have brakes. To stop, the rider puts his feet on the ground or between the seat and rear tire.

In Australia, Germany, the UK, Denmark, and many other countries, it is illegal to ride a bicycle without brakes on a public road.

Gear and Brake Adaptations for Arm Amputees

There are a variety of options for arm amputees who wish to try cycling two- or three-wheelers without prosthetics. Bike modifications include putting the brake levers and gear shifters on the dominant side.

The handlebar for the arm that is not there can be removed as in the figure above.

Other options for adaptation in cases of arm amputation include mounting the brakes behind the shoulder with a recumbent three wheeler.

For amputees who cannot operate brake levers or shifters mounted on handlebars, an alternative concept is the bum brake such as that used by quadruple amputee Jaye Milley at the 2012 London Paralympic Games. Devised by Pro Stergiou of Canadian Sports Centre and Dallas Morris of the University of Calgary, the brake is situated at the back of the saddle, in a T-bar off-the-seat post. To activate, the rider simply shifts his weight back toward the T-bar. These solutions or variations are equally suited to tricycles, recumbents, and handcycles.

From the Amputees

Victor Walther, Canada

Everyone, including amputees, has benefited from innovations in the industry, such as hydraulic disc brakes and a variety of shifter options (for arm amputees) along with a wider range of gears and pedal-shoe options (for leg amputees), as well as suspension (for everybody).

Jon Pini, UK

Up until recently I never had any adaptations on the bike. As I was growing up, we managed to put the gears, if they were three speed ones, on the left. I always just used one brake lever which was the left brake. This was always the back brake, so you didn't have the chance of just flipping over the bike as you would if you just used the front brake. But later on we did have modifications. On the last mountain bike I had, we put the two brake levers on the one side. That was made up independently by a friend of mine because at one stage a lot of cycle shops were unwilling to do it—probably due to litigation because if something snapped and the brakes didn't work you'd be in trouble. That was about 10 years ago. Since then you can actually get bespoke brake levers where one lever will operate two cables.

You can get new gearing systems which can be operated on one thumb shift or a twist grip. Obviously, gearing has become more complex as you've now got anything between 12, 15, 18, and 21 gears, and normally you have a selection on both sides. With the bike that I had, we had to combine the gears onto one side, so we had a twist grip which I could just twist back and forth and a thumb shift as well. The artificial side, which is my right side, was a simple passive hand which rests on the handlebars in order to gain that balance, confidence, and steering. It all helps. You need that extra support and balance going over rough terrain, particularly with mountain biking. The left hand did all the work with the brakes and gears, and I found that absolutely fine. I did struggle with drop handlebars. They were quite awkward. I did have one drop handlebar which I used, but very often I would just rest the arm on the top piece rather than the drop handle section. All my bikes have been on a straight stem and bar. I just found that more comfortable.

Srdjan Jeremic, Bosnia and Herzogovina

Srdjan usually uses mountain bikes with Shimano XT equipment specialized for hill and plain riding. Srdjan's friends made him a special glove he uses while cycling that attaches to both a bike and his residual limb. This glove helps him to keep good control of a bicycle. In addition, he has adapted his bicycle according to his needs, putting gear and brake commands on his right-hand side.

Further Reading
1. Bike frames: www.exploratorium.edu/cycling/frames1.html
2. How a bicycle is made: www.madehow.com/Volume-2/Bicycle.html
3. General design factors: www.dot.state.mn.us/bike/pdfs/manual/Chapter3.pdf
4. Bike frame materials: www.rei.com/learn/expert-advice/bike-frame-materials.html
5. List of bike parts: en.wikipedia.org/wiki/List_of_bicycle_parts

Things to Try for Yourself
1. Familiarize yourself with the different parts of a bike.
2. Visit a bicycle museum to learn more about bike developments.
3. Subscribe to a cycling magazine.
4. Visit a bike shop and ask to take a look at some bike parts.
5. Visit a bike recycling facility and take a look at their bike parts. Note the wear and tear aspects on them compared to the new bike parts in bike shops.

Did You Know?
1. The clipless pedal was invented in 1895 by Charles Hanson.
2. Charles Goodyear invented vulcanized rubber in 1844.
3. John Dunlop and Robert William Thomson are both credited with inventing the pneumatic tire in the late 1800s.
4. Edouard Michelin developed a detachable tire that could be held on the rim by metal clamps so that punctures could be repaired easily.
5. Tubeless tires were first patented in 1903 by P.W.Litchfield of the Goodyear company.
6. Grooved tires were invented in 1908 by Frank Seiberling to improve grip on roads.
7. The wheelbase is the distance between wheel axles or where the tires touch the ground. It is shorter on road bikes and longer in mountain bikes.
8. Bike handling sensitivity depends on the *trail*. This is the distance the wheel axle follows behind the steering pivot point. For easier sensitive bike handling there should be less trail; for greater stability there should be more trail.
9. Racing bikes tend to have no suspension apart from the little in the tires.
10. Suspension terms: preload, rebound, sag, lockout, bob, and squat. These are all terms used to describe suspension issues on bicycles. For example, bob and squat happen when the suspension isn't functioning effectively.

Funny Things Happen on Bikes

*There was an occasion on a Pollards Hill Cyclists ride (PHC) a month or two ago. Regular riders know how quickly or slowly all the other regular riders cycle or react to certain road and path layouts. We were going up a hill (so I generally know who is likely to overtake me going up hills), and one of the slower female riders who is usually particularly slow going uphill, but had been doing more cycling for the previous month (to and from work daily, in addition to the weekly PHC rides), said she was right behind me. About 5 seconds later, she said she was coming past me, and she zoomed past me going **uphill**. I nearly fell off my bike in amazement!*

Jim Bush, UK

Mirsad Tokić, Croatia

I was a deminer (a man who searches minefields) in a demining company for ten years. I made one mistake, stepped on a mine, and lost my left leg below the knee. Life as an amputee can be difficult because of lots of problems like taking a shower, sweating in summer, and running after my one-year-old boy. I liked cycling all my life, and there was no option—I had to try to ride my bike! That happened in a big park behind my house in Zagreb; I was very clumsy, and it was risky. I think I started with a bike in the same year 2007. (I know that I skied 11 months after accident.) In the beginning, there were some problems— fears of falling on the leg, turning on narrow paths. My greatest success was up and downhill on Sljeme, a little mountain near Zagreb. That was on paved road. Before the accident, I cycled through woods and off-road which was much more difficult.

Cycling up Sljeme

I woke up in the hospital after the mine accident, put a smile on my face, and told people around me: I will climb Sljeme with my bike again! Men around me felt pity for me. Of course, they thought I am in trauma. That idea was the medicine for my brain, the path to my target, my big ambition. The beginnings were shy with a mixture of thrill and a fear of falling. The main training took place on Jarun—a city lake with 6.3 kilometers (4 miles) of road for cycling, roller blading, and walking. I aimed to do about 50 kilometers (30 miles) in about 2 hours every second or third day for conditioning. First, I cycled in the hills above Zagreb. The next time I reached the first serpentine of Sljeme, one hour pedaling from home across the whole city. It was excellent training with very long and easy climbing. Next time was a sunny, cold autumn day—the perfect one. I reached the first serpentine again, took a break, and took off my prosthesis (yes, on the road). A forest worker saw me there while I changed cotton pads in the silicone liner (a very helpfully trick). He said, "svaka čast," which means "congratulations," and then he disappeared into the forest. And that was the trigger. About 14 kilometers (9 miles) of pure uphill and countless serpentines—it was a one-way road, and there was no turning back. Only beautiful forest lay ahead. I took another break in the middle and the third break at the top of the mountain. I have no picture of that! I can't explain my feelings—the man who can do anything. It was fast and cold downhill. I rode across the whole city without stopping to get home. Total distance was 47 kilometers (29 miles). Time— I don't know, and I don't care. I was so tired and satisfied!

Chapter 4

Bike Choices

The increased availability of different types of specialized bicycles, tricycles, recumbents, and handcycles has made it easier to find the right cycling equipment for all sorts of levels of amputation. Bike shops and bike manufacturers are more ready than ever to experiment with different modification possibilities to make your cycling experience safe, healthy, and enjoyable.

This section provides examples of different types of bicycles to investigate and experiment with as you start to explore the benefits of cycling for yourself. There are many options available all around the world, so check out your local bike shops first and take it from there. You never know, maybe you will end up having a bicycle collection that ends up looking a little like this:

→ Cartoon by Dave Walker **www.solpinsnaps.blogspot.co.uk/2012/10/cycling-cartoons.html**

There is a vast assortment of bicycles that amputees can try. The main consideration is how adventurous you are as a cyclist! If you used to cycle before, then dusting your old bike off might be an option. Before you do that, think about why you stopped riding it and whether it would be suitable since your amputation. Is it worth exploring other forms of cycling to give you time to get accustomed to it all again? Or are you confident enough to get back on your old bike? If you are totally new to cycling, then choosing a bike may present some initial challenges. The first thing to think about will be what sort of cycling you are looking to do. Some bikes are good for commuting, but not good for racing; others are good for off-road cycling, but not good for holidaying and touring. If you have never cycled before and are unsure as to the type of cycling you would find enjoyable, take the time to try out different varieties before you buy. In some countries, you may be lucky and find a bike rental center with a good range where you can hire a bike for an hour, a day, or a week. Alternatively, bike stores offer a possibility of short test rides on certain models.

Set yourself a realistic budget for your bike purchase. This should include the costs of repairing, maintaining, and insuring the bike. Compare and contrast as many bike features as possible before buying. The sensible parts to spend money on are the frame and the brakes. Plastic parts may damage quickly—best to avoid if doing a lot of cycling. It is important to get some idea of the amount of pedal effort the bike requires. Buying too heavy a model will make it hard work to pedal and may not be enjoyable for your first attempts at cycling. Bikes usually come already assembled and have a warranty. Read the manufacturer's guidance on the warranty limitations so you are aware of the things that are covered.

If the budget doesn't look like it can stretch toward a new bike with manufacturer's warranty, buy secondhand either through your local bike shop, a cycling charity, or a bike recycling facility. There is plenty of advice available at all these places if you want to discuss purchase options. If you want to browse other possibilities and are happy to undertake some repair work yourself or try a bike that might not be the perfect fit, then check out Internet auction sites, local adverts, and newspapers. Bikes do not have service manuals that provide an indication of how they have been used or maintained by previous owners.

Make sure any secondhand bike you buy is in good condition overall with very little wear and tear and is likely to fit you. Especially look for signs of frame damage, corrosion, rust, cable and brake defects, or other things that may make the bike dangerous to use. If there is rust on the outside, there may be rust on the inside of the tubes which causes frames to snap while in use. Ask the seller about age and previous use (weather and road conditions) and about falls or accidents.

Some well looked after older bikes last many years longer than newer models, but you may have to compromise on the weight of the bicycle and the latest gearing and brake developments or find ways to incorporate these into older models.

Technological advancements in online shopping and credit card use have allowed consumers to buy bikes from suppliers around the world. So, if you see a bike you like that is manufactured and supplied only from the Netherlands or from Japan, then as long as they export to other countries, you can put your order in using the Internet or telephone. Even with the currency conversion you might find a good bargain. Check the customs import tax and potential maintenance or repair costs as bike shops may be particular about repairing bikes not bought through their stores. Parts may be more expensive to source if the bike is not a standard range model.

The main aspect to consider if importing a bike from another country will be the gearing and braking system. Remind them (and yourself!) that you will need these set up for left-hand drive roads or right-hand drive roads, or, if you are an arm amputee, for whichever side is your dominant side. If you require substitutions to components, ask at the time of buying as you may get a discount and free fitting.

A good way of learning more and getting lots of expert advice and information when considering the buying decision is to visit a cycle exhibition or show where manufacturers of bikes and accessories are available to answer a lot of questions. There are usually a lot of bikes available to try out on small routes around the exhibition center. These events can get quite busy, so choose your day wisely. The beauty of visiting such exhibitions is that you are surrounded by experts. Most people who attend such exhibitions are highly experienced cyclists, not just the organizers, but the exhibitors and many of the visitors. You never know who you might bump into at such events, so keep that autograph book and pen at the ready and don't feel intimidated or shy of asking questions. Most charge an entry fee and parking fee if traveling by car. Disabled parking facilities are usually available. Booking in advance is advisable in the more popular events, and some days are busier than others, so go on a quieter day and enjoy it all at your leisure. Examples of the many bike fairs planned for 2016 include:

- EICMA, Italy
- International Bicycle Show, Canada
- 26th International Bicycle Fair, China
- GoExpo, Finland
- Euro bike, Germany
- Inabike, Indonesia
- Velopark, Russia
- Cycle Show, UK
- Interbike, USA

Bike Fit

A bike is not a one size fits all type of vehicle. The better the fit of the bike to the rider, the more comfortable and enjoyable the cycling journey. The process of bike fit generally involves compromises between comfort, performance, stability, acceleration, and speed. The contact points for the rider in all versions of cycling are the pedal, saddle, and handlebars. These are the areas that should be the

most comfortable and easiest to use. Don't buy a bike on which you are uncomfortable. You won't use it, and it will sit gathering dust or getting in your way, and you will wish you had never bought it. A bike that is too big for you will be difficult and dangerous to control.

One too small for you will cause discomfort or injury. The position of your body on the bike affects your riding technique. Don't keep trying to ride a bike in a position you're not happy with. Most cyclists need to readjust fit over time as they cycle. As the body ages or as the type of cycling changes, the fit of the bike needs to be altered.

For handcycles, the adjustments needed in order to fit the rider will be in the seating position (front/back), seat angle (lean back more or less), headset (nearer/farther away), and handgrips (fatter, smaller, side or top). Most of these adjustments can be made with an Allen key and a bit of tinkering.

For recumbents, the reach of the foot to the pedal is important. The knee should have a slight bend in it at full pedal extension. The crank should be the correct size to ensure the pedal does not hit the ground on rotation, and the seat should be adjustable in forward and back positions and level of recline. The handlebars should be easily reached and of the correct width for the rider. Too big, too small, too high, or too low may result in wrist, hand, or neck injury.

The angle of recline in both the handcycle and recumbent will affect visibility while cycling. The more reclined the rider, the less visibility they have of road conditions farther ahead.

For upright two-wheelers and tricycles, a number of sizing systems are used ranging from the use of manual mathematical instruments by a bike fit expert to computer-based versions that analyze a cyclist's data in digital film format. There are several variables that determine these positions:

- Distance from crank center or bottom bracket to saddle
- Distance from saddle to handlebar
- Saddle angle
- Relative height of saddle and handlebar
- Seat tube angle and saddle offset
- Handlebar width
- Crank length
- Handlebar drop on road-style handlebars

Two-Wheelers

It is best to wear cycling shorts for a fitting as these will allow better measurements to be taken. First, the fitter will ask some routine medical and riding questions to establish your level of cycling experience, type of cycling, injuries, and cycling goals. Then a physical evaluation is undertaken to decide levels of flexibility, strength, spinal weakness, curvature, and misalignment. Tape measurements are taken of trunk, forearm, arm, and total height along with parts of the body that are used while cycling. These allow the bike fitter to work out the contact points for the cyclist for the position of the saddle, pedal, and handlebars. A plumb-line is used to make sure the saddle position is correctly adjusted, and fine-tuning is undertaken at this stage.

Computer-aided bike fitting is becoming more popular. The cyclist's measurements and type of cycling they intend to do are entered into the program, either professional racing or recreational. The computer makes recommendations for seat tube length, top tubes, and handlebars. An enhancement is the use of camera technology. The camera enables 3D data capture along with software that provides an extremely accurate measure of the geometry of a rider and bike while cycling. The saddle, handlebars, and frames are all tailored to suit the type of cycling (e.g., mountain biking or road cycling). The anatomical shape of men and women differs markedly. Women generally have shorter legs and longer torsos. Usually, for mountain bikes and most other two-wheelers, there should be a clearance of 3 to 4 inches from the top tube and your body when you straddle the bike. It is best to choose the smallest possible frame, one that is lighter and easier to maneuver.

Saddle

The saddle shape can be measured by a device that you sit upright on. Memory foam in the device creates an impression of your sit bones. The saddle height should be adjusted to allow the rider to reach the pedals with a slight bend in the knees (30 degrees) even when the pedal is fully extended. Someone may need to hold the bike steady when you do this. The following is one recommended technique on a fixed stationary bike:

1. Sit on the saddle with one leg hanging free and your hips square.
2. Set the saddle high enough so that your other heel can just touch the pedal with your leg straight and with the pedal at the bottom of the stroke in line with the seat tube.
3. Pedal with the balls of your feet over the axle of the pedals. The height of the saddle should leave some bend in the knee at the bottom of the stroke.

This height may be too difficult for absolute beginners to feel comfortable with as it means that your feet should not touch the ground when you are on the saddle of a two-wheeler. It may be something to aim toward once you have mastered the basics of balance, steering, and control on a saddle set at a slightly lower height.

Changing pedals or cranks affects the saddle position and height. The saddle should be almost level or angled slightly upward. If it is angled downward, you will fall onto the top tube. The closer you can get to a level platform, the easier it will be to find the best position of saddle and handlebar. The farther over the handlebars your body is when you cycle, the farther forward the saddle has to be positioned to enable you to remain balanced. If your body is more or less upright when cycling, the saddle should be brought back away from the handlebars more. A good way of measuring this is to put the saddle in a position on a stationary fixed bike. The rider takes the hands off the handlebars. If they can remain upright and pedal comfortably with no strain in the back or arms or without falling forward, then the seat position is correct.

From the Amputees

Mark Ormrod, UK

I'd say the first thing to check on the bike is that you're positioned in it correctly. If you're not, you may be okay for a little while, but if you're putting in big miles, it's going to get uncomfortable unless you're in the best possible position.

Steve Middleton, Canada

For an above-knee amputee, the ability to touch the ground while seated is mandatory. A cycle shop can be a great help with all of this.

Cranks

As much body weight as possible should be carried by the pedals. The crank length should be sufficient to allow the rider to get past the 90-degree bend in the knee at the top of the pedaling stroke. This may require shortening the crank length, altering the type of crank system being used, or increasing the seat height. Crank length affects pedal movement. The larger the diameter of movement as seen with longer cranks, the more flexion experienced by your knee and thigh muscle. Choose a crank length that requires less knee flexion, especially for lower-limb amputees. This overcomes the problems of prosthetics limitations so your muscles work more efficiently. From research conducted by sports and biomechanical scientists, the optimum crank length for cardiac efficiency is 120 millimeters to 160 millimeters for most cyclists.

Handlebars

For recreational cycling, handlebars should be an inch or two above the saddle to begin with. It is important to be able to reach the handlebars comfortably with elbows slightly bent. The back should be leaning forward at around 45 degrees. For racers, the handlebars are positioned lower due to their aerodynamic positioning. In racing bikes that have dropped handlebars, these should be dropped down at a 10- to 20-degree angle from horizontal. The seat height and pedal position should be adjusted with the rider in racing position—aerodynamic, flattened back. Handlebar and saddle height depend on how quickly the cyclist wants to pedal and whether that body position can be maintained over a particular distance without injury.

Bikes and Accessories for Children

While there are handlebar seats and rear seats for very young children, as amputees, the safest options are possibly the use of a trailer or tag-along (trail-a-bike) for children once you are fully confident in your cycling ability. Trailers may be adjusted to fit other forms of bikes rather than just two-wheelers. They come with one or two seats, have a plastic covering which protects them from mud splashes and weather, and they convert into strollers when not attached to the bike. Children have space in the trailer for toys and drinks, and they are strapped in for safety.

Tag-alongs are part of a bike that has a bar clamp for the seat post of your bike so the steering is left to you. It is a form of tandem, but the child can stop pedaling if he gets tired. When choosing a tag-along, it is a good idea to take the child with you for a test drive before buying. The bar clamp (bracket) should be the correct size for your seat post. It is important that they listen to you while on the tag-along as it is easy to lose balance if they try to make sudden movements of any sort.

A common misconception for parents who buy their children cycles is to choose something that is too big for them with the idea that they will grow into it. Parents usually end up frustrated that their child will not use the bike or trike because they are scared of falling off. Check the weight of the child's bike. Are the brakes easy to use (e.g., with just your little finger)? Can your child reach the handlebars easily and put his fingers over the brakes sufficiently? There should be a chain guard on the bike to prevent shoelaces, clothing, or other items from getting caught. Cycles for children should not be too tall, the seat should not be too high, and the wheelbase should be wide enough to distribute their weight across the whole of the cycle.

Seats should be stable, and bicycles should have the options of attaching training wheels and push bars so parents can assist and support their child as they learn how to cycle. There are guide charts available on the Internet or from bicycle shops to help decide on the correct bicycle for your child.

Push bars (attached to the back of the bike) are a good safety feature for hills, descents, and traffic areas. Safety flags are also useful to ensure visibility. Children need to be instructed on looking after their bikes; however, most will want to test their own and the bike's limits. So be prepared to be a regular at the bike store and prosthetics clinics getting repairs and replacements of bike and prosthetics parts in their first years of cycling. As soon as your child stops growing in height, it is worth getting a proper bike fit done as that will reduce the effects of overuse injury later on in life. (See chapter 12, Common Injuries and Stump Care.)

To gain some ideas of the cycling you might like to try either with an older child, a friend or just by yourself, here is a brief overview of the different varieties and when you might use them.

Side by Side

These are ideal for introducing an amputee to cycling, especially for those who express a general fear of cycling. They consist of two recumbent bicycles joined together side by side to form a recumbent quad bicycle, allowing two people to ride together. An experienced rider can sit alongside the novice and talk them through various bike- and prosthetic-related issues as they pedal along a route. These are also good for older amputees who do not feel comfortable balancing on two-wheelers or tricycles. Their size limits use to wider roads rather than off-road and single dirt track use, but for total beginners and those who do not know the benefits of cycling, it is worthwhile. They can be hired at bike rental centers or are available to buy. Side by sides can be customized with rear child seats for a family outing, or even with lights, horns, sun canopies, cargo platforms for carrying shopping, and electric motor gear for extra power when climbing hills or accelerating from stationary.

Handcycle

A handcycle is powered by the arms instead of the legs. As arms are weaker than legs, handcyclists use the whole upper body to help provide power and achieve speed. They are used for commuting, touring, utility, recreation, and competing.

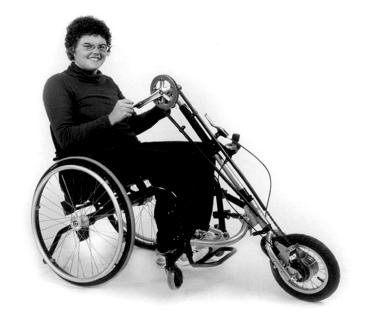

There are two types of handcycles: one that clips on to the

front of a wheelchair and one that the rider sits in. In clip-on handcycles, the rider is generally sitting upright in the wheelchair; sit-in handcycles come in either upright or recumbent styles. Wheelchair attachments are usually quite simple and can be manual, fully electric, or electrically supported. Most are designed to be easy to take on and off the wheelchair as required. For indoor use, they can also be fixed to become a stationary bike.

For competitive handcycling, nearly all riders use a sit-in handcycle. It is aerodynamic and allows better turning and acceleration than a wheelchair adaptation. Most have two rear wheels and one front wheel (delta), but some also come with two wheels at the front and the single at the rear (tadpole).

The aspects to consider when looking at different handcycle options will be the tires, wheels, brakes, suspension, front unit, overall shape, and whether it is an upright, recumbent, knees bent, or fully recumbent version. Having a variety of tire options is useful for the different types of road and weather surfaces that you may come across. If you cannot choose between the different forms of cycling, why not combine both? This allows you to use arm and leg power while cycling.

Before investing in a handcycle, whether new or second-hand, have a word with your local bike shop to see if they would be willing to undertake repairs and maintenance. The parts that need repairing or replacing from time to time tend to be the tires (punctures), sprockets, chain, and chain rings. Cables get worn if a lot of steering is done on uneven terrain. Paintwork will get scratched as handcycles are somewhat nearer to the ground as compared to upright two-wheelers and, therefore, more accessible to loose stones and gravel.

The frame may dent or break if using it off-road with very uneven or rocky ground. Handcycle manufacturers will also have recommended repairs and maintenance advice that will keep a new handcycle within its warranty obligations. In the longer term, you might prefer to do the basic maintenance yourself, but in the initial stages, it will give you some peace of mind to know that there are others around who can assist with these things.

The beauty of handcycling is that it can be done in lots of different places and in lots of different conditions. Whether it's racing, off-road, snow, or rain, if you want to handcycle in it, there is nothing to stop you.

There are handcycling organizations in many countries, such as Handcycling UK, Handcycling America, and Handcycling Europe, that hold introductory taster sessions and organize group rides during the outdoor handcycling season. Handcycling organizations also organize holidays and tours, so it is worth linking into your local organization for lots of hints, tips, fun, adventure, and advice on the best way to enjoy handcycling on or off-road.

From the Amputees

Joe Beimfohr, USA

I ride an Invacare Top End Force K. It is a kneeling handcycle, so I'm able to bear weight on my residual limb and use my core muscles to power the hand cranks. Each handcycle is custom built for the individual rider. I couldn't wear prosthetics with the riding position I use. Plus, we're always looking to ride with the least amount of weight possible. Since I bear all of my weight on

my one residual limb, I need to pad my knee so that I can stay in that position for long rides. I wear a volleyball knee pad and also use a customized seat cushion. I'm a hip disarticulation on my right side and don't sit level like most people, so I need to raise it.

Joe's Tips for New Amputees Considering Cycling

Attend either an adaptive sports camp or clinic and try different types of bikes. Your level of injury will determine what bike you can ride, but the bikes are so advanced these days that no one model is faster than another. It still all comes down to the rider.

Tricycle (Three-Wheeler)

Popular in many countries, these are used by both adults and children for leisure and transportation. Tricycles allow amputees to focus less on balance concerns and more on technique while out cycling. Because a tricycle is fully balanced when stationary, the cyclist is not under pressure to take his foot off the pedal when stopping as on a two-wheeler. The balance issues of uphill cycling are also reduced, even when going slowly. Falls and injuries are less likely to be an issue for a total beginner. The comfortable chair-like seat of the recumbent tricycle also reduces the doubts about saddle comfort and safety. Tricycles for adults include multiple speed gearing and front and rear brakes. For amputees of all ages who have not cycled before or have concerns about their ability to balance on a two-wheeler, the tricycle is worth trying.

If you have a two-wheeler that you do not enjoy riding anymore, it can be converted into a tricycle quite easily with a conversion set to form a recumbent tricycle.

Children's tricycles are the key to their independence and mobility. They enable a child to develop steering, pedaling, and control of a tricycle with an amputated limb or prosthetic device with reduced risk of balance issues. Children's versions usually have no brakes and tend to be made from plastic or, in some countries, bamboo, which is equally lightweight and strong, but does not rust like metal.

Tandem tricycles are a good option to consider for sociable cycling. They are usually recumbents with a detachable coupler for easy dismantling and transport. Some versions allow both cyclists to pedal at different speeds.

A good way to try your hand at tricycling is to join an association such as the Tricycle Association UK (or a similar one in your country) or rent a model from bike rental centers, or even direct from manufacturers. This site is a good source for bike rental: www.draisin.com/draisin-rental.

From the Amputees

John Thraves, UK

In the past, many trikes, the recumbent styles in particular, have been looked upon with disdain by the dinosaurs in the cycling clubs and organizations. I have two recumbent trikes: one is the HPV Scorpion FS, and the other is an ICE Adventure both with a Bionx system. I admit I have had to go down this road for health reasons, but I wish I had considered this mode of cycling much earlier.

During the last two years, a lot of development and research has taken place both in Europe and in America. The Dutch have done a lot of development with different materials and folding models, and the Germans with alternative forms of suspension, different wheel sizes and styles of recumbent. In all cases, manufacturing techniques and quality has improved enormously. There is certainly a demand for good quality brands and products. In fact, the British firm ICE with their new Adventure model was voted Trike of 2012. I have ridden this model, and it is very good—a superb finish, good road holding with full suspension, and comfort to match. My latest is an Ice Sprint with the latest crank drive system. Additional supports are available to help you mount and dismount with ease.

Robert Bailey, USA

I think trikes are wonderful for amputees. They give you the stability of three wheels. It is extremely comfortable. The most important thing is it takes all stress off your residual legs. I did have to make changes to the trike. I found the stock 170-millimeter cranks were too long, so I installed a 152-millimeter mountain bike crank. A trike cannot be "mashed." You have to spin, so it is easier with a fast cadence. Then I installed Q-rings by QRotor. These elliptical chain rings did a great job of banishing the dead zones on my pedal stroke. These dead zones are when each foot was fully extended on my trike. On an upright bike this would be when the foot was either at the top or bottom of the stroke. It was a big change that worked. I have to thank the Veterans Association (VA). They have always been willing to help me purchase parts.

Recumbents

Recumbents come in various options, depending on the type of cycling that is being done. They can be two-, three-, or four-wheel versions. Stationary recumbents can be found in a fitness or training center to use in the warm-up and cool-down phase of training. For general leisure cycling, an option to consider is the semi-recumbent bicycle. These are not designed for speed or performance, but they are comfortable and easy to use.

Recumbents can be adapted to enable off-road use if the route is wide enough without too many narrow or tight curves. For off-road use, they usually have large diameter wheels and higher gearing to enable better traction and climbing. Suspension and brake systems are also included in these models.

For racing and competition use, there are two different recumbent bike styles that are commonly used: low racers and high racers. Low racers are totally reclined and highly aerodynamic. High racers use larger wheels, so they require the cyclist to be higher up. They are easier to balance on at lower speeds. Recumbents can be part of a hybrid tandem where there is a mix of both upright and recumbent in one unit.

Upright Two-Wheelers

There are many different varieties of upright two-wheelers which may seem difficult to ride for some amputees, but once the techniques are mastered, they will find it equally, if not more enjoyable than many other forms of cycling. These are the different types of two-wheelers:

- Mountain bikes
- Road bikes
- Touring bikes
- Commuting bikes
- Time trial bikes
- Track bikes
- Tandems
- BMX and Cyclocross Bikes
- Utility bikes
- Folding bike
- Unicycle
- Electric Bike

Mountain Bike

The mountain bike is the most popular of the two-wheelers for most leisure cyclists. They are typically designed for strength and stability over uneven or rough ground. Balance is easier to achieve with fatter tires. Mountain bikes come in three versions: hard tail (no suspension), hybrid (front suspension), and full suspension (front and rear suspension).

From the Amputees

Mirsad Tokić, Croatia

I had a mountain bike for freeriding on forests and hills. It was stolen because I was not able to carry it to my flat on the first floor. Now, I have a road bike with 28-inch wheels. It has a bit of a different construction. Maybe that is the reason for the 17-millimeter cranks.

The photo shows me and my bike on a TACX trainer (www.tacx.com/) on my balcony. That TACX device is very good thing, but is very difficult for the brain because it is so boring.

Jon Pini, UK

I had a standard mountain bike—front suspension, nice lightweight aluminum frame. At the time, cantilever brakes were being replaced by V-brakes because they produce better force onto the rims, but now, of course, you can get disc brakes. You can still work one lever with two cables on certain disc brakes but not all of them. But the bike, apart from having the brakes and gearing altered, was a standard bike which I think most upper-limb amputees would be able to cope with. Whatever side is your sound side, you'd have to put all your brake cables and gearing onto that side to make it easier to control the bike. The biggest thing would be whether they are above or below elbow. Possibly an above-elbow amputee may need a specific arm to cycle, such as a straight arm to rest on the bars (i.e., no elbow joint involved), to give him more stability.

Mark Inglis, New Zealand

I ride a Lightspeed road bike as I love something unusual and the "feel" of the titanium frame but have ridden every type over the years. Currently, my mountain bike is a 29er single speed—no gears, just push a damn sight harder! Likewise, I've had every sort of MTB over the years. Just buy the best you can afford from a reputable bike shop. The bike might be a bit more expensive, but the service and good advice will make up for that in every way.

Road Bike

This is lightweight and built for speed and long-distance cycling along paved roads. It usually has a narrow saddle and dropped handlebars to allow the rider to lean forward for more aerodynamic cycling. There can be anything up to 33 gears, and gear shifters are usually part of the brake lever mechanism. Those with three chain wheels at the front make climbing easier. The frame is designed to be very light, lean, and compact.

Touring Bike

The invention of the bicycle opened up the world of transportation for vast numbers of people. Bicycle touring became a hobby, a holiday, and an adventure organized either by the cyclists themselves or by professional clubs for business or charity. *The Wheels of Chance*, a comical novel written by H.G. Wells in 1896, describes perfectly the freedom and exhilaration of cycling holidays and touring the countryside by bicycle.

A bicycle tour can be of any distance and time. Long-distance cycle touring over weeks, months, or years requires special touring bicycles that can carry the cyclist and his equipment. Such bikes have space for racks and panniers, extra water bottles, mudguards, and extra gearing. The tires are usually wider to take the weight and provide a comfortable ride over longer distances. Handlebars tend to be drop or butterfly to allow various hand positions. Bicycle trailers can also come in useful for equipment.

Commuting/City Bike

These are typically bicycles that take a person to and from their place of work to their house on a daily basis. They come with hub gears and chain guards, built-in locks, integral lighting, and rounded handlebar grips for upright riding. City bikes are heavier than road bikes and racers and are not so good on steep hills, but for general commuting in most cities, they are very efficient.

Time Trial Bike

Time trial bikes are particularly used for racing in velodromes or on roads. A main feature is the handlebar, known as the aerobar. Its shape allows the cyclist to maintain a low, tucked position for better speed and stability. The wheels are usually disks or have deep rims instead of spokes. The main aim of the bike design and rider position is to gain as much aerodynamic advantage as possible. They are similar to triathlon bikes.

Track Bike

These are fixed gear bikes used in velodromes for competition purposes. The modern track bicycle doesn't have a freewheel or brakes. There is only one gear, which is a low one, to allow quicker acceleration. Made from carbon fiber, it is extremely light. It has a higher bottom bracket so pedals don't scrape against the velodrome track surface. The wheelbase is quite short, and the seat and head tubes are set quite steep. Tires are usually tubular, narrow, and inflated to high pressures for speed.

Tandems

These are bicycles or tricycles designed to be ridden by two people, both of whom pedal. Riders typically are positioned one in front and one at the back. The rider in the front is known as the captain, pilot, or steersman. The rider at the back is known as the stoker. The rider in the front steers as well as pedals while the rider at the back concentrates on pedaling and enjoying the landscape. Tandems have double the pedaling power and are often better on the flat and downhill than a conventional bike. Uphill tandem cycling requires good pedal coordination between riders and is slower than a conventional bike. Tandems can be made for more than two people, and these are used in the entertainment and acrobatics industries. While most tandems have the cranks linked to enable timed pedaling by both cyclists, some models allow independent pedaling. A combination version of hand and foot tandem is also available for multiple disability or mixed able-bodied and disabled users. Tandems are ideal for blind cyclists as the stoker does not have to steer.

BMX and Cyclocross Bikes

BMX bikes are very compact two-wheelers designed for stunts in urban settings whereas cyclocross bikes are tough bikes suited to extreme off-road racing. They usually have knobby tread tires of a smaller diameter and sturdy robust frames. These bikes tend to get damaged, so it is not worth spending too much money on frames and fancy components due to the nature of the cycling undertaken. Most regular cyclocross enthusiasts have at least two or three bikes to see them through a season. Amputees do cyclocross and mountain biking off-road. They usually compete against able-bodied cyclists as there are not enough numbers of amputees doing this type of activity yet.

From the Amputees

Armin Köhli, Switzerland

I got my first (race) bike as a gift. A very old secondhand bike, steel frame, but nice. The second one was a cheap deal from my favorite bike mechanic. Steel no-name frame, but produced by a well-known manufacturer. Then I started approaching the manufacturers directly and got really good bikes for a good price—the initial steps of sponsoring. First made of aluminium, then carbon. (But I never got one entirely for free.)

My advice: Buy good quality if you can afford it. Not the best quality (Campagnolo Record or Shimano Dura-Ace or similar), because they are made for racers. That means they are extremely light, but won't live long. So don't take the lightest material, but buy good quality that will last for years.

Dan Sheret, USA

My first bike I rode across America cost about $600.00 USD. It was considered cheap by most bike standards, but it got the job done and was still useable when the trek was over. As your interest in the sport grows, so will your ability and desire to get better and more expensive bikes. While non-cyclists might consider five to six bikes excessive, for an avid cyclist, this is a normal amount of bikes!

Esneider Muñoz Marín, Columbia

I ride a conventional bike. I have prostheses on both feet, and I cycle with these. On my bike, I have no attachments or adaptations that could help my performance.

Nathan Smith, New Zealand

Mostly I ride my BMC road bikes for training and racing. But I also have two time trial bikes (one for racing and one for training), a track bike, and a commuter to ride with the kids. I require no adaptations to my bike.

Sara Tretola, Switzerland

For road racing, I ride either a Specialized or a MErida for time trials. And for track races, I have a track bicycle. This fixed-gear bike has no brakes and no gears and a drive train with no free wheel mechanism. This allows you to brake or control the speed with just your legs.

Utility Bike

These types of bikes are generally used for shopping or transporting people and goods over short distances, often in developing countries or big cities. Professionals who have to deliver, transport, or commute take up cycling as a practical method to complete their job. The main features include a step-through frame, mudguards, chain guard, and a kick stand so the bike remains upright when stationary. Parts are designed for strength and durability. Attaching trailers and other extensions such as child seats allows for flexible transportation. The cargo or trailer fixed at the back is a better option rather than a basket at the front for difficult road surfaces such as gutters and potholes.

Folding Bike/Trike

A bike that can be folded (or taken apart in an easy manner) makes it practical for general everyday cycling and is an option for amputees who commute in cities. When folded, they should be easy to carry and store in crowded areas or small spaces. This allows them to be taken on planes, into workplaces, and on trains or buses with minimal problems. Folding bikes can be more expensive than other bikes due to the technical difficulties of an easy folding mechanism that makes a lightweight, compact bike. Frames only come in one size, so all other aspects (seatpost, handlebars) are more adjustable. They can be folded in a number of ways: half- or mid-fold, vertical fold, or triangle hinge. Usually a flick of a latch or quick release mechanism enables the bike to be folded.

Unicycle

Unicycling has developed from an entertainment activity to a competitive sport and recreational pursuit. For an amputee who has never cycled, it is an ambitious prospect. For those who unicycled before their amputation, it is again simply a matter of adapting the prosthetic limb slightly and practicing as much as possible to regain the balance and coordination that was there previously.

→ **www.stumpsandcranks.co.uk/videos**

A unicycle has very few parts. The wheel is designed so that the axle is fixed to the hub. There are no chains, gears, or brakes. The pedals rotate the crank, turning the wheel directly. The frame is the shape of a front frame post of a two-wheeler, and this sits on top of the axle with the cranks attached to the end of the axle. There are a range of unicycles, such as freestyles, trials, mountain unicycles, giraffes, and long-distance unicycles. Due to the extreme nature of this type of cycling, a lot of safety equipment is recommended, such as helmet and knee and elbow pads. For more information, consult the International Unicycling Federation at unicycling.org.

Electric Bikes (E-Bikes)

An electric bike (e-bike) is a conventional pedal cycle with an integrated motor and battery. This extra power assists the rider to cycle different terrains without huge amounts of effort. E-bikes may be a way forward for amputees who are taking their first tentative steps into the arena of bicycles as a form of transportation or recreation. Moving away from car usage to other forms of transportation can seem rather daunting whether you are an amputee or not.

If you did not ride a bicycle before your amputation and are concerned about your ability to power up hills or ride longer distances without too much exertion or negative impact to your stumps while improving your cycling confidence and technique, then an electric bike can certainly support your efforts.

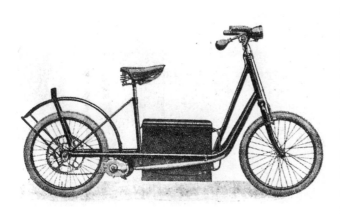

If you think the concept of the e-bike is new, then prepare to be shocked: Inventors have been trying to modify the power and range of the standard bicycle using things such as steam, lead acid batteries, petrol power, and compressed air since the late 1850s. That's over *150 years* of tinkering and blue-sky dreaming to give cyclists the transportation solution that is the electric bicycle of today!

Choosing an e-bike for an amputee requires similar thinking processes as for any other cyclist interested in trying an electric version of an old favorite. First and foremost, it's important for you to consider what you expect to do with the bicycle before you buy it. Are you going to use it to

- commute to work,
- take short leisure rides,
- tour or holiday,
- transfer loads and goods, or
- carry passengers?

Again, buying new or secondhand is something to think about. The best option for secondhand e-bikes is through a good local bike shop so you know it has been checked over properly. While more expensive than buying online, you know you can keep going back to them if things start going wrong. The quality of the bike is important as well as the quality of the electric system being used with it. It is better to get something that is of good quality on both those aspects so if the electric system did go for any reason the bike is still good enough for you to pedal until it can be fixed. A test ride is important when considering the purchase of any bike, but more so with an e-bike. Not only should you try it with the electrics, but it is advisable to try pedaling it without the electrics as well. Imagine the worst case scenario where the battery runs out, it is cold, dark, and wet, and you have miles to cycle to get home. Could you do it with that bike without assistance? Electric bikes, as a rule, are heavier than a simple two-wheeler or tricycle equivalent due to the motor and battery. There are also rules about the legal speed limit that can be cycled with these in some countries without it being subject to the rules of motor vehicles.

If buying online on auction sites, make sure they are trustworthy. These have buyer protection policies in place. Always email the seller to find out why they are selling the bike and try to get some usage history from them, too. If the bike has been well looked after, then it will be worth buying. Even after you have bought the bike, take it to a good bike shop to be checked over for any obvious issues. Buying secondhand is only recommended if you have existing knowledge of bikes and electric systems or access to such expertise through a good bike shop.

The two types of e-bikes are pedelecs and twist-n-go. The pedelec monitors the rider's pedaling rate, force, and bike speed and automatically adds motor assistance when necessary. The twist-n-go is a simple on/off switch or twist grip operated by the rider. They are both designed to provide assistance only when the rider is pedaling. The twist-n-go can be operated without pedaling if required, but doing this is not recommended as the motor is not meant to take all the effort of powering both bike and rider. Throttle-only power ultimately may not be good for the electrical system. The motors for pedelecs and twist-n-go systems can be mounted either in the hub of the wheel or within the crank and pedal area. Both are well enclosed and relatively quiet systems, so there should be little issue of dirt or debris from the road surfaces entering the mechanism.

Both systems use battery packs made up of electric cells. The main aspect during manufacture is that of battery matching. This should ensure that all the cells "wear" at the same rate and give roughly the same capacity to store energy throughout battery life. Battery packs have a limited life and will need to be changed every so often. The frequency of this will depend on the level of use and care. The efficiency of battery cells to store and deliver electrical energy is reduced with use.

They will require replacing after a year or two, so battery replacement costs of around $750 should be factored into your budget when deciding what to buy. Some battery packs come with a manufacturer's warranty for the maximum number of charge cycles that they can undergo. This is based on a full discharge–recharge cycle. Charge cycle information is designed as a rough guide only. A relatively small number of batteries on the more expensive models come with built-in software that records the number and level of discharges. Charging batteries is a complicated issue. Any time you put the battery on to charge, even if it is only half empty, is considered as a charge cycle. It is, however, considered better to charge the battery regularly from "not quite empty to full" rather than a small number of "totally empty to full" charges.

Batteries should be charged indoors in warm environments as cold weather affects the ability of the battery to produce electrical energy. In cold weather, it is best to keep the battery in a warm place and only fit it on just before you go out to ride so that it can still provide enough power. There are four main varieties of batteries: lead acid (still used in Far East and developing countries), nickel cadmium, nickel metal hydride (NiMH), and lithium-ion. Engineers are working hard to improve the weight, safety, and reliability of lithium-ion batteries, using different internal chemistries based on iron, manganese, and other elements. They are the battery of choice for current electric bike manufacturers. If the battery has a larger storage capacity, it may be heavier and take longer to recharge. Average charge times are between four and six hours for a full charge. This is decreasing with technological improvements in battery manufacture. Battery choice depends on how much pedaling assistance you think you are going to need. If quick charge times and cycling only a few miles a day are important, then a small battery will suffice. If cycling longer distances, then a larger battery capacity will be needed, but you may not be able to charge it up quickly enough to its full capacity. Stacked battery systems are another option whereby you save weight and charging time by using one battery, and if you need to go farther, add another battery. Most batteries have an approximate 18- to 38-mile range. The latest batteries deliver power for over 100 miles. A dashboard display on the bike shows information such as power level, battery remaining, and distance travelled.

The language of electricity is voltage (volts), current (amps), and power supplied (watts). There is a mathematical relationship between these that enables battery capacity to be understood whether it is quoted in amp hours (Ah) or watt hours (Wh). All figures quoted on batteries are usually rough guides only, and actual performance is usually less than quoted.

Choose bikes with good gears and smaller wheels as this offers less resistance during starting. There is a debate about the utility of suspension forks on e-bikes that are just going to be used for built-up road areas and cycle paths. They are expensive and add extra weight to the bike and may only be worth considering for mountain trail use or poorly developed road use.

While e-bikes may not be as environmentally friendly as a pedal cycle, they are better ecologically than a car or motorcycle. Choosing electricity providers who get their energy from renewable, sustainable sources can help reduce the environmental impact of using an electric cycle. Other options to consider may be setting up your own solar- or wind-powered facility to charge the battery.

If you are starting out in cycling and want to convert an existing non-electric bike, a twist-grip throttle system will usually get the bike moving on motor power alone, although there are a small number of very good pedelec retrofit kits out there, too. These are things that are best discussed with your local bike store mechanics as they may be able to offer a source and fit service (or you could negotiate one) at a reasonable price. Alternatively, there are existing variations of electric tricycles, recumbents, tandems, handcycles, self-balancing unicycles, utility trailers, and folding bikes, so the options are truly limitless.

Summary
It's a tough call choosing to cycle and buy a bike, isn't it? Do you drive your car to the gym and sit on an electric powered stationary bike with a TV screen in front of you which you stare at aimlessly without registering what's on it while churning on the pedals, or do you get on your bike and

- explore your neighborhood,
- absorb the fresh air of the countryside,
- visit friends and relatives, or
- simply go to different places and enjoy the sights, sounds, and smells of life as it hustles and bustles around you as you exercise your prosthetics, have fun, and relax all at the same time?

The answer to that could simply be that it depends. You may need to practice pedaling and gaining confidence on a stationery gym bike when you first start wearing your prosthetics (arm or leg). Later on, once the stump has stabilized in shape and size, it might be fun to start testing out your limbs with an electric bicycle, tricycle, or recumbent.

Being a new amputee combined with being a novice or non-cyclist is the ideal recipe for fun and laughter (or disaster—depending on your outlook!). It's where you will learn not only what you are capable of, but also how to deal with your prosthetic limb that has become a valuable part of you. Each time you try cycling with your arm or leg prosthesis, it is an opportunity to note and discuss with your prosthetist topics such as comfort, fit, alignment, and other issues. Once refined, these allow you to have as high a degree of functionality with your prosthetics as possible.

This section on electric bikes has been written with the kind assistance of David Henshaw and Richard Peace, authors of *Electric Bicycles: The Complete Guide* (Excellent Books, 2010). Their book contains excellent information on the history, technology, and the everyday practicalities of choosing and using different types of electric bicycles. Some of the material in this section has been reproduced from their book, the A to B website www.atob.org.uk, and www.excellentbooks.co.uk with their kind permission.

From the Amputees

John Thraves, UK

Electric drives are becoming very popular, and there are two outstanding systems available. The one that is now being preferred both here and in Europe is the Nuvinci drive. This system has been around since 2006 and is the subject of further development. The Bionx System, which is fitted in the rear wheel, has also been upgraded. The electric assist systems do suit the  *trike, but they have one weakness—steep inclines. Creech Hill has been conquered, but Kingston Hill, well that is another matter! I think an electric assist system such as the system I have with the crank drive would be ideal for an arm amputee. There should be no delay in the system kicking in; it should be there to assist as soon as pressure is applied. Use the Nuvinci drive fitted in the rear hub, no gear changing involved. I have tried this, and it works.*

There is always some kind of drawback and that is cost. Personally, I think the cost of these products will fall, but not by much; good batteries cost money, and supplies of the raw material is limited. But one of the big manufacturers in Switzerland is committing 20 percent of production to electric bikes in 2015 and already 20 percent of bicycles sold in Europe are electric in some form or other. Charging points is another issue, and at the moment in the UK, we appear to be lagging behind.

Funny Things Happen on Bikes!

The first amusing cycling story that comes to mind was on a training ride from Wandsworth, London to Newbury. Crystal (my wife) and I were riding with a friend, Mike, who was getting back into cycling, and we were trying to take a back-track route to avoid all the busy roads. Needless to say, I was getting us fairly lost and having to regularly stop and check the map. Mike had some fairly old clip-in pedals, and at some point, they must have broken. As a result, every time he twisted his left heel to click out, the toe of the cleat would stay stuck, and he'd end up falling over sideways. He was a strapping lad, locking down the Newbury 3rd XV scrum, so you can probably imagine both the heavy fall and the abuse I was copping every time we stopped. Why he never thought to use his right foot—old dog, new tricks? Crystal and I had just rolled through a T-junction, turning right, and we looked back to see Mike sprawled across the give-way lines underneath his bike and a line of traffic backed up behind him. We cracked up, rode on another 100 meters (330 feet) and pulled over to the left of the road among a row of trees to wait for Mike and for me to check the map again. You could see he was pretty dark as he rode up to us and pulled over. Our weak attempts at covering our laughter didn't help matters, and I could tell he was about to abuse me again for checking the map when over he went again, landing on his left with the bike on top, but this time a cloud of flies arose as he smacked into the dirt. However, it wasn't roadside dirt this time, but some big black and white roadkill! I'd never seen a badger in the flesh before, and now our mate was going to be wearing some of it all the rest of our ride.

Nathan Smith, New Zealand

Further Reading

1. Choosing a bike: www.thecyclingexperts.co.uk/get-cycling/buying-a-bike/choosing-the-right-bicycle/bicycling.about.com/od/howtoride/a/right_bike.htm
2. *BikeLife* magazine: bicycling.about.com/od/thebikelife/
3. Bike size guide for children: www.edinburghbicycle.com/info/sizing-guide-for-kids-bikes/
4. *Bicycle: The History* by David V. Herlihy (Yale University Press, 2004)

Things to Try for Yourself

1. Visit a bike shop and take a look at the different types of bikes.
2. Visit a bike fair or exhibition; sit on different bikes; play around with the different gears and brakes; and ask lots of questions.
3. Find a bike rental center (preferably one that deals with disabled cycling) and see if there are any suitable bikes that you can hire or book a lesson on.
4. Do an Internet search on different types of bikes available, their costs, and their upkeep requirements.
5. Dream of the perfect bike for you and do your very best to find it or make it!

Did You Know?

1. Baron Karl von Drais of Baden in Germany invented a Laufmachine in 1817. It was commonly known as a velocipede or dandy horse.
2. Tricycles and 4-wheelers were invented between the 1820s and 1850s.
3. The "bone shaker" was replaced by the "penny farthing" or "ordinary" in the late 1800s.
4. The first recumbent was recorded in Fliegende Blaetter in September 10, 1893.
5. The Fautenil Velociped was the first genuine recumbent.
6. Charles Mochet invented the four-wheel, two-seater, pedal-propelled car called the Velocar in the 1930s.
7. There are many tandem clubs around the world. Visit: www.thetandemlink.com/nationalclubs.html.
8. There are penny farthing clubs around the world. Visit www.thewheelmen.org.
9. Stephan Farffler (Germany) invented what is believed to be the precursor to the self-propelled wheelchair, handcycle, and tricycle in 1655.
10. The longest tandem ever made seated 35. It was 67 feet long.

Nezir Lupcevic, Bosnia and Herzogovina

Nezir suffered amputation as a young 10-year-old boy when he experienced a high-voltage electric shock that resulted in a high amputation of his right arm (to the shoulder).

The accident did not stop Nezir from learning new things, but it came with many barriers in his mind as he considered he was not able, among other things, to ride a bicycle and be like other young people.

At age 22, he learned to ride a bicycle because his job required him to travel a lot, so he "shifted all commands in his brain to the left-hand side" and never gave up, regardless of the obstacles he experienced. At the start, Nezir had some different experiences and feelings; it was really difficult to cycle and stay on a bike when big trucks would pass next to him, sometimes paying no attention to him or the fact that he has no arm. In those moments, Nezir's body would be overwhelmed with some kind of fear and yet complemented with pleasure for being able to ride alongside big trucks. Still, he never lost his main goal in life: to reclaim his position in a community where he lives and not to be dependent on anyone. To date, Nezir has overcome all obstacles, and he continues to enjoy his cycling in nature, thus forgetting all problems and barriers. He mainly cycles in beautiful places around his hometown and continues enjoying thrilling experiences on a daily basis.

Nathan Smith, New Zealand

I lost my left leg above the knee in April 2004. I was hit by a car while trying to cross a busy road. I also had quite a bit of metal work to put my hips back together. I met an above-knee mountain bike cyclist while in the walking school at St Marys, London. Once I could walk, I visited my cousin in Wales whose husband was into mountain biking, and he got me on a bike with clip-in shoes and cleats. A couple of laps around the local park, and I was back to London and started cycling out to Surrey for work (about 5 months after my amputation). I then got a road bike for a charity event from Lands End to John o' Groats. From there I was hooked. I did a couple of 100-mile events in Wales before  *heading back to New Zealand in 2006 and started racing with the local club. Before I knew it, I was in the New Zealand paracycling team being considered for Beijing 2008!*

Chapter 5

Necessary and Useful Cycling Gear

Buying a brand new bike that gleams like crystal and fits you well will certainly make you feel very happy. Wow! Only a few more necessary aspects to think about and organize before you go out in the spring rains for that all important bike ride!

Storage

A valuable aspect to consider is where and how you are going to store your bike. Safe storage not only prevents deterioration of bike parts due to weather conditions, but it also reduces the risk of opportunistic theft. Bike theft is a major issue in most countries. In Norway, around 60,000 bicycles disappear each year, never to be seen by their owners again. Most bicycles are stolen from places owners assume are safe. Experienced thieves take locked bikes in about 10 to 20 seconds. In the UK, a bicycle is stolen every minute, and less than 5 percent of those are returned to their owners. It is not surprising that cycle theft is found to be the single greatest deterrent to cycle use after fears concerning road safety.

Your home living space (or lack of it) will affect how you store your bike. If you have a family-sized house with a garden or garage, then locking the bike out of sight will be relatively easy. If you are intending to become a family of cyclists, then bike storage stands are a good space-saving solution to try. Bike pulley systems fitted to solid surfaces help to keep a bike high enough in a shed if you need the space for other things. They are easy to use and don't require you to be able to lift the whole weight of the bike.

Bike storage hooks, brackets, or folding bikes in suitable holders may be options to consider if your living space is very compact, and you have the strength to lift the bike up. For work-based storage solutions, bike cages are a good option. They can be situated in a parking garage, and cyclists who use these can be given a code for the combination lock. The cage should have a bike rack system inside so bikes are stored efficiently and securely. And if you are really lucky and live in a bike-friendly country, then covered multi-story bike parks are your best option.

Locks

Bike locks are an absolute must. They come in a number of varieties. Depending on the country you live in, insurers might require locks of certain standards to be used for your bike. Cable locks have key or numerical code options and come as either twisted or straight inner cable. A high quality U-lock is the best investment. Bike-specific chains tend to be heavy or expensive. Be sure to thread your lock through the rear triangle in the frame and, if possible, the rear wheel. Lock it to a fixed, non-removable structure, such as a lamp post or an iron fence. The best lock won't help if the bike is attached to something portable. Double

locking with a U-lock and heavy cable is a good idea. Lightweight cable accessory locks are also available. Take valuables such as money and cell phone with you rather than leave them with the bike.

Bike marker pens, security tags, and etching kits are also used to try to deter thieves and help identify the bike if it is retrieved. In some countries, bike owners in urban areas modify the bike design to make expensive bikes look cheaper in an attempt to deter theft.

Insurance

Bike insurance comes in many forms from various providers depending on which country you live in. It is a particular type of insurance policy that is intended to pay for repairs or replacement to your bike in the event of damage or theft or for damage or injury you cause to others. This is a very important aspect of bike insurance that you should include in your policy. It could ruin your life if you kill or disable someone while out having fun on your bike. As with all insurance policies, there will be a multitude of clauses and conditions that you should consider carefully.

- Things to assess include: Security conditions – what security are you expected to apply, such as locks and storage?
- Use of the cycle – will other members of the family ride the bike?
- Will you take part in competitions?
- Where will you take the bike?
- Are you covered outside your own country?

The amount to pay for your insurance will depend on the level of cover you choose. Some insurers only provide a form of legal expenses coverage that operates if someone else damages your bike. They will then seek to recover the costs from that other party. At the other end of the scale are fully comprehensive policies that will pay for theft of the cycle from the roof of your car, damage caused while taking part in competitive mountain bike events, injury caused to other people or damage to their property, and even injury to you if you come off the bike.

Choosing the right coverage for you and your bike is a very subjective process. Some people are more prepared than others to take risks. Many people choose to "self-insure." In other words, they take the risk themselves. If you have a bike that is worth $750 and feel you could afford to pay for repairs or replacements if it was stolen or damaged, you may choose not to insure it with an insurance provider. The more expensive the bike, the more likely you will want to protect your purchase by paying an annual insurance premium. This principle also applies to the likelihood of an accident occurring. If you regularly take part in cycling events and use your bike every day, the chances of needing repairs are probably greater.

If, despite all your best efforts, you find you have to claim against the insurance policy, make sure you make a record of what happened. This is particularly important when other people are involved, either because they have suffered injury or they have caused injury to you or your bike. Try and get witnesses to agree to provide a statement. Photos of the circumstances can also help make it easier to supplement the information required on the claim forms.

Notify the police in the event of a traffic accident or a theft, and notify your insurers as quickly as possible. Many policies have time limits within which you must present a claim. An excess is usually payable in the event of a claim. It is set at a limit that is designed to reduce the numbers of small claims made. In the UK, it is approximately £100, or it can be a percentage of the amount of the claim. Some insurers reward policyholders who do not claim on their policies over a specified period.

The legal position is different across the world, but many policies will also provide coverage in the event that the cyclist is considered to be responsible for damage to someone else's property or injury to another party. This could include circumstances such as hitting a vehicle, another cyclist, or a pedestrian. In some countries, the motor vehicle is always considered to be at fault irrespective of the circumstances.

If you are taking your bike abroad, you should contact your insurance company. Establish if you're covered there or if your policy can be extended to provide the cover you need. You should also check the policy to see if you need to take additional security precautions when you are away or if there are any transit conditions, particularly if your cycle is being transported by an airline.

Adapted or specifically designed bikes for amputees should be insured in the same way as a "regular" bike. When choosing an insurance policy, do some research. Consider your overall cycling requirements and look to match them to the cycling policies available. The Internet provides the ability to seek out the providers and, as cycle insurance is relatively straight-forward, enables the cyclist to compare the products available to them.

Written with kind assistance from Butterworth-Spengler, www./butterworthspengler.co.uk, a provider of bike insurance in the UK for over 25 years. It is not meant to be specific insurance advice on individual needs, but rather general guidance.

Helmet

Once you have your storage, bike locks, and insurance sorted out, it's almost time to start cycling. But not without that all-important helmet. Helmets are designed to protect the delicate areas of the skull and brain from heavy impact. Skull or neck injuries are life threatening and highly disabling. Helmet technology is constantly developing to keep those delicate areas well protected.

Hard concrete-based road surfaces and faster speeds at which cyclists generally try to cycle means the impact to the skull and brain can be devastating.

Helmet law controversy rages on among the rank and file of seasoned cyclists. There are claims that helmets make cycling less convenient, less comfortable, and less fashionable. Others suggest helmets make cycling more dangerous as cyclists experience a false sense of safety and engage in riskier riding behaviour. Helmets became compulsory in UCI racing from 2003, following another death of a cyclist at a race. They are legally required to be worn by children and adults in the following countries: Australia; New Zealand; Canada, depends on the province; Austria; Czech Republic; Croatia; Finland; Hungary; Iceland; USA, depending on the state; Sweden; Spain, some areas only; Japan; Malta; Portugal; Slovakia; South Africa; and South Korea. In some countries such as Israel, the law is not enforced, and in other countries such as Mexico, it has been repealed.

Some helmet materials deteriorate with age. Helmets should be replaced every five years or sooner. Helmets that have been damaged or involved in a collision should not be worn again. Check with the helmet manufacturer in your country; they may replace them for free if damaged by a fall or collision. When choosing a helmet, make sure it has an approved mark or sticker on it from the standards organizations relevant to your country. If buying from abroad, check that the country standards applied during manufacture are of a high standard. Do they have a tough outer shell, an impact absorbing inner layer, cooling vents, a comfort liner, strong chinstraps, and a secure buckle? Tightening devices allow a helmet to fit better around your head. They can be circular dials or clips on a rigid plastic strip at the back of the helmet. Adjusting these ensures your helmet fits snugly and does not move or slide around the head.

If you would like to keep people guessing whether you are wearing one or not, you could try these wonderful helmet covers. Designed specifically to fit all sizes of helmet, they are waterproof and have a place for a head lamp. They come in many different styles. Keeping your hair looking great after wearing a cycling helmet needn't be difficult. The flattened hair effect that you experience is due to the sweat from the scalp. An easy way to deal with such "helmet hair" is to take along dry shampoo and brush or comb to use when you reach your destination. Simply brush through and style.

Lights

Lights and reflective lighting should be used in and around the bike for riding in poor visibility and at night. Being visible from all directions and being able to see in all directions are important in such conditions. Check lights mounted on a bike from all sides to see if you are happy with their range. Lights should be mounted at the front and at the rear of the

bike. For good front vision, two lights are better than one. Aim one down so you can see the road surface clearly and aim the other a little higher so you can see ahead of you

clearly. Choose lights that can be adjusted in brightness so you can dim the amount of light coming from it. Rear lights can be continuous or flashing. Flashing lights use less battery power. It is important to be aware of the hours of burn time. This will depend on the quality of the battery.

LED (light emitting diodes) lighting has revolutionized the ability to cycle for longer and farther in the dark. They are efficient and reliable. When choosing which lights to purchase, consider the light density, the amount of heat produced by the light, and how long it is supposed to last. They can dim very quickly once the battery runs out. Choose lights that don't require a screwdriver to open the battery holder to make changing batteries in the dark that much easier. Where do you intend to use the light? For well-lit urban areas, the lights on your bike may not need to be as powerful as the type of lights you might need for a ride in a dark unlit forest, but choose adjustable lighting so you do not frighten or disturb any wildlife on such cycling expeditions. High-power lights produce a lot of heat, so they should only be mounted in casing that allows air to flow through and act as a cooling system.

Lights can be regulated or unregulated. Regulated versions will emit a constant amount of light across the whole burn time. These have a battery level indicator, and if the same amount of light cannot be emitted anymore, then the light will automatically switch off. Unregulated lighting fades over the time of use. They may start at full brightness but will start to fade after some time. There are various ways of charging lights. They can be powered by 1.5V batteries, rechargeable USB cables, or a lithium battery. Rechargeable units fit onto your bike frame which adds a little weight to the bike. Look for those that have a variable focus function that allows the width of the beam to be adjusted. Other options include Dynamo lights that fit onto your wheels and even fairy lights for your back pack.

Strap mounts, brackets, or similar will be required for lights to fit onto handlebars securely. They should be versatile enough to fit onto handlebars of different diameters and onto a helmet mount bracket.

Helmet mounted lights are useful as you don't have to move the handlebars around to light up areas around you. Be aware around other people as turning your head toward them might result in shining a bright light into their eyes. For a helmet light, a bracket will be required.

These can be attached to the helmet with a Velcro strap. Choose ones that are compatible with the bracket connection and specific helmet light. Some helmet lights come with the brackets included. The whole system should be as lightweight and as compact as possible to reduce the weight on your head and neck. Charging times vary for these (2-4 hours), and spare battery packs are available to hook onto your bike to make the burn time last longer.

Clothing

Now you've got the necessary things organized, it's time for that fun bike ride, isn't it? What are you going to wear? Did you know what you wear when cycling will affect how long you cycle? If you get wet and cold or too warm and overheated, you will be more inclined to stop cycling that day. In general, clothing and shoes should be sensible and designed to keep away from important areas, such as pedals, chains, brakes, or spokes. There is nothing stopping you from cycling in a long jacket or worksuit, a long dress, a skirt, trainers, high heels, or whatever else you want to wear as long as you are happy to perhaps sweat in those clothes and don't mind oil or grease on them from the chain and pedals. Cycling clips for trousers or long-sleeved loose tops may help to keep such clothing from getting caught in important bike mechanisms, but as a beginner, it's best to keep those types of clothes to change into when you arrive at your destination.

So what can you wear instead? It depends on the country you live in or want to cycle in. What is designed for cyclists in colder countries, such as Norway or Switzerland, may not be particularly suitable for warmer countries, such as Ecuador or Brunei. As fashion and trends develop, products offered from the cycling manufacturing community become more sophisticated to match. Consider how and when you intend to ride your bike and budget your clothing and accessory purchases accordingly.

While cycling, you generate around 10 times more heat than at rest, and you may feel up to 11 degrees warmer. Cycling-specific clothing has different purposes. Some items will be designed to keep you warm; others will be designed to keep you waterproof; and the third variety will be designed to allow airflow through the clothing as you sweat (breathability). It is better to dress in light layers that can be removed or added easily rather than wear one bulky item that may make cycling uncomfortable. On longer rides, take spare clothes in case the weather changes. Heavy materials such as jeans tend to absorb water quickly and stay damp for longer, so avoid these if cycling in wet weather.

For Cold Weather

The main areas of your body to protect against the elements are your torso, arms, legs, hands, and feet. Essentially you will need to look at wearing an inner layer of quick-drying fabric, a thermal layer, a wind breaker or insulating jacket, a cap or a headband under the helmet to keep the head warm, and gloves to keep your hands warm and dry. There are various high-tech materials used for outdoor pursuits that are suitable for use in cycling. They are manmade fabrics sandwiched into layers with other manmade polymer materials. Some of these have small holes in them that allow sweat to evaporate through them but keep rain out.

If it is very cold, you may need a balaclava under your helmet or something to protect your face from frostbite. When cycling in the dark or when weather conditions make visibility poor, the main aim is to see and be seen. Your bike should have reflective banding on it, and you should also wear reflective clothing. Insulating jackets and vests should be comfortable to wear. Make sure they do not have too much bulk or long tails at the back as this will restrict your ease of movement on the bike. Look for jackets that fit well around the neck area to prevent rain from getting in.

Some have pockets on the front, side, inside, or back of the jacket. Where you prefer the pockets to be is a matter of personal preference and may be something you consider more as you cycle. Having lots of pockets in a jacket may reduce the insulation properties of the garment. Lightweight, windproof jackets and vests usually have a water-repellent coating. They use a mesh fabric at the back for breathability and are a close fit to prevent water coming through. Some can be folded into a carry pouch and are wind and waterproof.

Half-finger gloves are essential as they protect against shock, vibration, and cuts during a fall as well as making it easier to remove sharp stones and other debris from your tires while out cycling. In cooler weather, use full-finger gloves. If it's very cold, mittens are better overall at keeping you warmer. The fingered variety can be worn under the mittens as a second layer. Half-finger varieties are also good to wear as  a layer under mittens. Bib tights are a good way to stay warm. They usually come in a thermal fabric which is stretchable and has inserts for wind protection. A full-length (all-in-one) reversible is a good option to keep warm under other layers. These have zippers in various places to make it easy to take shoes on and off and store small items. Many are reflective and have a fleece lining for added warmth. Cycling jerseys provide extra layering with bibs or all-in-ones. They can be short- or long-sleeved. Knee warmers and arm warmers are alternative ideas for cold weather conditions. The fabric expels moisture away from the skin. Cycling socks are now high tech with at least four fiber structures. They have a rapid drying and thermal layer as well as an elastic middle area for good fit. The open knitting ensures good breathability.

Winter cycling shoes have insulation for the ankle, offering varying degrees of protection from cold, wet conditions. Shoe covers are recommended for wet, muddy conditions as they will protect your footwear from the inevitable splashing. They consist of a waterproof rubber material and have inner fleece lining for warmth. They can be a tough or lightweight shoe cover, depending on road and weather conditions.

Clothing for Recumbent and Handcycling

Clothing is slightly different because of the seating position and the fact you are closer to the road. Insects can travel into your trousers or shorts more easily, rain will pool on your lap, and muddy water from puddles are that much closer to your face.

For handcycling, the feet and legs are kept in one position for a long time and will tend to get cold, so they will need layers of insulation. Products such as thermal all-in-ones and woolly socks are a must for cycling in cold or wet weather. Reverse Gear pants are unique in that they have weather-resistant panels on the back to repel rain and cold from the road due to the lower recumbent position. The overpants are also easy to take on and off because of zippers on the side of the waist and adjustable elastic in the waist. Your feet will get all the wind and spray as they stay in one position constantly while handcycling. To keep them well protected, wear over trousers, waterproof boots, thick socks, and gaiters. If you are intending to cycle in windy conditions, then put the overpants on before you set off as it may be difficult or frustrating to attempt this halfway through a ride.

When you have finished cycling in cold or wet weather, it is important not to let yourself get too cold. Change into dry clothing straight away and eat or drink something warm. Take dry spare clothing with you, and if it's windy, include a lightweight windproof top layer.

Accessories

Recumbent- and handcycling-specific panniers are available for carrying items. Panniers should be short and waterproof with lots of compartments to avoid dragging on the road. As recumbent and handcycling is nearer to the ground, it is important to use pennants, flags, or lights to make sure you are seen by other traffic. This especially applies to children's bikes.

Written with the kind assistance of Judi Bachmann. An excellent blog and diary on the website has lots of useful information for beginners:

→ **www.reversegearinc.com/blog/**

Hot Weather Cycling

In hot, sunny weather, it is paramount to use plenty of waterproof sunblock and wear tops and jerseys that allow the perspiration to evaporate. The neck area can be protected with a light scarf or similar, and it is useful to take some long-sleeved tops or jerseys for later on or if the weather cools down. Lips should be coated with sunblock and moisturizer to prevent chafing, and a light fold-up waterproof jacket will help protect against rain. Cycling shorts have lots of panels and are seamless in the inside leg. They come padded with chamois and antibacterial agents as the inside leg area is prone to chafing, blistering, and infection through sweating. Wearers of such shorts are advised not to wear underwear with these as that will prevent the chamois padding from working. It is important to change out of these straight away after a ride to keep the area infection free. If wearing lycra cycling shorts does not appeal to you, then sensible longer, looser shorts made out of cotton, linen, or other materials; bell-bottom trousers; or longer trousers that are not too flared are options to consider. Choose clothing without heavy inside seams to reduce risk of chafing and infection.

Cycling shoes come in various types. It is best to use a rigid shoe, without laces, and if you are not using cleats, it should have grip on the sole to help keep the foot on the pedal. Soles made out of plastic are prone to flexing whereas those made from carbon fiber or mixed materials tend to stay rigid. Rigid soles improve the power transmission from your feet to the pedals.

Specific cycling shoes are worth investing in once you have mastered the basics of cycling and are confident enough to try the cleat system of fixing the foot to the pedal. This allows the foot to work on the pedal stroke for a whole circle (i.e., pushing and pulling) rather than just on the down stroke. Modern shoes have threaded holes in the soles of the feet for the cleat which can fit into different pedal systems.

Clipless pedals are designed for mountain biking and road cycling. The mountain bike version is small and sits inside the sole of the shoe to allow for walking when dismounted. Most allow attachment of two screw-in spikes in the toe area for traction in mud or steep trails. Road versions tend to be bigger and make walking more difficult. Nearly all cycling shoes use the three-hole LOOK system.

Track cycling shoes tend to be very simple and rigid. For touring, it is often a compromise between having a shoe with a bit of tread to enable walking and a clipless pedal for efficient pedaling. The easiest type to walk in is the casual cycling shoe that comes with the Shimano SPD system. These are also available as sandals.

Makeup will usually run and smear while cycling due to sweating, so it is best to cycle without. It can always be applied when you get to your destination. Don't forget to use a good skin cleanser and light moisturizer first. Lipstick with a sun protection factor is advisable if you do not feel comfortable without any makeup. Mascara should be lightly applied and waterproof.

Eyes are delicate areas which, during cycling, have to contend with insects, sand, grit, wind, cold, rain, and bright sunlight. If mountain biking in the forest, watch out for low branches and thorns. If cycling in hot, dusty weather, watch out for sand, grit, or insects. Rather than risk damage to eyesight from exposure to any of these when cycling regularly, invest in a good pair of sunglasses. If you normally wear reading glasses to help with vision issues, then you require prescription sunglasses from your optician. Contact lens wearers can either keep their lenses in and use ordinary sunglasses or take the lenses out and use prescription sunglasses. When you go cycling regularly, take good care of your eyesight at all times. It may seem common sense as you read it, but remember you are going fast, and there is a lot to take in as you ride.

Good quality sunglasses have different types of lenses. Look for those that are specifically designed for high-impact activities, such as skiing or extreme cycling, as they should be more durable. These are broadly split into photochromic, polarized, or multi-layered. Photo-chromic lenses automatically adapt to changing light conditions. The lenses can adapt to let different percentages of the available light flow through them. In bright sunlight, only 20 percent of the light will be needed, whereas in darker conditions, 75 percent of the light will be needed.

Polarized lenses are good for bright sunlight. They eliminate glare and reflections. Multi-layered lenses require the user to change the lens manually, according to different light conditions. A clear lens is used when it is overcast or dark, orange or brown lenses help to relax your eyes, and yellow lenses add definition in poor light conditions.

Choose frames which are lightweight, robust, and flexible. Also, make sure the sunglasses are coated with an anti-rain coating so that the rain slides off the lenses while you are riding. Some sunglasses will come with rubber nose pieces, interchangeable lenses, and protective cases. Wrap around lens systems optimize protection against glare, dust, or wind from the sides as well as the front.

Extreme Cycling Clothing

For extreme cycling such as unicycling, BMX, cyclocross, and complicated mountain biking, the following safety equipment is essential gear: wrist guards, knee and elbow pads, helmet (full head), shin guards for metal pinned pedals, and gloves.

Abdul Qahir Hazrat, Afghanistan

Weekdays, I live, work, and study at AABRAR. Weekends (Fridays) and holidays, I live with my family. When I was 14, I was going to buy some food. On the road between my home and the market, I stepped on a mine. It was placed there by a Mujahedeen leader who was fighting the Taliban. It was in 1996 when the Taliban captured power. I lost both legs below the knees. There are still many mines all over Afghanistan because of the wars. I went to normal school until class 4, when I was 14 years old. Then I became disabled and had to stop school because the other students bullied me a lot and made it hard to study. As an alternative, I was offered study and

work at AABRAR through the Disabled Cycle Messenger Service. I am a cyclist postman, taking letters and parcels from one office to another. With my wage, I can support my whole family.

In general, in society, it is not easy for disabled people in Afghanistan. It is not like in other countries. Here there are no laws and policies protecting the rights of disabled people. Not for school and not for work.

Funny Things Happen on Bikes!

One day, I was in Kabul for a bicycle race for people with disabilities, and a lot of people with disabilities (PwDs) came from different provinces and districts of Afghanistan to take part in the competition.

While cycling during the race, a car which accommodated journalists and photographers was following me in order to take my pictures. The driver wanted to turn the vehicle to the other side of the road for photographers to take my pictures, but mistakenly the car touched my bike and caused an accident. I fell to the ground; my prosthetic limb separated from my body and was thrown away from me. The vehicle stopped, and the people helped me up. I was badly injured and near to losing my confidence, but the journalist, photographer, and physiotherapist provided me first aid and then encouraged me to start again. Their encouragement gave me good confidence, and I won! Now whenever I remember those moments, I cannot forget that amazing time that even after being knocked down I could still come first—it was so funny!

Habib Jan, Afghanistan

Other Useful Accessories

If you are just going on a short ride, keep a bicycle pump and repair kit with you. Tires have different valve systems on them known as Schrader, Presta, and Dunlop. Pumps come with adapters for these, and replacement valves and kits are available. Air cartridges are also an option when the tire has to be pumped up quickly.

A standard repair kit will contain some basic items that you will find useful if you get a small puncture or other small emergency while cycling. Most contain a spare inner tube and small tools.

When going out on a longer ride, a group ride, or if you are out and about in heavily populated areas, you might see an accident or require some form of first aid. It is useful to have a basic first aid emergency kit with you as well as your cell phone so you can request assistance quickly. Emergency first aid courses are available from many different organizations around the world, and it is a useful skill to have both for the workplace and for hobbies such as cycling. Course providers will show you ways to overcome the limitations of the amputation for the specific first aid procedure.

Cycling technology that measures your speed, distance, and heart rate and have built-in satellite navigation systems to help find your way around are becoming more popular. Earlier versions of cycling computers are simple to use if cycling for leisure and short trips. They have become increasingly complex as computer technology develops. If buying a newer high-tech model, choose one that is compatible with wireless technology and can be handlebar or stem mounted. Make sure it is either waterproof or has a waterproof cover. A method of padding is also advisable to prevent damage during a fall. Some providers enable you to turn your smart phone into a high-end bicycle computer. Having a camera attached to your bike or helmet will allow you to film the route as you ride along. For touring and wet weather riding, a set of wheel guards (also known as mud guards or fenders) is vital. These should be wide enough to prevent dirt and water from getting on you and the bike. Adhesive padding may be beneficial to protect the paintwork from flying dirt and debris along the frame.

To keep belongings safe, saddle bags or backpacks are useful. They should be lockable, waterproof, have enough compartments inside, and come in different sizes.

To attach a saddlebag to the bike, a T-buckle system that mounts directly to saddle rails might be required. It comes in different sizes to match the bag size. Backpacks should have lots of compartments and zippers that can be locked, good chest and shoulder straps, and be waterproof. Cycling-specific backpacks are designed for specific areas of the bike. They should be the correct size for the bike. Some have extra paneling on the backpack to protect the back during a fall. Bells and horns are good methods of alerting others to your presence. Cycling is a very quiet method of transportation, and it is good courtesy to make others aware when you intend to overtake them on narrow cycle lanes or public paths.

For touring, the following items are worth considering.

Panniers: These need to be big enough for everything you want to take, but not too big for the bike.

Bike boxes or bike bags are a must for air travel, ferry, and public transportation in some countries.

Roof racks or racks for the back of the car, motor home, or caravan and car trailers can transport up to four bikes. Other items that are necessary or useful to take while touring or considering longer journeys is covered in more detail in chapter 8, Choosing Routes and Planning Your Journey.

If you can't get outside to cycle, consider investing in a stationary bike, bike trainer, or a similar device that your bike can be fixed to. Some require you to remove one wheel whereas others require both wheels to be attached to the bike to keep it stationary. Putting such devices on a suitable mat will protect your floor surfaces while you cycle.

To get good advice on bike clothing and accessories, ask at your local bike shop, visit a cycling exhibition, ask other cyclists, or look online. If the item you are looking for isn't available through these usual channels, look online in other countries. Or, if you are convinced there is enough of a market for that product, think about how to manufacture, test, supply, and export it for yourself.

From the Amputees

Dan Sheret, USA

For the run-of-the-mill below-knee amputee, there is really little you need to become a cyclist. I would suggest using mountain biking shoes, even for a road bike. They are a better shoe for walking in when you are not on the bike. Road shoes are just too slippery for my taste. If your goal is to ride more, I recommend all the equipment any cyclist would have—shorts, shirt, helmet, gloves, and the best bike one can afford.

Steve Middleton, Canada

A road bike shoe normally has a stiff sole with a clip protruding from the sole, making it more difficult for walking. Mountain biking shoes are normally more flexible, wider, and easier for walking in. The mountain bike clip is recessed on the sole. Mountain biking shoes are ideal for straps, cages, and SPD pedals.

Further Reading

1. Sportswear company revenue: www.statista.com/statistics/241885/sporting-goods--sportswear-companies-revenue-worldwide/
2. Global electric bike sales data: www.statista.com/statistics/255653/worldwide-sales-of-electric-bicycles/
3. European insurance figures: www.insuranceeurope.eu/uploads/Modules/Publications/european-insurance-in-figures-2.pdf
4. Sports clothing: www.reportlinker.com/ci02121/Sport-Clothing-and-Accessories.html
5. Bike clothing: www.sustrans.org.uk/change-your-travel/your-bike/bike-accessories-and-clothing

Things to Try for Yourself

1. Visit a cycle exhibition to see the latest clothing and accessory ranges.
2. Take a look at clothing available from a bike shop near you either online or in person.
3. Try dressing for cold, wet weather cycling and see how easy it is to move around while wearing multiple bulky layers. Practice sitting down, pedaling, and walking while dressed in layers. If you are feeling adventurous, make the gear wet and then try sitting down, pedaling, and walking.
4. Take a look at the cyclists around your area. What sorts of things do they wear? Is that the look you would like to emulate or would you rather develop your own trend?
5. Chat to other cyclists about clothing, helmets, and lights to see if they have any valuable points to pass on from their experiences.

Did You Know?

1. Newburgh's *Physiology of Heat Regulation and the Science of Clothing* published in 1949 helped the industry develop thermoregulatory clothing.
2. Teflon is the name for a polymer that is very slippery. It is combined with nylon and other polymers to make Gore-Tex.
3. John Richard Dedicoat invented the bicycle bell in late 1800s.
4. Before the invention of torches and LED lighting, cyclists used gas or oil lamps to help them cycle when it was dark.
5. Sunglasses were first mass produced for the US in 1929 under the brand name of Foster Grant.
6. Vinyl, latex, and Gore-Tex are the most commonly known waterproof materials.
7. Wraparound sunglasses were first made in the 1960s.
8. Lycra is a synthetic fiber used for its elastic properties. It was invented in 1958 by Joseph Shivers in the US.
9. The very early helmets used at the turn of the 20th century were little more than a ring of leather around the head, a wool ring above that, and then leather padding in strips. In the 1970s, they were known as hairnets.
10. The materials used for making helmets in the 21st century are cork, balsa, and polystyrene.

Sara Tretola, Switzerland

I was born with only one hand; my right lower arm was missing on birth. The condition is known as Dysmelia in which, during pregnancy, the arm and hand does not form completely. In Switzerland, I don't feel discriminated against because of my disability. I work as a design engineer in medical technologies. I support the Theodora Foundation (Spital Clowns, www.theodora.ch/). I am also a sports consultant at the rehabilitation clinic in Bellikon. I became involved in racing through my father who was an amateur racer. On Sundays, he enjoyed taking one of us with him to the race. I loved these days out with my father. We discovered a common passion. That is how I started to compete in my first bike race in the Spring of 1997 at the age of 13.

Funny Things Happen on Bikes!

In winter, I train in a fitness center. For the gym (weight training), I use my normal battery-powered hand. Once, during an exercise in which I had a 20-kilogram (45 pounds) weight in my hand, it wouldn't open. The battery was empty, so the hand couldn't open. Now what? I didn't want to take the weight back to the house with me, so I used my left hand to prise open the prosthesis. Phew! What luck!

Sara Tretola, Switzerland

More Funny Things Happen on Bikes!

During the medal ceremony at the Paralympics in Athens in 2004, shortly after I received my bronze medal, my prosthetic arm fell off! Some people were shocked, and others smiled and laughed. My coach said to me "cool show (nice one)," but actually, it wasn't done on purpose.   *Sara Tretola, Switzerland*

Chapter 6

Cycling Basics, Part I

Learning how to cycle as an amputee is lots of fun! If you used to ride before your amputation, then you'll have to relearn some of the basics, but that should not be too difficult. If you've never ridden a bicycle or if you have a fear of cycling, whether related to the amputation or not, it will require more effort initially. However, once you get the hang of it, you'll wonder what all the fuss was about!

Depending on the level and severity of the amputation, you might decide to start off on a side by side or handcycle. With time and practice, you might try a tricycle or recumbent and then a two-wheeler. As your technique and cycling ability improve, so will your level of confidence. It might also be interesting to compare riding with and riding without prosthetics. How much you ultimately want to test your balance and cycling abilities depends on your own motivations.

It is a matter of personal choice whether to undertake activities in the same way as able-bodied people or develop different innovative ways of cycling that may be better suited to your amputation. If you can find others to try out or discuss different techniques with, then go for it! Explore, learn, discover, and, most of all, enjoy the incredible fun that cycling brings you.

There are a few options that can be considered when learning to cycle. One option may be to take some organized cycling lessons either from bike rental centers, cycling charities, or other organizations that promote cycling. These are usually advertised in newspapers or online through their websites. Dates, times, and prices of these sessions will vary depending on the content of the course. Courses designed for the general public tend to be centered around the use of a two-wheeler whereas those designed for disabled people tend to have a full range of cycles to try out (e.g., handcycle, side by side, tricycle, or recumbent). A good point of contact is your local disabled sports club or national disability sports federation.

From the Amputees

Habib Jan, Afghanistan

I went to AABRAR for one month of bicycle training. They provided me with a bicycle after completing the training. In that training, all the lessons were practical, and we learned how to ride on a cycle and how to repair small bits on our own bicycles. Since then I use a bicycle for fulfilling my own and family's needs.

These options are useful if you have no experience cycling at all and want the support and encouragement of a more structured learning environment. In some countries, children will learn about cycling skills in school, and it is worth spending that extra bit of time with them on weekends and holidays to develop these further. If your child is an amputee and attends a mainstream school rather than one specifically for disabled children, it is worth reminding the organizers to ensure the cycling instructor becomes familiar with teaching cycling skills to amputees.

Instructors should ideally have a recognized instructor's qualification and have passed any other requirements specific to the country they are teaching in. In the UK, for example, they are required to pass criminal records checks and protection of vulnerable children and adults. If you are an experienced amputee cyclist interested in becoming an instructor, discuss these requirements either with the country-specific cycling organization or the national disabled sports federation.

If you are worried about attending a cycling course and not being able to keep up with others in it, or are used to cycling but are out of practice, an option to consider might be to rent or buy the type of cycle you are interested in. Go to a suitable practice area, such as a local park or parking lot, with a family member or good friend and work it out for yourself.

This option is best if you have family and friends who know enough about cycling to support your attempts at mastering a bike. Having familiar people around you will help start you off on your learning journey, but attending courses, events, and charity rides all assist you to feel comfortable about social contact with strangers. This is worth spending time on as a way of getting used to societal reactions toward amputation.

Transporting Your Bike
In the very early stages of learning to ride a bike, you may have to transport it in a car or van to the area where you want to practice. Park the car in a space which allows doors to be opened fully so it is easier to take your bike out.

Lifting a Bike In and Out of a Car
If transporting more than one bike, place them carefully to avoid scratches. If you have put the whole bike into a car, then it is easier to roll it out. You may have to remove the wheels and cover sensitive areas like the derailleurs and greasy chain to fit the bike into your car. If you have laid a bike without wheels on its side, then tilt it upright and lift it out. Check that cables and chain are not twisted or caught anywhere if the bike is on its side. Because of the weight and shape of the cycles, it's best to work with someone to do this.

Lifting a Bike Off a Bike Rack Behind a Car
Recumbents, tricycles, and handcycles are heavy, long, and cumbersome. Work with someone to unlock the straps, steady the bike, lift it off the rack, and put it safely on the ground. Take care not to get the chain or cables caught in the rack. Contact points for holding the bike should be sturdy, fixed areas of the frame rather than moveable areas, such as pedals, wheels, or handlebars. For tandems, because of their length, it is better to use a trailer or a rack that fits onto a van or large family car.

Moving a Bike Off a Trailer or Van
Bikes fixed onto trailers are easily rolled on and off. If rolled on backwards, they can be rolled off forwards. If the bike is fixed upright in a van, then again it can be rolled down the tailgate. If it is on its side, place it upright and then roll it off. If the van does not

have a ramp, it will take one person to be inside the van and either one or two outside the van to carry it out and put it on the ground safely.

Depending on how the bike was stored, it may need putting back together again before you can ride it. It is advisable to perform bike safety checks before each bike ride. Instructions on dismantling, rebuilding, and pre-ride checks are described in chapter 11, Basic Bike Maintenance. If the bike does not need to be rebuilt and is fitted to you, give your brakes a quick squeeze, check tire pressure is correct, and get ready to cycle. If it is a bike that you have rented, check the seat height. Transporting your bike in public transportation for those early attempts at cycling might be a little ambitious unless you are very familiar with your prosthetics and public transportation systems in your country. This may involve carrying the bike up or down steps, over gaps, around narrow corners or through crowded spaces.

If you intend to do this by yourself, spend time getting used to the feel and weight of the bike before attempting to get it onto a bus, subway, or train and get someone to help you when necessary. If you are on public transportation with family or friends, they can do a lot of the manual handling for you until you are ready to try it.

Choose a Good Practice Area

In highly urbanized environments, there is limited public park space or open grass land where cycling is allowed. Always check with the local park authority whether there are any restrictions to cycling. If using a parking lot, make sure it is quiet with few cars. The place to learn should ideally have flat areas and gentle slopes. Cycling in tight spaces, on steep slopes, over roads with potholes, or with traffic can be something to work toward as you gain confidence on the bike.

For very young children, ideally choose a flat or slightly downward slope of grass to cushion falls. Grass provides resistance, makes balance and pedaling a bit difficult, and provides a soft landing. Alternatively, use protective elbow and knee pads for young bones if cycling on concrete, paved, or tarmac roads.

Take a look around the ground you will be cycling on. Are there lots of wet leaves, twigs, sharp stones, broken glass, potholes, gravel, humps, or bumps? If you are in a public park, is it full of dogs, parents and grandparents with strollers, other cyclists showing off their skills, and children with balls, baseball bats, or Frisbees? Will practicing cycling skills in such conditions work against you by increasing your stress levels? Will the hustle and bustle of popular park life enhance or reduce your overall levels of enjoyment? If you feel uneasy or uncomfortable, consider coming back when it is quieter or look for somewhere better maintained for that first attempt at riding a bike.

The discomfort may be because you are very new to amputee life, more self-conscious, and not confident enough to learn bike skills in a busy public park. Initially, your stumps will sweat causing them to shrink and you may not wish to take off the prosthetics openly in a public area to add socks or dry off the stump. The longer you live with your amputation, the more you will accept it as being a normal part of who you are. If you find it easier, choose a park that has some changing or restroom facilities so you can attend to the stump without distraction or embarrassment. Cycling is a good way of testing your comfort levels with the prosthesis and with the amputation. The initial frustrations you experience can be overcome in time, and you will find or develop your own coping techniques as you progress.

If teaching or practicing with a child, watch their reactions closely and keep asking them about the bike, their prosthetics, and their cycling. If they are nervous, they may decide to simply walk the bike back and forth and play with the bell, brakes, and pedals before sitting on the bike. Give them that space and time and enjoy being with them on their journey of discovery. It may be tempting to push them through certain aspects of cycling, especially if you didn't enjoy learning to cycle when you were younger, but keep your patience and good humor to deal sensitively with them, especially when they fall.

Putting on a Helmet

Make sure it is an approved helmet and does not have any signs of damage, such as dents, scratches, or cracks. Push all hair out of the face and back behind the ears to limit restrictions to your hearing. Tie long hair back neatly, place helmet on head, and fasten the side clips under the chin. There should be two finger-widths between your eyebrows and helmet. The chin strap should only fit one finger-width between strap and chin. Adjust the side straps so the buckles sit just below your ears—one strap in front and one behind in a V shape around your ear lobe. There should be no twists in the straps. Tighten any of these areas if they are too loose. Nod your head a couple of times to make sure the helmet does not shake loose. Arm amputees may prefer someone to put the helmet on them initially until they become more adept with their prosthetic, or they may simply decide to put the helmet on with their main functioning arm and hand only.

If the helmet slips upward at the front, tighten the front straps. If it slips forward, tighten the back straps. The helmet should feel comfortable and not press or pinch anywhere. When putting helmets on children, place your fingers under their chin to prevent the buckle from catching their skin. When you finish cycling, take off your helmet and store it safely. Try not to drop it on the ground or on a hard surface as this compromises the structural integrity of the helmet, thus making it less likely to effectively protect your head in the event of an accident.

Basic Cycling Skills

The skills required to ride a bicycle can be performed by amputees to a high level of competency. At the most basic level, you need to know how to:

A. Get on (mount)
B. Balance
C. Pedal
D. Brake
E. Change gear
F. Steer
G. Get off (dismount) when you have finished cycling

During these activities, keep control of the bike and pay attention to the amount of pressure going through the stump areas. Keep practicing the exercises until you can do them all smoothly without wobbling.

A. Get On (Mount)

1. Handcycle

First, make sure the parking brake is activated, and the handcycle does not move freely. The handgrips can be moved upward out of the way. Straddle an upright handcycle with your body weight on your dominant side if you are a leg amputee. If that is not comfortable, try doing the same from your weaker side to see which works better for you. For a recumbent handcycle, remember you will be trying to sit lower to the ground. If cycling with legs off, sit on the ground next to the handcycle, remove legs, shuffle over, and raise yourself onto the seat with your arms. Or mount the handcycle with legs on and remove them once seated, whichever method feels more comfortable. Either store your legs on the back of the bike or give them to someone to put away safely. Arm amputees should have enough lower-body control to be able to straddle a handcycle or recumbent easily. They can then attach their prosthetic arms to the handgrips.

2. Recumbent

Make sure the recumbent is in a low gear, and the brakes are pressed. Straddle the frame with your body weight on whichever side you find works best for you, weaker or dominant if you are a leg amputee. Lower yourself carefully into the seat by moving your legs forward and keep hold of the handlebars. You may require an additional hand rail if the seat is very low, or initially let someone hold the recumbent steady until you get a feel for mounting. For arm amputees, they should have enough lower-body control to mount a recumbent using their good arm for balance and control if necessary. The prosthetic arm can then be fixed onto the handlebars. To test the sturdiness of prosthetic arms while cycling, arm amputees can try using them for support during mounting as long as they put their weight through the upper body gradually, maintaining balance with their lower body while doing so.

3. Tricycle

While someone holds the tricycle steady by pressing on the brake levers, step across the tricycle frame. Sit on the seat, making sure you can reach the floor with your feet and pedal backward comfortably. Once you have done this a few times, practice holding the brake levers yourself and stepping across the frame. If you are an arm amputee, attach or rest your prosthetic arm on the handlebar.

4. Two-Wheeler

There are a few two-wheeler mounting techniques. The one described next is the most basic bike mounting technique. Other techniques can be tried once levels of confidence and balance are improved. If experiencing difficulty with this as a free-standing bike, try fixing the bike on a trainer or similar and practice mounting a few times. Then try mounting the free-standing two-wheeler. If balance is very poor, try using the stationary bike in the gym and do some core muscle work to build strength and balance before attempting a free-standing two-wheeler bike mount.

a. Arm Amputee

Attach or rest the prosthetic arm on the handlebar, but do not put your stump into it. Make sure the brakes are to the good side, and press them to keep the bike steady. If the bike is large and the seat is high, lean the bike toward you a little. Lean forward toward the handlebars and swing your leg either over the seat post or top tube or through the tube area if it is a step-through bike. Straighten up and sit on the seat, keeping brakes pressed throughout. Slot your stump into the prosthetic hand. Once you are happy with the arm movement as you mount the bike, you can try mounting with your stump in the prosthesis.

b. Leg Amputee

Press both brakes and hold the handlebar to keep the bike steady. Keep the body weight on the good leg if a single-leg amputee or on whichever leg works best if a double-leg amputee. Lean forward over the top of the handlebars and swing the prosthetic leg over the seat post, over the top tube, or through the tube area on a step through bike. Place the prosthetic leg on the ground, straighten up, and sit on the seat, keeping the brakes pressed at all times.

5. Tandem

When learning tandem cycling for the first time, the captain should practice riding without anyone else on the bike to get a feel for the length, weight, turning circle, and braking. For the captain, the mounting technique involves straddling the bicycle frame and sitting on the seat at the front of the tandem. Put the dominant foot on the pedal at a 45-degree angle from the ground and push down as hard as possible to gain enough momentum to move the bike. Another method is to start with the non-dominant foot. Try them both out to see which one works best for you.

Once this has been mastered, the stoker can mount. The brakes should be pressed by the captain throughout. The bicycle frame needs to be between the captain's legs with both feet firmly on the ground. The inner thigh supports the frame, and legs are kept wide enough apart to prevent the pedals from hitting you. The stoker mounts by straddling the bike frame behind the captain and resting his dominant foot on the pedal. Body weight should be centered as much as possible. The stoker signals to the captain that they are ready, the brakes are released, and both captain and stoker pedal hard to move the bike. An alternative method is for the stoker to put both feet on the pedals rather than just the dominant one. This is useful if the stoker is a leg amputee. Again, try these out and see which one is better for you.

6. Unicycle

Rest the unicycle next to a fence that is an appropriate height. The pedals should be at the 4 o'clock position for your dominant leg and the 10 o'clock position for your weaker leg. Tilt the unicycle toward you, rest the seat between your legs, and squeeze it with your thighs. As you squeeze, place both hands on the fence and face your body and the unicycle forward. Place your dominant foot on the pedal at 4 o'clock, push with your other foot, and sit on the seat. Pedal and rotate the wheel a quarter turn backward as soon as you get on the unicycle. Once you have mastered mounting with the fence, free mounting can be tried. This involves placing both hands on the seat instead of a fence or using your arms to help you balance as you mount. Arm amputees will have to try doing this with their good hand only initially and experiment with the prosthetic arm once they are comfortable with using it. Above-knee amputees may not get the hold they require from the prosthetic to mount without the use of support. Alternatives to a fence are a handrail or narrow hallway walls. **A unicycle is the most difficult bike to ride for both arm and leg amputees. Only attempt it if you are very accomplished at riding other types of bikes and want to challenge yourself.**

7. Without Prosthetics

If cycling with leg prosthetics, these can be used for stability on mounting and dismounting as well as take some of the effort out of pedaling. If the leg prosthetic is not something you want to cycle with, mounting can be done with or without it. Initially, straddle the bike with the prosthetic on, and then take it off while resting on the saddle and store it safely on the back of the bike or give it to someone to look after. Once your balance is better, you can hop to the bike and mount without the prosthetic.

For arm amputees, cycling without prosthetics requires them to use one arm for mounting, braking, gearing, steering, balancing, and dismounting. Initially, mounting the bike can be done without an arm, either with someone helping or, when the upper body is strong enough, by the amputee themselves.

From the Amputees

Armin Köhli, Switzerland

- *Lean bike toward you, holding on to both handlebars.*
- *Cross one leg over the back wheel so you face the handlebars and straighten bike.*
- *Put that foot on the pedal (at the top of the turn).*
- *Press down on the pedal to generate momentum.*
- *Straighten the bike and get on the saddle (as you push down on that pedal).*
- *Put the other foot on the pedal and carry on cycling.*

Rajesh Durbal, USA

I have been a triple amputee all my life. I have always cycled, but just for fun. I have special cycling road legs which are shorter so I can maximize my power to the pedal and use the entire pedal stroke. Braking and shifting gears are put on one side, so I only use them with my left hand. I ride a Felt triathlon bike. I get on it like any other person does. I put my leg over the bike, step into the pedal, and then I take off. I usually have one pedal clipped in, push off, and then sit on the seat.

Mark Inglis, New Zealand

Mounting: Leg over with the pedal at about 45 degrees forward—not at top—push and seated then mostly need to up and down stroke the one side clipped in until I can get the other side clipped in. Far more commonly, though, is I lean up against something, clip both in properly, then go—trees, fences, power poles, cars—whatever is handy. Really the only technique when starting off on an uphill. Dismounting—just unclip and get off. Not hard! Occasionally fall off, even easier!

Nathan Smith, New Zealand

I am a left above-knee amputee (AKA). I ride a two-wheeler. To mount, I stand on the right side of the bike and swing my prosthetic leg over the saddle. Once straddling the crossbar, I bend down and clip my prosthetic foot into the pedal using my left hand while my right hand squeezes the brake. I push off with my bum on the saddle, and then clip my right foot in once moving.

To dismount, I can only clip out my right foot. I come to a complete stop, and then lean the bike to the right with my right foot on the ground and unclip my prosthetic left foot.

John Thraves, UK

I ride a recumbent trike (i.e., two wheels at the front, one wheel at the back). I approach the trike from the front, straddle the chainwheel, and using standing aids, sit down on the seat. When I dismount, I use the standing aids to lift and support myself from the trike with my arm and hands. The standing aids can be supplied by manufacturers such as ICE and HPV.

Sara Tretola, Switzerland

I am an arm amputee. I get on my bike in the normal way. I click my right foot into the pedal and then sit on the bike as I set off.

Victor Walther, Canada

For arm amputees, it doesn't really matter what side you stand on or how you get on the bike. Generally speaking, it helps to stand on your strong leg or side and lean the bike toward you, and then swing your leg over the back wheel, placing your foot on the pedal.

The only tip I can think of is to stand on the prosthetic or weak side, then attach your hook first before jumping on.

As for special or stunt mounts, there is a special superman mount used by racers after a crash. Basically, you put both hands (or hand and hook) on the handlebars and run alongside of the bike. Then literally jump or dive onto the bike (you end up stretched out with your arms in front of you and your legs dangling behind).

B. Balance

Balancing is easier on side by sides, tricycles, recumbents, and upright handcycles, especially if cycling straight ahead. Balance issues may arise when turning or cornering with these types of bikes. On two-wheelers, tandems, and unicycles, it is more difficult to balance if you have never cycled before or if your muscles are deconditioned or weak, even when trying to go straight ahead.

1. Two-Wheeler

A simple technique to help you balance is to sit on the bike, making sure both feet are flat on the ground. Push with alternate feet back and forth along the road until you feel steady. If the pedals get in your way, remove them. Then try pushing yourself along fast, gliding with your feet up in the air. Your body will lean slightly into the curve to keep balance while you steer with your hands. Next, try leaning your body toward either side to see what that does to the direction the bike moves in. If you find yourself starting to fall to the right, regain your balance by steering the bike to the right and vice versa for the left.

When you have practiced that a few times, reattach the pedals if you have removed them (see chapter 11, Basic Bike Maintenance). Try putting one foot on a pedal while pushing the ground with the other foot. Change the foot on the pedal and then try putting both feet on the pedals and turning them. The faster you go, the easier it is to balance, but do not go too fast initially. Keep the bike under control at all times.

The same technique can be used for children. Rather than trying to run beside them, holding onto their saddle while they wobble about, remove their pedals and ask them to just use their feet to move the bike. When they are better balanced, put the pedals back on and let them try pedaling. Stabilizers can be used as an alternative.

If you find it difficult to coordinate your balance on a free-standing two-wheeler, practice on a stationary gym bike or a bike fixed to a roller. Then try again on the free-standing bike once you feel ready. Alternatively, switch to a tricycle, handcycle, or recumbent that places less demands on balance.

2. Tandem

This is achieved by making sure the stoker does not move around on the back of the tandem or lean on either side while cycling. As long as the captain is an experienced and competent cyclist, the stoker can remain balanced under the captain's control of the tandem. The main aspects to get right are the starting, stopping, changing gear, and going over bumps. These are the points where the balance may be shaky when first attempted. They should improve with practice.

3. Tag-Along

If using a tag-along for your child, impress on them the need to listen carefully to your instructions. Sudden, violent steering movements to either side will make you lose balance. This is more likely to occur if the child is bored of cycling, and it may be better to stop, rest, and do something else for a little while and then get back on when refreshed.

4. Unicycle

The way to balance on a unicycle is by pedaling forward or backward in small movements and tilting the body either forward very slightly or being upright. The unicycle is the hardest of the cycle variation to balance on and takes lots of patience and courage to master.

From the Amputees

Jon Pini, UK

I am a transradial congenital amputee. I started learning to use a bike with stabilizers as any other child would between ages 2 and 3. When I was around 5 and 6, my parents thought it was time to take the stabilizers off. I then started to learn to ride a little bike without my arm, believe it or not, on a little side road next to the bungalow where we lived. I just used to go back and forth there. Balance is the big thing as it would be with lower-limb amputees, but certainly with upper-limb amputees there is a lot of balance put through the arms obviously with steering of the bike itself. I just learned through sheer determination and repetition and managed to get the balance to hold on to the bike, and away we went.

Mona Krayem, Germany

I had both my legs amputated below the knee about one year ago due to an accident. Before I cycled quite a lot, but obviously it is totally different without legs and with prosthetics. After I came back from rehabilitation with my first prosthetics, I tried to ride my old bike again—at least give it a try. The therapists and doctors couldn't say whether it would still be possible, and I didn't meet anyone who rode a normal bicycle with the same amputation (only one-leg amputees or others riding a handcycle or tricycle). This was actually rather discouraging as I couldn't even get on the bike without falling or sliding off the pedals and losing balance, let alone talk about riding or getting off without a mess!

I started looking for a tricycle in a special store as not cycling at all was definitely not an option for me. I tried it, and it was all right, but it was not the same feeling as my bicycle. That was when I met another girl who had both legs amputated below the knee as well. She'd been riding a normal bike for years, even in the city. I was motivated to practice again as well, at least I knew now that it **must** be possible somehow.

Shortly after that, I heard about Armin Köhli and all the amazing cycling he does and got in touch with him. He invited me to visit him in Switzerland so we could do a little training session. And that's what we did!

I'm also fascinated by how little my stumps are actually stressed through this movement. It's more gentle than walking, for example, and expands your range enormously.

C. Pedal

To get the best pedal technique, make sure you have a good bike fit. If wearing cleats, position them correctly relative to your foot. Feet should be centered on the pedals, they should not be too far forward or too far back. Knees and toes are best placed so they are not directed into the bike frame or excessively outward while pedaling. Prosthetic leg users may not be able to feel where the "feet" are on the pedal and find overcoming the "dead spot" of the pedal stroke difficult if not wearing cleats. Pedaling requires your muscles to be activated in a certain sequence. The aim is to develop a rhythm or cadence in which pedals turn smoothly at a regular pace. There is no "best" pedaling technique. Different riders use their most natural technique and refine it by doing it a lot. It might be worth trying out the different pedaling techniques when you first try to cycle so you understand the differences, but most people find it easier to stick to their natural pedaling technique. Using an inefficient pedaling technique will make cycling jerky and uncomfortable.

1. Handcycle

Hold the handgrips ready and release the brake. Turn using a forward motion. Turning the handgrips on a handcycle is the equivalent of pedaling a two-wheeler. Your back, chest, and shoulder muscles will play some part in this movement. Make sure the force applied through each arm is similar, even if one of these is a prosthetic. Getting suitable rhythm and speed will make it easier to control the handcycle.

2. Recumbent

Activate the brakes and put your dominant foot on the pedal. Pull the pedal backward until it is approximately straight up. Push back against the seat to assist in moving the pedals, release your brakes, and put the other leg on the pedal.

3. Two-Wheeler and Tricycle

Hook your foot under one pedal and bring it back to the 2 o'clock position. Rest your foot on it and push down hard. Put your other foot on the other pedal, catching it as it rotates, and carry on pedaling.

Pushing pedals with equal force on both sides rather than just using your stronger side ensures your body remains still on the bike. A gentle pace allows you to control the bike. This can be increased gradually to 60 to 100 rpm. The legs should work in a natural sequence in which, as one leg finishes an action, the other leg starts that action. Think of making circles with your legs. Avoid pounding by using these circular motions to smooth out the pedal stroke and also reduce the strain on your muscles. Having severe restrictions in movement around the hips, lower back or legs will reduce the effectiveness of the pedaling action. Your posture on the bike will impact on your breathing and pedaling. The technique will change, depending on the terrain. If you are going uphill, you will pedal differently to a downhill or a flat surface. If you pedal at faster speeds, your technique will change as compared to slower speeds.

There are three main pedaling techniques. The most common is where the heel starts to drop after the 12 o'clock position and around the 3 or 4 o'clock position the toe starts to drop until it reaches the 6 o'clock position. After this the heel rises again.

Some cyclists dip their toes so they can sit higher on the bike, but they have less foot leverage. The body weight tips forward so the rider has to sit farther back and higher to reduce the impact on their upper body, arms, and hands.

Others dip their heels more at the beginning of the stroke. The foot is used more, the knee is extended more, and the stroke is shorter. The seat is usually lower for this technique with the rider sitting forward on the seat.

It is important not to pull up forcefully on the pedals for long periods of time when seated to ensure a pain-free back. It is natural to pull up forcefully when standing up off the seat or when accelerating in a big gear while seated. "Biting hard" (pushing hard) into pedals creates power and speed—save that for those big races!

The aim of considering pedaling when you first learn to cycle is so you can stop thinking about it the more you do it. Eventually you become less conscious of pedaling (in smooth circles!) and focus more on how to navigate your way along the course, especially at speed. As long as you can identify functional issues, such as muscle weakness, just push down on the pedals and let the brain work out the rest. The stronger and more flexible you are, the easier this will be.

4. Tandems
In a tandem, pedaling may be synchronized or non-synchronized. When each rider is pedaling at the same rhythm, they are said to be in phase. If the leg lengths and strengths of riders are similar, then in-phase pedaling is suitable. If leg lengths and strengths of riders differ, it is better to set up the crank and pedal system to work out of phase so both riders can ride to the best of their own rhythm. Bike fit should be designed around the captain as he will be responsible for braking, steering, changing gears, and direction.

Without Leg Prosthetics

This requires the stump to either be fixed at a platform or hanging loose if too short. The good leg is fixed into the pedal by a cleat, and the rest of the body moves forward and backward to assist with balance. A cleat or clipless system means that the pedal is working on both the down and the up rotation to move the wheels.

5. Unicycles

After mounting, hold the fence and sit up straight. Pedal by leaning your entire body forward. Move your body and the unicycle as a single unit as just bending your upper body from the waist will throw you off balance. To pedal backward, sit up straight and pedal in short quarter turns backward. Do not lose balance or lean backward as you may experience a dangerous fall. Once you feel comfortable enough pedaling backwards or forwards, let go of the fence and try it without support.

From the Amputees

Steve Middleton, Canada

To begin cycling, start off slowly and practice on grass, where the falls don't hurt so much (you must plan on a few in the early days). Wear your helmet. With your good leg firmly on the ground, swing the prosthetic leg over the bike, and then get seated. Find a post on one side to lean on to start. Trial and error and a helper enable this learning process to happen. Once moving, position the good foot into the pedal. Alternatively, use a post to put both feet on the pedals to start. This will require practice, but will become second nature.

John Thraves, UK—Starting and Pedaling an Electric Bike

There is no difficulty with a throttle control system. You just twist the throttle like a motor cycle and off you go. Pedal assist is slightly different. The system reacts through a sensor to the pressure applied to the pedals and kicks in with the assistance when you reach a certain speed (2-5 mph). The assistance continues until you reach 15 mph. Some systems, such as hub motors, are fitted in the front or back wheels. Crank motors are fitted on the crank drive but operate the same way. (I have both types of system all fitted to my trikes.) Because of my age (71 years young!), balance has been a problem; therefore, starting and stopping is much safer with the trike.

D. Brake

1. Two-Wheeler and Tricycle

Test which lever controls which brake. Whether the right lever controls the front brake and the left lever controls the back brake or vice versa will depend on the country you are cycling in. This can be done by lifting the front of the bike, spinning the front tire, and pressing each brake lever individually. The back brake is usually best used by absolute beginners or young children as they progress to a bike with brakes, as it is a gentler action.

The front brake is better at stopping the bike, but may cause injury if used by beginners unaware of its braking power. Once confident, it is better to get used to using the front brake more as the stopping distance is less than with the back brake. When confident using both brakes, you will not worry as much if either of them fail. To get an idea of the braking potential of your bike, walk with it and, at different speeds and intervals, press each brake in turn and then press both together suddenly. This will not be the same as having the weight of your body on the bike when you brake, but it will give you some indication of it.

When the brake lever is on the back of the seat, simply press back with your body to activate the brake.

If the braking system is on the pedals, bring the pedals to where they are almost level with your feet. Press down on the pedal that is farthest back as if you are going to pedal backward. This should slow down or stop the bike, depending on how much pressure you apply. For children's bikes, teach the child to slow down the bike by reducing the force of pedaling or by backpedaling. Put a foot down on the ground once stopped.

Try to anticipate when you want to stop, slow down the pedaling, and squeeze gently on the brakes. Apply approximately 75 percent of the braking to the front wheel and 25 percent to the back wheel to stop you from skidding. Rest your weight on one pedal. When practically stopped, take the other foot off the pedal and place it on the ground. Do not press the brakes and put your feet down as the bike is still moving; it will cause you to hurt yourself on the bike frame as it stops and you continue moving forward.

As you apply the brakes, move your body toward the back of the bike. Braking on descents requires effective speed control and weight transfer toward the back of the bike to prevent wheel lock. In an emergency, be careful if braking quickly and suddenly as there is a risk of your body going over the handlebars. In wet weather, allow more space and time for braking.

If you feel the wheels lock up, release the pressure on the brake levers a bit to keep the wheels from rotating. In most cases, as long as you brake gently, you can use just one brake lever, mainly the front one. This only works on good paved surfaces. If you are on wet, slippery, muddy, or bumpy surfaces or on a steep descent, it is better to use the back brake more and the front brake less. If going downhill around a corner too fast, gently squeeze the brakes to slow down enough to gain more control. Sudden braking will cause the wheel to slip.

2. Recumbent

If the recumbent has front suspension, the front brake should be applied gently first followed by the back. As you slow down, remove feet from pedals, keep your knees bent and raised, and place your feet on the ground as the bike stops. A technique used by racers in low recumbents is that of putting a gloved hand on the ground rather than their feet when they have come to a stop. The recumbent must not be moving at that point as it may tear the glove and the skin of the hand. If the brake is located behind the shoulder, press back on it with your upper body to activate it.

3. Tandem

The captain signals to the stoker to stop pedaling so that the tandem slows to a speed suitable for the captain to press the brake and put one foot down on the ground. This involves the captain getting off the seat and the stoker remaining steady in position with both feet on the pedals. Once the captain and stoker are better coordinated, they can both put a foot on the ground—on the same side of the bike.

4. Handcycle

If this is an attachment to your wheelchair, then just turn the handles backward to stop. If it is an upright handcycle, turn the handles backward. Be careful if braking suddenly as your body might fly into the front mechanism.

5. Unicycle

Allow the unicycle to coast while keeping your feet on the pedals. Lean forward slightly and press the pedals backward until you stop moving. Then to keep stationary and balanced, either move your body and feet back or dismount.

From the Amputees

Robert Bailey, USA

Riding unilateral AK or BK is not that big a problem. You can clip in the prosthetic foot and use your good foot to disengage when you have to stop. Bilateral BK is more difficult. I use Crank Brothers Eggbeaters. They are easy to engage. You just slap your foot onto the pedal, and it will "click" pretty easily. The hard part is stopping. It is not a natural motion. You have to think ahead. You push down and turn to disengage. Do it 10 seconds earlier than normal. I keep my foot lightly on the pedal and then reach for the ground with it. I use the left foot because it is longer and more stable than my right.

Steve Middleton, Canada

The good foot always comes off its pedal to the ground first. Depending on seat height, you may have to lean the bike slightly to get the foot flat on the ground. Then remove the prosthetic foot, either by pulling the leg out of the strap and cage or by twisting the prosthetic leg from the hip to disengage the clip-in cleats.

Jim Bush, UK

My bike is an entirely standard bike, and I haven't had one stolen since approximately 1986 (8 years before the accident when I fell off a mountain in New Zealand, so maybe people who see me get off the bike think that it must be a special one!). The only "adaptation" is that I have toe clips and straps on both pedals; the right one with the prosthetic foot is strapped in tightly to stop the foot from "wandering off."

I also need a toeclip and strap on the left pedal because the left leg does most of the work (although the prosthetic leg does seem to help maintain momentum), so it needs a toeclip and strap to pull up against. The strap on the left pedal is not done up tightly as I need to put the left foot on the ground if I want to stop.

E. Change Gears

Keep your eyes on the road ahead when changing gears. Most bikes require you to pedal as you change gear. To change gears when the bike is stationary, lift it up, manually rotate the front wheel, and shift the gear lever. Move up-or-down gears slightly earlier than needed to ensure a smooth cycling rhythm. Start in a low gear and change up and down as the terrain changes. Practice in a traffic-free area with few obstacles. Words commonly used for gear changing are upshift and downshift. Use low gears for uphill riding, shifting down the gears gradually in plenty of time. The lowest gear is for the steepest hills. Work down the gears gradually when intending to come to a stop. If you are bouncing on your seat when pedaling fast, go up one or two gears. Do not pedal too slowly when in higher gears or cycle with gears at the highest end of the range as this may damage the chain.

1. Handcycle

Turn the gear either up or down while the bike is moving. Make sure the chain is under some tension and moves smoothly over the chainrings. Only change gear when moving forward, not when stationary or when pedaling backward.

2. Tandem

On a tandem, until both riders become familiar with each other, the captain signals to the stoker when they are going to change up or down gears so the stoker can increase or decrease the speed of pedaling accordingly.

3. Unicycle

In a unicycle, to accelerate, apply more force to the pedals and tilt forward a little. To slow down, sit up straight and reduce the force on the pedals. Do not bend backward as you might fall.

F. Steer

Steering affects how you turn a corner, especially at speed. It is important to be able to steer the bike (whichever variety) around obstacles, debris, potholes, people, and other objects that are on the route you are taking. Steering is controlled by the handlebars and the body. Some variations of cycles are front steer, and some are back steer. A bicycle that is self-steering is one that turns the way it is leaned.

1. Handcycle

There are two different types of steering: fork steering and lean-to steering. Fork steering is used in the upright handcycles where you turn the wheel (using the handgrips) in the direction you want to go. Lean-to steer is used in recumbent handcycles in which the rider uses his body (trunk muscles) to lean in the direction he wants to go. The front wheel moves with the seat.

2. Tricycle

To steer, turn the handlebar in the direction you want to go. It will not respond to the direction in which you lean as other bikes might do. Do not try to steer around corners at high speed as the tipping point in a tricycle is reached at such speeds.

3. Two-Wheeler

There are two methods of steering for beginners. The first is balance steering which requires you to use your shoulder and body rather than your elbow when turning the handlebars. The second method of steering is known as counter-steering. This involves moving the bike very slightly opposite to the way you think it should go due to the different gravitational forces that are working on it as you steer away from a straight line. The movement makes you lean your body into the turn. A conscious or exaggerated counter-steer helps you lean into a sharp turn quicker.

a. Counter-Steering Right

Turn the handlebars slightly to the left. Lean your body slightly to the right. This will cause the bike to turn toward the right, and then, when you straighten your body back up, the bike will follow a straight path again.

b. Counter-Steering Left

Turn the handlebars slightly to the right. Lean your body to the left. Straighten up when the turn has finished. Using the handlebars only while keeping the rest of the bike straight to steer left or right should only be used to get through narrow spaces or when going very slowly. On a straight, wide road, practice moving the bike toward the left and right gently while traveling forward along the straight line.

When you reach the end of the line, turn the bike around and do the same exercise going back to the starting point. This helps accustom you to steering left and right in both directions.

Beginners will find that they swerve or wobble along in a snake-like pattern when they first start to learn how to pedal and steer effectively. Being uncertain about how to steer may result in them slowing down. This makes it difficult to keep balanced on the bike and steer at the same time, and this leads to wobbling or swerving.

4. Unicycle

This involves the cyclist correcting the way they are "falling." This is done by moving the wheel with their lower body underneath their center of gravity. By leaning or moving the arms subtly, the beginner cyclist can steer until they learn how to use their lower body to steer.

5. Tandem

This is controlled by the captain who leans the way he wants the bike to turn. The stoker must remain in a steady position throughout the lean and when the bike returns to the upright position.

G. Get Off (Dismount)

Once the bike has stopped and you have one foot on the ground to steady it, it is time to dismount. When you first start to learn to cycle, the seat may be lower down than normal, and you will come to a seated stop. Free the foot which is your dominant one from the pedal and let it steady you on the ground. Keep hold of the brakes, stand up, and swing your leg over the seat post or through the frame and on the ground. You may need to lean the bike toward you to do this if it is high.

Once you have increased the seat post height, then you have to be able to slow the bike down, stand up off the seat, lower the dominant foot off the pedal and onto the floor as you stop, and swing over the second leg while leaning the bike toward you. This is a more advanced technique that requires balance, coordination, and practice.

If you are cycling without prosthetics, then you may need to stop where someone is waiting with your prosthetic limb before dismounting, if it is a leg. There are other advanced stopping methods which involve getting off the bike while it is in motion. These should only be attempted if you are fully confident of your ability on the bike as timing and balance are key to avoiding injury. For beginners, until you can stand happily on the pedals while cycling, it is worth keeping to the basic dismount methods. Try more difficult methods on soft surfaces, such as grass or a mattress, in case you fall.

On recumbent and handcycles, always put the parking brakes on before getting off.

1. Tandem

The captain should communicate with the stoker to let him know that they are stopping. There are only brakes on the front of the tandem, so the captain presses the brake levers, takes his feet off the pedals, and puts them on the floor. The captain remains straddling the frame to keep it upright and support the weight of the stoker as they dismount. The stoker only takes his feet from the pedals and dismounts once he has the signal from the captain. Once they are more coordinated, the captain and stoker can take their feet off the pedals at the same time from the same side of the bike.

2. Unicycle

The dominant foot pedal should be at the highest position. Transfer your body weight to the lowest pedal. Look forward and hold on to a handrail to steady yourself. Step down with the dominant foot first, and then step off the lower pedal. Timing is crucial. Do not force the seat to move backward, but rather tilt yourself slightly backward and let the seat fall by itself with your legs ready to catch the bike between your thighs. As you get better at unicycling, instead of holding a handrail or fence, simply hold the seat with both hands; dismount as you do this to catch the unicycle and prevent it from falling. It takes a lot of practice to get that confident.

From the Amputees

Steve Middleton, Canada

The emphasis is on practice, practice, and practice before heading out on the road. As proficiency is gained, raise the seat higher to create better leg extension, but to dismount, tilt the bike at an angle to the ground (toward the good side) to place the foot firmly on the ground.

Jim Bush, UK

I ride two-wheel bikes (currently a mountain bike or a Brompton folding bike). I get on all bikes by standing on the left-hand side of the bike, put the weight on my left leg, swing the right (prosthetic) leg around and over the back of the bike, and then sit on the saddle. I have toe clips and straps on both pedals, and I strap the right (prosthetic) foot tightly into the toe clip and strap to stop that foot from moving. Than I push off with my left foot, and after a couple of turns of the pedals, I get the left foot into its looser toe clip.

I need a toe clip on the left pedal so that I can pull up as well push down on the pedal, because this leg does most of the work. I used to think that the right (prosthetic) leg was strapped to the pedal and just "going round for the ride," but I think the right leg can maintain momentum although the left leg does do most of the work.

The strap on the left toe clip and pedal is looser because this is the foot I want to get free from the pedal and put on the ground when I stop. This is handy in the UK (especially in urban situations) because the curb for the pavement is on the left-hand side of the road. Where there is no raised surface I can just about reach the ground if it is at the same level as the bike wheels, or on slopes I can stop so the upslope is on the left-hand side of the bike. (Nearly 20 years of practice as an amputee cyclist now doing approximately 6,000 miles per year probably helps!)

Very occasionally (only 1-2 times per year now!), I find my center of gravity on the right-hand side of the bike. I can't get my right foot clear of the pedal in time, and I fall to the right. People behind me have said it looks comical as I am clearly fighting to get my weight over to the left but then topple over to the right. These "crashes" invariably occur when I am stationary on the bike, and this is why I always wear an elbow pad on my right elbow only.

I get off both bikes in the same way as I get on. I stop, put my left foot on the ground, loosen the right toe clip and pedal strap, get the right foot off the pedal, get off the saddle, and swing the right leg around and over the back of the bike while putting all my weight on my left leg.

Robert Bailey, USA

I love the trike because it gives you stability and will not damage the residual legs (easily). It really did take a while to learn to ride on two wheels. I could have done it much earlier, but I just love riding on three too much. When I came home to Baton Rouge, Louisiana, I looked at that Rivendell bike. I had ridden it from time to time, but it was tough. Finally, I decided enough was enough. I experimented and found the right combination of pedals, feet, shoes, saddle, and handlebars. A week before I wrote this, I rode 40 miles through the hills north of Baton Rouge. It was the first extended ride on two wheels. This week I did something even better. I found a way to ride with clipless pedals. I can ride normally on any of my upright bikes.

First Attempts at Cycling

Mona Krayem, Germany

 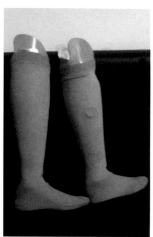

Especially in the beginning, it was really hard for me, and I had to practice and concentrate a lot, particularly while getting on and off the bike. So that's what I still do and what is still the most difficult for me (but as I mentioned I'm still at the very beginning). We started with a tandem bike just so I could get a feeling for being on the bike and riding with the prosthetics. That same day we made a trip with a single moutain bike and with a racing bike with clipless pedals the next day. I was enthusiastic.

Even though I knew that there was and is still a long path in front of me, I was really amazed about how much is actually possible again and that the improvements come even faster than I ever imagined. I still have to—and want to—practice a lot. Back in Munich, I've done a few longer rides, and now I'm even riding in the city again, which is such an enormous gain of independence, mobility, and quality of life for me.

Tran Duy Khanh, Vietnam

Riding a cycle is not easy to a starter without a disability; a two-leg, destitute amputee is not an exception. I can still remember the time I walked on two plastic feet; my body was so exhausted just trying to move forward. The muscles seemed to be worn out, and the stumps hurt when I tried to pedal. Repeated falls from the bike resulted in stump infection and a broken bike. I felt tired and scared of the bike and the prosthesis, and often I could not have a meal after training. Sometimes I thought about giving up riding the bike. However, the worry of lying in bed and being dependent on my relatives motivated me to continue learning to ride. I decided to overcome myself and my pain.

Eventually I could ride a bike! I counted the days, and it took three months to successfully graduate from the bike training course with me as coach. I was so thrilled when I could ride two rounds on my bike and did not fall down. The feeling of champion grew in me when I covered the distance of 100 meters (330 feet). Gradually I could ride farther, and the bike became my friend during my travels. It was the prostheses and the bike that helped me move around and attend social events as well as work. I believe that effort creates success, and it is true for most people with disabilities.

Margaret Biggs, UK

***200 MILES ON A TANDEM: A RIDER'S STORY**—Excerpts from an incredible tandem ride through Wales as written by Wyn Jenkins. Reproduced with the kind permission of the Douglas Bader Foundation. The full transcript is available at www. douglasbaderfoundation.com.*

Day 1: Holyhead
As we stood at the port in Holyhead, holding the tandem for the pre-event photoshoot, all sorts of doubts were starting to kick in. We knew that if we could coordinate our push to get the tandem moving, we'd be fine on the flat; in fact, we knew that we could bomb

along as it is a very fast bike. The unknown factor would be the hills that we'd have to encounter, especially on day 3 on the way down to Lampeter. Would we, between us, have the necessary "grunt" to get this steel-framed beast to the top of each climb, or would we need the help of other cyclists to push us up?

We are both right-sided amputees—Maggz below knee and me above—so we had to click our prosthetic legs into the cleats before getting into the starting position. I then had to get on the saddle (on tip-toe) with our prosthetic side at a quarter past three position on the pedals, and then after a 3-2-1 countdown, we'd push away, and Maggz, having the benefit of a knee joint, would generate enough downward pressure on her prosthesis to get the cranks moving. Once we had momentum, we were away, but we always had to be vigilant when stopping and invariably looked for a curb or bank so that we could unclip on our "good" side and coast to a stop.

Gemma Trotter and Colin Davies, both above-knee amputees, joined us on their own bikes along with able-bodied cyclists from my club in West Wales—CMC. Sandra and Peter, both club members and owners of County Cycles, were also riding with us, as well as providing the technical back-up. Support vehicles were driven by my wife Marg, Gemma's husband Rob, and Marianne and her husband Jeff.

The first part of the ride passed uneventfully. We used this time to get used to communicating with each other—"stop pedaling;" "pedal;" "change down/up;" "signal;" "push hard/slow down." We'd found very early on that communication was vital. On one occasion, I didn't tell Maggz that I was going to stop pedaling, the result being that her prosthetic leg came adrift of the cleat holding her leg onto the pedal. Apparently, it was quite a sight seeing her right leg going into frantic mode!

Day 2: Porthmadog to Machynlleth

We approached Harlech and the first solid climb of the day up to the town. The castle looked majestic as we approached on the lower slopes, and to our amazement, our steady tempo in an easy gear made the climb disappear very easily, and we were soon entering the narrow town streets. We were immediately behind schedule, and the wind was getting stronger as we finally left Harlech. It's lucky we left early that morning because by the time we'd battled our way down to Barmouth in a strong headwind, the rain had also started to fall. With even stronger winds due later in the afternoon, we didn't waste too much time having lunch before heading off across the railway line and footpath on the wooden bridge across the estuary. Just as we got to the other side

of the estuary, we stopped to allow everyone to catch up—a momentary stop, and I thought that Maggz was still on the back of the tandem. After we'd regrouped, I got in position and counted down in the usual way and pushed off. There wasn't the usual burst of power from the rear, but I put this down to Maggz having another of her private picnics or texting Wendy with regular updates of our progress. I heard some shouts from behind but ignored them as I set about picking up some speed. The tandem was feeling decidedly sluggish, though!

The shouts were now becoming quite frantic, and when Maggz failed to give me her usual running commentary, I realized that she was missing. I'd left her behind, and she was very unimpressed as the tandem took off without her.

Day 3: Machynlleth to Lampeter

Jeff's app was right—the rain was horizontal, and you could barely stand up in the wind let alone ride a bike! There were grim faces all round with some advocating a delayed start to give the weather a chance to ease, while others just wanted to get on with it, adopting the philosophy that once you're wet you're wet, end of! There were no guarantees that the weather would improve, so a decision was made that we'd head off at 10:00 am. So far, it was the weather making the ride hard even though we also encountered some stiff climbs. The going was a lot harder as we headed in land. We were escaping the teeth of the gale but were about to encounter our first steep climb with a 17 to 18 percent gradient and over a mile long. There's no easy approach to this hill; you're straight onto it and straight up! There's a short respite after a quarter of a mile when you can pull onto a forestry road to get your breath back before you tackle the next really steep bit. With heart rates hitting 180 bpm, we pushed hard over the steepest section, and once over, we could relax and use an easy rhythm for the remainder of the climb to the top. It was with a great deal of joint and personal satisfaction that Maggz and I, together with Gemma, conquered this major challenge. It was a tough climb for able-bodied cyclists, so it was especially rewarding for the three of us to get up it without stopping! We turned south after the climb, and any thoughts of an easy ride down to Tregaron were soon forgotten as the gale that hit us kept downhill speeds below 10 mph. It was hard going!

Although I'm an amputee with a reduced power level, I can still cycle with the other club members on equal terms. What I love is the fact that no allowances are made for my disability, nor would I want any. I pride myself that I can get up 99 percent of the hills in our area using a Compact front chainring and a 32-tooth rear cassette. Changing from a round chain ring to Rotor Q-rings and cranks enabled me to ditch my old triple front chainring. I can keep a high pedaling cadence on the hills and generate a good amount of power on the flat. I love my bike, and when I'm cycling, I often forget about my disability completely.

The Final Day

With lunch coming to a reluctant end, we headed off on the final 30 miles to the Mumbles, Swansea. As we got nearer, I suddenly started to feel quite emotional. As we approached the finish line, I felt immensely proud that we were sending a really positive message to others in the limbloss community. We had ridden the length of Wales with able-bodied cyclists who didn't see us as amputees, but as individuals who happened to enjoy cycling. While it's important to educate people to see past a disability to the individual beyond, it's equally important for disabled people not to see themselves as victims. There's an incredibly happy life to be lived if you're prepared to meet the challenge of making it so.

Funny Things Happen on Bikes!

I always used to enjoy mountain biking. When I was doing my prosthetics training up in Oswestry about 10 to 11 years ago, I took my bike up with me. One of my friends who was training there at the same time was also into mountain biking. I bought a local map and could see the cycling trails on it, so one day we both decided to go mountain biking in the hills and mountains of mid-Wales. We were going really well and thought we'd hit gold with this particular part of the mountain range until we found out we were in the middle of a quarry with dynamite holes ready to be blasted! You can imagine we soon scampered out of there! I don't know if we had taken a wrong turn. I always remember that, thinking "oh no, these are dynamite holes, let's get out of here!" Luckily, we did find the correct trail after that. We had taken the wrong turn, but thank god it was a Sunday, so nobody was working there at the time.   *Jon Pini UK*

Further Reading

1. *Everyone Can Learn to Ride a Bicycle* by Chris Raschka (Random House, 2013). Ideal for children.
2. *Learning to Ride With "The Bits"* by Harvey Nix (Reading Matter, 2007). Ideal for children.
3. Beginner's courses www.cycleskillstraining.co.uk/trainingcourses.html.
4. Learn to cycle at a mature age: www.theguardian.com/lifeandstyle/2006/oct/21/familyandrelationships.family5.
5. Handcycling by Disabled Sport USA: www.disabledsportsusa.org/handcycling.

Did You Know?

1. Mark Twain wrote "Taming the Bicycle" about his attempts to learn to ride a penny farthing.
2. A well-known quote from "Taming the Bicycle" is "Get a bicycle. You will not regret it. If you live."
3. The hardest part of learning how to ride a bicycle is the pavement (ouch!).
4. Too much fear is bad for your riding technique whereas too little fear is dangerous.
5. *Cyclophobia* is the term that describes the fear of bicycles.
6. "I will overcome fear of bicycles" is from the album *Self Healing Affirmations* (for meditation, relaxation, and hypnosis), set 32 by Sound Health.
7. "Riding on My Bike" by Madness is a song about a cyclist on a charity ride.

8. Cycling jokes are a useful way of entertaining children while they are learning how to ride.

9. Learning how to cycle provides freedom of mobility, freedom of space, and independence from others.

10. Albert Einstein is reported to have had his "eureka" moment about his Theory of Relativity while on his bicycle.

Things to Try for Yourself on a Flat, Paved, or Well-Maintained Surface
Get on the bike.
Get off the bike.

Get on the bike, start, and stop, steadying the bike if a two-wheeler.
Get on the bike, start, stop, and get off

Start, speed up, slow down, and stop.
Start, speed up, speed up, and speed up, then slow down, speed up again, slow down, speed up, and keep alternating this to practice gears.

Get on the bike, start, pedal, stop, get off the bike, and turn it to face the direction you came. Get back on the bike, start, pedal back to original point, and stop, steadying the bike if a two-wheeler.

Get on the bike, start, pedal, stop, get off the bike, and turn it to face the direction you came. Get back on the bike, start, pedal back to original point, stop, and get off.

Get on the bike, weave along a straight painted line or similar, stop, and get off.
Get on the bike, curve right, straighten, stop, and get off.
Get on the bike, curve left, straighten, stop, and get off.

Get on the bike, curve left, then curve right, straighten, turn around on the bike, then curve right and then left, straighten, stop, and get off.

Tran Thi Ngoc Linh, Vietnam

One summer day, sitting on my old bicycle, I attempted to ride again. With a little bit of embarrassment and hesitation, I got my bike to roll. I was so happy to discover that I could take the first steps on the bike five months after my accident and with one arm left. I spent days with an inferiority complex about my situation, hiding from people after my accident. I felt different from my relatives and friends. It was hard for me to pedal again as before. The first time sitting on the seat, I threw my body off balance. I considered lowering the seat so that I could put my feet mostly on the ground while seated. This kept me from falling while cycling. I shifted the bell to my right hand so that I could use it if necessary. Gradually, I could balance the bike with my single arm, and the pedals turned round and round. It was hard to describe my feelings at that time. A bit of happiness encouraged me to be more self-confident to move forward and rise above my life. Afterward, I could ride my bike to school and the market and pay visits to my neighbors. Eventually, I was able to travel by bike everywhere I wanted. From the day I could ride the bike again, nothing stopped me from thinking of myself in the same way as others without a disability. I was enabled to do whatever I did before. Only thing different was that I needed to try harder. I could ride the bike again but had to be more careful to avoid bad situations on my roads. Now, as a student, I ride my old bike to the university every day, with my single arm, confidently and happily.

Chapter 7

Cycling Basics, Part II

It's time to add some variety to your cycling. Getting on, starting, stopping, and getting off should come naturally to you by now. This chapter covers lots more interesting bike skills.

A. Turning corners
B. Cycling uphill
C. Cycling downhill
D. Cycling in a straight line
E. Looking behind
F. Taking a hand off the handlebars
G. Reaching for a water bottle and snacks
H. Signaling
I. Falling off
J. Riding out of the saddle

The more you try them, the easier they will become, and you will soon be looking to try out the expert stuff! Don't forget the helmet and those all-important bike safety checks. At the very least, make sure your brakes work, your tires have the correct pressure in them, and the seat height is comfortable for you.

A. Turning Corners

Try cornering and turning as often as you can. Create your own circuits in parking lots, playgrounds, or quiet streets. When you have got the basics, try making it more difficult by holding one hand behind your back, and for the really advanced, try cornering while standing on the pedals.

1. Two-Wheeler

Look in the direction you want to go as far beyond the corner as you can see. Lean your body gently into the turn, putting some pressure on the outside pedal (leg) and inside handlebar (arm) to keep the bike as upright as possible. Keep your

knees tucked into your body by squeezing the bike with your thighs as you go around the corner. Touch your brakes lightly before going into the turn, and then stop pedaling, keeping the outside pedal down. Keep the inside pedal up; this will stop it from hitting the ground as you lean into the turn. If you brake too late (i.e., when you are in the turn), you may skid, lose control, or fall. Start pedaling only when you have come out of the turn, otherwise toe overlap might result. Toe overlap is when the front wheel and toe touch, causing loss of control or a fall.

The smaller the frame of the bike, the more this occurs. Start off doing as wide a turn as possible to give you lots of time and space to get used to the feel of it.

As you learn to control the bike, make the turns sharper. The tighter the turn, the more you have to lean the bike in toward it. Only try taking turns and corners at speed when you are confident doing them at a slower pace. When taking sharper turns or going faster around corners, approach at a wide angle and start turning when you see where the sharpest point of the turn is.

Once you have mastered turning and cornering on either side, add a bit of variety by choosing narrower turns, hairpin turns, and turns or corners that require you to go downhill or uphill at the same time.

For cornering or turning maneuvers, you are reliant on friction produced between the tire and the ground. Road surface, brakes, rims, spokes, and wheels can all affect this. Choose the correct tire profile for the weather and road surface. Turning on surfaces such as gravel, sand, ice, snow, or wet pavement may cause the bike to skid.

2. Tricycle

Make sure your speed is not too high, and turn the handlebars into the direction of the turn. The front wheel will go in that direction, and the rest of the tricycle will follow. Straighten the handlebars as you come out of the turn. There is no need to turn your body. Going too fast at the turn may cause the tricycle to tip over.

3. Handcycle

Lean-to handcycles require you to lean your body quite a bit into the turn. Fork-steer handcycles require you to turn the handles in the direction of the turn. Straighten the handles or your body once you come out of the turn. Doing this too quickly or at too high a speed may cause the handcycle to tip over.

4. Recumbent

The process is the same as for an upright bicycle, but it is important for the rider to make sure that his feet do not interfere or get stuck in the under seat steering, forks, or tires. This may cause bruising or broken ankles if at speed. Recumbents require a larger turning circle than upright bicycles, and tight corners can be a concern for the new rider. Lean slightly forward a few inches and into the turn. Keep your back stiff and rigid if turning at low speeds.

5. Tandem

The captain is responsible for communicating when a turn or sharp corner is coming up, usually by counting down (3, 2, 1). The direction of the turn or corner is signaled with the hand (left or right), and if there is a need to reduce gearing and speed, that, too, will be communicated by waving the arm downward. This allows the stoker to prepare for the captain to lean into that direction and use the pedal positioning as for a two-wheeler. The stoker should keep a steady body position on the back of the bike and pedal position as for a two-wheeler unless the captain indicates they should also lean. Tandems are longer than normal two-wheelers, so the turning and cornering maneuvers will take more space and distance. The captain then signals when they are out of the turn or corner, and they return to pedaling normally.

6. Unicycle

The hips are used to turn the unicycle to the left or right. The sharper the turn, the quicker the hip movement needed in order to keep your balance. Hold on to a fence or railing the first few times you attempt to pivot on the wheel. Once you have the technique and are confident to try it without support, use your arms to swing in the direction opposite to the way you want to move. Tilt the body slightly in the direction of the turn and keep the body weight centered through the seat.

B. Cycling Uphill

First, choose very gentle, uphill slopes with relatively wide, straight gradients. Try walking up the hill with the bike to get some idea of its steepness. The easiest uphill technique involves building up momentum on the flat area of the path, leaning forward into the uphill, and if necessary (if you can), standing up in the seat.

Uphill starting requires a lot of practice. If the road surface is wet or has loose gravel or other debris, then be aware of creating "wheelspin." This is mainly experienced by those who ride off-road, but it can also happen on paved roads if the uphill is very steep. To overcome it, the body weight should be forward and steady pressure applied to the pedals. Having tires with good tread is vital for off-road, uphill cycling. Pedaling uphill is challenging for all cyclists. Go faster up small hills and keep doing this until it becomes easy. Increase the length of the climb and keep trying to get faster while seated. For more advanced uphill cycling, try standing in the pedals as you get to the top of the hill. Staying seated on longer climbs uses less energy and also involves the sit and hip muscles rather than the pelvis area, which carries the main weight during standing. Sit up as high in the saddle as you can and keep the hands as wide apart on the handlebars as possible. Keep the upper body and chest open to assist breathing. Keep shoulders back and open.

1. Two-Wheeler

As a beginner, concentrate on pedaling up a hill while sitting on the seat all the way up. The gradient will require you to lower the gear you are using. As the gradient gets steeper, you will find yourself stopping, getting off the bike, and walking some of the way up. With time and practice, you will soon be cycling all the way up. Once you start finding those easy, look for steeper hills. Add in corners and turns as you progress.

2. Recumbent

These have a poor reputation for uphill cycling. Start practicing on short climbs and then increase the length of the climb before increasing the steepness or gradient. Try to keep a steady pedaling rhythm or cadence.

3. Tandem

It is best for both riders to use a high cadence and a low gear in order to pedal uphill. It is more difficult than a single two-wheeler because the tandem is heavier.

4. Handcycle

When cycling uphill, expect the speed to drop dramatically in a similar fashion to two-wheelers. Arms and shoulders are generally weaker muscle groups, so turning those handles will require more effort. Again, starting with gentle inclines and then building up the steepness gradually will make it all more bearable.

5. Unicycle

Riding uphill involves leaning forward into the steepness of the hill. Pedal with half-wheel revolutions, regain your balance, and repeat. Shift your body weight forward of the unicycle at each wheel revolution. Mounting on a hill is done by turning the unicycle across the hill, gaining your balance, and then turning the unicycle back toward the hill (either with small jumps or a three-point turn), keeping your body weight forward when facing the hill again.

From the Amputees

Mark Inglis, New Zealand

As a below-knee amputee, a real advantage is being able to stand up and sprint or climb hills. You do need to use modern clipless pedals (MTB ones), though, as it is critical your prosthetic foot is anchored to the pedal, with some "float." Only a good clipless pedal will do that.

Steve Middleton, Canada

Starting uphill requires a post or helper to start and is difficult for novice cyclists. An option is to start downhill and then turn around. Though, this is not too popular on long hill climbs. Most above-knee amputees are unable to stand up in the pedals; therefore, having low-gear ratios on the bike are necessary for cycling steep hills. Depending on the length of your stump, the prosthetic-leg side is simply a stabilizing procedure and may only do a little of the grind work.

C. Cycling Downhill

Choose areas with gentle slopes. If you can't ride to the top, walk the bike to the top of the slope. Make sure the area at the top is relatively flat to make it easier to mount the bike. Walk the bike back down the slope to get some idea of the steepness on the way down and what it does to the bike. Walk or ride the bike back up the slope.

Keep brakes pressed lightly as you go down. Take your feet off the pedals altogether the first time. Then try it with your feet simply resting on the pedals. When you are comfortable, try pedaling down the slope. Repeat these steps as many times as you need to get used to the speed and level of decline. Don't put your feet onto the ground to slow yourself down or stop. Use the brakes and get used to how much you have to press the levers to control your speed.

Pedal down the slope and onto the flat area and continue biking along the flat surface. Brake to a complete stop and try putting only one foot out to hold yourself upright on the bike. When you can do this in a straight line and on steeper slopes, add in a bit of variety by increasing the number of slopes and adding in corners and turns on the downhill slopes. Practice making gradual turns and then sharper turns. This will prepare you for the serpentines that you see the experts tackling on all those wonderful mountain locations around the world.

Starting on a Slope
Bike up and down the slope several times until you're comfortable with both. When you feel confident enough to do so, bike halfway up the slope, come to a complete stop, and restart pedaling upward. Once you can do this easily, try it on more challenging terrain.

D. Cycling in a Straight Line
It is important to be able to cycle in a straight line so that you do not confuse others around you by weaving in and out unnecessarily on a road or cycle path. This is especially important when cycling in regular traffic. It is an advanced skill as it needs to be done without wobbling around.

Balance and moving in a straight line on two-wheelers, tricycles, and unicycles comes from the interaction between the shoulders and arms supported by the pedaling action of the hips. For handcycles, it is the arms and shoulders that "pedal." To cycle in a straight line, make sure none of these areas are tense. Reduce the grip on the handlebars if squeezing them too tightly. Look straight ahead into the distance, keep your head up, and do not look down at the ground. Practice by following a straight painted line or place some cones in a straight line and cycle next to them.

It is easier to cycle in a straight line if going faster, but to really test your skill, an advanced exercise to try is to cycle as slowly as possible and keep the bike upright and straight without wobbling. Cycling slowly makes the steering harder to control, so keep in a low gear while pedaling and apply the brakes on and off gently at intervals. An advanced course that teaches you this skill is the instructional paceline ride. This is a skill that is useful for group riding. A paceline can be single or double. Each rider lines up behind one another, and the rider in front sets the pace. After an agreed time (seconds or minutes), the front rider pulls off to the side and joins at the back of the line. Then the second rider sets the pace. This rotation of rider at the front carries on down the line throughout the length of the ride. The double paceline (double echelon or rotating paceline) has two lines of riders, but one line goes faster than the other. The front rider in the faster line drifts off toward the back of the slower line. Trying these cycling skills is only advisable once you have fully mastered the basics as the people that take part in such rides are usually racers or experienced road users who want to improve their existing technique.

E. Looking Behind

Another advanced exercise to try once you have mastered cycling in a straight line while looking forward is to try to look over your shoulder. To do this, drop your chin to your shoulder, turn your head to look behind you while holding your arms and handlebars steady, and keep cycling in a straight  line ahead. You may need to drop the opposite arm to your thigh if you cannot maintain a straight line while looking back. Keep the movement quick and controlled and make sure you have a good focus of what is behind you. Racers look under their shoulder in order to maintain a straight line, but this is not easy or comfortable to do.

One practice technique often used is to have someone behind you holding up a certain number of fingers. As you cycle forward, they shout when to turn your head, and you let them know how many fingers they are holding up. Do this for both sides—left and right—and for longer distances away from the person. Also try to increase the amount of time you can look back and cycle forward in a straight line (1 second, 4 seconds, 10 seconds, etc.).

Looking Around You

This is skill that is necessary, especially when cycling in traffic, in groups, or when there are others around, in order to prevent accidents and to be aware of (and enjoy) the environment you are traveling through. You can scan with your eyes or your head. It is worth being able to turn your head from left to right (and right to left) while you cycle to gain a better sense of balance. If you are in a race, you might decide to just keep your head down and focus on the narrow field of vision ahead, but try to be aware of the actions of others around as well.

F. Taking a Hand Off the Handlebars

Being able to cycle by controlling the bike with just one arm is sometimes necessary, especially when you need to signal that you want to turn in a traffic area. Start off slowly by simply lifting one hand off the handlebars and returning it back to its original position. Do the same with the other hand. Increase the amount of time you can keep the hand off the handlebars.

Once you can take one hand off, try moving it away from the handlebars onto your thigh. Drop the arm down next to your side if you feel more confident. Do this with the other hand and arm, too. Then try lifting one hand off the handlebar and putting it out to the side as if you are signaling. Repeat with the other hand.

For arm amputees, the prosthetic side may be fixed to the handlebars. That is the side of the body that has to take the weight when taking the dominant hand off the handlebars. If cycling without arm prosthetics, then taking your dominant hand off the handlebars becomes problematic as effectively you have no hands on the handlebars, and it is best to confirm the legal position on this in your own country before attempting it.

G. Reaching for a Water Bottle or Snacks

An advanced skill is to eat and drink while continuing to cycle rather than stopping and getting off. In the beginning, it will be useful to have those natural breaks in your cycling to assess how you and the prosthetics are doing. After a while, though, once you are confident with taking your hands off the handlebars, you will want to try some of these advanced skills. To reach down for a water bottle, take one hand off the handlebars and reach down toward your seat post. Keep your head looking in the line of travel. Put your hand back on the handlebars if you become too wobbly. Keep reaching down and back up until it becomes easy. Try it on alternate hands to see if you find one side easier. Try it on a flat, straight area first, then on an uphill or downhill, and then while curving or turning. Next, progress to actually taking the water bottle from the holder and replacing it while still cycling. If you can take a water bottle from its holder, take a drink, and replace it all while maintaining your direction of travel, then you are doing really well!

A similar technique can be used to get a snack from your pocket. Take your hand off the handlebars and put it on the outside of your pocket. See how long you can keep your hand there. Then put it back on the handlebars. Keep doing this until you can keep your hand on the pocket for long enough to reach into it, take out a snack, eat it and then put the wrapper back. Again, for arm amputees who ride without prosthetics, check the legal position of attempting this as both hands will be off the handlebars at that stage.

H. Signaling

Once you progress to being able to take one hand off the handlebars and maintaining the bike in a straight line, practice signaling. To signal, you have to combine looking over your shoulder, looking ahead, holding your hand out in the direction you want to turn, and then, with both hands on the handlebars, looking over your shoulder again before you make the turn. Do this in plenty of time, not just as you approach a turn. As this is an advanced technique that is used for cycling on roads with other traffic, it is best to attend a road safety course that teaches you correct positioning, signaling, and maneuvering before attempting to cycle in road traffic. These are usually organized by local authorities at regular intervals and sometimes take place in specifically designed centers that mimic road signs, markings, and traffic lights.

For arm amputees, once you have mastered being able to control the bike with the prosthetic side, the dominant side can do the signaling. Alternatively, if wearing a prosthetic hand that is simply resting on the handlebars, practice signaling with it. If you do not cycle with prosthetics, your core balance has to be incredibly strong to be able to take the dominant arm from the handlebars. This is a very advanced skill, but it is better to clarify the legal position on this before attempting it as technically both hands will be off the handlebars.

I. Falling Off

As a beginner, you will fall. Starting, stopping, and turning are where you are most likely to experience falls, but they are the perfect opportunity to test how well you can get back up again and carry on cycling. There are five stages to a fall:

Stage 1 = shock. The rider realizes he is falling or about to fall.

Stage 2 = negotiation. Stage in which the rider tries to prevent the fall by taking control of the bike.

Stage 3 = acceptance. The rider accepts there is no chance of recovery and he will fall.

Stage 4 = salvage stage. Try to fall as gracefully as possible to avoid injury.

Stage 5 = recovery. You need to overcome frustration—both physically and mentally.

To limit the damage that could be caused either to your stump, your prosthesis, to the rest of you, or to the bike, it is worth looking at some falling techniques. The main directions that you are going to fall off a bike are usually either forward over the handlebars or sideways. With unicycles, there is the added risk of falling backward.

Over the Handlebars

This occurs if your front wheel gets stuck in something on the road surface, if you ride into a solid object, or if you press your front brake too hard to stop. At that point, the bike has stopped, but you keep moving. When this happens, get your hands up, extend your leading arm (not the hand) toward the ground to absorb the impact, tuck your chin into your chest, and protect your head with the other arm. Do not let your head or spine hit the ground. Even if you have a helmet on, aim to protect your head as you fall. As you hit the ground, keep rolling over until you are on your back. Try not to impact your shoulder or hip. Be prepared for the bicycle to fall on top of you.

High Side Fall

This usually follows an attempt at coming out of a slide or skid on slippery road conditions. The back wheel that was skidding and had no grip suddenly grips again and lifts the front of the bicycle upright. At this point, you fall over the side. When this happens, let go of the handlebars and push the bike away from you. Make sure you are not falling on a hard curb or against a solid wall that could damage your head or cause more serious injuries. Tuck your head in with the outside arm and let the leading side of your body go limp to help absorb the impact.

Low Side Fall

If you take a corner too quickly, the bike will slide out from underneath you. As the bike goes down, rotate your upper body to face the direction your bike is sliding in. Drop your inside shoulder, turn onto your back, or put your feet out to act as brakes. Care should be taken not to twist or sprain the ankles while doing this.

Straight Sideways Fall

For total beginners, this fall can happen at any time and is usually due to a lack of concentration and balance. Falls that happen slowly can hurt more than those that happen at speed as there is little momentum to roll your body out of it. To avoid hitting the ground straight on and damaging your elbow, hip, or knee, lean away from the ground, keep your body upright, push your bike down in front of you so that the bars and inside pedal hit the ground before you do, and then roll over the bike onto the ground.

Try as much as possible to anticipate the fall. Learn to ride in such a way that you do not fall as often and keep practicing bike-handling skills to more advanced levels so you limit the risk of falling. Things to practice include slow speed handling, sudden direction changes, cycling without hands on handlebars, cycling one-handed, and turning tight corners.

Practice riding with most of your body weight over the pedals rather than the handlebars or seat so if you do fall, you can land on major muscle areas, such as your bottom or thigh, rather than areas that are more prone to injury, such as your neck, hands, or arms.

Falls happen in seconds, and it is difficult for the rider to anticipate or prepare to fall. Wearing good protective clothing will reduce the injuries experienced. Always protect your head and neck areas by covering them with an arm, hand, or shoulder. Use the arm, shoulder, and hand areas to provide momentum to roll onto other body areas which can take the impact more. Try not to land stiffly on the upper body and especially not on your hands as it could lead to wrist injury.

To practice such falls, it is worth getting an old mattress and trying these techniques out for yourself so that you learn to recognize and anticipate when you might fall. Separate your bike from yourself as much as you can during a fall so it does not hurt you by landing on top of you. Also keep looking for areas where you can get a soft landing if you do have to separate from your bike. When falling off a recumbent, due to its lower center of gravity, riders usually land on their thighs or bottoms.

How to Get Up After a Fall

If the fall is minor and you did not hurt yourself, follow the steps outlined here. If the fall is more of a major one with bleeding or severe pain, do not try to move yourself unnecessarily to prevent further injury to areas such as the back or neck. Request first aid and further assistance as described in chapter 12, Common Injuries and Stump Care.

1. Dislodge from the bike if it is on top of you or if your feet (or prosthetic arm) are clipped into the bike. Get someone to assist if necessary and available.
2. Double check all over for cuts and scrapes. Then stand up by using your dominant leg to take your body weight.
3. Perform bike safety checks as outlined in chapter 11, Basic Bike Maintenance. Especially check tires, brakes, gears, handlebars, and the seat in case these have been dislodged out of position.
4. Check your prostheses. If they are broken, do you have a spare set with you or will you need some assistance returning home?

How to Overcome Fear After a Fall

After a fall, you may feel shaky and nervous about getting back on the bike. Take a couple of deep breaths, sip some water, or rest a bit and keep the fall in perspective. If it was simply a question of slow timing or not seeing an obstacle, then those issues can be easily remedied. Get back on the bike once you are steady and relaxed again, and gently ease back into pedaling. Stay positive and focus on the road ahead. Frustration and anger at yourself for falling are all natural reactions and will dissipate once you go through the sequence of events that led to the fall and understand how not to let it happen again. The more you can laugh about the fall, the easier it is to get over it and move on to the next cycling challenge.

Emergency Dodge Maneuver (Advanced Method)

This is useful for avoiding hazards without necessarily changing road position and causing a worse situation. It is a basic safety method that every cyclist should be able to do.

To do this:

Look ahead, identify the hazard, and note its distance. Focus on riding a straight line while moving your bike around it. As you approach, jerk your front wheel around it and then back again. Your body must continue straight over the obstacle while your bike moves around it. A more advanced method of doing this is by standing up in the pedals, keeping them both level. Lift your weight off the saddle and lean forward, allowing the back wheel to move around or over the obstruction.

From the Amputees

Habib Jan, Afghanistan

I can ride without prosthetics. It is much easier to ride with prosthetics in crowded areas, because it helps keep me balanced and less likely to fall. If it is not crowded, I may ride without prosthetics. I have fallen off my bike many times! I remember one time, I was carrying 56 kilograms (123 pounds) of things needed for my family, such as potatoes, onions, tomatoes, and wheat, but on my way home, there was a pothole on the road. My bike was out of control, and I suddenly fell to the ground.

Joe Beimfohr, USA

I'm lucky to have not had an accident yet. I've seen plenty during races, though. I tend to be cautious, and I spend a lot of time doing skill drills on my bike so I can learn the balance and tipping point of my bike.

Mirsad Tokić, Croatia

Yes, I did fall because of the SPD pedals, and I didn't have time to disconnect the shoes to prevent the fall. Anyone who cycles with the SPD system experiences a free fall from their bike (it's an unwritten rule—ha, ha). Standing up to ride is a truly big challenge. I can do it, but it is very hard.

J. Riding Out of the Saddle

Riding out of the saddle allows you to put more body weight through the pedals as well as allows you to change your position on the saddle if riding long distances. It is used to help accelerate and to help cycle uphill. It uses

more muscles and energy. To do this, it is best to practice on a stationary bike or fixed trainer so you can feel the way the muscles react without risking a fall.

Put your knees as far forward as possible and tilt the bike. Tuck in your bottom and put as little weight as possible through the handlebars and as much through the pedals as possible.

Standing on the pedal will force it downward, but to pedal, you need strong muscles in your legs and ankles to be able to create the correct pedaling motion without dead spots or breaks in the rhythm. The head and body should be as still as possible with the bike swinging from side to side. Make sure someone is nearby in case you turn the bike over at this point, even though it is stationary.

Do not be too rigid; relax and keep a light grip on the handlebars. Putting more force on the handlebars through the hands can help support the body weight by using the upper body. Hips should be positioned vertically over the pedals when the crank is straight forward. Knees will almost be touching the bar. Keep your hands as wide apart and as far forward on the handlebars as possible to remain in control. To become more advanced, ride slowly in a high gear and build up the amount of time out of the saddle—first on a flat area and then on small inclines. Work on it a little at every opportunity and keep at it. It will hurt the muscles as they develop the strength that they need, but it will be worth it. Practice alternating standing up and sitting down as you cycle along to keep the muscles and the blood flow active.

This should only be attempted once a suitable level of upper-body fitness has been achieved. The body weight remains balanced if it is squarely over the legs and feet when doing this. Proper positioning protects the spine and helps efficient breathing. Shoulders should be rolled back and down to open up the lung capacity.

Using Cleats, Toe Clips, or Straps
These require some practice, and the easiest way to do this is, again, using a stationary or fixed bike on a trainer—or even as stoker on a tandem. Make sure you concentrate as any distraction will result in a fall. Keep cages and straps loose until you are sufficiently confident with getting into and out of the pedals to tighten them. If riding with prosthetics, keep the locking mechanism of the cleats at a very easy level; you will need to click out quickly and will not have sufficient power if it's too tight.

From the Amputees

Steve Middleton, Canada

Attaching the artificial foot to the pedal can be achieved by toe straps or toe cage for single-leg amputees and once confident with clipless pedals (SPD type). A beginner should start with a strap or cage. Only when proficient should you consider clip-in style pedals. SPD clips stop the prosthetic foot from moving entirely. The clip-in pedal system requires pressing the shoe clip (part of the cycling shoe sole) into the pedal clip to engage. Twisting the foot from the hip is required to disengage the shoe and can only really be achieved if the good foot is firmly placed on the ground. Toe straps and cages are part of the pedal. See a good cycling shop for advice and help. A good bike pro will help align the pedal and foot position.

When I first started cycling using my socket, I would wear a strap around my waist that went to a buckle on my socket to hold it in place. I did this for quite a while until I was confident my socket was a good fit and would stay on. Once I removed the waist strap, I was always concerned my leg might still come off. Because I wear a suction socket, I had to frequently drain my sweat. I also carried a pull donning sock with me, just in case. I initially sweat for the first 20 minutes, and then I seem to stop. I know others have to use antiperspirant deodorants for stumps. Talk to your prosthetist. Because I wear a suction socket, I am easily able to just stand up on my pedal (on the prosthetic side) and push the suction valve to let the sweat drain out through the valve. Alternatively, get off and drain the leg. If you are using a liner, your only option is to remove it and dry it out before proceeding. If you wear a one- or two-ply sock, your options are to carry a spare and, when necessary, replace the sock with a dry one or wring out the wet sock. If you feel your liner is separating from the socket, a quick and easy fix is to use a strip of Velcro and stick it to the liner and the socket. If you use biking shoes, look at mountain bike shoes because the cleats are recessed to make it easier for walking.

On a Stationary Bike

- Practice getting on and off the bike and fixing the feet into the pedals.
- Then practice pedaling with them.
- Then practice reaching down to release them and getting off the bike safely.
- Try putting the cleat position on different parts of your shoe to see if it makes a difference to your cycling technique.
- Try locking your foot onto the pedal while pedaling with the other one.
- Try pedaling with one leg only.

Once you can do all these things easily on a stationary bike, choose a grassy area where the landing will be soft if you do fall and try all these things again with a free-standing bike.

New cyclists tend to go through the same learning curve in different ways. Common issues include:

- Seat too low
- Mounting and dismounting awkwardly
- Foot in the wrong place on the pedal
- Poor balance and wobbling
- Using the wrong gear
- Not braking
- Using the wrong lane
- Not using lights at night

- Not using reflective clothing at night or in poor weather conditions
- Having poor turning and cornering techniques
- Braking sharply on descents
- Not maintaining bike properly (flat tires, rusty chain)
- Going too fast too soon
- Avoiding hills and steeper gradients

From the Amputees

Jon Pini, UK

I have fallen off the bike a few times. There was one particular time I can remember when we were mountain biking in South Wales. We were going downhill, and I hit a tree stump. The bike went one way, and I went the other. I went over the handlebars, but I was lucky enough to land in bracken and heather. My arm was still on because I had a suspension sleeve on that day to give me extra grip. What you tend to find is that if you are going downhill and going over rough terrain, very often you have to absorb the shock through the stump. Normally, I've gotten self-suspension, and if your limb is being moved up and down all the time because of the terrain, it can weaken that self-suspension link. So having an auxiliary suspension just enhances things to make sure the arm doesn't come off or come out of the socket, for instance. So basically I would have fallen off the bike in the same way a person with two arms would have—the bike went one way, I went the other, nothing was broken, and everything was fine. You check your bike and get back on just like any other person.

But, of course, if I'd broken my arm (as in, the prosthetic arm), maybe I wouldn't be able to get back on the bike, so there is that risk. But then, if I had broken my arm, it could have been my natural arm, and that could have been even worse. You are just as likely to break your prosthetic arm as you would your natural anatomical arm. Your hand could break from the socket, or the socket could crack.

Confidence is a big thing. As you get used to cycling, confidence levels increase, and you develop a rhythm. You become more natural and fluid in your technique. At the forefront of my mind is always to make sure I am not going to be attached to the bike when I come off because the resulting injury could be worse. That's why I use a normal passive arm attachment. The last thing you want is the bike flying on top of you as you are falling off. Some professional and semi-professional racers may want their arm clipped on to give them extra stability. That may be a matter of personal choice as professionals clip their shoes into the pedals so very often; even though they may be quick release, they could still be attached to that bike if they crash or fall. There might be some sort of quick release system for arm amputees that someone may have developed for those cyclists.

Nathan Smith, New Zealand

Everyone falls when they're first getting used to being clipped in, and when you're a newbie amputee, there is only one way to fall. Luckily, these are mostly only when you're traveling at low speed or coming to a stop. In London, while commuting, I've braked too hard and gone over the hood of a car, clipped the inside of a turning bus and gone tumbling down the sidewalk, lost the front wheel in a sewer grating, and been left lying in the middle of the road.

My worst crash was in a 120-kilometer (75 miles) race in Hamilton, New Zealand. I got dropped from my bunch during a long climb and was trying to chase on the downhill. I was fairly fearless on descents up until then. I was hammering it hard and went into a left-hander too quick. It was wet, and I applied too much rear brake. The bike was sliding beneath me toward the median, and as I was trying to lean it back, I went down hard onto my left side, spinning across the opposite side, and crashed into the banking only a second before a car came up the opposite way. The bike was a wreck. Thanks to landing on my prosthesis, I escaped with just some cuts and bruises, but the pain from the bolts in my left hip was with me for weeks. My confidence with descending was rocked for a couple of seasons. To overcome it, I talked to some more experienced riders who told me to not bother with the rear brake when descending in the wet. I then used to pick out the best descender in our training rides and tried to follow what they were doing for as long as I could. My confidence is not quite back where it used to be, but I like to think I'm a bit wiser because of the crash.

Further Reading

1. Introduction to tandems: cyclingabout.com/tandem-faq-everything-you-ever-need-to-know/
2. *Watch Your Line: Techniques to Improve Road Cycling Skills, Second Edition* by Alan Canfield (CreateSpace Independent Publishing Platform, 2011)
3. Uphill cycling tips: www.bicycling.com/training-nutrition/training-fitness/uphill-ease
4. Uphill cycling tips: www.bicycling.com/training-nutrition/training-fitness/fly-hills
5. Dos and don'ts of cornering: www.cyclingweekly.co.uk/fitness/training/bike-handling-techniques-improve-cornering-148960

Things to Try for Yourself on a Flat, Paved, or Well-Maintained Surface

Get on the bike, cycle straight, turn left, and continue cycling.
Get on the bike, cycle straight, turn right, and continue cycling.

Get on the bike and try narrower turns and curves in both directions.

Try to cycle in a straight line as slowly as possible.
Try to cycle in a straight line as quickly as possible.

Try cycling with one hand behind your back, alternating hands.

Weaving In and Out of Cones

1. Arrange a line of cones. Space the cones apart from each other and ride through them from one side to the other. Try it without touching or knocking down the cones. Then try it by clipping the cone with your pedal. Then, if that becomes easy, bring the cones nearer to each other and repeat.
2. Arrange two lines of cones in a V and try and ride between them without hitting the last pair. As your confidence increases, move the final pair closer and closer together. As they get closer, you have to start thinking about pedal position, too.

Braking

Pedal a 100-foot (30 meters) distance at an average speed. Then apply the brakes and come to a smooth, non-skidding stop within a distance of 10 feet (3 meters) without losing control. Repeat at a faster speed. Note the increase in distance required to stop. If you're riding a bike equipped with hand brakes, remember to apply the rear wheel brakes first. Note: UK law requires that a bike be equipped with a brake that will enable the rider to make the braked wheels skid on dry, level, clean pavement.

Circling

- Ride several times around a circle measuring 15 feet (4 meters) in diameter.
- Then ride several times around a figure-eight course formed by two circles.
- Practice adjusting your balance as you change directions.
- Make the circles and figure-eight smaller and smaller to make it more advanced.

Tour De Forces Charity Bike Ride

Excerpt reproduced with the kind permission of Invacare UK, Mark Ormrod, and Paul Shearsby.

→ **www.invacare.com**

Mark Ormrod has written a book about his amputations titled, Man Down (Corgi, 2010). It won The Royal Marines Historical Society Literary Award, 2010

→ **www.markormrod.com**

September 1, 2012, saw the start of the Tour de Forces bike challenge. This was an event where Mark "Rammers" Ormrod achieved his dream of handcycling around the coast of the UK. Due to the injuries Mark sustained in Afghanistan, he undertook the challenge on an Invacare Top End Force2 handcycle, sponsored by Invacare UK.

Mark and his team started in Plymouth, tracking the east coast of the UK, passing through Folkestone, Grimsby, Aberdeen up to Inverness, and coming back down the west coast through Lancaster, North Wales then heading back down and completing the journey at Plymouth covering a staggering 3,000 miles. All this to raise funds for their chosen military charities, The British Legion, Royal Marines Association, BLESMA, and Semper Fi Fund.

Their journey ended in October 2012, when a wet and weary team crossed the finish line having completed their task, and Mark achieved his dream of being the first triple amputee to handcycle around the coast of the UK.

Mark Ormrod

I became an amputee in 2007 while serving with the Royal Marines in Afghanistan. I stood on an Improvised Explosive Device which severely damaged three of my limbs. I ended up having both legs amputated above the knee and my right arm amputated above the elbow.

When I was training, all I could use was a static bike in the garage because I couldn't ride outside on my own as I wouldn't have my prosthetic legs on while on the handcycle. If I had a flat or blow-out or accident while out there on my own, I would have been stranded. So I had no choice but to put the static bike on the hardest setting in my garage and just train on that all the time. So I had no idea what I was actually capable of. I wasn't using a speedometer or mile counter or anything. I was just cycling for an hour, hour and a half, two hours at a time. So when I got out on the road, I said to myself, "Right, I am going to do 10 miles, and that is probably going to tire me out."

Remember, I only had one arm to power the bike as the prosthetic didn't really provide power; it just helps steady the wheel. I did that 10 miles the first day, and it was very hard because it was the first time I'd encountered undulating ground, and it was constant.

But then I got up the next day and did 35 miles, and I was just doing between 35 and 50 miles every day, and that's just the way it continued for the whole journey.

One of the toughest parts of the tour for me was when I got to Scotland, and we were doing a 40-mile section, finishing in a town called Ayr. At the end of this leg was a ferry port, so there were a lot of HGVs and freight trucks around on the roads trying to get to the ferry. The last 4 miles or so was all uphill. It was a spiraling uphill, so as you reached one corner, rather than leveling off or going down, it just kept going up and up and up. So I was obviously very very slow, but what wasn't so slow were the HGVs flying past me from behind, trying to get to the ferry port. I had a safety rider on a two-wheeler wearing high visibility clothing as it was quite overcast and murky up there. As I went around one of the corners on that uphill stretch, a HGV came tearing around and obviously hadn't seen us at that point and nearly wiped me out. I would have been squashed like a bug, but luckily my safety rider was there covering me. It was emotionally draining as well because we'd nearly completed the ride, and every time you turned the corner, the road just kept going up and up. It messes with your head because you think that it must flatten out eventually, or what goes up must come down. Obviously, it did eventually, and that was fun, but it went on a lot longer than I thought it would.

Coping with the weather was the hardest thing, but there were some funny things that happened because of that. In Scotland, it was raining very heavily, and I didn't want to put too much clothing on as I tend to overheat while cycling. It had been another long day—a 35-mile stretch—and we were going up and down the hills, and I was quite close to the end of the ride again where I was due to finish in the next 4 to 5 miles. We were going down a hill, and I went through a puddle, and, obviously, being on a handcycle is a lot different to being on a regular two-wheeler. The puddle came up to my belly button, so I got completely soaking wet! Then, as I was going down this hill, I jammed my brakes on the brake lever and started squeezing more and more until eventually it popped! So I could hardly see anything because it was raining so heavily, my brake liner had just snapped, and I was soaking wet flying downhill on a main road in a wooded forestry area. My safety rider was behind me on a two-wheeler, and there was a HGV behind him. I had to steer my bike as fast as I could into a brick *wall, and I couldn't tell him what was happening because there was so much noise from the rain and the trucks that he wouldn't have heard me, and I couldn't do hand signals because I've only got one arm. So I just slammed my bike into a wall at about 30 mph, and my safety rider slammed into the back of me and fell on top of me, crushing me with his weight. And, again, we nearly got squashed by a HGV that went winging down the road beeping at us. I had to stop about a mile short on that stretch because of the brake failure and trashed bike.*

With things like Facebook, where we advertized the UK Tour, absolute strangers that we didn't even know were inviting us to stay with them on the way. It was amazing (and weird) as these people had never met us, and the husband and wife would cook us massive banquets of food and set up their spare rooms and do all our washing for us and let us use their bathrooms even though we were covered in mud and junk off the roads.

Sport has a big part to play in rehabilitation of amputees; they just don't realize it. Getting out in teams, meeting people, and doing stuff really lifts your morale. It gets a little bit hard now and then, but I get a lot out of it personally—setting challenges and trying new things all the time to see what I can do and what's available.

The only downside for me at the moment is working out how to do 30 to 40 miles on my own, especially if I have a flat or injury while out on the road. While I can technically fix flats and change wheels on my own, I could also land myself into a lot of trouble doing so.

Cartoon by Martin Proctor who donated his fee to the Royal Marines for this work. Mark Ormrod has kindly provided his permission to be caricatured.

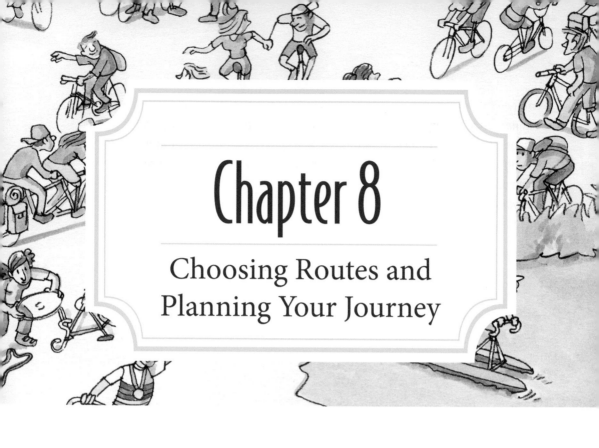

Chapter 8

Choosing Routes and Planning Your Journey

Cycling in the great outdoors is an adventure to be relished and looked forward to for some people and an absolute chore for others which they would gladly avoid. Outdoor exercise has great benefits in improving concentration. Exercising in green areas, such as in parks, or more rural locations helps to keep blood pressure, stress levels, depression, as well as heart disease under control. In fact, outdoor exercise is second to laughter in aiding recovery from illness or trauma.

When deciding where to cycle as a beginner, it is important to use similar thinking and planning methods used by experienced cyclists who travel much longer distances. Do this, even if at the very beginning of your cycling journeys all you are intending to do is go down the street to the local shop for some milk and bread. Does it sound strange to you? Remember, if you are a relatively new amputee combined with being a seriously new cyclist, all those simple activities you might have taken for granted suddenly take on a new meaning in terms of challenging your method of achieving daily living goals.

These planning challenges will be different depending on whether you live in a sprawling city or rural or semi-rural areas. In areas that do not have dedicated traffic-free bike paths, spend some time mastering the basics of cycling technique and learning the highway laws as they apply to cyclists. It is very important to maintain your own safety and the safety of others on the road if you decide to cycle with other traffic on a regular basis. Be very clear about issues such as cycling on pavements, road positioning, signaling, cyclist's and pedestrian's right of way, as well as cyclist or motorist liabilities during accidents. The highway laws are specific to each country and must be legally adhered to if you start feeling confident enough to try cycling more regularly on road networks or across country or state borders. Even if you are very used to road traffic conditions in other vehicles (e.g., motorbike, car, truck, van, bus), riding a bicycle in traffic is very different. It's worth getting those tips and refreshers from those who regularly do it before trying it yourself by attending a road safety course for cyclists. They are generally free to attend.

Your lifestyle before amputation or before you decided to take up cycling will also make a difference to how you plan your route for cycling. Undertaking shorter distances may be advisable initially to allow your stump to get used to the effect of cycling, reducing the chances of soreness and infection. Some of these issues are covered in chapter 12.

If you used to simply jump in the car and drive everywhere using only a satellite navigation system to guide you, then the challenge of switching to cycling and simultaneously attempting journey planning techniques becomes somewhat greater. Driving a car often involves longer distances than those used by pedestrians or cyclists. In your early days as a cyclist, you may take the same roads as you used to in a car out of habit until you learn how to navigate your way around other routes. Satellite navigation systems for walkers and cyclists often detail such options so it is becoming easier. There may be a need to refamiliarize yourself with outdoor life. The effects of the weather, the different feel of the traffic on a bicycle as compared to being in a car, and the slower pace (70 mph versus possibly 5 to 10 mph as a new cyclist) may conspire to confound your cycling efforts at first.

If you are intending to replace a car journey with a bike journey, then time these on a weekend or in the evening to make sure you get an idea of how long such trips are going to take you. Making the trip by bike may take a little longer initially as you look for quiet streets and cycle lanes, but it will be more interesting and scenic as you avoid the usual traffic routes. If cycling on the road is unavoidable, do not stay too near the curb. Keep at least one foot between your bike and the side of the road or the lines of parked cars.

This increases your visibility, helping to avoid getting hit by car doors that open suddenly. Also, cars pulling out of street junctions can see you, and other road users can overtake you at a slower, safer speed. Try not to weave in and out of parked cars. Keep your cycling consistent and safe. Make sure you plan some stops along the way—

at a shopping area, for example—where you can get drinks, snacks, or access to other facilities if you need to. The more you cycle, the farther you will be able to cycle. Finding suitable routes for you will then become easier.

The main aspects to consider when planning any cycling journey are the route, the distance, the gradient, and the weather. While there are lots of different factors that can affect all of these, the main ones are outlined here.

Route

The choice of route depends on how confident you feel as a cyclist. When starting out from not being able to cycle at all, it is important to choose as many relatively flat, quiet traffic-free areas as possible, such as public parks and small traffic-free country lanes, to get the feel of the bike and your prosthetic limb(s). These generally have good tarmac or general paved areas that make it easier to get used to being on a bike without too many complications or distractions. There may be a few near where you already live, but you may have to ask around or search online to find such areas. When choosing a public park, make sure to check with them first as some prohibit cycling within their grounds.

What does your local park look like?

Is it like this?   *Or like this?*

If it is like the first image, there is a lot of work to do to get it back to the beautiful way nature was intended to be, isn't there? Perhaps it's something you can help with. Cycling and environmental groups often work together on such issues, and simply providing feedback on the general condition of areas will assist tremendously.

Next, consider if it is a familiar route or unfamiliar route. How well do you know the place where you are about to cycle? Is it somewhere you have been to often so you know the layout, the surface, and the people who might be there, or is it somewhere you have never been before? Start off by cycling in areas that you are very familiar with to build up your confidence levels. Cycling such routes will help you focus on mastering the basic cycling skills, as outlined in chapter 6, rather than worrying about simply being lost. Only venture out to new and unfamiliar areas when you are more skilled with cycling skills (chapters 6 and 7), bike safety checks and repairs (chapter 11), and the prevention and treatment of injuries (chapter 12) so you can really enjoy learning about your surroundings and testing out what you have learned.

When first cycling outdoors, try to avoid using extremely narrow paths and being too near unfenced rivers, steep drops and hills, or sharp corners on routes. It makes for hilarious story-telling and entertainment for your family and friends as you call the emergency services to bail you out, but, in the interest of your own safety, these are things that can all be tried later when you are fully in control of your bike.

Start off by taking routes that are simply straight ahead or in a circle, coming back to the same point. Then start adding in turns or forks in the route for a bit of variety as well as to test your orienteering skills. Once you feel confident, make routes a bit longer and add in more turns, corners, and gradients. Keep to traffic-free areas.

Cycling and walking require different orienteering skills than driving. When driving, most main roads and directions are well sign-posted. In built up areas streets usually have name signs visible at the end of the street. This may not be the case for cycle routes or small country lanes, and you will have to rely on your sense of direction and navigational skills to cycle the route and get back home safely. Even if you have the latest in technology to help you, here is a quick refresher on map reading, navigation and orienteering skills that might come in useful in case the satellite navigation system lets you down.

Maps

A map is a way of drawing the landscape features around you in order to find your way around safely. Most are drawn as if looking at the area from the sky. Advances in science and mathematics alongside greater global exploration and mobility have allowed for the creation of accurate, finely detailed, and widely available maps of most areas around the globe. These satellite or aerial photographs can be printed on paper or viewed digitally on a computer or other device. Maps come in all types and in all levels of detail. Those designed for motorists show road networks clearly. Those designed for hikers or tourists show landmarks, small paths, and camping grounds. For cycling, it is best to use a map that has a waterproof covering on it so it does not get damaged by the weather conditions. Folding a map is a trick in itself, especially when windy or raining. Fold it so the route you are on is clearly visible at the top, easy to refer to, and kept out of direct wind or rain.

How to Read a Map

A good map will have a high level of accuracy in the information it shows. Maps are all drawn to a certain scale; a unit of distance on the map represents a particular distance on the ground. The scale measurement is shown as a ratio (e.g., 1:25,000). This means one centimeter (or other unit of measure) on the map equals 25,000 centimeters or 250 meters (or other unit of measure) on the ground.

The first number is always 1, and the second number can be anything from 10,000 to 190,000 to 1,625,000. The larger the second number, the larger area of ground is shown, but a lot of detail may be missing. The smaller the second number, the smaller the ground area, but with a lot of detail. This is especially important when choosing the routes you are going to cycle. For navigating your way around a town or city, a 1:10,000 scale would give good detail. Cycle paths are more likely to be shown on these. The scale of the map also helps you work out the distance you are traveling.

The next thing to be able to work out from the map is the direction. You need to know by how much you are going to travel up, down, left, or right (degrees north, south, west, or east). The words to familiarize yourself with here are *latitude, longitude, coordinates,* and *grid references.*

Latitude refers to the amount in degrees north or south of the Equator. These get smaller the farther away they are from the Equator. Longitude refers to the amount in degrees east or west of a point termed the Greenwich Meridian.

A way of showing how flat or steep the ground is (along the route) on a map is by contour lines. Contour lines show the height of the ground above sea level. If they are close together, the ground will be steep; if they are farther apart, the ground will be relatively flat.

Contours depict hills, saddles (a ridge between two peaks), valleys, spurs (a narrow neck of high land extending into a river valley), or cliffs. They show the gradient up and down (slope), the slope angle, and the direction a slope faces.

As it is impossible to show all features in great detail on a map, most have a key of symbols in a legend. The main symbols to be familiar with are roads, mountains, rivers, lakes, railways, forestry, parks, towns, cities, and buildings.

It is useful to have a compass as well as a map. This provides valuable information on the direction of travel. There are four main points to a compass which are known as the cardinal directions of north, south, east, and west. The halfway marks in between these (e.g., southeast, northwest) are known as the intercardinal points. There are different types of compasses, each designed for particular uses (e.g., on land, in air, or at sea).

A compass is split into 360 degrees. Usually, the needle pointing north is red at the end. To read a compass:

- Hold it steady away from phones, zip fastenings on pockets and bikes as these affect its magnetic field.
- Place between your face and waist with your arm in a comfortable position. Your elbow should be bent and held close to your stomach.
- Look to see where the needle points.
- Turn your body and you will see that the compass rotates but the needle stays pointing in the same direction.
- To find which direction you want to travel, line the arrow with the end of the needle that depicts north.

Using Compass and Map to Plot a Route

To do this:

1. Figure out where you are: Find two landmarks and look for these on the map. Align the map so the landmark in front of you is on top of your map. Draw a straight line down from that point. Now draw another line from the second landmark to meet the downward line. Where they meet is roughly where you are. Closer features and landmarks will make it easier to be more exact with your location.

2. Find your destination: If you just want to go from one place to another, it is simple to plot a single route. If you want to take in more than one destination, you need to plan your route more carefully. In both instances, bear in mind how much time you will need to get there.

3. Use the index and the scale to work out the expected traveling time: Check this at intervals to make sure you are on track.

4. Plot the route using a pencil and make a note of checkpoints along the way: Double check where the turnoffs are as missing a turn may take you off course.

If the map and compass are not available, then some of the very early orientation methods may prove useful. These include using the sun, moon, stars, or wind to tell what time it is or in which direction you are going.

The sun rises from the east, is highest in the sky at midday, and sets in the west. The only place where it is exactly on east and west is at the Equator. From the position of the sun, you may be able to work out roughly which direction you are traveling in and how much time there will be before the light fades. The sun also helps with orienteering through the use of shadows. The easiest method to try is placing a stick upright into flat, even ground and angling it toward the sun so it casts no shadow. Wait some minutes, and a shadow will appear as the sun moves around. The shadow will be facing roughly east to west.

A watch can be used to find out the direction of travel when the hour hand points directly at the sun. Care must be taken to not look directly at the sun. The imaginary line that goes halfway between the hour hand and the 12 o'clock mark will run north to south.

Satellite Navigation

A system of satellites orbit the Earth, and small electronic receivers determine the longitude, latitude, and altitude of their signals to a high degree of precision. Typically, four or more satellites must be visible for accurate information. Basic GPS systems only show a position. Most systems, however, will compute speed and direction as well as other useful route information. Changes in speed and direction may be slightly delayed or inaccurate, but more advanced systems now overcome this.

Satellite navigation systems (sat nav) for cyclists have to be robust. The most obvious place for a sat nav is centered on the handlebars to maintain balance. A bulky device on the handlebars increases the weight and stability of the bike. The device should be weatherproof, durable, and fall proof, and the screen ideally should be readable in sunlight. The method of strapping the device to the handlebars should not be too complicated so it can be taken on and off the bike to reduce opportunistic theft when parked. As the handlebars experience some turbulence on rough road conditions, the device should be stable on the mount as it is difficult to read a jolting screen. The difficulty for many will be choice of route. For beginners, the satellite navigation system should direct

them to cycle specific paths and traffic-free areas, whereas for advanced cyclists who are used to and don't mind cycling with traffic, it can work out the quickest or shortest route to the destination.

For such cyclists, lane guidance and junction information may prove useful. Some basic systems are available as applications on a smart phone. Using these may be convenient for short journeys, but they tend to use up a lot of battery power. A high-quality, dedicated satellite navigation system can provide more than 12 hours of use on a full charge.

Distance

So how far do you want to cycle? Around the world? Around the USA? Around Africa? Around New York or Tokyo? You will want to do at least one of these things as soon as you realize you *can* actually ride a bike. Everyone does—deep down, if you ask them, each and every one of us has a goal that keeps us motivated to keep cycling. It's good to have such goals and a real accomplishment to achieve them. In the early stages of cycling, though, choose shorter routes. Doing a few of these will increase your confidence and improve your familiarity with the bike. Definition of **shorter** in this context means start off in terms of half a mile or kilometer. Progress to 1 mile or kilometer, 2 miles or kilometers, 5 miles or kilometers, to 10 miles or kilometers gradually over a number of consecutive cycling sessions.

Some amputees underestimate their ability to cycle and set themselves small distances only. They may attempt a longer distance which they hadn't contemplated previously as their cycling improves, or they may plateau at a certain short distance and are happier working more on their cycling technique and pace rather than trying to cycle longer and longer distances.

Others will set themselves a long-distance target straight away. For avid car, train, or airplane users who regularly travel 100 miles or more each way to work, such very short distances may not be a part of their general everyday vocabulary or thought processes; it may take a little effort for them to get used to. Splitting up the overall distance into sets of smaller distances at each session will result in a better sense of achievement and more positive experiences of cycling.

If you set yourself too big a distance to reach and don't complete it, then you will feel more frustration and negativity toward yourself, your prosthetics, and your cycling ability. At that point, it may be tempting to give up the activity altogether, and it is important to ensure that you obtain enough support to keep yourself motivated. If long-distance cycling of thousands of miles is your fundamental aim, then you will be able to do it. Some amputees have, and their stories are in this chapter. It requires a very high level of fitness and motivation to be able to do such cycling feats. If at the point of your amputation or at the time you decided to try cycling you do not have a good level of overall fitness, those areas will need to be worked on before you can do long distances comfortably. Build up the length of your cycling route gradually and steadily, and don't forget to consider the return journey! That way, whatever is going to happen to either the bike, to you, or to your limb(s) happens in manageable ways that you can easily control. Design yourself a cycling goal chart or calender to keep you focused on the distances you want to master.

Gradient

Always riding on flat routes can get boring, can't it? There will come a time during your cycling journey when you will want to tackle some gradients. We are not talking about cycling up Mount Kilimanjaro here (which has been done already, by the way, though not by an amputee yet) or whizzing around the Alps à la Tour de France (done by some amputees on holiday and not during the race itself, by the way). During the early stages of cycling and getting used to prosthetic limbs, you should be aiming for smaller gradients. Proficiency in these will naturally lead you to steeper hills and curves, but in order to be successful at those, you have to work on the correct cycling techniques and have prosthetics that fit well.

Here is a general idea of gradient values to help you prepare for those climbs:

- **0%:** A flat road.
- **1-3%:** Slightly uphill, but not particularly challenging. A bit like riding into the wind.
- **4-6%:** A manageable gradient that can cause fatigue over long periods.
- **7-9%:** Starting to become uncomfortable for seasoned riders and very challenging for new climbers.
- **10-15%:** A painful gradient.
- **16% and up:** Very challenging for riders of all abilities. Maintaining this sort of incline for any length of time is very painful.

Downhill slopes are given negative gradient values. These are average values. In reality, gradients at different points along the climb may be steeper or shallower for certain sections and involve cornering, curves, and turns. The narrower these are, the more difficult it is to do them without falling or injuring yourself, especially as a beginner. During an uphill, there are three main forces acting against the cyclist: wind resistance, road friction, and gravity. These have to be overcome to move forward and upward. The heavier the person, the harder it is to climb quickly as more power is required to move the body weight over the same distance.

When choosing the route and distance, be aware of how many inclines there are and how steep they are. They will affect whether you cycle, walk, or take public transportation to get up them.

Weather

Rain, sun, wind, fog, ice, sandstorms, blizzards, hurricanes, thunder, lightning, and tornadoes—which one of these seasonal variations will you have the most *fun* cycling in? That is purely up to you! Blowing about on a bike in a tornado may look good in a movie such as *The Wizard of Oz*, but I doubt it is to be recommended in real life.

The serious message here is:
Consider how much of your time is currently spent shielded from the weather either in a heated or air conditioned building or vehicle. How much time do you currently (or did you before your amputation) generally spend outdoors and feel the full impact of the weather on your body? Was it for short periods or longer periods? Did where to go in your leisure time depend on whether it was raining (indoor venue) or sunny (outdoor venue)? How much time on average do you spend outdoors in extremely hot, dusty conditions? Would you say you are a fair weather person or an all weather person?

If you are an individual who goes from your front door directly to your car parked in front of the house, adjusts the air temperature to your personal comfort level for driving, and then parks right outside the building you are working or shopping in, then you will find it a particular challenge to be so *exposed* to all manner of different weather conditions when you are on a bicycle. More important, these weather features can and often will change throughout the length of your journey. Even if you are just going around a small park for a practice ride, it may start off sunny and warm and end up raining quite heavily. This isn't so bad on a short journey, but it is important to consider such things for those longer rides that you will want to go on eventually. The weather affects your prosthetic limbs, the rest of your body, your cycling, and your mood. No matter how well you try to prepare for these things with extra clothing, it can be very unpredictable in some geographical areas of the world, so check the local weather conditions carefully before you set off.

Clouds

Cloud formation can be used to predict different weather patterns. A clear, cloudless sky means no rain, snow, hail, or ice to watch out for while cycling. Clouds can be water or ice or both. They can trap heat in the atmosphere or block out the sun. There are four main types of clouds—nimbus, cumulus, cirrus, and stratus—which are defined by their shape, color, composition, and height.

Cirrus clouds are found at very high altitude and are made of ice. They are wispy or hair-like and are also the white bands or streaks that line a clear sky. They signify fair, pleasant weather.

Cumulus clouds are puffy heaps of white clouds. They can indicate stormy weather with lightning, thunder, or tornadoes. Stratus clouds are low, gray clouds that resemble fog. They can cover the whole sky and produce rain or snow. Nimbus clouds are dark gray, low clouds full of water. At the start of your route, there may be very few clouds, but on a longer bike ride, keep checking for changes in the clouds as you travel along so you are not caught out by unexpected storms, hail, or sleet.

Cycling in Wet Weather

There are two golden rules for cycling in wet weather:

1. Dress for it.
2. Make sure your bike is suitably prepared.

Wet weather clothing should be breathable and should keep you dry and warm. If you are wet, you are likely to become cold.

Use a hood for your head and boot covers for your shoes to prevent rain from making those areas cold. Being able to see clearly despite the rain means having the correct eye protection. Anti-fog products may help.

The areas of the bike to double check are the brakes, gears, tires, and lights. Using mud guards will prevent the rain from splashing back from the tires onto your body or face. Changing to a heavier, fatter tire and reducing the tire pressure a little will help you stay on the bike. Brake pads can be easily worn down due to the grit on the roads. Check them regularly if cycling in wet weather. Rainbow-colored patches along the surface of the road suggest oil may be present. Do not apply the brakes heavily or turn if cycling along such surfaces. Be extra careful around cars in wet and poor visibility conditions. Metal surfaces, wet leaves, and painted traffic markings all become slippery in the rain. Stopping requires longer distances. Water on the road may be deeper than it appears, and your chain and bottom bracket may become rusty if you ride through deep water. When cycling around corners, go slower, shift your weight to the outside pedal, and try to keep the bike more upright by leaning your body into the turn. Puddles can mask potholes, so avoid them if possible as they can cause damage to your wheels. Wipe down the bike after use to prevent rust and keep the chain lubricated.

Cycling in Snow

Snow tires, spikes, and chains are options to consider if you want to cycle in snow. Again, letting some air out of the tires increases their grip on the road. Use mud guards and make sure your brakes and gears are working properly. Dressing for cold wet weather is essential, especially for your fingers as they are used for operating your brakes, and you don't want them to feel numb with cold.

Fresh snow offers a natural resistance while pedaling, so your legs have to work a bit harder, but at least if you fall it will be a soft landing. Being the first to make cycling tracks in freshly fallen snow will remind you of the excitement you felt as a child when you first saw snow. When cycling on ice, slow down, keep your body weight to the back of the bike, only use the back brake, and remember that stopping distances will be longer.

Don't brake while turning, and use your body rather than the handlebars to steer. Avoid icy roads in any circumstances. It's almost impossible to keep balance, and the fall will be very hard.

If you hit icy patches such as tire tracks caused by cars or other bikes, keep the body weight back and let the front wheel of the bike go gently in whichever direction it needs to over the tracks. Wipe down the bike after use to prevent rust.

Cycling in Sand

Sand can be dry, wet, or even frozen. Wet sand is easier to cycle on than dry sand. It takes more effort from your legs, and the wheels may slide around while you remain stuck. Distributing your body weight differently on the bike may help you cycle through. The deeper the sand, the more chance of the bike becoming stuck. The tires should be wide with good knobby grips, and the tire pressure should be reduced to improve grip.

Cycling in a Heat Wave

When it is extremely hot, it is important to protect your skin with very good sun protection. Drink plenty of water regularly and wear light, breathable clothing. Tire pressures can be higher than in winter or wet weather cycling. Watch out for tacky areas of tarmac that have melted in very hot weather. Dust and grit on your bike can be reduced by regular cleaning and lubrication.

Your Checklist

For those initial small escapes on the bike to run errands or explore the countryside, go through a simple checklist, such as the following. Whether you write things down or simply run through these things in your head depends on you.

* What/where to cycle?
* What do you want to be able to do when you get there? (e.g. sightseeing, shopping, movies, meeting friends)
* Which route are you going to take?
* When are you going to do it?
* How long is the journey?
* Are there any food, drink, telephone, restroom or public transportation facilities around on the way if needed?
* What will you do in case of a flat tire or accident?
* Are you going to cycle alone or with others?
* Do you have enough spares of stump socks, liners and inner tubes to see you through the journey?
* Are there any safety issues that you need to consider?
* What is the route like — full of potholes or well maintained?
* Do you have the correct clothing for the weather forecast?

Cycling Days With Children

Once they have mastered the basics of cycling, children tend to look forward to the suggestion of a bike ride. For younger children, make sure these don't end in tears and tantrums by keeping distances shorter than you would normally cycle. Keep them off the roads and out of traffic. Finish at a place they consider a treat, such as the beach, a playground, or park where they can play, eat ice cream, and refresh themselves for the return journey. Cycling with their friends or other amputee children is an added stimulus, and drinks or treats (e.g., nuts, seeds, dried fruit, cake, cookies, and salty snacks) along the way keep the outing fun.

Extra clothing, a first aid kit, and a flat repair kit are useful to take with you to ensure everyone enjoys messing around on their bikes. As they become older and learn how to deal with traffic situations, keep children on the inside of you on a road or have one adult in front and one adult behind. Schools that offer cycling courses cover the following:

Level 1—How to control bikes away from traffic or cars.
Level 2—How to deal with traffic on short journeys on roads, such as cycling to school.
Level 3—How to deal with a wider variety of traffic situations and road conditions.

Plan longer cycling days with teenagers as a regular family activity. Getting them involved in route planning and general preparation will provide them with the skills and confidence they need to continue undertaking such cycling expeditions on their own or with friends.

Bike Touring or Holidays

If you are seriously considering doing some real long-distance exploring on your bike, it is useful to consider the following aspects before venturing out on that epic adult journey:

1. Planning the route
2. Making sure you have enough money or can access funds as you travel around
3. Considering health and safety issues, especially if traveling alone or if prosthetics require repair or replacement
4. Obtaining all the correct insurances and visa permits for the areas you want to travel to
5. Making a list of risks you may face along the way and how you intend to deal with them

Alternatively, if that sounds a little too responsible and boring, why not simply quit your job, get a bike, and start pedaling? Who knows where you might end up and what wonderful tales of mystery and adventure you will have to tell when you return? Bicycle touring can be as adventurous and exciting as you want it to be. The following are some of the ways cyclists tour in the 21st century:

Lightweight: The cyclist carries the minimum of equipment and a lot of money. Food is bought along the way, and overnight accommodation consists of bed and breakfasts, youth hostels, or small guesthouses.

Ultralight: The rider carries his own equipment and is self-sufficient, but there are no frills, extras, or luxuries included along the way.

Fully loaded touring: The cyclist carries everything he needs, including camping equipment.

Expedition touring: This sometimes involves traveling through developing nations, and the bicycle is heavily loaded with spares, tools, and camping equipment.

Supported touring: Cyclists are supported by a motor vehicle that carries most of the equipment. It may include guided tours, luggage transfers, route planning, meals, and rental bikes.

Day touring: These are rides that cyclists might do themselves or in an organized group. The purpose may be to raise funds for charities. They may or may not require overnight stay, depending on the distance to be cycled.

Baskets and rucksacks are used to carry much of the equipment if there is no support vehicle, so it is worth practicing cycling with these before setting off on that epic journey. They affect how you balance on the bike, and the extra weight makes the bike heavier

to pedal, especially uphill. The more training and preparation you do both physically and mentally, the less of a struggle it is when you finally set off.

To pack baskets for a long-distance journey, put clothing in one and food and medicines in another. Putting valuables such as passport, phone, and money in a plastic bag will keep these things from getting wet.

A suggested basic equipment list is shown here for long-distance cycling in open terrain where there is little in the way of amenities. It is neither complete nor is everything compulsory.

Cycle computer	Spare tubes (more than one)
Flat kit	Hydration packs
Bike pump	Tire levers
Spoke spanner	Multitool kit
Identification	Lightweight jacket
Space blanket	First aid kit
Sunblock	Lip balm
Energy bars, snacks, packets	Map and compass
A full water bottle	Thermos of hot drink in cold weather
Flashlight	Wristwatch
Sat nav	Whistle to attract attention

Cell phone in plastic bag plus a spare fully charged battery

For those longer journeys, taking in enough energy and fluids becomes a priority. Bakeries, farm shops selling fresh produce grown on site, bars, and restaurants may be your choice of fuel, or you may decide to take along your own supplies. Keep them in a cool box on your bike to maintain freshness while you are out and about, and make sure you pass enough places to replenish these as you cycle along. Even with detailed planning and organizing, it is useful to accept that not everything in life can be accounted for or managed. It is best to allow enough flexibility in your schedule to deal with emergencies, delays, and general day-to-day living issues as well as all those fun, exciting things that might crop up on the way. You might come across a new area you wish to explore, and there may be interesting people—other amputee cyclists even— to meet there. The beauty of the scenery, nature, and wildlife might mean you decide to stay longer in some places than originally expected. The more flexible your route planning, the more you will be able to take advantage of these and other fun things along the way.

Inevitably, you will need replacement parts and spares, so finding out where bike shops are is often a good idea. Keep equipment costs manageable by looking for good quality secondhand equipment online or in charity shops. Much of this equipment may or may not last the whole journey, so keep some money budgeted for replacing these, too. Overall, keep your travel plans as simple and as flexible as possible so you get the opportunity to pedal where you choose along your main route. If you are the type of person who equates simple with boring, then add in a few complications and diversions along the way to make it more interesting for you.

If setting off on that incredible journey does not appeal, you might be tempted to consider an organized cycling trip where a lot of the planning, scheduling, paperwork, and arrangements are all taken care of. All you have to do is cycle and enjoy it. There are many versions of cycling trips to choose from. Many restrict numbers within the group, and others have support for large numbers of riders. While most cater to able-bodied cyclists, there are options to travel with disabled cyclists, or negotiate aspects of a tour to suit your disability. If you can interest existing tour companies to offer more cycle touring trips specifically designed for disabled cyclists, it may be a way of increasing your touring options. It would also allow you to enjoy the tour more fully than trying to keep up with seasoned able-bodied tourers. Most vacation tours for able-bodied cyclists require you to be able to cycle anything from 50 miles a day for at least a week, so make sure you can do this within your pre-trip training in different weather conditions before booking.

From the Amputees

Jon Pini, UK

There some good trails around a few areas of Wales—plenty of cycling and mountain biking trails in mid Wales. I used to cycle a lot. I am in the process of getting another bike and want to do more cycling around the Gower; there are some nice side tracks there. It varies; some days I'd look to go on a proper mountain biking trail, and other days I would be quite happy to go off on little side roads and just do 20 miles uphill and down dale. It varied on the weather, of course, and it varied as to how enthusiastic I was feeling on the day.

Mark Inglis, New Zealand

Look for a grassy park for your first ride (softer when you fall off, which everyone does), especially when getting used to proper pedals. Then, try and stay off roads until you are very confident. Nearly all councils will have information on dedicated bike trails, especially within city limits. Find them, and then ride!

Sara Tretola, Switzerland

In Emmental, there are lots of cycle routes which have no or little traffic on them. They would certainly be good for disabled cyclists at beginner level.

Steve Middleton, Canada

While cycling, load bearing on the socket is minimal. Depending on the type of socket, there are a number of considerations. When wearing a socket liner system, consider carrying extra socks, liners, and draw socks. Be aware of chafing areas in the socket, and deal with these immediately. Riders wearing a suction socket may need to stop frequently to drain the socket of perspiration. I suggest carrying a spare pull sock for emergency. If wearing socks, these may become damp from perspiration and need changing on longer distances. Discuss all concerns with a prosthetist before embarking on any lengthy journey.

Stumps and Cranks Book Interview with Armin Köhli, Switzerland (Summer 2013)

1. Do you take your bike by plane when you go on bike tours?

I avoid it if I can. I hate packing the bike, and I hate cleaning my bikes. Whenever possible, I rent a good bike (did so in Crete; check crete-cycling.com). Renting bikes is fine; although, sometimes you don't find the exact quality that you're looking for or that you're used to (i.e., tires!). But for the tours, I had my own bikes, of course.

2. If hiring bikes were an option in countries, do you have to arrange such ahead of traveling due to time required for adaptions?

Not necessarily for adaptions, but just to be sure that they have bikes available (depending on the seasons, of course). There are training destinations with well-developed infrastructure for cyclists and bike rental, such as Mallorca, Cyprus, Andalusia (Chiclana), Catalunia (Giverola), all across Italy (such as Cesenatico, Riccione), but, if you dig a bit, you'll find other places like Crete and Sardinia. And whereever there is good terrrain for mountain biking you'll find dealers that offer bike rental (in the Alps, in South Africa, etc.). It gets more difficult in developing countries, but at least in capitals or big cities you might find good dealers or guided tours. Lebanon has a "critical mass" in Beirut, and there's also a (tourist) program, "Beirut By Bike." Quite active is a club in Jordan: Tareef Cycling Club (https://twitter.com/Tareefclub). They accompanied me from the Syrian–Jordanian border to the Dead Sea in 2007. They are bike lovers and should know if anything exists in the Arab world.

3. Have you been anywhere where you can remember seeing some good beginner's routes?

Sure! In Switzerland along some lakes (Greifensee)

The famous Donau trail (mainly Passau–Vienna)
  → **www.danube-cycle-path.com/austrian-danube.html**

Tuscany could also offer some nice, although hilly routes with limited traffic.

Inntal Cycle Route might also be an option.
  → **http://rad-donau.de/en/inntal-cycle-path/**

Also, in northern Germany (Brandenburg, Mecklenburg-Vorpommern) there must be almost car-free, flat trails along rivers and lakes
  → **http://en.wikipedia.org/wiki/EV7_The_Sun_Route#In_Germany**

In general, look for rivers, lakes (usually flat terrain), and for little or no traffic. So either a tourist area that specifically promotes cycling or very remote areas.

Dan Sheret, USA–San Francisco to New Hampshire (and Beyond...)

The pain and weariness for the last two days fell away from me as I rounded the last corner and finally saw the Atlantic Ocean stretching out as far as I could see. I found myself yards away from the beach access I had spent two months trying to reach. With one last pedal stroke my riding was done. "How many millions of turns of the pedal crank had passed since I started in San Francisco?" went through my mind as I made that last revolution. I slowly coasted to a stop and unclipped my left leg from the pedal and then reached down and unclipped my prosthetic leg on my right. Hoisting my bike on my shoulder, my eyes were brimming with tears. I walked those last few steps of my long journey to the water's edge. As I made my way through the crowded beach, I was joined by my fellow riders. We became a curiosity for the families enjoying their summer beach vacation. A group of 30 laughing, crying, shouting, cyclists standing in the warm surf is not an everyday occurrence on a New Hampshire beach in July.

I stood stunned for a moment, unaware of the press of people around me and of the cameras of the media closing in on my spot on the beach. There would be time for them later. This was my spot. I earned it. There was one last thing I had to do before I was descended upon. I steadied myself with one hand on the bike that had taken me all across this vast country. I reached down and stripped away the cover to my leg and pulled my stump from the carbon fiber socket of my prosthesis. The tears of joy were blinding me now, and I lifted my carbon and titanium leg as high as I could in victory. "Yes!" I said over and over. "Yes, I did it!" Fifty-two days and 3,800 miles earlier I left a foggy beach in San Francisco on June 8, and here I was in Portsmouth, New Hampshire, on the last days of July, my travels completed. Or so I thought...

A decade has now passed since that summer of 2003, and in that time, I have cycled some 30,000 miles in 15 countries and across 3 continents, bringing a message of hope and awareness about limb loss. I had the fortune to be one of a handful of amputees that had up to that point cycled across America. Today, amputees by the thousands regularly cycle great distances and perform other amazing athletic feats. What was once rare and newsworthy is becoming commonplace and expected.

Kiera Roche, UK

KIERA'S BIKE DIARY—An excerpt from the Egypt Bike Tour, reproduced with permission

→ **www.limbpower.org**

We arrived in Cairo in the early hours of Monday evening after a two-hour flight delay. Mike Paterson, a double below-knee amputee, and I had the usual airport shenanigans, setting off the metal detectors on the way through customs. We stayed at a hotel in Cairo, which reminded me of a holiday chalet. Our rooms were at the farthest end of the complex, so I struggled with my suitcase, spare leg, and travel bag until I spotted a porter who took pity on me, thinking I was a weary packhorse. Once I'd unpacked and plugged the C-leg (a computerized leg made by Otto Bock) into the wall socket, I was ready for bed. The next morning was a fantastic opportunity to see the pyramids, something I have wanted to do for as long as can remember, but I had to drag myself out of bed at what seemed like the crack of dawn. However hard I try to be quick, it just takes me longer to get ready because I have to wash the socket sleeve of the artificial leg with antiseptic wipes, put on the sleeve and a stump sock, and finally don my artificial leg, which isn't always easy.

After breakfast, we gathered our belongings and headed to the bus for what we thought was a long bus trip to the pyramids, so I nearly fell off my leg when I walked out of the lobby into the bright sunlight to see the pyramids staring back at me. It was the most bizarre sight, standing in the middle of a street in a built-up city, looking at the most talked about historical construction in the world. It somehow reduced their magnificence.

After lunch, we flew from Cairo to Luxor where we joined the Nile Queen, our home for the week. Staying on a boat on the river Nile was a lovely touch and added a hint of romanticism to the trip. Those of us who had brought our own bikes had the wonderful task of putting them back together, while the other bikers were fitted with their bikes.

This all took place on the deck of the Queen and was a great bonding experience, and gallantly, many of the chaps offered their services as temporary bike mechanics, and together we put the Pink Lady back together.

During dinner, we were given a rundown of the next day's itinerary and informed that we needed to be up at 6:30, which meant a 5:15 wake-up call—yes, 5:15! I'm not quite sure how I actually made it out of bed, got washed and dressed, put my cycling clothes and cycling leg on, and made it to the deck on time, but I somehow did. The biggest difficulty I have as an above-knee amputee is that I weight bear from the ischial bone (bottom bone) and the socket which encases the bone, interfering with the motion of cycling and throwing me off the saddle on each rotation, not a comfortable option for 400 kilometers (250 miles).

My prosthetist, Richard Nieveen, and I devised a plan to cut the socket back and load the weight bearing in other areas, which would be more comfortable for cycling but uncomfortable for walking. So on the first morning, I had to negotiate my way, not only off one boat, but through a number of different size and, therefore, different height boats. Nile boats are similar to barges; they line up next to each other to dock, so to get to the shore, you walk through the lobbies of each of the boats that have docked before you. Quite an interesting experience when each boat has its own metal detector at the entrance and exit; after a few days I simply sidestepped the detectors and went on my way.

The first days cycling was mainly off-road, and where there was road, it was covered in potholes and rather large rocks to negotiate. The Pink Lady would have shivered, curled up in a ball, and refused to move had it been organic. We started on the first leg of a 115-kilometer (71 miles) day which was a lovely ride apart from a small incident involving a car, Cathy, me, and a donkey cart. Fortunately, I was next to the donkey cart, and I held on to steady myself and managed to stay upright on the bike. A promising start, I felt. I was warned that the first section after lunch would be difficult because it *was a road that had been dug up and not resurfaced and that I might struggle; this only spurred me on. I wasn't quite prepared for how difficult it would be and the distance it would cover—approximately 8 kilometers (5 miles) of struggling to cycle across gravel and pebbles, some as big as those on Brighton Beach. After about 5 kilometers of pounding, my wrists and bottom couldn't take any more, and I conceded defeat and jumped in the van. To my relief, I wasn't the only person who had found the section too difficult as Cathy and Mike jumped in the van with Tony and me to enjoy the scenery. I was disappointed that I had missed about 12 kilometers of the day's ride, but we got back on the bikes and cycled the next section.*

Day two was on a much smoother surface. It made such a difference being back on my bike, and I had a really enjoyable morning ride. Mike and I were somewhat of a novelty to the locals with our hi-tech limbs. People would shout hello as we cycled past, see my leg, and either look surprised or excited and cheer us on. I was amazed at the positive attitude toward disability displayed by the locals. They were both supportive and helpful.

We cycled back to the boat for lunch and some rest and recuperation. In the afternoon, we headed north, cycling through small villages. The local children were fantastic, shouting excitedly and running alongside the bikes, waving their arms in the air and shouting, "Hello!" "Hello!" "Money!" "Pen!" Some of the adults were a bit more suspicious with the odd stone being thrown. One or two people were hit on the bottom with sticks (sugar cane poles). Chris was cut on the leg by a stone which looked more like a small rock! A minute pebble hit me on the head, but I hardly felt it.

On day three, we cycled 120 kilometers (75 miles). This was the toughest day, with much of the cycling against a strong headwind as we headed northbound along the east bank of the river Nile. I had to take a couple of rest breaks along the route due to some sores on my stump.

I was amazed and delighted that I had reached this far before I started to feel the effects of the socket rubbing against the skin. I would like to thank Assos for their superb chamois cream for getting me this far, not to mention my prosthetist, Richard.

We were near the end of our cycling. I didn't need to worry about keeping energy reserves on the last day, so I just cycled at my own pace. I could watch the world go by and just enjoy the ride. It was lucky that I had some energy left because the 7-kilometer ride into the Valley of the Kings was hard work. The entire leg was uphill, but what made it really difficult was the illusion created by the valley that you were cycling on the flat. In some places, it even looked like we were on a descent, but when you stopped pedaling, the bike would stop. We were cycling into the midday sun, which also took its toll, as the heat was overbearing, and there was no breeze. Tony and I had to stop a couple of times while I had a drink of water and caught my breath. The scenery was incredible, and I had to pinch myself to make sure that I was really cycling into the Valley of the Kings.

Although this section was hard, I enjoyed it the most and felt a sense of achievement as I turned the last corner and saw the bus lot full of tourist buses. We descended the Valley of the Kings as our final descent of the challenge. It felt like we were in a novel and had just solved the mystery and decided to descend the hill with our legs in the air. If I could have swung my legs in the air for the whole descent, I would have. We passed through a small village to reach the finish line, which I crossed a couple of times because I didn't want it to be over.

Robert Bailey, USA

Two beginner's rides:

1. *Tammany Trace is located across Lake Pontchartrain from New Orleans. It is 28 miles of cycling, hiking, and horse trails built along an old railroad right of way. Since it was built for trains, there really aren't any steep climbs. Beautiful, small, southern towns line the Trace. The best time to go is in the fall or spring. I would try for around Easter. The azaleas will be in full bloom. Summer is very hot and humid in south Louisiana. It is a great ride for a beginner amputee.*
2. *An equally beautiful, but much hillier, ride is north of Baton Rouge, Louisiana in St. Francisville. St. Francisville is in the heart of plantation country. The word millionaire was invented for the antebellum plantation owners of Feliciana Parish. There are dozens of old homes. Several of them can be toured. There are a few highways with speeding trucks, but most of the country roads are safe and serene. Some of those hills are good climbs. Be sure you have the gears to handle it.*

Further Reading

1. Bicycle route mapping site: www.bikely.com
2. Cycling fitness app: www.mapmyride.com
3. *Collins Ultimate Navigation Manual* by Lyle Brotherton (Harper Collins, 2001)
4. Google maps: www.googlemaps.com
5. *Navigation: Techniques and Skills for Walkers (Cicerone Mini-Guide): Using Your Map and Compass* by Pete Hawkins (Cicerone Press, 2007)

Did You Know?

1. 2015 is the 20th anniversary of the Sustrans National Cycle Network, UK.
2. EuroVelo is the European Cycle Network managed by the European Cyclists Federation.
3. There are 14 EuroVelo routes crossing most of Europe.
4. www.walkjogrun.net is a very detailed website for cyclists, walkers, and joggers in China which shows inclines, downhills, and turns as well as satellite maps.
5. The Ruta Austral in Chile is set in the mountains and runs for over 1,300 kilometers (800 miles).
6. The Sun Moon Lake in Taichung, Taiwan, is an easy cycle ride around the largest lake in the country.
7. The EuroVelo 6 is an easy cycle route at the Loire Valley in France and around the Danube.
8. The North Sea Cycle Route opened in 2001. It is 6,200 kilometers (3,853 miles) and crosses the UK, Netherlands, Germany, Denmark, Sweden, and Norway.
9. In January 1936, an arm amputee, Walter Greaves, set off from Bradford on a specially adapted bike that had a single brake lever for both wheels and a twist grip gear changer all on the one side of the handlebars. Twelve months later, he had cycled 45,383 miles (73,036 kilometers) around the UK.
10. Thomas Stevens was the first person to circle the globe on a penny farthing (1884-1886).

Things to Try for Yourself

1. Cycle to and from local shops or to work.
2. Take part in charity rides or other group rides by cycling, helping out, or just being part of the crowd.
3. Try night rides, bike dinners, or full moon rides, but make sure you have lights on your bike.
4. Join "Slow Up" in Switzerland—a car-free day which is good for beginners: www.myswitzerland.com/en-gb/switzerlandmobility.html.
5. Stelvio Day, Sellaronda Dolomiti, and Slow Up Albula are car-free passes in the Alps for more advanced cyclists.

Shafiqulla Samim, Afghanistan

I have been an amputee for almost 17 years. I think I was 8 or 9 years old. One day in 1996, I was going to school and faced a bomb explosion in which I lost my left arm. Before my amputation, I was so young I couldn't cycle, but since my amputation, I ride a regular two-wheeler made in China for accomplishing my daily needs. I don't have any adaptations on the bike. I have a prosthetic limb, but I don't use that for cycling. It is a plastic arm. I don't use it because it is very heavy, and I cannot control it while cycling. It is much easier cycling without prosthetics. One time that I remember, I had my children on my bike. I wanted to take them sightseeing to a garden in Nangarhar province, so it was a fantastic ride we had. We enjoyed it a lot and spent the whole day there. I felt good regarding my bike ride and that I was carrying children without any challenge to my body. My children were also very happy and enjoyed the bicycle trip, too. On returning home, my wife and whole family appreciated that like other normal people I can also ride the bicycle without any difficulty.

Funny Things Happen on a Bike!

Yes, it happened. Once I was cycling along a road in the city of Jalalabad; surprisingly, I heard an explosion. First, I became very scared and thought that some serious accident occurred very close to my surroundings. Then, fearfully, I tried to pedal my bicycle away from that place. However, it was then that I noticed my own cycle tube blast that made the sound like explosion. All the people around me were laughing at me, and I was so embarrassed. I took my bike to a bike mechanic to change the tube. Whenever I remember that accident, I laugh at myself.

Shafiqulla Samim, Afghanistan

Beginner's Routes

There are some well-known routes around the world that you can explore at your leisure. The following routes are in the easy to moderate category, and you can make them as long or as short as you wish.

Australia: Kings Park and Botanic Garden, Perth

An option for the family outing when cycling with young children. Plenty of entertainment along the way.

Brazil: Flamingo Park, Rio de Janeiro

A route along parks and beaches with cycling and walking lanes available in some parts.

China: Tongzhou Canal, east bank to west bank

10-mile (16.5 kilometers) simple, flat route with views of the Grand Canal along the way; traffic free. Very few supply outlets en route, so take food and plenty to drink with you.

Europe: Danube Cycle Path

Follow the EuroVelo 6 through countries such as Switzerland, France, Germany, Austria, Slovakia, Hungary, Serbia, and Romania.

Rhine Cycle Route from source to sea

Follow the Rhine through six countries: Switzerland, Liechtenstein, Austria, Germany, France, and Holland.

Japan: Shimanani Kaido to the islands

A spectacular cycle path with stunning views.

Thailand: San Saeb Canal, Bangkok

It is possible to cycle both sides of the canal and enjoy the sights of the water taxis as they go back and forth. There are also guided tours into the countryside available.

USA: Mount Vernon Trail, Washington D.C.

18 miles (29 kilometers) long, mostly flat with a hill at the end.

Chapter 9

Nutrition Plan

The simplest aim of healthy nutrition is to enjoy good, tasty food and drink refreshing drinks on social occasions, on your own, or during family meals. These should fulfill the criteria of adequacy, balance, calorie control, nutrient density, moderation, and variety. To be adequate, the food eaten should contain the nutrients considered essential to maintaining health. Balance is achieved through calorie control where the amount of energy consumed is equal to the amount used in daily living. Moderation enables you to keep balance by not eating or drinking too much or too little. Each country around the world has its own favorite staple ingredients and recipes that are served up regularly day upon day. Variety is achieved by choosing lots of different foods and drinks to add interest and reduce food boredom.

Food and water are vital energy sources that enable cells to function, muscles to contract, and other body processes to occur. Making and eating nutritious, healthy, balanced meals can be as easy or as complex as you want it to be. Learning about nutrition and food manufacture, storage, or preparation can be as fun and exciting as learning about cycling. Both could improve your health and well-being with some very positive side effects.

Eating the right foods in sufficient amounts promotes skin healing, reduces risk of infection, and provides energy for mobilization. For amputees with diabetes or high blood pressure or those who smoke or are obese, consulting a nutritional expert may prove beneficial. Such professionals examine your current eating habits in depth to work out suitable nutritional plans. Particular food preferences related to ethics and religious beliefs as well as food allergies are taken into account.

A nutritional plan is sometimes confused with the term diet. People diet for many reasons: to gain weight; lose weight; maintain weight; train; compete; or for health reasons, such as diabetes and food sensitivity. The word *diet* comes from Old French *diete* and Medieval Latin *dieta*, meaning a daily food allowance. The Greek word *diaita* means a way of life, a regimen. Modern interpretations still imply restriction and abstention which may explain why people do not stick to them. Rather than follow a diet, make food choices for healthy and nutritious living through an optimal or personalized nutritional plan.

What, specifically, does an amputee require in their nutritional plan to function healthily or improve cycling ability? Cycling increases the amount of energy the body requires, and loss of energy and fatigue can result. In general, your nutritional needs will depend on

- level of amputation and other medical problems,
- general lifestyle,
- body size and shape,
- metabolism, and
- frequency, duration, and intensity of training.

Important Nutrients

What you eat helps you power the bike. Components in food that provide energy and support growth and repair of body cells are termed *nutrients*. Nutrients can be essential, nonessential, or conditionally essential where those not normally required can become essential for life under certain conditions. Essential nutrients are not synthesized by the body and are required for critical processes of growth, health, and survival. Without them, disease and death occur.

There are at least 40 essential nutrients, including the following:

- Water
- Amino acids — histidine, isoleucine, leucine, lysine, methionine, phenylalanine, threonine, tryptophan, valine
- Fatty acids — linoleic, linolenic
- Minerals — calcium, phosphorus, magnesium, iron
- Trace minerals — zinc, copper, manganese, iodine, selenium, molybdenum, chromium
- Electrolytes — sodium, potassium, chloride
- Vitamins — ascorbic acid, vitamin A, D, E and K, thiamin, riboflavin, niacin, B_6, pantothenic acid, folic acid, biotin, B_{12}
- Ultratrace elements

The majority can be obtained from these categories of foods: legumes, grains, fruits, vegetables, meat, poultry, dairy, fish/shellfish, and fats/oils. To get started in fueling correctly for cycling, the following are important: water, carbohydrates, proteins, and minerals. Appropriate nutritional adjustments may also improve cycling performance.

Water

The adult body is 60 percent water by weight. Men have approximately 10 percent more body water than women as the female body contains a higher proportion of body fat. While cycling, sweat evaporates from skin to produce a cooling effect; 1 liter of sweat removes 573 kcal of heat. Some people sweat more than others at the same cycling intensity. Exercise increases the size of the sweat glands so they can secrete more sweat. High sweat rates while cycling cause dehydration and increase the internal body temperature and heart rate. Up to 1 °C increase in body temperature can be produced with high-intensity cycling. A liter of oxygen breathed in produces 4 calories of heat of which 1 calorie is used in pedaling. If body temperature keeps rising, muscle enzymes and contraction processes will cease within around 10 to 15 minutes, resulting in muscle and brain fatigue.

Exercising for a long time without replacing fluids increases the risk of muscle cramps. The temperature of the body should not rise over 40 °C (104 °F), otherwise heat exhaustion or heat stroke will occur. These are both life-threatening conditions that damage vital organs such as the brain, liver, or kidneys. Regular cycling can help regulate body temperature. Endurance cyclists may have lower starting skin temperatures due to the efficiencies of regular intense cycling. This is a form of heat loss conservation that maintains energy levels.

Drinking enough water regularly throughout the day is vital for general health and sports performance. Optimal fluid intake is measured by urine. If it is clear and plentiful, then the person is adequately hydrated. If it is bright yellow and in small quantities, the person should drink more. Hydration tablets may be an option in some circumstances. The sensation of thirst is an indicator of needing more fluids. The mouth or throat may feel dry. Overdrinking can cause similar symptoms to dehydration. Significant dehydration can be avoided by drinking safe amounts of water and electrolyte replacement fluids. Half of this comes from food, such as soups, pears, and melons.

In general, the daily amount of fluid required for different types of physical activity levels are approximately the following:

Resting: 2 L to 4L (35-45 °C)
Light work: 4 L to 6 L
Moderate work: 5 L to 8 L
Heavy work: 6 L to 10 L (more will be needed if very hot)

Heat-related illness is one of the major causes of death in populations that exercise at intensity in hot countries. Drinking lots of fluids well before cycling in the heat as well as during it will keep the internal body temperature system working efficiently. Increasing the volume of blood by drinking fluids can improve performance in cycling. Time trial performance data shows a 10 percent improvement in results when the body is fully hydrated. Adding glycerol to fluids keeps more water in the body. It is available from pharmacies, food stores, or bodybuilding companies. When drunk with 1 or 2  liters of water sometime before cycling, 1 gram/kilogram of body weight of glycerol may protect against heat stress when cycling in hot climates. Be careful using it as it can upset stomachs. Low levels of physical fitness and lack of acclimatization to the atmospheric conditions increase the probability of experiencing problems due to exercising in the heat.

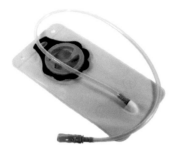

It is important to get used to drinking during cycling. Either stop and drink or attempt to drink while cycling. It is a question of confidence and practice as to whether you can maintain position and speed while reaching down for the water bottle, as mentioned in chapter 7. Drinking from a bottle also requires you to put your head up, reducing visibility if done while pedaling. An alternative fluid replacement device is the hydration pack (water bladder or CamelBak) that is carried on the back. A filter or straw is positioned at the side of the mouth, and you can sip from this. It allows you to carry on cycling without worrying about dropping the water bottle or falling while reaching for the water bottle.

When starting out, consider the length of the session. Is the ride going to be long and strenuous enough to warrant a sports drink, or is water going to be sufficient? Is there a way to keep the drink cool enough for the duration of the ride, or is it better to stop somewhere en route to buy something cold and refreshing?

Carbohydrates

These are the body's main fuel source. Classified as simple or complex, they are also known as sugars (glucose), starch, glycogen, and fiber. Glycogen is stored in the liver (80-100 g) and muscles (300-900 g) and converted to glucose to use as an energy source. The daily recommended amount of carbohydrate is 300 grams in a sedentary person. Elite competitive athletes consume more than 1,000 grams per day. Because glucose fuels brain and blood cells, 130 grams of carbohydrates should be eaten each day to keep the brain functioning. Complex carbohydrates should provide around 60 percent of calories for cycling. The aim of eating carbohydrates is to replenish muscle glycogen stores.

Proteins

These are made from building blocks called amino acids. There are 20 common to proteins; 11 of these can be synthesized by the body and are termed nonessential; 9 have to be obtained from the diet and are termed essential. High-quality protein contains all essential amino acids, whereas low-quality protein has some missing. Some examples are listed here. The number 1 means it is 100 percent complete (high quality) protein containing all the essential amino acids. Anything less than 1 is considered an incomplete (low quality) protein as it is missing some essential amino acids.

Milk protein = 1
Beef = 0.92
Soy protein isolate = 1
Kidney beans = 0.68

Animal protein is high-quality protein, and tofu and soy products are the most popular high-quality, non-meat protein. During cycling, protein consumption should be kept low as it takes longer to digest. Maximum safe amounts of protein are around 1.8 grams/kilogram of body weight per day. Endurance cyclists have reported taking around 3 grams/kilogram of body weight per day of protein. A good food with adequate amounts of carbohydrate and protein is low-fat milk. Protein is classified as either a fast absorber or a slow absorber. For example, whey is a fast protein found in milk that the body uses rapidly. Casein is a slow protein also present in milk. Soy protein is not as good at protein synthesis as milk protein.

Minerals

Minerals are classified as macro or micro (trace elements). There are six macrominerals that are essential to health, such as sodium, chloride, potassium, calcium, phosphorus, and magnesium. These are needed in larger quantities (>100 mg per day) than microminerals (trace elements), such as zinc, iron, copper, manganese, selenium, fluoride, and iodine. Very small amounts of trace elements are needed by the body (< 100 mg per day).

For mineral replacement after a hard cycling session, drink a commercially available sports drink containing sodium and glucose, add salt to meals, or eat a salty snack (e.g., salted chips or peanuts). Processed foods and meats contain large amounts of sodium. Examples include sauces, pickles, and ready-made meals. This will ensure you are not dehydrated before cycling on subsequent days.

The natural low acidity (pH) and high sugar content of sports drinks increases the risk of dental problems if teeth are not cleaned and maintained properly. This is more likely in those who train and compete heavily and rely on sports drinks to plug gaps in their nutrition or rehydration plans. Addition of calcium to such drinks may help balance out the low acidity. Using products containing fluorine (fluoride) may help protect the teeth from erosion due to sports drinks.

Iron plays an important role in oxygen transportation during prolonged exercise. It helps deliver oxygen to muscles in blood hemoglobin. Iron is lost in sweat, urine, and through bleeding within cells. Endurance and prolonged cycling or heavy schedules increase iron demands up to 70 percent. Sports anaemia is a condition seen in some athletes where hemoglobin in blood is diluted by heavy training. A few days of rest returns blood volumes and hemoglobin levels back to normal. A 10 to 15 percent fall in blood volume is typical for moderate-intensity exercise due to the pressure to maintain blood flow to active muscles. In some cases, iron and vitamin B supplementation may be required.

Digestion, Absorption, and Metabolism

Once food and water are consumed, they are digested and absorbed through the gastrointestinal tract—a long, 6- to 8-meter tube that travels from the mouth to the rectum. Nutrients released during this process have to be transported, stored, or used. The mouth chews and breaks up food to increase the rate of digestion and gastric emptying. Food takes between one to four hours to leave the stomach and is eliminated from the body after a maximum of 3 days. Digestion is quicker in the mouth than the stomach. Around 30 to 40 percent of carbohydrates are digested in the mouth and stomach. Foods have strong effects on gastric emptying. Fat reduces gastric emptying. The amount of carbohydrate in a sports drink affects the rate of gastric emptying. 2 percent solutions empty slower than water, and 8 percent solutions slow it down even more. Minerals are not absorbed well. Only 35 percent of calcium, 20 percent of magnesium, and 14 percent of zinc are absorbed from food. Absorption of iron depends on whether it's from an animal or plant source. Animal iron is 15 percent absorbed whereas plant iron is 10 percent absorbed. More than half of calcium and phosphorus in food is excreted in the urine.

Hyperacidity (i.e., acid leaking from the stomach) is a common problem in cyclists due to their aerodynamic sitting position. Foods that can contribute to hyperacidity include chocolate, peppermint, fatty foods, coffee, and alcohol. Foods and beverages that irritate a damaged oesophageal lining, such as citrus fruits and juices, tomato products, and pepper, also should be avoided. The energy available from food is dependent on the body's ability to completely digest and absorb it. On average, 97 percent of carbohydrate, 95 percent of fat, and 92 percent of protein is completely digested and absorbed.

Metabolism

This is the term used to describe chemical reactions in the body that convert food into energy. Metabolism builds up body tissues and energy stores as well as breaks them down to generate more fuel. Diet and training affect the rate of metabolism during exercise and resting. Muscle fitness and cell fitness improve with exercise. In low-intensity (aerobic) exercise, fat is the main fuel source. Carbohydrates are the dominant fuel source during high-intensity (anaerobic) exercise. When the body is at rest, amino acids contribute around 15 percent to energy expenditure. This falls to 5 percent during exercise due to carbohydrate and fat oxidation. Around 60 to 75 percent of the energy from food is used by the body while sedentary. The liver, brain, kidney, and heart use the highest amounts. Muscles use 20 percent of energy if not being used for physical activity.

For cycling, it is important to eat and drink enough. The average energy utilized while cycling is based on cycling pace.

	kcal / hour / kg
Leisurely (< 10 mph)	4
Light (10-11.9 mph)	6
Moderate (12-13.9 mph)	8
Fast (14-15.9 mph)	10
Racing (16-19 mph)	12
BMX or mountain:	8.5

Energy Use

The human body does not use energy from food efficiently. In cycling, 20 percent is converted to power, and 80 percent maintains body stability and produces heat which leaves the body. There are particular metabolic processes which cyclists refer to such as the lactic acid (Cori) cycle, ATP, and oxygen processes. The lactic acid cycle is important because of its accumulation in muscles post exercise, which causes pain.

Nutritional Plan Goals

What is going to be the purpose of your nutritional plan? Do you want to lose weight or gain weight? Do you want to control diabetes or other medical conditions? Do you want to train and compete? Try different plans and adapt them to suit your tastes. Try out other plans and measure the results. Nutritional plans to control diabetes focus on incorporating foods that stabilize the insulin levels in the body throughout the day whereas those used for heart conditions incorporate very low amounts of saturated fats. To increase the chances of sticking to them (if not to the letter, then at least the principle), devise different plans for different seasons or for different months. Take into consideration issues such as eating out either at restaurants, friends' houses, or on the go during a busy training or work phase. Deciding on suitable food substitutes for those occasions means you don't miss out on socializing or compromise your nutrition goals.

Using a nutritional plan can help you become more organized about what you buy, eat, and drink, thereby reducing food waste and saving you money. Make the time to check fridges and cupboards regularly to prevent duplication, and check the state of the food in case it needs to be eaten or frozen.

Plan your meals, check recipes for ingredients, and then go shopping (on your bike even!) just for things that you need. Learn more about how to use leftovers and different cooking, freezing, and preserving techniques to make your food budget go that little bit further while adding a bit of creativity and interest to your meals. If you don't think you will be up to cooking straight after a heavy training session, choose easy, quick nutritious meals for those particular days. Alternatively, prepare it all the night before or, better still, persuade your husband/wife/partner/friend (or anyone else who will take pity on you!) to make the meal that day.

Factors to take into consideration when deciding on meals:

1. How much time do you have for food preparation?
2. Do you eat regular, balanced meals at home or usually just snack on junk food all day?
3. Do you buy all your food as ready-made meals, eat mostly in restaurants, or buy fresh ingredients?

If you didn't grow up in a household that made four-course meals, three times every day and time to cook is limited, take a look at some of the cooking programs on the Internet or television. There are plenty of recipe books from well-known chefs in each country as well as cooking competitions and other hospitality programs to provide you with ideas and inspiration on how to make those meals appetizing, exciting, and delicious within your nutritional plan. Recipes are getting quicker to cook; ingredients from around the world are more readily available; and microwaves can sometimes be your best friend (after your bike, that is). If you don't have a cupboard full of exotic ingredients, herbs, and spices and want to find quick simple ways to feel like you are a Michelin Star chef, just play around with a few classic ingredients listed on the next page.

Italy: tomatoes/oregano
France: wine/garlic
Greece: cinnamon/lemon
China: soy sauce/ginger

These will add plenty of variety and interest from around the world to your meals and you will feel more confident making delicious, healthy food for cycling. Include in your nutritional plan food you want to take on a bike ride: energy bars, drinks, and those real food options. If you are more of a leisure cyclist, then planning a picnic or barbeque with other cyclists and taking along homemade (or ready-made!) muffins, fruit loafs, deli meats, and other delicious appetizers stored in cool containers to retain freshness will make both the training and the nutrition lots of fun!

Nutritional Guidelines

To help develop a nutritional plan, useful tools are available, such as nutritional guidelines, nutritional databases, and food labeling. A food label on a product indicates the number of calories in a serving as well as the amounts of fat, carbohydrate, and protein. Certain vitamins and minerals may also be stated on the label.

Nutritional guidelines are based on six different food groups: fruit, vegetables, grains (bread/cereals), dairy (milk/cheese), oils and protein foods (meat/fish/eggs).

Vegan guidelines are based on four food groups: fruit, legumes, grains, and vegetables. The recommended servings are:

- 3 or more servings of fruit
- 2 or more servings of protein-rich legumes
- 5 or more servings of whole grains
- 4 or more servings of vegetables

Nutritional values will be different for pregnant or breastfeeding women. The suggested calorie intake for children is around 1,400 kcal.

For more physically active individuals, calorie intake and proportion of nutrients will be higher.

For example:
Endurance cycling = 4,370 kcal
Tour de France cyclists use up to 6,000 kcal per day.

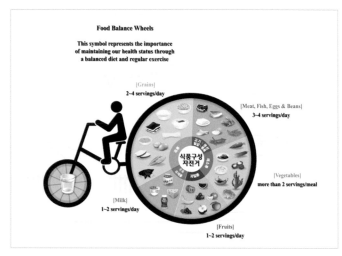

Food Balance Wheels

This symbol represents the importance
of maintaining our health status through
a balanced diet and regular exercise

[Grains]
2–4 servings/day

[Meat, Fish, Eggs & Beans]
3–4 servings/day

식품구성
자전거

[Vegetables]
more than 2 servings/meal

[Milk]
1–2 servings/day

[Fruits]
1–2 servings/day

In the initial stages as an amputee, depending on your existing body mass and severity of amputation, your energy intake may need to be higher (10-50%) to help with rehabilitation goals.

As the body becomes more efficient, energy consumed can be reduced to prevent unnecessary weight gain. The challenge of using dietary guidelines is converting the information into appealing meals within limited household budgets. The transferability over geographical and cultural borders is an added complication.

When adopting particular food or dietary practices, being able to follow these in different countries may prove challenging. For cycling, it may mean you bring your own food to races and charity events rather than take advantage of the food provided on site. Some places allow external food to be eaten on site; others generally don't. Usually a quick phone call or email to the event organizers letting them know of any dietary restrictions allows them to accommodate those requirements into menus where possible.

Nutritional plans for weight maintenance advocate 2,000 to 2,500 calories per day. Breakfast, lunch, and dinner should be around 500 calories each and snacks around 250 calories. If intending to cycle regularly, get used to eating and drinking before the feeling hungry or thirsty. Aim for a mix of real food and energy bars to add variety, and refuel correctly after a long ride (i.e., within the first 30 minutes of finishing cycling). The key ingredient is to keep the plan realistic enough to maintain over a couple of months without losing the fun and joy of replenishing your energy levels.

Eating and Cycling to Lose Weight

If you are using a nutritional plan to lose excess weight, then the amount of energy consumed throughout the day must be less than the amount of energy you are using. This is achieved by smaller portion sizes and switching from high-energy density foods to low-energy density foods (e.g., fried potato switched to boiled or baked potato). Main meals should average 375 calories and snacks 187 calories. Do not skip meals such as breakfast or lunch. Instead, maintain a schedule of three meals a day with snacks in between. Ensuring all your meals have some element of protein in them helps keep you full. Another way of feeling full is to add fiber. Fiber is plant parts that cannot be digested or absorbed by the human body. Adding fiber to food reduces digestibility through the digestive system. Recommended fiber intake is 20 to 35 grams per day. Fiber-rich foods (e.g., bran, peas, beans, and lentils) are suitable while training as they also require you to drink more fluids. Indulging yourself at social occasions is not a problem if you stick to the plan the rest of the time. Drinking alcohol with meals will make it more difficult to lose weight. It may dehydrate you or increase your appetite, making long-term healthy weight loss even more of a challenge. If you are accustomed to drinking alcohol with food, invest time in finding suitable refreshing alternatives you can enjoy without affecting your nutritional goals.

Alongside a nutritional plan, it is important to undertake adequate levels of exercise to stimulate the metabolism. Bike riding for about an hour at around a heart rate of 65 percent maximum is reported to reduce your appetite by temporarily releasing natural appetite-suppressing hormones. To further benefit from this, develop it into longer timeframes on the bike at a steady pace. Delaying eating for an hour after exercise helps with weight loss as the body burns more fat during this recovery phase. Fat metabolism is also higher the day after cycling if you do not replace these fats by eating unhealthy fatty foods after exercising. Substitute carbohydrates and proteins instead. An adequate amount of healthy fats is required, so do not avoid fat altogether. Simply structure the plan to avoid or significantly reduce the amount of unhealthy fats you eat. The best results are achieved if you aim to progress slowly rather than looking for quick results from fad diets. Changing everything you eat and drink all at once may result in you falling back to your old nutrition patterns. Substituting one food or drink at a time, maintaining, and then progressing to other foods may make it easier to adapt to dietary changes as a longer-term goal.

Eating and Cycling to Gain Weight or Muscle Mass

For weight gain, the amount of energy you consume must be more than you use and often higher than the 2,500 calories recommended for sedentary people. If you are a new amputee and have both weight loss and muscle building goals, then work on your weight loss first. Adding weight as fat is always easier than adding muscle. Converting excess fat to muscle adds bulk rather than leanness or tone, and this may frustrate your cycling performance.

The body adapts to the amount of food entering your stomach. Adding lean, toned muscle involves exercising correctly. If you notice your levels of fat creeping up, increase the amount of cycling you do to burn off the excess. To gain muscle, high-quality, fast-digesting proteins need to be eaten alongside the training. This protein can be obtained from food or bodybuilding powders. They can be drunk either before or after exercise or as an occasional meal substitute. They are soluble in milk, juice, or water, and flavors vary. Muscle building is assisted if protein and carbohydrates are eaten very soon after exercise. Carbohydrates and fats in muscle building nutritional plans should be healthy options, not junk food. Other supplements, such as creatine, zinc, or vitamin B, may be taken if necessary.

Eating for Endurance Cycling

The important nutritional aspect with regard to endurance cycling is making sure you have enough energy before, during, and after the bike ride with sufficient amounts of carbohydrate, fat, and protein in your nutritional plan. Pre-ride nutrition and post-ride nutrition prepare you and help you recover sufficiently. Make sure the meal you eat the night before an endurance ride is substantial in carbohydrates to store up glycogen levels. You will also need to drink a lot of fluids the day before and eat a good breakfast. Experiment with different foods, gels, and energy bars to test how much your body can consume and digest on training rides and what it prefers or reacts unfavorably to. These will vary person to person, and what may suit someone else may not suit you. Gels are a concentrated form of carbohydrate and better digested if you take them with fluids.

During very long endurance rides, vary what you eat and drink as you will not enjoy just sweet things or just salty things all the way. Find the mix that works for you and take along food and drink you like rather than things you don't. If you are very new to endurance cycling, it will take some trial and error to discover what fires up your muscles enough to complete a long ride. It is advisable not to try anything new on the day of the event. Do all your nutritional experimenting in advance of the big day, and you will enjoy it much more. Check the ingredients on energy bars as some contain high levels of fat which the body digests very slowly, and others contain lots of sweeteners which can cause stomach upsets. Prolonged endurance exercise may reduce the ability to absorb large quantities of food. Endurance cycling in tough terrains requires you to consume a vast amount of carbohydrates which isn't easy as well as making fluid intake more important. As you can usually only carry two water bottles, it is worth investing in a hydration pack which makes it easier to take sips along the way. Drinking small amounts of these fluids regularly to keep the amount of fluid in the stomach high may also reduce the negative effects of slower gastric emptying.

Carbohydrate loading (described in eating for competition) is worth trying. Once you are cycling, eating and drinking in the first hour will take some willpower after carbohydrate loading. It is best to take small amounts of food and drink every 30 minutes.

Beginners may prefer to stop and refuel whereas experienced cyclists tend to refuel on the bike. When trying this, make sure you can breathe, eat, or drink safely while turning the pedals. Don't try to refuel while going uphill, for example, as all your oxygen and energy will be needed for your muscles. For endurance rides on consecutive days, the post-ride meals have to be designed to replace as much carbohydrate, electrolytes, fluids, and protein as possible. This should be started within the first 15 to 30 minutes of finishing cycling and continued after the post-exercise meal.

Between 6 to 20 grams of protein is advised for endurance cycling in those first 30 minutes and 2 hours after the last meal. As it is usually difficult to eat lots in one go if you are exhausted from cycling, drinking a high-carbohydrate sports drink and grazing on high-carbohydrate foods at regular intervals after you finish riding may make it easier to keep nutrients in your stomach. This will provide you with plenty of energy to cycle the next day.

Hitting the Wall

The body only contains enough nutrients to fuel a moderately intense bike ride for around 90 minutes. Eat and drink before you actually feel hungry or thirsty to keep your sugar levels up to reasonable levels on longer rides. This will allow you to finish it safely and enjoyably. When cyclists don't fuel along the way or make the wrong food choices that do not provide energy to their muscles quickly enough to carry on cycling, they hit the wall, or bonk. The medical term for this is *hypoglycemia*. It also occurs in people with diabetes.

The amount of glucose in your blood becomes very low as it has been used to fuel the muscles to cycle. You will notice it in your leg muscles. They feel very heavy, and you may sweat or shake a lot. It also affects your brain as you will be unable to think clearly and might be irritable, hostile, confused, or disoriented. There are many more symptoms which are documented on the Internet and medical journals. To treat these, take in some quick absorbing carbohydrates as a drink or eat some sweets high in sugar. It is better to stop cycling while refueling if you are experiencing symptoms. Carbohydrates are the best form of energy replacement as fats and proteins do not metabolize in your body fast enough to provide the glucose you need. Your sense of balance may be affected if you let symptoms go too far, so it is better not to be on a bike at that point. Before getting back on the bike, make sure all the symptoms have cleared; you are fully aware of your surroundings; or are not weak, lethargic, or lightheaded. Only continue cycling if you have enough carbohydrate-rich foods and drinks to take with you, and make sure you eat and drink at short intervals throughout the ride.

Eating to Compete

A nutritional plan for training and competing is influenced by the type of activity, such as high- or low-impact sport or endurance sport. There are specific phases: preparation, competition, and transition. Small, frequent meals are advocated with glycogen and protein replenishment being the priority. Fiber-rich foods should be avoided up to a day or longer before a cycling event as they reduce the ability of the body to produce energy from the food consumed. To provide enough glucose for competing, carbohydrate-loading may be tried. This involves eating large amounts of carbohydrate (60-70% of total calories) and reducing the amount of training before a competition. The difficulty with carbohydrate loading is the increase in water stored. This technique is beneficial when cycling up to two hours. Eating or drinking carbohydrates a few hours before and then 45 minutes to 1 hour before cycling is recommended. In events that last one hour, drink a sports drink containing 4 to 8 percent carbohydrate.

Examples of foods and drinks that can be consumed for recovery include:

*   1 liter sports drink
*   1 1/2 energy bars
*   3 bananas

Fruit juices and soft drinks have high quantities of carbohydrates (more than 10%). The type of sugar in the drink is important. Glucose is more readily metabolized than fructose or dextrose. Drinking around 500 milliliters at regular intervals before and after cycling and taking small sips every 10 to 15 minutes while cycling should help maintain fluid levels. Guidelines on fluid and food intake related to competition are available from the relevant cycling organization in your country. If the priority is rehydration, then low levels of carbohydrates and electrolytes are recommended. A cool drink with a little glucose and sodium in it during a cycling session certainly makes it easier to drink enough to keep hydrated. If cycling daily, fluids drunk after exercise need to stimulate thirst and replace lost electrolytes. Sodium keeps the feeling of being thirsty over a longer time. Another healthy way to increase fluid intake is by drinking plain water and eating soups or water-rich fruits, such as melon. Caffeine and alcohol are generally discouraged as they stimulate urination. After the event, replace carbohydrates and proteins as per endurance cycling.

Overcoming Appetite Loss

As you get older, your taste in food and drink changes. Things you used to like may not have the same appeal, or you may go off them altogether. This is quite normal. It becomes a concern when you lose your appetite for extended periods of time. This might be due to the trauma of losing your limb. It may be your way of reacting to stress or depression. Being ill or recovering from major operations can affect your ability to eat. As far as cycling is concerned, if you cycle to the point of exhaustion, you may not feel able to enjoy food or eat enough for more cycling. It may reduce your enjoyment of cycling if this happens too frequently. If your cycling performance is not meeting your expectations or has been particularly difficult, this will lower your mood, putting you off eating. Common sports conditions, such as anorexia and bulimia, can occur, especially in children and young adults, so monitor eating patterns closely if they take up competitive cycling. If the loss of interest in food is linked with loss of interest in daily activities, seek medical or professional advice.

Stimulating your appetite may require some effort on your part and those around you. If you are dissatisfied with the way you cycled, then don't dwell on it. Write it all down or tell someone who might understand or advise; then put it all behind you and look ahead to eating to improve your performance. You can analyze and work on it all later when you have more energy. Your enjoyment of eating may return faster if you eat in good company rather than alone, but it is important that others don't try to force you to eat or stress about your food intake. Pleasant dining ambience; eating in a relaxed, friendly restaurant; or generally experiencing fun during mealtimes may be the ingredients you need to reawaken your taste buds to the pleasure of good nutrition.

The choice of restaurant can influence you, too. If you have totally lost your appetite, then an all-you-can-eat buffet might not be the place to visit. When you are well and hungry, a large portion may be something you enjoy, but when you are off your food, it is better to request smaller portions so you feel more inclined to eat rather than be daunted by the amount on the plate. Somewhere that is too formal and reserved may not provide the fun and relaxation you are after. A place where strong smells and sounds of lots of food preparation surround you may also put you off. Visiting a few different restaurants in your area may be required. To rediscover your appetite, try to eat things you know you enjoy for a short while, even if they aren't particularly healthy, until you get used to eating regularly again.

Or, if you used to enjoy preparing food yourself, make the things you like in different ways—as a dessert rather than a main course or as a savory rather than a sweet meal, for example. Looking at different ingredients and presenting food differently may stimulate your interest in eating and drinking again. Making sure you are getting enough fluids through soups, smoothies, juices, or just water will help short term until you get your appetite back for more solid foods. If you cannot face either cooking or eating a main meal, graze on small snacks until your appetite returns. Reduce the amount of fiber in your diet for a short time to stimulate hunger. To help you monitor your eating patterns, keep a food diary. If these things don't work or if you are very underweight, specific high-calorie nutritional supplements and professional advice may be necessary.

To Supplement or Not to Supplement

Dietary (nutritional) supplements are classified as vitamins, minerals, herbs, botanicals, amino acids, and other dietary substances. Definitions vary between countries. They are widely used in sports of all types in an attempt to improve performance. There are over 800 supplements available, and many elite athletes take more than one product. Manufacturers often claim the product increases muscle mass, aids fat loss, and improves stamina. Achieving weight loss and muscle mass is often difficult through ordinary diet and exercise, and nutritional supplements that speed up the process will always be sought after. But be careful: Many supplements are mislabeled, contaminated, or contain ingredients that may be banned by sports authorities.

Evaluation of manufacturers' claims and the product purity are important aspects in deciding whether to supplement or not. To evaluate supplements, think about your overall diet. Is it adequate and balanced, or not? You can also check with a health-care or nutritional professional before taking the supplement to reduce difficulties of side effects and interactions with other medications or your training schedule.

When researching and evaluating web-based information on the supplement, check that the site is run by a reputable medical or health-related association. Be aware of organizations who put information on sites simply to market the product. that the site has been recently updated, and reference sources for claims made on the site are published in reputable scientific journals. If the claims sound exaggerated, unrealistic, or promise a quick health or fitness fix, then they probably are suspect. This especially applies if you consider developing your cycling abilities to competition level. Doping controversy has indicated contamination of allowed supplements with banned substances. Some supplements may claim to have anabolic steroid properties such as androstenedione. While this is widely available in some countries without controls, it is a banned substance by the International Olympic Committee (IOC).

Caffeine and Creatine

Caffeine is a stimulant that has been used for many centuries. Coffee, tea, cocoa beans, and cola nuts are the main natural sources of caffeine. It is often added to other products and foods. Caffeine is quickly absorbed, and the effects are reported to last between 2 and 10 hours. Some is excreted in the urine, and large amounts are excreted in sweat. It is thought to improve performance with around 3 to 9 milligrams/ kilograms of body weight. Coffee is the most popular form of caffeine. 75 percent of all caffeine consumption is in the form of coffee. The method of preparation affects the caffeine content of coffee. The benefits of coffee as compared to pure caffeine have still to be adequately researched. Caffeine at high doses can cause agitation, headache, restlessness, and high blood pressure. In 2004, the IOC took caffeine off its list of banned substances.

Caffeine content in different drinks:

Instant coffee (150 ml)	40-108 mg
Starbucks grande (480 ml)	550 mg
Iced tea (360 ml)	22-36 mg
Red Bull	80 mg
Homemade espresso (150 ml)	40-90 mg

Creatine is a popular supplement used by over 80 percent of elite Olympic level athletes. It occurs naturally in the body and can be synthesized in the liver or kidney if necessary. 95 percent of creatine is in muscle, with the rest in brain, liver, and kidneys. While creatine may improve performance, it is most effective in those that do not have high concentrations in the body. It is synthesized and excreted in equal amounts. For example, if 2 grams/day is consumed, then 2 grams/day will be excreted in the urine. If less creatine is consumed, the body conserves what is left and does not excrete it. Foods containing creatine include fish and red meat. Vegans and vegetarians cannot obtain such amounts through plant foods, so they are dependent on synthesizing it in the body. Creatine can cause side effects, such as nausea, vomiting, diarrhea, kidney and liver problems, and muscle cramps.

There are numerous other nutritional supplements. Taking a trip to a health food store, pharmacy, or sports specialist or simply browsing the Internet and sports magazines will help you become familiar with their claims and risks.

Young Adults

Children and teenagers have different nutritional needs than adults. It is important that the high amounts of energy they use is replaced adequately in the diet. The energy they consume has two functions:

1. To help them grow into healthy adults
2. To help them perform in their sport

To help develop healthy eating habits in children, try to set a good example in the things you eat and drink. Children benefit from scheduled mealtimes which revolve around family or friends. As children's stomachs are smaller than adults, the portions you give them should be appropriate. You may, without realizing, be putting too much on their plates which leads to stress when they cannot eat it. Introduce as many new foods to them while they are young so they are not afraid to try out different textures, colors, and flavors. Making fun meals and involving them in food preparation or setting up to be ready for meal times may help them to be more interested in what they are eating. When they first take up cycling as a sport, they might be tempted to simply reach for sports gels, energy bars, and quick snacks rather than full meals. Packing easily portable nutritious snacks and drinks for those in-between moments will help them eat and drink enough to prevent deficiencies or develop eating disorders. Involvement in sports such as cycling is a useful way of showing them the benefits of good nutrition. Young people have a higher tolerance to exercising in the heat, so adequate fluids must be consumed. Flavored drinks or soups may be more palatable than plain water.

Overall, incorporating nutrition that optimizes health while learning about cycling will greatly improve your ability to cycle farther and faster without fatigue or aching muscles. Good quality nutrition information is obtained from journals and scientific magazines. Mass media messages have a tendency to exaggerate facts around nutrition. Conditions such as diabetes, cancer, cardiovascular disease, and obesity can be improved with appropriate food choices in combination with adequate exercise. A balanced nutritional plan is recommended for amputees who want to take up cycling, whether for leisure or for competition.

From the Amputees

Mark Ormrod, UK

I just took on board as many good calories as I could. I would say it was 60:40 carbs:protein, but obviously cutting out the rubbish. It was all self-administered; I don't have in-depth knowledge of nutrition, but I know the basics, and I know what my body needs to perform its best. There was nothing particularly difficult about sticking to it. The beauty of doing the event was that I got to eat a lot more than I normally do, and I like to eat!

I think it is a very good idea to consult nutritionists and trainers if you are a complete novice with no prior knowledge. A lot of people think you can just get by drinking glucose drinks or eating energy gels, and to be honest, they should be the last thing you put in your body once you have eaten proper, wholesome food and drunk plenty of water. Too many gels and sports drinks will end up taking you out of the game. I don't have any special utensils for cooking or eating; I just use my everyday split hook. If you have a great-fitting arm that works well, there is no real need for any of that stuff (in my opinion).

Rajesh Durbal, USA—Hitting the Wall

One Saturday, I rode 85 miles (137 kilometers) with a group of friends. I hadn't been on the bike much in the last 2 months, but I wanted to test myself to see how much fitness and mental toughness I had in me. It was a fast pace and felt good. We went through a little town and saw new sights that I have never seen before. It was hot and humid, and the sun was beating down on us as each minute passed. I hung in with the group until mile 70. I started to "bonk," which means I didn't have enough calories in me to hold the pace and effort. My legs started to cramp, and I started to get dizzy. I powered through and finished strong. It's at that very moment I discovered I still have the mental and physical toughness to be a powerful force that knows no defeat.

Robert Bailey, USA

The new thing is Lowfat Chocolate Milk. It does make sense. Full disclosure—they are one of my sponsors. Here is a website: gotchocolatemilk.com/science.

Other then that, I just try to eat fruits, veggies, protein, and some carbs. If I am on my yearly pilgrimage to Iowa, I make a point of eating more carbohydrates. Though, at RAGBRAI, you have lots of opportunities for pie, ice cream, porkchops to die for, and corn (it is Iowa, of course).

Sara Tretola, Switzerland

I do food combining. At noon before a workout, I only eat carbohydrates, and in the evening after a workout, I only eat proteins and vegetables. After 6 p.m., I do not eat any more carbohydrates. My coach told me about food combining. It's something that I have learned about by reading sports nutritional articles and by asking nutritionists questions. The nutritional plan I developed myself. It requires a lot of self-discipline. Especially in the evening, not eating carbohydrates is difficult as I like to eat bread. In order to control my weight for racing, I had to learn to eat less bread. This was and still is very difficult. If you decide to follow a nutritional plan, it is always important to make it fun, otherwise even the best diet is not much use. From my own personal experience, recommending adaptations for kitchen and eating utensils would not be useful. People quickly develop their own techniques, and it amazes me each time at a race how people do things similarly without prior knowledge of each other. Instinct plays an important role.

Victor Walther, Canada

While I was racing, I was fortunate to be part of the PowerBar Elite Team which provided me with a complete nutrition plan along with food supplements. Although I was racing downhill, my daily conditioning and training was the same as a cross-country rider. The only difference was the timing of the gels and supplements. For a downhill race, you would take a gel (sugar and caffiene) before the start of the race instead of the middle or end of a cross-country race. The best way to combat boredom and frustration is variety. Sometimes you need to cheat on or change your diet. Sometimes you need to ride different trails or just go for hike. The only time you really need to consult a nutritionist or trainer is when you want to start competing or training for a special event. There are not only health benefits, but also performance benefits to proper nutrition and training. I don't think general eating and cooking techniques are necessary as arm amputees.

Some Sample Nutrition Plans to Try

The following websites detail nutritional plans and recipes. Mix and match the information to suit your own personal needs, and then let others know what you think about such plans. No doubt you will also find some of your own favorite recipes to substitute into these, too.

→ www.gatorade.co.uk/nutrition-and-training/cycling

→ www.bengreenfieldfitness.com/2013/07/easy-meals-for-busy-athletes/

→ www.thepaleodiet.com/sample-menus-for-endurance-athletes/

→ www.cyclingtips.com.au/2011/08/weight-loss-for-cyclists/

→ www.livestrong.com/article/318146-asian-meal-plans-to-lose-weight-in-7-days/

→ www.diabetes.org/mfa-recipes/meal-plans/2012-10-Asian-Flavors.html

→ www.besthealthmag.ca/best-eats/nutrition/7-south-american-superfoods#EQKGQ4Ey38AFpqFA.97

→ www.muscleandfitness.com/nutrition/meal-plans/28-days-lean-meal-plan

Michael Caines, UK (www.michaelcaines.com), is an arm amputee who has twice been presented the Michelin star rating for his restaurants in the UK. He appears regularly on *Saturday Kitchen* and *MasterChef*. He has written *Michael Caines at Home* (Century, 2013). His recipes also appear on www.bbc.co.uk/food/chefs/michael_caines. He has been awarded the honor of Member of the British Empire (MBE) by Queen Elizabeth II. He has kindly provided two recipes for this book. Enjoy preparing and eating them!

Michael Caines

Penne Pasta With Spinach, Gorgonzola, Pine Nuts, Broccoli, and Mascarpone
Serves 4

50 ml extra virgin olive oil

500 g penne pasta

100 g baby spinach

50 g toasted pine nuts

100 g purple sprouting broccoli

100 g mascarpone cheese

100 g gorgonzola cheese

Salt and freshly ground black pepper

Method:
1. Cook the pasta in salted boiling water until al dente.
2. In a sauté pan, add half the olive oil and bring to a moderate heat. Add the purple sprouting broccoli and stir-fry for 3 to 4 minutes or until it starts to soften. Add the baby spinach and stir-fry until it wilts.
3. Add the mascarpone, toasted pine nuts and gorgonzola. Heat through.
4. Add the cooked pasta to the vegetables and cheese and mix well. Season, drizzling with a little more extra virgin olive oil before serving.

Leek and Potato Soup

300g peeled potatoes, cut to a medium dice size
400g leeks, chopped and washed
200g sliced onions
100g butter
1.5 litre water
100g chicken bouillon
Bouquet garni (parsley stalks and thyme wrapped in celery and leek then bound with string)
Salt and pepper

Method:
1. Place onions and leeks in a saucepan, along with the butter and cook until soft without colouring them.
2. Add water, chicken bouillon, bouquet garni and potatoes and bring to the boil.
3. Season with salt and pepper, reduce the heat and simmer for 30 minutes.
4. Remove the bouquet garni then blend with a hand blender until smooth.
5. Finally pass the soup through a sieve and correct the seasoning if required.
6. Serve..

Further Reading

1. British Nutrition Foundation: www.nutrition.org.uk/healthyliving/basics
2. Nutrition guide for cyclists: www.active.com/cycling/Articles/Nutrition-Guide-for-Cyclists
3. *Quick and Easy Workday Dinners* (Murdoch Books, 2002)
4. Nutrition for children: nutrition.about.com/od/nutritionforchildren/
5. *Linda McCartney's World of Vegetarion Cooking: Over 200 Meat-Free Dishes From Around the World* by Linda McCartney (Bulfinch, 2001)

Did You Know?

1. 7 million tons of food is thrown away every year in the UK.
2. On average, bananas contain around 30 grams of carbohydrate.
3. A banana has more than 450 milligrams of potassium, helping to prevent muscle cramps.
4. An average Tour de France cyclist burns around 350 to 700 calories per hour.
5. 50 grams of long-grain brown rice has 182 calories, 3.8 grams of protein, and 38.4 grams of carbohydrate.
6. 28 grams of rice noodles has 101 calories, 1.8 grams of protein and 24.2 grams of carbohydrate.
7. 50 grams of spaghetti has 181 calories, 6 grams of protein, and 38.5 grams of carbohydrate.
8. Breakfast cereals, cheese, and bread are regarded as processed foods.
9. Oily fish include salmon, herring, sardines, trout, tuna, and mackerel.
10. The pufferfish, a Japanese delicacy, is so poisonous that chefs have to be specially trained to prepare them.

Things to Try for Yourself

1. Invite friends over and cook a good meal, have a picnic, or barbeque.
2. Visit and support organic farms in your area.
3. Attend a fresh food festival.
4. Visit your favorite restaurant or try another totally new dining experience with people whose company you enjoy.
5. Subscribe to a cycling magazine for specific nutritional advice.

Try Growing Your Own

If you were already a gardener and grew your own fruit, vegetables, and herbs before amputation, then your main challenge will be adapting your garden area to make it easier to continue growing your own produce.

This can be done by raised beds and using wheelbarrows and other lifting equipment to avoid too much pressure on your stump. If you grow food on an allotment or in a community garden, you will have to ensure that you are able to bend, lift, carry, stand, kneel, dig, and weed for longer periods of time. This is more demanding than growing produce in a window box or small area of your garden so be prepared to ask for assistance if you are having difficulty. Farming is also possible after amputation.

Amputee, Cyclist, and Farmer
Despite Everything—There With a Bicycle

Swiss farmer, Alois "Wisi" Zgraggen lost both arms in a work accident 11 years ago. Nevertheless, he took over his parent's farm—and also rides a bike.

He introduces himself as "Wisi," stretches out what is left of the stump (approximately 15 centimeters [5 inches] in length) of his left arm in welcome, and turning his head toward the house, says, "Come in!"

Wisi's recumbent tricycle is next to six bikes belonging to his wife and their four children. They are situated in front of the family-sized house where they all live along with Wisi's parents. "We like to go walking or cycling. It's not ideal to cycle on the road without hands on a two-wheeler."

While investigating this further, they ended up in a bike shop in Kriens where they encountered the inventor and *Velojournal* technical editor, Marius Graber. He knew how to rebuild a recumbent tricycle in such a way that Wisi could control and steer it himself.

"Not with your hands under the seat, but with shoulder steering, and then there was the extra challenge of gearing and backpedaling and braking that had to be done with the feet. It works well now." The Velo—a Hase bike—is a converted standard model, says the powerful 36-year-old. "My wife, Angelica, gave it to me six years ago as a 30th birthday present."

The accident in which Wisi Zgraggen lost both arms occurred on October 16, 2002. He was 25 years old at the time, and the farm still belonged to his parents. Wisi and his father were pressing bales of hay on that day. When the round baler suddenly got stuck, Wisi wanted to quickly fix the problem while the engine was running. He stumbled; the roller pulled his right arm inside. He tried to free himself, fell back again, and the roller pulled his left arm inside. And in the next few minutes, both arms were torn.

As his father came to help, Wisi gave him precise instructions; he should turn the engine off and on again, several times. "That was the only way he could free me. I was absolutely clear in my mind [fully conscious], right up to the moment the helicopter ambulance came. And I didn't bleed a bit, probably because the blood vessels were closed due to the friction."

He's not sure, but he says, "What is certain is that the Lord my God sent the best of all his guardian angels."

Back to the Baler

Wisi Zgraggen has already told the story "several thousand times." That started at the hospital. He says, "I received a lot of visitors, and everyone wanted to hear exactly what happened. I only realized afterwards that talking about that day has helped me to handle it all. I was responsible and had to learn to forgive myself."

Eleven years later, sitting at the kitchen table, a father to three sons and a daughter, he knows much better what is important in life, says the attractive blonde man.

"The accident has grounded me. Before, I would put work before everything else. There were lunches where I didn't even sit down. That must not be."

Today, he makes more time for his family. In speaking of his wife, he says, "she has supported me all these years and given me the strength to continue. But first, I had to want it; Angelica and everyone also had to see that I wanted to. You can't pull someone who is feeling dreadful out of that hole against his will."

While at the site of the accident, as they waited for the helicopter ambulance, he said to his father that he wanted to take over the farm anyway and by converting it from milk production to cattle farm, it should be possible. And they have done just that. Today, it is mainly small Irish Dexter cattle that Wisi farms on the Bielenhof at Erstfeld, Canton Uri. The meat is sold directly by the family to private buyers, and from time to time to the Hotel Tiefenbach on the Furka Pass.

Since 2008, when his father badly broke a leg, Wisi operates all the machinery on the farm, except for one: "The two-wheeled handtractor needs both hands to work it. But I am operating the round baler again." The one that cost him both his arms. He uses his stumps, his shoulders, and his knee to help him operate the machinery.

To get to Bielenhof, you go down a narrow road that the farmer knows inside out. Even as a small child on school days, he would cycle four times per day, back and forth. "We all learn to cycle here at an early age, even my children. My youngest already cycled as a three-year-old around the yard."

"It might look a bit odd to see such small tots cycling around," laughs Wisi. And then he says, quite seriously, because this article is written for a cycling magazine and because this small road that leads from his farm to Erstfeld is part of the National North–South bicycle route:

"Some cyclists feel that the road belongs to them. Especially the racers. They rarely stop at the side of the road and give way." But moaning and shouting is not actually Wisi's way. He much prefers to give others strength. And for that, he doesn't need many words. You merely need to look at him.

For information on Bielenhof, bookings, and orders visit:
→ **www.bielenhof.ch**

→ **www.dexterzucht.ch**

Written by Esther Banz, in Velojournal, Switzerland, and translated with the kind permission of Esther Banz, Velojournal, and Wisi and Angelika Zgraggen.

Available at: http://velojournal.ch/archiv/jahrgang-2013/ausgabe-3/2013/trotzdem-mit-dem-velo-da.html.

Srdjan Jeremic, Bosnia and Herzogovina

Srdjan Jeremic was born in 1968 and lives in Eastern Sarajevo. He was a member of the Army of Republika Srpska, and in 1993, he suffered injuries from grenade shrapnel which resulted in amputation of his left fist. Today, Srdjan. is 80 percent disability group IV. From his early youth, Srdjan aspired for sports, and he did some cycling before the war and sustained injuries. He cycles on a recreational basis. Although Srdjan does not participate in any competitions, he still manages to cycle some 10,000 to 12,000 kilometers (6,200-7,500 miles) every year which keeps him fit and in good shape. Srdjan uses every opportunity to go cycling throughout the country and the region. He visited neighboring Montenegro and cycled to the highest peaks of the most picturesque mountains around Sarajevo (Igman, Jahorina), river canyons, and other scenic places around the country. As he mainly cycles on mountains, he is in a position to enjoy beautiful scenery in a way no person can experience while in cars. He feels free, does not think about problems life brings on a daily basis, and cannot fully describe overwhelming feelings inside him. In his own words, Srdjan will continue cycling and enjoying the world around him for many days to come.

Chapter 10

Training Plan

The fitter you are, the easier it is to accomplish daily living tasks. Losing muscles in your limbs through amputation requires your body to adjust and compensate for such loss. In order to use your prosthetic limb daily (all day, every day, for many hours, as amputees in this book will tell you), your remaining muscles have to become stronger. The amount of training will depend on how severe the amputation is and what you want to be able to do in life. Alongside the need to develop physical capacity to use a prosthetic limb daily, there may be a need to lose weight or reduce the impact of diabetes or heart problems through regular exercise.

If you are already a highly athletic amputee who enjoys all forms of sporting activites and would like to work toward a sports or fitness qualification, there are plenty of options (and advice) on the Internet and at your local leisure center or sports college (higher education facility where the main subjects taught are sports). You never know, you may end up training the next Paralympic amputee! If you are new to amputee life or not yet so keen on being physically active, *keep reading*.

Why Train?

Improved levels of strength and fitness prevent complications from poor posture (standing style) and gait (walking style) which can lead to back pain or spinal abnormalities. Posture, gait, and joint range of motion affect arm and leg amputees to different degrees. Proper posture minimizes stress and maximizes strength of joint movement. Succesful rehabilitation following amputation is best achieved with a mixture of muscle building, balance, stretching, and cardiovascular exercise. Exercises introduced in the early stages of rehabilitation following amputation are very low impact in nature, undertaken without prosthetics, and require very little equipment. Often a towel, sand bag, and resistance band are all that is required.

The responsibility to continue sufficient levels of exercise for better prosthesis use rests on the amputee, his family, friends, and work colleagues. If you were physically active before amputation, you might continue with your previous activities with or without modification. For sedentary, non-motivated amputees, a consultation with a physical therapist or fitness instructor may be required. A qualified fitness trainer or physical trainer works in a fitness center or gym or in some countries, delivers a personalized home-based exercise plan for individual clients. Following a fitness test, the trainer develops a training plan, demonstrates each routine, and assures it is performed correctly. The trainer regularly monitors exercises are being done safely, correctly, and effectively. In the initial stages, because of the lower physical capacity of a deconditioned amputee, exercises may require adaptation. This will be reflected in the training plan when the stump is still healing and shrinking. Once the prosthetics have stabilized, a larger amount of training may be attempted. Success depends on the commitment and motivation of the individual. More difficult exercises can be added to the training plan when fully conversant and confident in using the prosthetic side of the body. There is also the potential of exercising without prosthetics and from a wheelchair to varying levels of difficulty.

Fitness instruction for group settings is often organized as a sequence of weekly classes, each with a particular exercise theme. There is no reason not to join exercise classes designed for able-bodied participants. Inform the instructor before attending a class, and work with them to ensure you are performing exercises safely or develop techniques around the amputation.

General guidelines state that young people between the ages of 5 and 18 should undertake at least 60 minutes of moderate or vigorous intensity activity per day. This should be supplemented by three days per week of muscle and bone strengthening activity. Adults ages 19 to 64 should attempt 150 minutes of aerobic activity (e.g., cycling) a week and muscle strengthening activities on two or more days a week. Fit adults 65 years and older should attempt to maintain these levels of physical activity.

Types of Training Plans

Training plans are a good way of developing structured and focused routines of physical activity into a daily, weekly, or monthly schedule. This is especially important if you are sedentary by nature with a tendency to substitute other things rather than exercise. If the exercises seem boring or hard work, vary routines to keep interest and motivation levels high. There are various types of training plans, the main ones being general fitness, weight loss, and competition. While the actual content depends on the person, the following routines are invariably included in a training plan:

- Warm up
- Stretching (develop flexibility)
- Cardiovascular or aerobic (develop power, coordination, speed and agility)
- Strength (develop muscle endurance)
- Balance (develop posture)
- Cool down and recovery

Training plans for general fitness split the amount of strength, cardiovascular / aerobic, and flexibility into equal distribution across the day, week, or month of the training plan. Exercise routines are varied on a regular basis within the plan to ensure a full-body workout is achieved. For weight loss, high-intensity exercises that increase heart rate and breathing rate are required. For cycling competitions, different training plans are used. The competing season plan focuses on preparation to compete, and the off-season plan enables proper recovery and readiness for future competition training. High levels of performance in cycling take many years of well-planned, methodical, and challenging training. Elite, high-level, competitive athletes spend a major part of their day in some form of training for their sport. For the majority of amputees who want fitness levels that enable general daily living activities to be carried out easily, the amount of time spent in the gym or on a bike will not be as intense as an elite athlete. The benefits of training begin to disappear after only two weeks of inactivity. Muscular endurance declines, flexibility is reduced, and further inactivity negatively impacts heart muscle and the cardiovascular system. It is important to keep active even when (or especially because) you are an amputee.

Why Train on a Bike?

All forms of bike riding increase core muscle strength, stamina, fat reduction, and overall balance skills. Cycling could also help develop the muscles needed for better walking, balance, and posture. Cycling uses the majority of muscles in the body and, mixing it with other forms of exercise, provides you with a full-body workout. Upper-body strengthening of the shoulder and arm muscles can be achieved on a two-wheeler, tricycle, or tandem by standing or leaning forward. Handcycling develops upper-body and core abdominal muscles.

Using a bike for physical exercise incorporates fun while improving your fitness and cycling performance. Varying intensities, including and repeating intervals, doing sprints, climbing hills and mountains, or pacing yourself with your own time trials are all fun and exciting ways to liven up the drudgery of physical exercise. Take time to mix cycling with other exercises for a balanced workout.

When thinking about a training plan to develop cycling skills, consider the following:

- What do you want to achieve? General fitness and mobility? Preparing for a bike holiday? Crossing a continent? Or competition? If so, at what level and for what kind of race?
- Where do you live? Do you have different terrains you can choose from to integrate into your training? Are there hills around you, mountains, or is it all flat? Do you live in a big town where you can only interval and sprint between traffic lights? Would it be better to use public transportation to get out of town to train or is cycling to the outskirts a nice, adequate warm-up?
- Are there roads with little traffic that allow you to train as you want and where you don't face the noise and stench? Are there long, straight stretches where you can keep pushing, without needle curves or other obstacles that let your heart rate and your breathing go down?
- What would stop you from getting bored? A beautiful landscape? Changing terrain? Company? Pushing hard? Improving performance? If so, why not take a few test laps on a hill or along a river and measure your time every few weeks? And what annoys you most, and how can you avoid it?
- How much time can you invest in an average week? 1 hour? 3 hours? Or more? And how often can you train? 2 x 45 minutes, or 2 x 3 hours? What time suits you most? Do you like to start your training with the rising sun? Or do you prefer to get home in the mild light of the sunset?

- What are your options in bad weather and winter? You don't mind rain and hail? Great! But if you do mind, can you stick to your training plan? Are you flexible enough to move training from Monday to Wednesday? If there is ice and snow, is there a spin class in the nearby gym? Do you have a fixed bike in your room? Or are you happy to do other sports, such as running, cross-country skiing, or swimming?

With these basic questions answered, you can start preparing your own training plan. The examples provided at the end of this chapter might help you. They need not be followed completely and may require adaptation to suit your particular situation or motivation for training. If you have a good working knowledge of training and fitness, then experiment using safe training techniques and measure the results. Don't forget you need to plan time not only for training, but also for showering, changing clothes (and possibly liners), and cleaning liners. Depending on the weather and road conditions, you might need to give the bike a quick clean. And last but not least, you might be tired after all that hard training. Calculate time for recovery as well!

As your aim is to work on improving your cycling ability, think and plan your training in cycles. Write out a training plan for yourself.

First, set your goal for each training session. Use the following as examples:

- Endurance
- Force and power
- Stamina
- Riding technique
- Active recovery
- Discovering nature
- Goals could be something like: Cycle 30 miles every weekend and 75 miles per week.

Time yourself on these and try to reduce the average time on each ride so you get quicker. Set the timeframe and number of cycles.

For example: 4 cycles of 4 weeks each.

Cycle 1: 4-week timeframe
Week 1 = 3 hours of training
Week 2 = 4 hours
Week 3 = 6 hours
Week 4 = 7 hours

Then plan time for recovery and start the next cycle with a slight increase in the number of hours you train.

Cycle 2: 4-week timeframe
Week 1 = 4 hours of training
Week 2 = 6 hours
Week 3 = 7 hours
Week 4 = 8 hours

Use the training plan to guide you on what to work on day by day and week by week. Set yourself at least one long, slow recovery ride and give yourself one day off. Increase the intensity as you train. For example:

- Low intensity in week 1
- Increase intensity in week 2
- Go further in week 3
- Go back to the intensity level of week 2 in week 4

With 3 or 4 cycles completed, you will reach a level of speed, endurance, and general fitness that will make you feel stronger than ever. If that all sounds too complicated, then simply play around and vary things as much as you want. Do whatever makes you gasp for breath, laugh, smile, and most of all, makes you enjoy cycling!

Correct Technique

The importance of correct technique when undertaking any form of physical training cannot be overemphasized. There may be a tendency to use too much weight, use the wrong muscle groups, or undertake exercises too quickly, too slowly, or for too long. Perfecting technique takes time and effort. Correcting technique errors reduces the risk of injury and makes the workout more efficient. Bad habits can develop over time, and unlearning these is often more difficult than learning good technique habits. Recording a workout or asking a trainer to monitor your technique are good ways of checking that the exercises are being performed effectively.

Strenuous physical activity that begins abruptly can cause injury. Three aspects of training that people tend to skip are the warm-up, stretching, and cool-down. These should not be overlooked when training for any reason, whether for competition, general fitness, or weight loss. A typical training session should consist of the following components:

A. A. Warm-up
B. B. Stretching
C. C. Main exercise
D. D. Cool-down with stretching

A. Warm-Up

The warm-up improves performance by preparing you mentally and physically for the more strenuous exercise ahead. It prepares the heart gradually and safely to work harder during the main exercise routine. Warm muscles contract and relax easier and quicker, and oxygen is released quicker into muscles at higher temperatures. Blood is diverted away from the digestive system to the muscles being exercised, and unwanted waste products are removed. Joints are better protected as more synovial fluid (lubricant) is produced to improve shock absorption.

The warm-up can last from 10 to 30 minutes, involving some low-impact cardiovascular exercise at a light intensity. It may cause a little perspiration, but should not cause fatigue. On particularly cold days, it may take longer to warm up. Cycling at a steady low speed is a useful warm-up before tackling the main elements of your training plan. Warming up all other muscle groups by light exercise is also advisable.

For example, do the following in a warm room:

- 5-10 minutes slow cycling
- 5-10 minutes stretching
- 10-15 minutes drills for specific muscle groups

B. Stretching

Stretching should be included for around 5 to 10 minutes. Stretching should not hurt or feel uncomfortable. Hold each stretch for around one minute. It should be done to the point of slight tension in the muscle. Do not bounce the body during stretching. If muscle range of motion is reduced, more flexibility training restores function. If joint range of motion is reduced, the muscles and tissues around it have to be lengthened carefully.

If cycling at intense levels on a regular basis, stretching is crucial to balance out muscle tension at joints. Muscles should only be stretched once they have been warmed up as they become elastic and relax more easily. During the warm-up, dynamic stretches (i.e., slow, controlled movements with full range of motion) should be undertaken. They should only be performed gradually. Examples include hamstring stretch, calf stretch, shoulder extension, neck stretch, trunk rotation, as well as others. Instructions for these can be found online or in training manuals.

Alfred Kaiblinger, Austria (http://1a1b1r.com/)

Before my accident, I was already well known as a triathlete. During the 1990s, I used to train with my local cycling club in Tulln. After the accident and during the two-year rehabilitation period, I started paracycling. Cycling was the best sports opportunity. Since then I have been active in cycling and especially paracycling. I competed successfully in many races over the years, culminating in the Paralympics in Athens in 2004 where I came in 8th. I have also been very active in committees, such as the IPC Disabled Cycling Committee and the UCI Paracycling Committee, over those years. My cycling history is available on my website for those interested in it.

Since 2006, I have had problems in my stumps with phantom pain and nerve loss. The prosthetics no longer fit well, and the muscles don't work as well in the prosthesis. I now attempt to simply keep moving. The amount of time and effort people invest in their cars, they should invest in their own (personal) motor—their body.

My motto is: Move yourself; your body is made for it!

C. Main Exercises—Cardiovascular, Muscle Strength, and Balance
1. Cardiovascular

Breathing correctly improves exercise ability, and exercises that increase heart rate and breathing rate are cardiovascular exercises. Cardiovascular exercise is known as aerobic activity if it is rhythmic, continuous activity that uses oxygen for energy release in the muscle. The aim is to increase the ability of the large muscle groups, the heart, lungs, and blood vessels to improve endurance. It should only be performed to the level where there is no extreme discomfort in breathing. A good test to try is the "talk test" If you can do the exercise and talk comfortably, then you are working to a reasonable level. Undertaking such exercise on a regular basis improves heart volume and rate, breathing, and blood flow to muscles. The heart muscle controls the flow of oxygen to other muscles, and the fitter the heart is, the better the athletic performance. It also improves the ability of muscles to use oxygen effectively to supply energy for movement. The ability of the blood to carry away waste and carbon dioxide out of the muscles improves. Smaller blood vessels are developed, and more hemoglobin is created to enhance the transport of blood to the areas it is needed. This makes your body more functional and efficient. Cardiovascular fitness is measured by heart rate and oxygen consumption among other factors. The terms used to describe the intensity for such exercises are percentage of maximal heart rate (e.g., 60-90% of maximum heart rate), lactate threshold, and VO_2max.

Heart Rate

Measure maximum heart rate to make sure you are training effectively for cardiovascular fitness. It improves with time and training so you know you are getting fitter. There are at least seven variations of the equation that can be used to work out maximum training heart rate. A basic version is to subtract your age from 220.

For example: 50-year-old = 220-50 = 170 beats per minute

For cycling, you should be training at 65 to 85 percent maximum heart rate; this is worked out by:

From equation above: 170 x 65% = 110 beats per minute (minimum target heart rate)
170 x 85% = 145 beats per minute (maximum target heart rate)

An alternative to maximum heart rate is a good training heart rate, calculated by subtracting your age from 180. Normal resting heart rate is between 60 to 80 beats per minute.

Lactate Threshold

An alternative method of testing fitness is to use the lactate threshold heart rate. This is suggested to be at around 85 percent of maximum heart rate. It is the point during your workout where you can't speak easily and fatigue is setting in.

VO$_2$max

VO$_2$max is a measure of the amount of oxygen being used by the muscle tissues during a training session. The more oxygen you use, the more energy you can produce. It is a good indicator of aerobic capacity and exercise endurance. It is expressed as a percentage (e.g., 60% VO$_2$max) measured in milliliters of oxygen used in one minute per kilogram of body weight.

Increasing the aerobic intensity of training impacts cycling cadence, speed, efficiency, power, agility, and coordination.

Cadence

Cycling is an activity that uses cyclic skills. The actions involve repetitive movements which are duplicated for long periods of time. Each phase is repeated in the same order. For example, when pedaling, the downstroke is followed by the upstroke, and this is repeated over and over again. Cadence is your pedaling speed measured in revolutions per minute (rpm). A smooth pedal technique will improve your cycling enjoyment and your efficiency. Typical pedaling issues are mashing or spinning. Mashing involves pedaling hard in high gears at low or moderate cadence. Spinning involves pedaling hard on low gears with high cadence. A way to monitor your cadence is through the use of a cadence meter that can be easily attached to the bike. A useful drill is cycling in a lower gear than you would normally choose and increasing your pedal revolutions slowly. Increase the pedal frequency until you start to bounce in the saddle; reduce it so you no longer bounce; and then slow back down to your normal rate.

Speed

To develop speed for racing, interval training is recommended. This is a fast form of cycling training that pushes you physically and mentally to the limit if you pedal intensely enough. It involves warming up on the bike, and then alternating between hard and easy pedaling for short bursts of time (e.g., 30 seconds). The cadence should be kept very high—above 100 rpm. Each set should be five intervals with a few minutes of easy recovery cycling in between each set. Working up to five or more sets will increase your speed and stamina for sprint-style competitions. Sets may be repeated or stepped up or stepped down in intensity. You will certainly feel it in your muscles, and it is best reserved for those who are fit and strong! To be effective, it should not be done more than twice a week. Give enough time for recovery in between.

Efficiency

When you first start cycling, pedaling may not be smooth or efficient. A typical issue for leg amputees using prosthetics is overcoming the dead spots of the pedal stroke to produce a smoother rotation. Efficiency uses less energy to travel the same distance. Pedal stroke efficiency can be measured on indoor computer cycles. A series of 30-second one-leg drills at low cadence on a stationary bike on low resistance setting can improve the amount of work each leg does with regard to the pedal stroke. Alternatively, slow frequency revolutions on a small incline where you are concentrating on applying equal force through each pedal stroke can help smooth out dead spots.

Power

Strength combined with speed provides the body with power. Maximum short bursts of power take up to 0.70 seconds to produce in well-trained athletes. In cycling competitions, a cyclist has to be able to generate the highest possible force in the shortest possible time to accelerate ahead of the rest of the field. The more power generated, the faster the bike will go over a given distance. Power can be measured with a good cycling computer. Improving cycling power as well as muscle and cardiac endurance requires cycling up hills. This involves maneuvering a heavy object (your bike and your body weight) in a relatively large gear at a steady rhythm (cadence) or speed for an extended period of time. Even walking up a hill with your bike will produce some muscle effect in those early days before you become fit enough to cycle up them. Increasing climbing distance gradually helps improve the power and endurance development of your muscles. Riding into the wind (headwind) or through a crosswind can also provide a good deal of resistance to help develop endurance and power. Your ride will be exhilarating, if nothing else! This type of work can also be done on a trainer or stationery exercise bike with a resistance program built into it.

The effort level should not be set too hard otherwise it will be ineffective. Staying seated in the saddle when going uphill and changing up and down gears regularly improves muscle endurance and power. To build leg muscles, use short intervals of intense speed or resistance followed by recovery periods. When toning leg muscles, cycle at moderate speeds for longer periods.

Agility

Agility enables the cyclist to change direction quickly while keeping balance, strength, speed, and body control on the bicycle. It requires some practice. The level of agility can be higher if the cyclist has developed enough speed and power. On a bike, agility can be practiced by moving forward, backward, upward, round corners, turns, changing direction, going through cones, accelerating, and decelerating. Balance and core strength are tested fully during such actions. Sprinting, relaying, and cycling around an obstacle course also develop and test agility. To develop agility in an individual, timing, coordination, balance, direction changes, and suppleness are areas of training that can be incorporated into the training plan.

Coordination

Coordination is how well the body works together. It requires your eyes and brain to synchronize with the rest of the body on the bike. Throwing objects at a target as you pass it on a bike is a good way of developing this skill. Riding in opposite directions while throwing objects as you pass also tests coordination and balance.

1.   Muscle Strength and Endurance

Muscle strength and endurance are important fitness training aspects. Strength is how much force your muscles can exert; endurance is how often your muscles can repeat that exertion of force. Muscles can only work to the limits of their capacity (i.e., the strength and ability to push, pull, or lift a weight). All daily living activities require muscular strength. See if you can work out which muscles you use for the following:

- Opening a bottle
- Carrying shopping
- Climbing stairs

For amputees, these basic tasks seem difficult at first because of muscle deconditioning following surgery and lack of physical training of other compensating muscle groups. Muscles work all day long to some extent, supporting body weight even when sitting down.

Many forms of cycling, apart from handcycling, use the lower-body muscles: quadriceps, gluteals, hamstrings, and calves. All of these work together to give power when pedaling. The majority of muscles in the leg are considered long muscles as they stretch great distances. The largest muscles in the leg are the thigh and the calf. The main joints used in cycling (apart from handcycling) are the hip and knee joint with the ankle joint used to a limited degree. The hip and spine are important for balance on the bicycle. The hip joint is one of the most flexible joints in the entire human body. Hip muscles provide movement, strength, and stability to the hip joint, hip bones, and thigh.

These forms of cycling also use upper-body muscles, such as the arms and shoulders, to support the weight of the body on the handlebars (triceps) and in pedaling uphill (biceps). Muscles in the back and abdomen are used to stabilize you on the bike, improve cycling efficiency, and eliminate energy waste from side-to-side movement. The abdominal and oblique muscles work the most. Increased abdominal strength, thereby, releases pressure from the lower-back muscles.

Depending on the severity of amputation, the major leg or arm muscles, or a combination of these muscle groups, could be lost. This alters the center of mass of the amputee and affects balance and posture on and off the bike. If cycling without prostheses, the rest of the body requires conditioning and training to compensate for the loss of muscles and joints. If cycling with prosthetics, the rest of the body adjusts its technique to enable the prosthesis to function appropriately.

For handcycling, the muscles and joints used are those of the upper body. The major muscles used are the chest, upper back, shoulder, neck, and abdomen. Due to poor technique and deconditioning, we may overcompensate by using the wrong muscles at the back of the neck and shoulders to perform actions that should be done by deeper neck muscles attached to the spine. This can lead to tightness, pain, and headaches.

Exercises to activate the deep anterior neck flexors must be done slowly and carefully in order to engage the correct muscle groups.

Muscle strength and endurance is related to the type of muscle fibers present. There are two types: slow-twitch (type II) and fast-twitch (type I). The ratio of fast- to slow-twitch fibers in muscles cannot be substantially altered, but they can be trained to work more efficiently.

- Average sedentary person = 40% slow-twitch/60% fast-twitch
- Average active person = 50% of both
- Extreme endurance athlete = 90% slow-twitch/10% fast-twitch.

Slow-twitch fibers sustain effort over long periods of time by using oxygen to break down carbohydrate and fat for energy. They are in muscles used for endurance activities. Endurance levels depend on how well these fibers are developed. Endurance training involves repetitions of activity—for example, 2 to 3 sets of 10 repetitions of each exercise in succession with a brief rest (30 seconds) in between.

Fast-twitch fibers exert large amounts of force over short bursts of time in muscles involved in strength activities. They have poor aerobic endurance when compared to slow-twitch fibers as they produce energy by not using oxygen and, therefore, fatigue quickly. To improve the capacity for strength in muscles, an exercise should be repeated 10 to 12 times with 1 to 2 minutes of rest in between. Strength training should not be repeated on specific muscles more than once every 48 hours in order to prevent injury or overtraining. For cycling and prosthesis use, do low-intensity strength training—low-weight and high-intensity endurance (longer time/number of repetitions) training.

The first set for both slow- and fast-twitch muscle development should be considered the warm-up. These aspects can be trained on a bike with power and cardio-intensity cycling. Without a bike, the type of equipment required for muscle strength and endurance training can vary from free-standing dumbbells and barbells to full-size weight machines. For children, use very light free weights, medicine balls, or their own body weight. Keep all exercises low to medium volume and very low or low intensity. If such equipment is not available in your area, why not improvize by using the things around you? A wooden pole, a metal bar, a bike frame, a rubber ball, a big rubber tire, a phone book, a large textbook, or a wheel all weigh a certain amount. You may have to take a bit of an educated guess at the approximate weight of these, and they may be awkward in shape or size, but don't let that stop you. As long as you use safe lifting techniques, it might make a good change from the gym.

To make sure you lift safely, keep feet parallel and at shoulder width to maximize balance. Keep technique controlled and build speed gradually once technique and flexibility have increased. Start slowly with the very lightest weight.

Work the larger muscle groups first then the smaller muscle groups to prevent early fatigue. Train opposite areas of the body to develop all muscle groups equally. Muscle training within a training plan usually involves splitting the different muscles into upper body, lower body, and core muscle areas. Workout sessions can involve all body areas or specific body areas. Selecting one exercise for each major muscle group promotes balanced muscle development. Performing each exercise through the full range of motion of the limb or joint will improve muscle strength and joint flexibility. Muscle groups should be trained in an organized, systematic fashion by doing each exercise for the muscle group together. Do not jump back and forth between the muscle groups during the session.

When developing muscle strength and tone, 8 to 12 repetitions at 70 to 80 percent maximum resistance is a good plan. If muscles are fatigued, lighten the weight for the next set. Moving weights up and down during sets tests muscle strength and endurance. As muscles adapt, the weight may be increased progressively over time. This makes the muscles work harder and increases strength and tone. Increasing the number of repetitions is often better than increasing the amount of weight lifted. This ensures lean, strong muscle is created rather than bulky muscles that make you heavier on the bike.

2. Balance

Balance exercises on a bike involve riding in a straight line and riding in figure-eights. Balance exercises in a gym or at home develop posture and stability. Balance training is made quicker and easier with kettlebells, resistance bands, and medicine balls. Using such equipment to exercise without prosthetics and from a wheelchair is well worth exploring. Yoga, tai chi, Pilates, and the Alexander technique are all good tests of balance. These improve musculoskeletal system coordination, pain relief, performance enhancement, and improved breathing. Balance on a bike is best tested by riding a unicycle, two-wheeler, or tandem. Standing up on the pedals is a very good test for balance and muscle tone. Where joint problems and complications prevent exercising in such ways, water-based exercises may be a gentler alternative.

Back and Spine

The back and spine need to be developed for strength and endurance if undertaking a lot of cycling. The back muscles help the cyclist generate power during the pedal stroke as well as stabilizing the pelvis and spine during pedaling. An exercise such as the stability ball extension is a useful one to try regularly before and after a cycle ride to help ease those areas.

D. Cool-Down

Once the training session is completed, it is just as important to cool down. Cooling down helps dispose of waste products, such as lactic acid, reduces muscle soreness, and allows the heart to gradually return to normal resting rate in a safe way. This decreases the chances of fainting or collapsing if strenuous or high-impact exercise is stopped abruptly. The main function of cooling down is to aid recovery and promote relaxation.

Slowing down the speed of the exercise gradually while keeping the body moving over 5 to 10 minutes or longer will allow the heart to adjust the blood flow to the muscles appropriately. Gentle, easy-paced cycling is a good cardiovascular exercise to use during the cool-down.

For example, in a warm room:

* 5 to 10 minutes cycling, pedaling slowly on a lower gear
* 5 to 10 minutes static stretching

Stretching (During Cool-Down)

When heart rate and breathing is under control, stretching can be done. Stretches performed at this stage are static. Stretching assists the body in its repair process by reducing stress and tension developed in muscles during the workout. If the main exercise session involved strength or resistance training, then new muscle will have been built. Such muscles need to be lengthened and flexible to increase range of motion. The aim is to overcome the automatic tightening of a muscle following exercise. This is done by holding the stretch gently for 10 to 20 seconds and not bouncing, pulsing, or overstretching the muscle.

The stretches are designed to work deep within the muscle to realign muscle fibers to their normal range of movement. This realignment of muscle tension across joints assists in posture and balance improvement. The muscles are warmest during this time, and all muscle groups that have been exercised should be stretched. Breathing out as the muscle is being stretched allows the muscle to lengthen smoothly. Breathing deeply during the cool-down allows more oxygen to enter the body.

Total-body workouts require stretches for all muscle groups. Stretches can be modified to make them more or less difficult. Single-joint stretches are easier than multi-joint stretches. If an element of balance is introduced, the stretch becomes harder to perform. For example, standing on one leg may be difficult for a leg amputee.

Regular stretching increases circulation to muscles, reduces lower-back problems, and improves posture and mobility. This brings nutrients to joints and improves coordination. Flexibility training undertaken two or three times a week can help maintain mobility levels. Three popular forms of increasing flexibility and core strength are yoga, Pilates, and tai chi which can be modified to take into account amputation or prosthetics use. Try adding these into your training plan and see if they make a difference?

Rest and Recovery

Once all the hard work of the training session is complete, two important facets to remember are rest and recovery. When exercising for the first time, it is best to start slowly and build up gradually with plenty of rest in between. This allows the body enough time to adapt. The sooner the recovery from fatigue, the better the chance of improving performance during the next training session. Recovery strategies include getting plenty of good quality sleep and ensuring the body is well nourished with carbohydrates and proteins and has enough fluid replacement. Rest is physically necessary so that the muscles can repair, rebuild, and strengthen. Muscles require between 24 to 48 hours to repair. Recovery time allows glycogen stores to be replenished.

There are two categories of recovery: short term and long term. Short-term recovery is also known as active recovery and occurs after exercise during the cool-down and immediately afterward. Quick recovery comes about when you listen to your body. If you are feeling sore or feeling okay, this will affect whether you should train again the next day and the type of training this should involve. If you are feeling sore, then stretch the area and work on other aspects that do not involve those muscles to any great extent or choose a gentler activity such as swimming. If you are feeling fine, continue with your training plan.

Long-term recovery techniques involving hydrotherapy, water immersion, or compression garments are more often used by elite athletes. Alternating hot and cold showers or baths should be done within 30 minutes of the training session. The cold exposure should be less than one minute, the hot exposure for around four minutes. Massage can also assist in recovery by increasing blood flow to fatigued muscles and stretching soft tissues. This removes toxins, relieves tension, and relaxes muscles. For simple finger or thumb massage, use oil on bare skin and lie down or sit in a comfortable position. Relax your body. Make circular motions on the skin, starting at the lower end of the body and working up toward the heart. Start off gently and then press deeper, using your knuckles if required.

Overtraining

If insufficient time is given to rest and recovery, overtraining syndrome can result. Fatigue and underperformance may be symptoms of this as you may feel tired or have sleeping problems, headaches, loss of enthusiasm, and decreased appetite. Training strenuously over long periods of time can result in poor health and infection. Try the following to minimize this:

- Include 1 or 2 days of resting recovery in a week.
- Avoid extremely long training sessions as a total beginner. Split a 3-hour session into 2 x 1.5 hours (morning and evening) and do not do more than 2 hours in one training session.
- Eat a well-balanced diet with enough total energy, carbohydrate and protein. If dieting to lose weight or if fresh produce is unavailable, consider supplements.
- Drink carbohydrate sports drinks or eat energy gels or bars before, during and after prolonged workouts to reduce some of the adverse effects of exercise on immune function.

Mental Toughness

Mental toughness is built up gradually by many different techniques, and in cycling, it is usually through the design of competitive challenges. These test the endurance, stamina, determination, and technique of the cyclist in different environments and circumstances.

Elements that all cyclists learn to deal with are frustration, lack of confidence, and coping with pressure as well as being able to perform even if things are not going their way. Understand what causes you fear, shame, anger, low confidence, or frustration about your performance and know that being overcritical of yourself can be destructive. Frame these emotions in a constructive, forgiving way instead to remain mentally tough. It is often easy to get distracted or overwhelmed by stronger opponents or confrontational situations. Learning to deal with such events is an essential part of mental toughness preparation.

Thoughts, feelings, concentration, decision making, dealing with pressure, exhibiting courage, discipline, self-determination, and confidence can all be worked on in different training sessions. A training diary is a useful and fun tool for this. Make a note of the training format, duration, distance (or weight or number of repetitions), average speed, your weight, your feelings, positive and negative aspects, and weather. Write down whatever you think is important to work at so you can compare, learn, and see improvements. This will help you be more focused, driven, and prepared.

An element of competitive spirit is always helpful to enable you to gauge how well you are doing against others of a similar amputation level. It can be motivating and inspiring even if you are initially in awe of what others can achieve if they set their minds to it. Training with others helps you to recognize and correct strengths and weaknesses. Being independent and determined to succeed will enable you to learn what needs to improve and how to train as well as provides you with the satisfaction that you achieved it because you enjoyed doing it as compared to having achieved it for a trophy or praise from those around you.

Staying Motivated

Motivation is a big factor in achieving success and maintaining exercise. If the reasons to exercise are not sufficiently motivating or the activity is not motivating, there is a risk of failure. No one can remain motivated forever, and sometimes you need those around you to provide support and encouragement. The longer the timeframe before the result is seen, the greater the risk of not achieving it. If you find yourself making excuses not to train or to give up on a particularly tough part of the training, this may be a sign of fatigue. In such cases, reframe your thoughts to be more encouraging to help you finish your training. Take a quick break and eat or drink something to help you get energized. If you do have to stop, then make a note of where this was and try to beat that next time. The only time not to force yourself to train is if you have an injury or are in severe pain.

Different strategies to try include:

- Putting the training plan somewhere where you will look at it every day (e.g. on the fridge)
- Making time to start training, reassess priorities if necessary. If things get in the way, train anyway or readjust the schedule and start training again.
- Setting small goals and achieving them for each training session.
- Telling someone about the training and asking them to follow you up on it.
- Rewarding yourself when you have achieved the goals; if they are cycling related (e.g. cycling accessories or tickets to cycling events) that will keep you focused.
- Working out to music or podcasts.

- Finding a training partner.
- Taking part in an intensive weekend training camp.
- Taking part in or attending a competition or organized cycle ride; having other cyclists around you will provide the impetus you need to keep up with the training.

If you have just done lots of cycling, you may get to a point where you don't want to look at the bike, let alone ride it. This is normal. Simply take a good break from it for a couple of days, do something totally different instead, and then come back refreshed and ready to ride. Combating boredom by cycling indoors can be achieved by developing videos such as those found at www.cyclingtips.com.au/2011/09/the-sufferfest-from-the-beginning/.

Special Consideration

This chapter was written with the expert assistance of Armin Köhli.

From the Amputees

Mark Ormrod, UK

To be honest with the team I was in, there was never really much chance of being bored as everyone was always up for making the event fun. While cycling, I would throw my iPod on and listen to some music, or if I was on a leg where there were mile markers, I would use them as goals to see if I could reach the next one quicker than the last. Lack of motivation was overcome by the thought that I was lucky to be doing it. Thinking of people who were too severely injured to take part spurred me on.

Robert Bailey, USA

The more in shape I got, the better my heat tolerance became. Losing 80 pounds did not hurt. Now sweat does not collect under the liners. I used to have to stop every hour or two to empty my liners (before losing weight and becoming fit). I do sweat, of course, but the legs don't seem affected.

Sara Tretola, Switzerland

I think of the goals I want to reach and those I have already accomplished thanks to my strong willpower. And every now and again I treat myself with something nice, such as a spa treatment, or I do something with my family.

Victor Walther, Canada

The best way to combat boredom and frustration is variety. Sometimes you need to ride different trails or just go for hike. Consult a fitness trainer when you want to start competing or train for a special event. There are not only health benefits, but also performance benefits to proper nutrition and training.

Stumps and Cranks Book Interview With Alfred Kaiblinger, Austria

1.   How do you know when or if you need a cycling trainer?
If you want to reach national or international level in paracycling, then it's best to have a cycling trainer as they know what the requirements for the sports are and how to achieve these.

2.   What's the biggest mistake that beginners make in training?
The biggest mistake new entrants into parasports make are to expect too much too soon. For example, in 2015, they say, "Next year the Paralympics are in Rio. I want to be there." It usually ends in demotivation, and I saw it happen exactly like that in Austria once. It is better for the first two years to race in your own country and in C1 races in neighboring countries, and then see if you make it to the national team, the qualifying rounds of the World Cup or World Championships, as well as to see where you are better and where you have more of a chance—on road or on track, in time trial or road races. Road races are a big challenge for arm amputees. In time trials they don't have pressure from other racers, and they can go at their own pace.

3.   When can you start training?
That depends: If you trained regularly or have taken part in performance sport before the amputation, then you can start intensive training quickly, centered on your actual performance level. First a check over by a sports medic or trainer and then a particular training plan. That will reduce a lot of the training errors, help you get prepared up to race day, and most importantly, stick to the schedule for recovery.

4. What should a training session involve and look like?

A training session depends on the goal you want to achieve from it. Do you want to or need to improve or stabilize the basic endurance ability? If so, cycle at low intensity for two to four hours. If you are preparing for competitions, then it's about doing enough long, easy warm-up cycling, special high-intensity intervals, and testing out routes similar to competitions—for example, more downhill, more active recovery in between, and cool-down on the bike afterward. It also, unfortunately, means that you can't improve all conditioning skills, such as endurance, strength, and speed, at the same time.

5. Is it better to train in a group or alone?

It's usually more motivating to train in a group; you are more likely to participate and train and not look for excuses not to train, such as bad weather. For track time trial competitions, train alone at your own time trial pace from time to time. For all road races, it's the opposite: Get used to cycling in a group and train at all intensities and routes, otherwise you are not training specifically for competitions.

Sample Training Plans for You to Try

The following websites detail exercises and training plans for amputees and cyclists to try. Mix and match them to suit your needs. No doubt you will find your own favorite exercises to substitute into the plans, too.

→ www.icrc.org/eng/assets/files/other/icrc_002_0936.pdf

→ www.brianmac.co.uk/dynamic.htm

→ www.helpguide.org/articles/exercise-fitness/chair-exercises-and-limited-mobility-fitness.htm

→ www.active.com/cycling/articles/a-sample-3-month-training-plan-for-cyclists?page=2

→ www.bicycling.com/training-nutrition/training-fitness/ride-strong-all-year-long

→ www.bicycling.com/training-nutrition/training-fitness/your-training-plans

Further Reading

1. Preparing your mind: www.active.com/cycling/articles/improve-your-cycling-train-your-mind
2. *The Amputee Coach* by Cathy Howells (Global Publishing, 2009)
3. Yoga for cyclists: www.bicycling.com/training-nutrition/training-fitness/essential-yoga-cyclists
4. Training plans for beginners: healthyliving.azcentral.com/beginner-training-plans-exercise-bike-2474.html
5. General cycling training articles: www.pezcyclingnews.com/toolbox/

Did You Know?

1. On average, 40 percent of the body is made up of muscle.
2. Walking and running is actually the process of losing and catching one's balance.
3. The heart is the strongest muscle in the body. It is the size of a fist.
4. The human body has more than 650 muscles.
5. By the age of 80, sedentary people lose about half their muscle mass.
6. If you cycle at a slow pace for half an hour, you can burn between 75 and 155 kcal.
7. One hour of massage equals seven to eight hours of sleep.
8. Massage therapy was first officially offered as a medical service during the Olympic Games in Atlanta in 1996.
9. Swedish and deep tissue massage are the most popular forms of massage.
10. On average, an adult breathes around 126 to 190 gallons of air per hour. During exercise this, can increase to 2,378 gallons per hour.

Things to Try for Yourself

1. Visit a recreation center or fitness center and take a look at the different fitness activities they do. If there are yoga, Pilates, cycling workouts, or a gym, see whether they appeal.
2. Check out televised workouts or workouts streamed on the Internet that you can do from home.
3. Discuss with other cyclists their experiences of workouts—especially overtraining and recovery.
4. Try out different training plans. Develop your own or try some of those on the Internet.
5. Investigate the fitness trainers in your home town. Ask them to help you develop a plan that you will enjoy doing.

Steve Middleton, Canada (www.morethanmobility.ca/index.html)

Cycling for leg amputees presents a number of challenges, but from these challenges, the cyclist can reap many rewarding, pleasurable hours of fun and sightseeing! You are no longer limited in seeing places. Cycling provides a freedom of movement and independence that can only be limited by one's own will to get out there. As an above-knee amputee who has been cycling for over 10 years, cycling has provided me independence.

As a road cyclist, one is able to join cycling groups and clubs, participate in events, and take part in self-guided cycling tours in countries all over the globe. Amputee road cyclists are free to increase fitness and endurance and make full use of the prosthetic leg. Find what works for you. Enjoy freedom of movement, touring, and traveling.

For example, cycling through Italy or France uphill to walled cities and monasteries, discovering history firsthand, and then cruising through fine wineries can be wonderful as the ride back down is thrilling. Alternatively, mountain biking has enabled me to see the back country and mountainous remote area's of third-world countries, inaccessible by car or bus. Willingness to persevere and push yourself are a must to becoming a confident mountain biker, and be ready as falling is inevitable! Biking in the back country of Peru and experiencing the wonderful people and villages along with my family has been an enriching opportunity I had never dreamed possible as a new amputee. With the same delight and thrills I am able to join my able-bodied cycling friends for weekend rides challenging up and down steep terrains.

Steve Middleton experienced a cycling accident in 2000 that resulted in multiple operations and an above-knee amputation. He mastered walking, swimming, cycling, golf, and skiing after amputation. He volunteers at sports and community events and helps new amputees interested in sports. Visit **www.amputees.vch.ca/bios/Steve.htm** for more information.

Chapter 11

Basic Bike Maintenance

As with any gadget you buy, the only way to make it last is to look after it. The same goes for your bike. Get into the habit of checking your bike regularly to guarantee many years of hassle-free riding without major problems. It will last much longer than your car, iPod, tablet, toaster, or microwave for that matter!

This section of the book explains the common bike maintenance issues you will encounter as you keep cycling. The tools and techniques to do these basic maintenance tasks skillfully and enjoyably are illustrated. Most amputees make sure they get to know their bike repair shops very well as not only do they have the expertise to repair and service your bike for you, they are also very good at providing advice and tips on numerous cycling-related topics.

It is always helpful to have someone around to do the bike safety checks, lifting, carrying, and repairs when you first start cycling. It isn't compulsory to be able to do any of the things outlined in this chapter as long as you are out cycling in good company and can get the support when you require it. As you progress with cycling and get more used to your prosthetic limbs, you might want to challenge yourself to try bike checks, repairs, and maintenance out of curiosity or for self-sufficiency. Once you get into the habit of inspecting your bike on a regular basis, you will soon get to know the minor adjustments and repairs you can do yourself and those you need to ask the bike repair staff about.

The natural tendency for amputees when undertaking any physical activity is to overcompensate for the loss of a limb by using the opposite limb, back, and shoulder areas more. When handling a bike, observe and practice correct manual handling techniques to make it easier on the rest of your body and your prosthetic limb.

Manual Handling

To perform bike checks and repairs, you will inevitably have to be able to lift the bicycle and carry it some distance. You will also have to be able to kneel, bend, or stand for some of the time that you are carrying out repairs. Such movements, if not done in particular ways, can lead to further injury and strain on your body. Muscle, tendon, and joint injuries can be caused not because of the weight of the bicycle, but because of the amount of times you pick up and carry the bicycle, the distances involved, and any twisting, bending, stretching, stooping, or other awkward postures adopted while using a bicycle.

Before you do any manual bike handling, think of ways to make it easier. Is the bike being stored in a cluttered, awkward to reach area such as at the back of a storage cupboard behind all the children's toys? Will you have to lift the bicycle above head height to hook it onto the wall? Are there items on the bicycle that can come off to make it lighter in weight before you lift it, such as panniers, racks, or baskets? Added complications occur when you try to lift while outside in very cold weather if there are strong winds, poor lighting, or if wearing restrictive clothing. If you are lifting the bicycle with someone helping, it is important to coordinate and communicate during the lifting and carrying processes so that you both reduce your chances of injury.

Before lifting, think and plan ahead:

- Are there any obstructions that need to be moved out of the way?
- Can you lift the bicycle yourself or will someone have to assist you?
- Or will you be assisting them?
- Will you need to stop and rest halfway if carrying the bicycle some distance?
- What sort of grip are you using to hold the bicycle? Is it comfortable or awkward?

As bicycles come in all sorts of shapes and sizes, the weight is only one aspect of manual handling that you will encounter. In general, it is important to get a good hold on the bike. This means that you don't just lift with your arms and shoulders, but support the weight of the bike by holding it close to your body. The heaviest part of the bike should be close to your waist for support from the rest of your body as you lift. Leaning against a wall while you lift can provide support to your body. Arm amputees have the added fun of trying out different bike lifting techniques that test their prosthetic arm or their stump. If you want to play with lifting techniques as a leg amputee without your prosthetics, you may need to sit on the floor and then lift or move the bike.

If it is a recumbent or a children's bike, then it is important not to stoop to get a good grip. Feet should be flat on the floor and slightly apart to maintain balance, and the back, hips, and knees should have a slight bend in them. Squatting (knees and hips fully flexed) is not recommended as it can cause back strain.

Avoid jerky movements while lifting and walking. Make sure you feel in control of the bicycle and your prosthetics as you lift. If the load is too heavy and causes your back to bend or arch, put it down and seek assistance. Shoulders should be level and face the same direction as the hips. Turning should be done by moving the feet rather than by twisting the body. Look ahead in the direction you are intending to move the bicycle rather than at the bicycle or at the ground. When you are ready, put the bicycle down and then adjust its position.

Here are some examples of manual handling actions to work on as amputees when using bicycles.

1. Lifting a bicycle onto a repair stand, storage stand, or wall hook:
    This task involves stooping, lifting, and twisting movements.
2. Lowering a bicycle onto the ground from a repair stand, storage stand, or wall hook:
    This task involves lifting, twisting, and lowering movements.
3. Carrying a bicycle along a flat surface:
    This task involves lifting, carrying, and walking movements.
4. Carrying a bicycle up steps:
    This task involves lifting, carrying, walking and steadying movements.
5. Carrying a bicycle uphill
    This task involves lifting, carrying and walking movements.
6. Carrying a bicycle downhill
    This task involves lifting, carrying and walking movements.
7. Carrying a bicycle on an uneven surface
    This task involves lifting, carrying, steadying and walking movements.
8. Lifting a bicycle over a fence or wall (as in pedestrian walkways that are too narrow or high for bikes to get through)
    This task involves lifting, steadying, twisting and lowering movements.

Even if you do not carry or lift your bike, you might have to push or pull it while out cycling—up a hill, for example. It is better to push (walking alongside the bike) rather than pull (walking backward pulling at the handlebars) and to be in full control without stooping over the bike (recumbent/small bike). Pushing a bike up a slope along uneven surfaces or soft ground can be more difficult and require more force. Keep your feet well away from the bicycle pedals and go no faster than your natural walking speed. Do not twist your body in toward the bike or away from it. If pushing a bike down a slope, keep control by activating the brakes to prevent the momentum of the bike increasing to more than your natural walking pace.

At all points, always seek assistance if you feel that you are not comfortable putting these sorts of pressures through your stumps (arms or legs) or have existing back or other joint problems. What sorts of things can you do to reduce the amount of twisting, lifting above shoulder height, or carrying your bike over long distances?

How to Dismantle and Reassemble a Bike

This is often required if you need to take your bike on public transportation or to store it if space available for bike storage is limited. The following instructions apply to two-wheelers. If you have a tricycle, recumbent, or handcycle, check with the manufacturer, and they should supply you with clear packing and reassembly instructions. They may recommend particular bike boxes or cases, too, that are more suited to the bike's design.

Dismantle

Tools: Pedal wrench; 4-, 5-, and 6-mm Allen wrenches (hex key); packing tape; bubble wrap; small bag to store parts

1. Deflate your tires and remove any accessories, such as water bottle holders, bags, panniers, bike computers, and lights.
2. Remove the pedals by shifting the chain onto the smallest chainring and largest rear cog. The right pedal may require a counterclockwise motion with a pedal wrench, and the left pedal a clockwise motion with a pedal wrench.
3. Loosen the bolt around the seat post, mark where the seat post fits by taping the area, and then remove the seat post by pulling it upward. Remove the saddle and seat post and place the bolts and washers safely in a small bag.
4. Open the quick release levers or the cable ends of the front brakes to make the cables loose.
5. Remove the handlebars and take the handlebar off. Place the bolts safely in a small bag.
6. Take off the front wheel by unlocking the quick release mechanism and removing it from the fork. If there is no quick release lever, then use a wrench to loosen the wheel nut (turn counterclockwise) and then take the wheel off.
7. Use lots of bubble wrap, cloth, or padding to cover the components and frame once in the box.
8. Use a fork protector block between the dropouts to prevent damage to the fork.
9. Pack all tools for reassembly in your luggage and tape up and label the box securely.

Reassemble

Tools: 4-, 5-, and 6-mm Allen wrenches (hex key); lube; 15-mm open-end wrench or pedal wrench; packing tape

1. Open the box but be careful not to use a knife as it may cut through the contents.
2. Remove the bike and all contents carefully. Lay them all out neatly so you can get to the correct parts quicker.

3. Remove any bubble wrap or packaging and inspect the items for dents, paint scratches, or other shipping damage. If there is damage, contact the freight handler.

4. Install the front wheel in the fork with the quick release on the non-drive train (chain and gearing) side. Close the quick release to secure the wheel. It must be closed tightly. Double check the wheel is fully inserted and properly centered, otherwise unfasten and reinsert.

5. Install and center the handlebars. Keep cables clear and untangled. Align the handlebars for height and correct position in relation to the bike and tighten with the bolts.

6. Install the seat post into the frame, adjust it to the correct height, and tighten the bolt securely with an Allen wrench.

7. Reconnect the brake to the fork crown or, if it is a V brake, by inserting the front brake cable noodle into the holder. Squeeze the brakes a few times to check they are working properly.

8. Insert the pedals in their correct positions (i.e., right and left). Forcing the wrong pedal into the crank may ruin it. Apply a few drops of lube to the pedal axles. Put in the pedal marked R, turn the axle clockwise by hand to start fitting it in the right crank arm. Turn the axle counterclockwise with the left pedal marked L. Finish tightening both pedals with a pedal wrench. Make sure they are tight.

9. Reattach the accessories (e.g., water bottle, lights, computer, bags, and panniers).

10. Inflate the tires. Take a quick test ride to make sure braking, gear changing, and bike fit are correct.

Tool Kit

The following are the recognized *must haves, shouldn't be without*, and *what do you mean you forgot* it items when you go out on a bike ride.

- Spare tube
- Hand-operated pump and air cartridge
- Patch kit and tire levers

If undertaking homebased repairs, remember that where and how you store your tools, their combined weight, and any body twisting while lifting, reaching, storing, or carrying them can impact your muscles and joints in the same way as manually handling the bicycle. Try to organize your workspace and tool storage area so that such problems are kept to a minimum. This is more important if you decide you would like to work in a bike repair shop or bike rental establishment as the number of times you will be likely to lift, carry, and store items will be considerably more.

For homebased bike maintenance you will also need:

- Spanners
- Allen keys
- Screwdrivers
- Pliers
- Foot pump
- Bike stand
- Degreaser
- Hand cleaner

Never use clamps on lightweight carbon composite or aluminium bicycle frames. Clamps such as those found on bicycle work stands and car racks can damage the frame.

- Grease
- Oil
- Polish
- Chain lubricant
- Cleaning cloths or rags

Bike maintenance can be split into three activities: checking/prevention, cleaning, and repair. How often you check, clean, and repair will depend on the type and frequency of your cycling. If you cycle short distances on good roads in clean areas on fine days only, then the need for cleaning and repair will be minimal. If you cycle mainly off-road in muddy areas or in all weather conditions on many different terrains, then you are more likely to check, clean, repair, and replace parts as they will wear out quicker.

Bike Safety Checks

Before setting off on any variation of bike, it is important to perform the pre-ride basic safety checks. These help ensure the bike is roadworthy and reduce the possibility of injury or bike breakdown. At the very beginning of your journey into the wonderful world of cycling, a bike mechanic would perform these checks for you. As you progress with cycling over time, however, whether you are an arm amputee or a leg amputee, it is worth trying to do these checks for yourself. It is a good test of balance, coordination, and grip.

Bike safety check courses are offered by bike shops or bike rental centers as well as cycling charities. Checks can be done in any order you choose, but it is worth sticking to a routine each time to ensure you haven't forgotten anything. It may be helpful to have someone assist with this at first until you get accustomed to it.

Bike Safety Checks for a Handcycle and Recumbent

Most of these safety checks are done by a mechanic, but before each ride, it is worth checking the following:

Brakes—Make sure the brake levers operate correctly and the brake pads are in contact with the wheel when activated.

Cables—Check that none are worn out or loose. Get them tightened or replaced if they are.

Wheels—Check that these are not bent out of shape and turn smoothly. They need to be trued or replaced if they are bent.

Tires—Check that they are inflated to a suitable tire pressure and there is nothing sticking in the tread, such as loose stones or glass, that might cause a puncture as you ride. If the tread is worn out, you will need to replace the tire.

Frame—Check over the frame for signs of damage or wear and tear. Do not ride the handcycle or recumbent if there are cracks in the framework.

Gears—Turn the front wheel and change gears up and down to make sure they are working correctly and that the chain does not come out of position.

Safety flag—Check that it is firmly attached, visible at height, and intact.

Mirrors—Adjust the angle and wipe mirrors so you can see out of them clearly.

Lights—Put lights on and check the distance that you can see them from. Make sure the light cover is not broken or cracked.

Bell—Test the bell to make sure it is working.

Loose spokes, bolts, and nuts should be tightened or replaced.

Bike Safety Checks for a Two-Wheeler, Tandem, or Tricycle.

Checking these items and recognizing when they need replacing or repairing comes with practice. It is always better to take a couple of minutes to do these checks rather than risk injury through bike part failure.

Handlebars—With front wheel between the legs, try to twist and then rotate handlebars. Tighten as needed to secure in a straight position. Bounce the bike a few inches off the ground. Loose nuts, bolts, and spokes will be revealed.

Saddle Position—Twist saddle. It should be tight. Make sure that there is enough seat post left in the frame (2 inches at least). The maximum extension line should not show.

Frame—Sit on the saddle. Do both feet touch the ground? *As a totally new learner* and non-cyclist, the saddle may be positioned low enough so your feet can both touch the ground comfortably. Once you have mastered the balance and control of the bicycle, the saddle height may be increased to the correct fit for your size. With someone holding the front wheel and handlebars, can your feet reach both pedals and rotate them backward comfortably?

Tires—Press down hard on the tires with your thumb. If they are easily pressed, they may need more air. Only inflate to the manufacturer recommended pressure. Check around the tire for any stones, sharp objects, or dirt. Check the tread.

Handgrips—Must cover the handlebar ends with no metal showing.

Frame/Fork—The frame should be sturdy, straight, and secure with no evidence of damage.

Chain—This should not hang loosely or be set too tight.

Reflectors and Lights—Check these are mounted securely on the bike and are visible from a distance.

Brakes—Take a look at the brake pads for signs of wear. Brake pads should only touch the rims when the brakes are activated. Press the brakes and push the bike forward. Do they feel secure, or does the bike still roll? If they are hand brakes, is there 1 inch of space between the handbrake lever and the handlebar?

Bolts/Quick release levers—Check that the bolts and quick release levers on the seat, seat post, handlebar stem, and axles are tight.

Axles—Check bearings for looseness by shaking the wheel from side to side.

Gears—Lift the front wheel off the ground and, while turning a pedal, try out all the gears to make sure that the chain remains on the sprockets when changing.

Spokes—Check and replace loose, bent, or broken spokes.

Wheels—Front wheel should be centered in the forks and not touching the brake blocks. Lift the bike up, spin the wheel, and look for wobbling or hopping as it passes the frame or brakes. Only allow for half a centimeter of wobble at the maximum. Repeat with the back wheel.

Bell—Attach a bell if cycling in high traffic areas.

Bike Safety Checks for a Unicycle

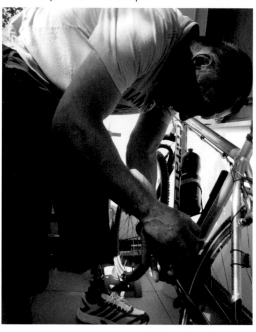

Check tire pressure and wheel, saddle position, and adjust the mirror.

Usually your pre-ride checks will be limited to the tire pressure, brakes, and lights. And unless you experience a fall or incident while out on your bike, you will limit your post-ride checks to tires, brakes, lights, and amount of dirt to be cleaned off. Once you have used your bike for a few rides, there are some post-ride checks to do in order to keep it roadworthy and well maintained. Manufacturers of new bikes recommend the following after every long or hard ride or after every 10 to 20 hours of riding:

- Squeeze the front brake and rock the bike forward and back. Everything feel solid?
- Lift the front wheel off the ground and swing it from side to side. Feel smooth?
- Grab one pedal and rock it toward and away from the center line of the bike; then do the same with the other pedal. Anything feel loose?
- Take a look at the brake pads. Starting to look worn or not hitting the wheel rim squarely?
- Carefully check the control cables and cable housings. Any kinks? Fraying?
- Squeeze each adjoining pair of spokes on either side of each wheel between your thumb and index finger. Do they all feel about the same?
- Check to make sure that parts and accessories are still secure, tighten any that are not.
- Check the frame, particularly in the area around the tube joints, the handlebars, the stem and the seat post for any deep scratches, cracks or discoloration.

Every 25 to 50 hard off-road hours of riding or 50 to 100 on road hours of riding, take your bike to your bike repair shop for a service. If you find it confusing to think in terms of the number of hours or miles of cycling you're doing, then try this alternative:

Every week check your tires, brakes, lights, handlebars, and seat are all in good working order and well fitted.

Every month check the tread on tires, the brake pads, the gear, and brake cables. Lubricate the chain.

Every year take your bike to an experienced mechanic for a thorough service.

Cleaning Your Bicycle

Manufacturers of new bikes recommend cleaning the bike and lightly oiling the chain after ever long or hard ride, if the bike has been exposed to water or grit, or at least after every 100 miles. Wipe off excess oil, and lubricate according to your climate.

If you only cycle very short distances irregularly in relatively clean areas, then you won't have to do much to the bike after the ride apart from give it a quick wipe with a damp cloth and dry it. Things can stick to your bike (and to you sometimes!)—mud, grime, insects, animal feces, and chewing gum. For more muddier, all weather cycling, if you are not up to cleaning your bike as soon as you come back, then it certainly should be done the next day. It takes very little effort and possibly a little bit of time, but it is a vital (though often neglected) part of getting to know your bike and to discover potential damage.

Tools: Water, brushes, cleaning products

1. Wash off the major areas with plain water to loosen any heavy dirt and grime. Start at the top and work down. Clean under the seat and wash accessories separately.
2. Use a cleaning pad or specialist brake cleaner to clean out all the debris from the rim.
3. Alternatively use a pressure washer on the tires and rims only, not on the rest of the bike.
4. Use a specialist bike cleaner or car shampoo to remove the worst bits of dirt.
5. Use a suitable brush to remove dirt from sprockets and chainrings. Dry the chain with a damp cloth and grease if necessary.
6. Wash off the cleaning fluids with water.
7. Use a water dispersing product to remove water away from the drivetrain and dry the bike with a clean cloth.

Changing a Wheel

To remove a wheel from the bicycle, mount the bike on a bike stand. Open the quick release system and pull the tire free. If you need to do this while out on a ride, remove the wheel and carefully lay the bike flat on the ground or stand it on the fork if it is not a windy day. There are more complicated wheel systems (bolt on wheels) that require tightening and loosening of nuts, bolts, and washers as well as alignment of cables and brakes when refitting the wheel. The quick release system is the easiest one to learn basic wheel removal on before progressing to the others.

1. Hook your thumb around the lever and pull hard.
2. Turn the lever a couple of times while holding the thumb nut if the wheel does not fall out.
3. To refit the wheel, pull the forks out a little to fit the wheel in between them. Tighten the wheel nut to steady the tire.
4. Push the quick release lever back toward the wheel to lock it in place. This may require some force. Try to point the lever to the back of the bike.
5. When removing and refitting the back wheel, take care to position it correctly past the gearing system. Put the highest gear on the rear before removing the wheel so it is easier to find the correct position when fixing it again.
6. Spin the wheels when they are back on the bike. They should move smoothly without too much noise. Lift the bike slightly and hit the wheel to see if it's really well fixed.
7. Inspect the rim for signs of cracks or other damage.
8. Inspect brake pads for signs of wear and clean them with a cleaning pad to remove any grit or debris.

Replacing Inner Tubes

1. Deflate the tire.
2. Push the tire beading in toward the center of the rim. Do this on both sides of the rim. Use tire levers if necessary to hook the tire over the rim at different positions along the wheel.
3. Reach into the tire and pull out the tube all the way around. Remember the valve—pull out the valve gently from the wheel area.
4. Check the wheel rim all the way around. Ensure spokes are not sticking out into the rim as they will cause a flat.
5. Tires are usually directional, so make sure the arrow is pointing in the direction of travel of the tire when you fit it on.
6. Lift one side of the tire over the wheel rim.
7. Inflate the new tube a little until it can just about hold its shape.
8. Push the inner tube over the rim. Take care when lining up the valve through the valve hole.
9. Tuck the tube into the tire all the way around.
10. Work the tire bead over the rim with your fingers and, if necessary, a tire lever. You may have to deflate the new tube completely again. Be careful if using a tire lever as you do not want to damage or puncture the tube.

11. Make sure the tire is well positioned all over the rim and inflate. It should be centralized over the rim properly, and the valve should be at right angles to the rim.
12. Inflate fully to the manufacturer's recommended tire pressure.

Repairing a Flat Tire

Bits of glass, nails, sharp plant materials, and small sharp stones can all puncture the material of the tire and inner tube as you cycle along. To fix this on the spot, either use a repair kit and follow its instructions or change the inner tube and pump the tire up. The flat can then be repaired at home or at a bike shop.

1. First remove the wheel and inner tube.
2. Locate the puncture in relation to the tire using the valve as an indicator. How far from the valve is the puncture? This can be done by pumping up the tube and listening for air escaping or putting the inflated tube in a bowl of water. Escaping air will cause bubbles to form. Finding the puncture requires some patience if it is a very small or slow leak. Stretch and compress the tube under the water to see if that shows where the puncture is any more easily.
3. Run your hands around the inside walls of the tire. Examine the tire tread. Look for cuts and sharp objects that might be stuck in the tire either on the inside or the outside. Remove anything that is found with pliers.
4. From a flat repair kit, apply a thin layer of puncture repair glue around the hole and let it dry somewhat.
5. Peel off the foil backing from the puncture repair patch and press down firmly onto the tube. Work from the center outward.
6. Stretch or fold over the patch to release the covering, and peel this off.
7. Reinflate the inner tube so it retains shape, and mount the tube and tre back onto the bike. Reinflate to manufacturer's recommended tire pressure.

Inflating Tires

1. Check the valve system (Presta or Schraeder) and put the corresponding adaptor onto the pump. Some pumps have adaptors that fit both valves. On Presta valves, remove the dust cap and undo the knurled nut. Press the valve with your finger. You will hear some air escape when you do that. Now fit the pump. On Schraeder valves, undo the cap and fit the pump on.
2. To fit the pump, push the adaptor onto the valve. Make sure it is aligned correctly. Steady with your hand and do not push the adaptor too far onto the valve.
3. Pump the tire until firm. Squeeze between thumb and finger to check. Inflate to the manufacturer's recommended tire pressure.
4. Undo adaptor, put all caps back on valves, and tighten them. Do not overtighten securing rings as this may lead to a flat. Refit dust caps.

Chain Care

There are two steps to chain care: degreasing and relubricating. It is important to keep the chain clean and lightly lubricated. There are different types of lubricant. A dry lubricant washes off in the rain easily so has to be reapplied more often, but doesn't pick up dirt. A wet lubricant requires more cleaning as it picks up some dirt, but it lubricates better in wet weather than dry or wax lubricants. Wax lubricants go on wet, they dry as a thick layer that doesn't pick up dirt, but they wash off quickly in wet weather.

Degreasing

1. Clamp the chain cleaner to the bottom of the chain and pedal backward to clean it. It can also be cleaned with a brush, a toothbrush, or damp cloth. (Or, apply the degreaser from the inside of the chain, spraying downward onto the lower chain. Turn the crank backward and cover the whole length of chain. Spray down onto the top of your rear cassette and chain wheels and leave to work for a couple of minutes.)
2. Rinse it all off with water.
3. Scrub the chain clean.
4. Dry the chain.

Relubricating

1. Hold a cloth under the lower chain.
2. Apply lubricant drop by drop, link by link (turn crank backward).
3. With a clean cloth, wipe along the chain, working the lubricant into all the joints, crevices, and pivot points.
4. Lubricate the brakes and gears (including levers) at their pivots. Be careful not to get brake pads greasy.

To make it easier to perform bike maintenance:

*   Don't over tighten bolts or pedal threads.
*   Don't leave the seat in the seat post for months at a time—it might seize or corrode.
*   Mark the seat height position on the tube before removing it.
*   Clean the area free of grit and dirt and grease the area well to keep it easy to adjust.

These are some of the very basic maintenance procedures that you will come across as a beginner. Most of the processes described in this chapter can be found as illustrations on the Internet if you require them. As your cycling experiences become more adventurous, you may find it useful to be able to do more complex maintenance procedures, such as changing brakes, removing and replacing chain sets and cranks, and changing headsets and forks, or you could just do as everyone else does and find a good bike shop that does it all for you!

From the Amputees

Joe Beimfohr, USA

I use bike shops when needed, but I have become a self-taught mechanic and can now replace all my cables and tune up my bike. It saves time and money, but most of the time we aren't anywhere near a bike shop when we need one, so it's good to know how to fix and maintain your equipment.

John Thraves, UK

I do my own repairs unless they are too difficult in which case the local bike shop helps me out. I change my tires and mend punctures, but the electrics I leave to the experts. So far I have had no problems. I think this is because I have chosen good quality suppliers. I am still assessing the latest crank drive on the ICE Sprint.

Mark Inglis, New Zealand

It is really important to be as independent as possible, so the first thing that a new cyclist should do is learn about their bike; bike shops often run courses. Don't be the "disabled" person expecting help! I do nearly all my own maintenance, but I have significant experience. If you are new, get your bike checked regularly at a bike shop—safety must be number 1. There should never be a reason why prosthesis is a hindrance to normal work like bike maintenance.

Nathan Smith, New Zealand

Mostly, I do my own bike maintenance, but I'll get the pros to help with bike setup and fixing my wheels.

Sara Tretola, Switzerland

The simple repairs I can do myself. Before the start of the competition season, I give my bike to a mechanic for a total check.

Victor Walther, Canada

I spent the first four years (1990-1994) researching products, buying bike magazines and picking bike shop owners brains (there was no Internet). I taught the industry about bike modifications for disabled riders. It is more important to know how to do the necessary modifications than being able to do them. Any competent bike shop mechanic can do the work. Other than pumping air in tires and lubing chain, I don't do the major repairs or modifications (I lost my dominant arm and have carpal tunnel syndrome in my hand and wrist).

Pre-Ride Checks

Basically, just like riding techniques, bike maintenance and pre-ride checklists are the same for everyone. Things like lubing the chain, checking tire pressure, wheels, handlebars, brakes, and cranks are pretty simple. However, things like adjusting gears and changing and repairing flat tires can be quite difficult, especially if you don't have a bike stand and proper tools.

Once your bike is setup, before each ride, you generally check the chain (to see if it needs lubricating; tire pressure; spin the wheels, checking for damage (you can see if the wheels are warped); and then pull the brakes, gently rocking the bike back and forth (this is to check the brakes, handlebars, and headset). Then it's a quick little spin in the parking lot to check out the gears and suspension, and away you go.

Further Reading

1. *Bike Repair Step by Step* by Rob Van der Plas (Van der Plaus Publications, 2002), www.vanderplas.net
2. *Mountain Bike Maintenance* by Mel Allwood (Carlton Books, Limited, 2004)
3. *Richards' Ultimate Bicycle Book* by Richard Ballantyne and Richard Grant (Dorling Kindersley, 1992)
4.   Manual handling legislation, UK: www.hse.gov.uk/msd/manualhandling.htm
5. How to clean your bike video: www.youtube.com/watch?v=hsk7Cj3HoEQ

Did You Know?

1. You can park 15 two-wheeler bicycles in a car parking space.
2. Maintaining a bike costs 20 times less than maintaining a car.
3. The first patent for a wrench (spanner) was granted to Solymon Merrick in 1835.
4. Allen wrench was originally a trademark of Allen Manufacturing, USA in 1943.
5. Half of all the parts of a typical bicycle are in the chain.
6. Recycling bicycles and bicycle parts is becoming more commonplace. Visit www.re-cycling.co.uk/.
7. Shimano and Campagnolo are two well-known names in the bike parts world.
8. A list of five of the best bicicyle repair books can be found here: bloombikeshop.com/articles/best-bike-repair-books.php.
9. The most expensive bike in the world in 2014, the Butterfly Trek Madone, was designed by Damian Hirst. It cost $500,000 and was coated with hundreds of real butterfly wings.
10. Re-cycle Bikes to Africa sends used bikes to Ghana, Kenya, Zambia, and South Africa. Visit www.re-cycle.org/about/history for more information.

Armin Köhli, Switzerland

Through Africa in 120 Days

The Tour d'Africa 2004 is over. Rob van der Geest won, Will Bonne came in second, and I was proudly third. My official time for the 11,268- kilometer (7,000 miles) race was 426 hours and 15 minutes. That means my average speed was 26.44 kilometers per hour! Add to that the transfers and the convoys in and out of towns. Because I had already lost my cycling computer in Sudan, I had to depend on other people's calculations. In total, I cycled 11,750 kilometres (7,300 miles) from Cairo to Cape Town in 99 race days. 35 of those days we cycled over stony, sandy, or muddy slopes and the rest was on tarmac roads. We went up and down, too—the total climbing must have been over 60,000 meters (37 miles).

Time off from prosthetics during the Tour d'Afrique.

My hamstring muscles were rock hard in the last two weeks, my brain was tired, and the bike desperately needed a full service. I had 18 punctures, 5 spokes had to be changed, the second chain and second cassette were broken, and the front suspension absolutely wrecked.

Even the back suspension had to be changed quite early on. The gears moved very badly, and the front gears took around 10 seconds to change because of some rubbing and crunching of cable and its mantle, casing, and cover. (We already changed it in Kenya as sand and dirt plays havoc with gear systems.) Two pairs of slick tires and two pairs of mountain bike tires were totally worn through, and one of the slick tires had already begun to decompose.

Ultimately, everything broke that could break. The travel bag ripped open and the aluminium suitcase lost its reinforced corners due to the thousand times it was shaken, tossed to and fro, and soaked from the rain. Sand penetrated everywhere. My prosthetic feet had begun to decompose at the back.

The last few days spent in South Africa were the most memorable. Dull, dreary desert turned into one of the most beautiful sights of the tour as we suddenly came through the morning mist to the Olifants River. To avoid the motorway, we even made a 50-kilometer (30 miles) detour over slopes and steep climbs and even some along spectacular scenery. Finally, we cycled along the coast to Cape Town. We didn't need to worry about obeying traffic rules this final time as the police gave us full right of way through Cape Town.

Translated excerpt from *Tour d'Afrique*, written by Armin Köhli May 16, 2004. The full transcript is available on www.tourdarmin.ch.

Chapter 12

Common Injuries
and Stump Care

Cycling is a relatively low-impact and safe activity. Physical activity in general puts stress and pressure on joints, tendons, muscles, ligaments, and other areas, including the heart and lungs. For amputees who follow more sedentary pastimes, taking up any physically demanding activity for the first time may, at some stage, result in injury. Many countries advise people to consult a physician before starting any exercise if you are not an active person or have existing medical conditions in case there is a need for precaution. To prevent injury as much as possible, ensure your body is well warmed up and stretched beforehand. Recovery and cool-down are important parts of injury prevention and should not be left out. Both aspects are described more fully in chapter 10.

If you are intending to cycle regularly alone, in group rides, at events, or even just with family on vacation, it is worth learning the basic principles of first aid to assist in case of accident or injury. Basic first aid is taught to the general public in many countries around the world. It is best to choose a provider approved by businesses and organizations within your country so you can use those skills in the workplace as well as while cycling. Well-known ones include:

Red Cross and Red Crescent	**www.redcross.int/**
Respond Right Asia	www.**respond-right-asia.com/**
First Aid Africa	www.**firstaidafrica.org/**
St John Ambulance	www.**sja.org.uk/sja/default.aspx**

Assisting in accidents or injuries will not only require first aid knowledge, but it will also, in some cases, require first aid equipment. Taking a first aid kit with you on a bike ride may be as normal as taking a pump, flat repair kit, and helmet. Always check the contents of the first aid kit to make sure it is suitable and complete. In some countries, a minimum contents list is available from first aid organizations that may help to form the basis of your kit. You may need to add certain things to this, depending on the cycling situation.

Injury Categories

For amputees, common injuries can be split into the following categories:

A. Stump
B. Bike setup and technique
C. Accidents and falls
D. Weather

A. Stump

Common stump issues that amputees experience are heat, perspiration (sweating), soreness, skin irritation, and back pain while wearing prosthetics all day for daily activities or while cycling.

Daily Stump Care Routine

The main aims of stump skin care are to prevent infection, maintain skin mobility, and decrease skin sensitivity of the amputated limb. It is best to develop a regular routine of skin inspection, desensitization, and skin hygiene to keep skin supple and mobile enough to continue wearing prosthetic limbs on a regular basis. To inspect the skin, a mirror may be necessary for areas that are difficult to see directly. Check stump areas every night for pressure sores, cuts, bruising, or swelling and treat straightaway. Look for ingrown hair follicles, protruding blood vessels or bleeding, blistering, weeping or tearing of the skin, and dry flaky areas.

Increasing the roughness of materials that you rub against the stich line and stump will help develop skin toughness (i.e., desensitization) and the ability to tolerate rough materials and pressures more readily. Good hygiene levels keep stump skin healthy. Wash stumps every night and dry well. Rub a good moisturizer cream into the stump, but do not rub into open wounds. Talcum powder can be used to absorb moisture during exercise. Clothing should be breathable to reduce overall sweating. Excessive dry stump skin can be counteracted by drinking plenty of water and using heavier moisturizing creams which may have to be prescribed by a medical practitioner.

Abrasion and Blistering

These result from sweating, rubbing, and shrinking experienced by the stump as you pedal. Sweating is a normal reaction to regulate body temperature. Within a prosthetic socket, the sweat has nowhere to go and pools around the skin of the stump in the liner. Prolonged sweat build-up causes the skin to soften, blister, and tear.

Skin that is about to blister will look red and feel warm. Fluid fills the space between the two layers of separated, blistered skin to reduce the impact of the continued rubbing. In more severe cases, the area can become infected. As you become fitter, sweating will decrease when doing the same amount of cycling, reducing the chances of blistering. If you then increase cycling intensity or distance or add in other physically demanding activities, sweating is more likely to occur again. Shrinking stump volume is a normal effect of exercise as the circulation goes to the parts of the body where it is most needed. When this happens, more socks are required to pad the liner and fill the extra space between the socket and stump to retain control over the prosthetic. To reduce the chance of blistering, you can remove your prosthetics and liners at regular intervals throughout the day during whatever activity you are involved in. Wipe off excess sweat around the stump and liner with a clean dry cloth or preferably with an antiseptic tissue. Let your stump skin "breathe" for a few minutes and then put the prosthetics back on.

If you are a very new amputee, this is more likely to be necessary for the first couple of years, until your body fully adapts to your activity levels with prosthetics, or you no longer sweat as much. If you have been an amputee and cyclist for longer, you may only need to do this once a day, if at all. Drink plenty of water to replace the fluids you are losing because of sweating. Some amputees find applying antiperspirants on their stumps useful. These are available in spray, roll-on, or lotion form. Reapplication may be required throughout the day. It is important to wash the stump at the end of the day to allow the skin to breathe and prevent blocked pores or infection. Building up all activity levels gradually over time will help reduce the risk of blistering. Blister pads and dressings with padding inside them are useful to alleviate pressure around a blistered area while using prosthetics, but the best treatment is keeping the area open to the air and letting it heal completely.

Bruising and Swelling

If the skin is soft with sweat and you put further pressure on the stumps, there is a risk of soft-tissue injury around the area which could result in bruising or swelling.

Soft-tissue injury is treated by rest, ice, compression, and elevation (RICE):

Rest—Remove the prosthetic limb and liner and clean with antiseptic or antibacterial soap and water.

Ice—Cool the area down by pressing an ice pack on it for 10- to 15-minute intervals for an hour or two. Place the ice pack in cloth or other material to prevent it from damaging the skin through direct contact.

Compression—Bandage the area firmly to reduce further swelling.

Elevation—Rest the limb slightly higher than heart level to encourage blood flow away from the bruised area and to further reduce swelling.

It may take some weeks to heal depending on the extremity of the stump, especially if there is poor blood flow to the area. This may require some prosthesis-free time while the healing takes place. Restart the activity as soon as the stump is fully healed to help the skin adjust to the level of pressure around those areas over time.

Soreness and Redness

Redness, scarring, and lines develop around the top of the prosthetic where the liner rubs against the skin, where the top of the prosthetic socket digs into the skin, and where there is friction during movement. This is normal when first getting used to the prosthetics as the skin has not had a chance to toughen up. In hot weather and with prolonged liner and prosthetics wear throughout the day, the red areas could react with sweat build-up, blister, or tear the skin.

A good moisturizing cream should be applied to the area, and stumps should be kept prosthetic free for short periods of time throughout the day to help prevent these. Things that have been tried by cyclists include chamois butter, lanolin, petroleum jelly, glycerin, tea tree oil, and body glide. (The product may be marketed as a "sitting cream" for cycling, containing soothing ingredients to prevent soreness and infection.) Reapplication is necessary over the course of the day if cycling long distances.

Stitch-Line Issues

Depending on its position, sweating and high levels of activity can cause the skin around the stitch line to separate. This area will be prone to blistering and tearing if left untreated.

Prevention includes drinking plenty of fluids, using lots of good moisturizer around the stitch line, and monitoring your activity levels on a regular basis. Reorganize the way you do things if necessary. Keep activity levels high, but alter the way you do them to reduce sweating. Treatment may involve surgical reshaping of the stump around the stitch line. This requires the amputee to keep prosthesis-free for a few weeks afterward.

Stump Swelling

The stump may swell up after a lot of activity to such an extent that the prosthetic limb does not fit. This may be due to the cycling intensity, the return of higher levels of blood flow, and fluid circulation to the limb area after exercise or hormonal changes in the body. Keep the prosthetics off, rest, elevate the stump, and exercise it gently after resting. Keep the stump level (do not hang it downward as more fluid will pool around the area) and drink plenty of fluids. A compression sock may encourage fluid to flow back toward the heart.

Back Pain and Spine Issues

Spine injuries (e.g., scoliosis) are common in amputees due to posture imbalance because of the weight of the prostheses and altered walking techniques that rely on intact limbs and muscles rather than putting body weight or pressure through the stump. Incorporating appropriate rest periods during daily activities; using good sitting, walking, lifting, and carrying techniques; and strengthening the back and core stomach muscles to improve posture with prosthetics use will reduce the occurrence of such injury.

Contractures

These are the restrictions of movement that amputees experience due to shortening or structural changes in the connective tissues of the body. The joint may be severely restricted or freeze in one position. These are problematic as they may not be able to wear the prosthetic limb due to fatigue and pain. Steps taken may be shorter than normal due to restriction of joint movement, and trunk twisting may occur, resulting in back pain. Prevention is through activities such as stretching and cycling. At least five to six hours of physical activity per day is required to maintain normal joint movement. Treatment involves ultrasounds and casts to stretch out the joint, but results are limited. Support devices can be used but do not improve the range of movement to any great extent.

B. Bike Setup and Technique

Overuse injuries are common among all cyclists as most have experienced at least one or more injury. Amputees, in general, tend to overuse their intact limbs which may lead to strains and fractures of those areas. The majority of injuries tend to be relatively minor and can be treated easily with a little first aid. The repetitive movements of the arms and legs in cycling, especially when undertaken regularly or over long distances, can cause discomfort or injury. Areas of the body susceptible to injury in handcycling include hands, wrists, shoulders, elbows, and upper back. For other types of cycling, the neck, shoulder, elbow, knee, lower back, buttocks, and hips are susceptible. In most cases, stop cycling for a little while until recovery has taken place. Ease back into it gently and then build up gradually to your normal cycling capacity to reduce the risk of further injuries. During the first three days following an injury, avoid heat, alcohol, and high-impact exercise and do not massage the area.

Lower-Back Pain

It is important to build up strength in the back and core stomach muscles to help support the upper body as you cycle. Cycling involves sitting in a particular position for extended periods of time which may place pressure on the spine. Lower-back pain is typically seen in those who adopt the aerodynamic performance cycling position. Bend more from the hips to achieve aerodynamic positioning rather than just the spine and check saddle height. If the saddle is too high, it can make your pelvis swing from side to side, increasing the strain on your back.

Alternate from the aerodynamic to sitting upright position during a cycling session to relieve tension in the spine. Ensure handlebars are not too far away, causing you to over stretch. The bike frame should not be either too small or too big.

Most causes of low back pain are muscle, ligament, or joint related. A thorough medical consultation is recommended if back pain is frequent or severe. Symptoms include tenderness, spasm, stiffness, numbness, leg muscle weakness, or pain. Treatment of back pain includes rest, acupuncture, TENS, massage, back braces, or painkillers. TENS machines use electric currents to stimulate nerves that are under the skin. TENS stands for transcutaneous electrical nerve stimulation. They are used for mild pain relief instead of medication or alongside some medication. Electrodes are placed on the skin, and different strengths of electric current are applied to the area to reset the muscle contraction and reduce pain.

Acupuncture is a Chinese healing remedy using fine, sterile, single-use needles at specific points along the body. There are 12 major energy pathways in the body, and if there is a blockage in one of them, pain and illness result. The needles redirect the flow of energy to relieve the pain. It is used for all types of muscle and joint pain, including neck, shoulder, elbow, hand and wrist, back, hip, leg, and knee pain.

This should be followed by improving muscle strength and endurance as well as balance and gait exercises once the pain and inflammation have healed. Exercises can also be prescribed for your lower back and pelvis. Improving your deep abdominal core muscle strength will improve your stability and resistance to back pain.

Iliotibial Band (ITB) Syndrome
This is the result of a number of factors:
- Inadequate warm-up
- Poor technique and posture
- Increased distance
- Sprinting too quickly
- Weak hip and gluteal muscles
- Repeatedly bending and straightening the knee while pedaling

Knee problems are the most common injuries reported by cyclists. The cartilage under the knee cap may become irritated, or the knee cap may be misaligned and rub against one side of the knee joint, causing pain. Forward position of the knee and leaning forward during cycling, especially at high intensity, may increase your risk of ITB syndrome. Healing time varies from 2 to 4 weeks for mild symptoms, 7 to 8 weeks for average symptoms, and 9 to 14 weeks if symptoms are severe. Continued cycling with an ITB injury can make it chronic.

To prevent this, the saddle must be set up so the knee is not pushed forward or backward too far during the pedaling motion. The saddle should be high enough to get full leg extension. If it is too low, then a larger knee flexion angle is required which may lead to knee overuse injury. There should be approximately a 25- to 30-degree bend in the knee at the lowest pedal position. At the highest pedal position, the knee should not be bent less than 70 degrees. A compression bandage or sports tape can support the knee while cycling.

For arm amputees: If using cleats, ensure the shoe can rotate slightly to improve force transfer from the legs to the pedals and prevent knee injury. The pedaling technique you use should activate your hamstrings, hip flexors, and lower-leg muscles to prevent excess force on the knee from just using the quadriceps muscles alone. Leg amputees require shoes that do not rotate in cleats as you can lose stability, especially on the prosthetic side.

Good pedaling technique using all remaining leg muscles is essential to prevent knee injury. If the cranks are too long, the knee bends too much on the upstroke, and this can cause pain or injury. Using the correct gears for the type of cycling you are doing will prevent you from overworking the legs. The muscles around the knees need to be strengthened with resistance exercises. If cycling in cold weather, cover your knees and keep them warm.

Tendonitis

Tendonitis of the knee is inflammation of the tendon where it meets the bone under the kneecap. This is usually the result of a sudden twist or an attempt to break a fall. Swelling, redness, bruising, and pain may be present. Treatment is RICE (rest, ice, compression, and elevation) with remobilization exercises once the swelling has gone down. It can take up to six weeks or longer to heal and may recur if exercise is started too early in the recovery period.

Foot Numbness, or Recumbent Foot

Foot numbness occurs when the feet have been in one position for a long time without movement as in handcycling, for those using recumbent bikes, or if shoes do not fit properly in other forms of cycling. If the cleats are too far forward, there is more pressure on the ball of the foot, and this causes numbness if kept that way for a long time. Cycling at high intensity can cause more pressure to be put on the foot. Cycling shoes should not be too tight.

To treat foot numbness, get off the bike and walk around for a while, change your pedal stroke to spinnning or push pedaling, change your cleat position, or wear better fitting cycling shoes with additional insoles in them. If the foot is arched significantly during pedaling, move the seat nearer to the pedals. If the numbness is caused from nerve compression in the hip, move the angle of the seat to shift the pressure to other areas of the body. Changing pedaling technique by applying pressure to the ball of the foot for part of the pedal rotation can help reduce the numbness. Loosen shoes and straps if they are too tight, but not so loose that they rub and cause blisters.

Wrist Numbness

Symptoms of wrist numbness include pins and needles, pain, and swelling. It is caused by gripping the handlebars tightly for long periods of time which causes pressure in the nerves, ligaments, and tendons of the hand. Poor upper-body posture, having the saddle angle too low at the front, or bending the wrist at the handlebars rather than keeping them in a position where the hand and forearm are aligned can result in the nerves and blood vessels becoming trapped in the wrist area. The effects may sometimes feel worse at night. To prevent this, avoid too much padding on the handlebars and holding the handlebars too tightly as you cycle. Change the position of your hands on the handlebars regularly if cycling for long periods of time.

Treatment includes shaking the wrist, resting the hands, wearing a night wrist splint, and physiotherapy. Recovery exercises focus on grip, pinch, wrist rotation, hand range of movement, and forearm strength. Therapies to try include ultrasound, acupuncture, TENS machines, and massage.

Saddle Numbness and Soreness

Saddle-related discomfort in the groin, upper leg, or bottom is due to friction against the saddle and the rider's weight being carried on the soft tissues between the sit bones. Blood flow to the area is reduced due to the pressure on the blood vessels and tissues, resulting in numbness, tingling, and possible sexual dysfunction. Symptoms can last a few days if severe. Sitting in one constant position for long periods of time can also cause saddle soreness.

Treatment and prevention of saddle numbness include using an ice pack for around 10 minutes following a bike ride and adjusting the saddle padding, width, length, or position on the bicycle to allow redistribution of pressure around the sitting area more evenly. Altering sitting position or standing up out of the saddle for brief periods while cycling all reduce the occurrence of saddle numbness. Cycle regularly to build up resistance to saddle soreness.

Prior to cycling, some people apply corn flour or corn starch to the sitting areas of their body to absorb sweat. Other options include wearing well-padded cycling shorts while riding and applying chamois, petroleum jelly, shea butter, or zinc oxide creams around the sitting area of the body to act as a barrier to friction. Keep these body areas as clean as possible before and after a ride. If cycling long distances, change shorts along the way to reduce chance of infection or chafing.

Chafing is damage to the skin caused by friction. It is best not to keep cycling if the chafed area has not been treated as it can get worse quickly. After cycling, change out of cycling shorts and wash and dry them well. Apply antiseptic cream to any sores and cover with padded dressings to keep the pressure off them. Choose a dressing that has a ring cut out of it for the sore.

Infections such as crotchitis can be experienced by women when chafing of the genital area is combined with moisture, warmth, and poor or over zealous hygiene. This results in irritation and inflammation of the vaginal area with redness, itching, and pain. After cycling, it is important to change out of cycling clothes and clean the area well. Wear breathable fabric, especially breathable underwear, and loose-fitting trousers or dresses to allow enough air into the area. If foul-smelling discharge is present in those areas (in men or women), bacterial or yeast infection may be present. Medical advice should be sought with regard to the use of appropriate antibiotic or antifungal treatment for such conditions.

Neck Pain

Curving of the upper back and hinging at the neck causes compression and results in pain felt in the neck, head, upper back, and shoulders. This could lead to numbness and tingling in the arms. To prevent this, bend forward from the hips rather than the upper back. Keep the neck long and aligned with the line of the back. Neck exercises and spine exercises are useful strengthening tools for these areas. Relax your upper body while cycling. Keep the elbows slightly bent to improve shock absorption and reduce neck strain. Hook your index and middle fingers over the front of the brakes to reduce the pressure going through your arms and fingers. Change hand positions regularly, shake out your arms, and roll your neck and shoulders. Bike fit adjustments (e.g., saddle position) may need to be made if you have to crane your neck to see while leaning forward. If your helmet is too far forward on your head, you could be tilting your neck back to help you see. Adjust your helmet accordingly. Make sure your sunglasses are not too far down your nose so that you have to tilt your head and neck to see clearly.

C. Accidents and Falls (Trauma)

The majority of injuries following an accident or fall tend to be cuts, bruises, scrapes, and swelling. Ensure you have had a tetanus injection and booster within the last 10 years to reduce infection risk. In fast cycling, a collision increases the risk of breaking collar, wrist, or other bones. The best prevention is to try not to fall, but if you do, use the basic principles of first aid to attend to the injury. Falling techniques are described in chapter 7.

Basic Treatment of Surface Wounds

Examine the wound. If it is a shallow, surface wound, remove any large foreign materials around it, such as pebbles or sticks. Be careful when removing these from inside the wound as it will increase the amount of bleeding. Clean the area with lots of water and a very mild soap. Sterile salt water or sterile swabs are available from pharmacies in many countries. These are good to have in a first aid kit if cycling where there is lack of ordinary clean water en route.

Thorough wound cleaning may be painful, but is necessary to prevent infection. A small dressing may be sufficient to cover it if the ride is not going to take long. For longer endurance rides where medical assistance may not be readily available, ensure your first aid kit contains antibiotic creams and a range of dressings. Cover the wound with a very thin layer of antibiotic cream or ointment using a clean swab. Apply a clear, breathable adhesive dressing. If the cyclist is allergic to adhesives, use a bandage to secure the dressing in place. Check the wound and change the dressing daily if levels of physical activity, exposure to dirt and dust, or sweating are likely to be high. If dark yellow, green, or brown pus develops with fever and pain, seek medical advice. Keep the wound covered until full healing has occurred and protect the area with high SPF sunscreen.

If the wound is very deep with lots of bleeding, put pressure on the wound area to reduce the bleeding (bandage it tightly if necessary), raise the affected area above chest height, and seek medical assistance.

Insect Bites and Stings

These are common in the summer and can result in accidents, falls, or allergic reactions. If something flies into your helmet, stop and remove it. If it stings you, remove the stinger from your skin, apply an ice pack, and check for the development of any allergic reactions.

If you know you are allergic to stings, carry a sting kit with your general first aid kit that includes an EpiPen and antihistamines. Make sure you know how to use it, and if someone else is with you, show them what to do and how. Allergic reactions do not take long to occur and can be fatal if not treated immediately.

Fractures

The arms and hands are often used to break a fall from a bicycle, so wrist, elbow, and collarbone fractures are common. Hip fractures are also common, but spine fractures are less so. A fracture is a broken bone. The bone may stick out from the skin, or the broken area may look deformed. There is a lot of pain, and bleeding may be severe. There are a few scenarios to consider. The first is when you might be the rider and have fractured some part of your body. The second is when you are nearby when such an injury has occurred to someone else.

If you think you have fractured a part of your body and are still conscious and in pain, request help from others and call emergency services straight away. If you are alone, try to stop any bleeding if you can reach your first aid kit without moving or damaging the injured area further. Bandage the area firmly as described next to stop the broken limb from moving around or causing more pain. Be aware that the pain may be severe and send you into shock, so try to get someone to help you quickly.

If you suspect a fracture in someone else, call emergency services immediately as hospital treatment will be required. Do not move the injured person. If you are on a main road, ask for help to redirect traffic around the injured person. First stop the bleeding by applying pressure to the wound and bandaging firmly. Use a clean cloth or sterile bandage, or if you do not have a first aid kit with you, improvise by using some clean clothing. Elevate and immobilize the injured area with padding and bandaging to prevent unnecessary jarring and pain. Apply ice packs for pain relief, and keep the injured person warm by covering with coats and jackets. If they feel faint or dizzy, lay them flat onto the ground and, if possible, raise their legs to prevent them from going into shock. If they fall unconscious, check that their airways are clear and they are breathing. If they stop breathing, start chest compressions and resuscitation breaths until help arrives.

Muscle Cramps

This is a contraction of the muscle that doesn't go back on its own. It is painful and can be relieved by massaging the area or stretching and relaxing the area. Cramps and spasms can happen in any area of muscle. The back or front of the thighs, back of the lower legs, arms, hands, and abdomen are areas where cyclists can experience cramping. In extreme cases, whole-body cramps can occur. Muscles that are cramped or spasm feel very hard. Exercising in extreme heat, dehydration, and muscle fatigue are common causes of such cramps. Drinking electrolyte-containing fluids before cycling can help prevent muscle cramping. Having high levels of fluid intake generally will prevent dehydration from causing muscle cramps, especially in hot climates, where electrolyte replacement salts, such as magnesium or potassium, should be drunk during or after intense long endurance training. When a cramp is experienced, stop the activity, stretch, and massage the area until the cramp stops. Stretch regularly after exercise and warm up correctly before exercise.

Sprains

The joint between the collarbone and shoulder blade can be sprained during a fall or by going through potholes at speed. Spraining this area will result in bruising, swelling, pain on lifting the arms upward, or loss of shoulder range of movement. Resting the area will reduce the pain after a few days. Full healing of the ligament takes up to six weeks. Using a sling, shoulder brace, or tape will help prevent further damage as it is important not to overuse it while it is healing.

Once the area has healed sufficiently, it is important to remobilize and strengthen the shoulder area. Exercises should start off being gentle and then gradually building in intensity to prevent the chance of reinjury. Severe cases may require joint surgery and post-operative rehabilitation.

Strains

These are normally treated by the RICE method described earlier in this chapter. The three most common strains are described here.

Hamstring

This is the area along the back of the leg consisting of three muscles that are activated when the leg bends at the knee. Hamstring strength can be improved by appropriate exercise. If increasing the training load, ease into it gently. If hamstrings are overstretched, they can be torn or strained. Pain, bruising, and tenderness can be felt around the area as well as heat and swelling.

Calf Muscle

A calf strain is pain in the lower part of the leg that feels as if it has popped. There is pain, swelling and bruising, and difficulty walking. Minor calf strains take between two to four weeks to heal fully. The most severe can take up to three to four months and require medical attention. The calf needs to be non-weight-bearing at this stage, so you may need to use crutches or a wheelchair for a few days. It takes six weeks for a torn muscle to reattach itself. During this time, appropriate therapeutic rehabilitation should be undertaken. Reinjury can be prevented if recovery and return to the sport are gradual.

Gluteal Tendinopathy

Gluteal tendons connect the gluteal muscles to your hip bone. These tendons can become inflamed due to poor hip and gluteal muscle control from physical deconditioning or inactivity. This may occur when you first start cycling as these muscles will not be sufficiently prepared for such activity. Hip–pelvis instability can result. Symptoms include hip pain, tenderness, redness, warmth, muscle stiffness, and loss of strength in hip area. It may be worse at night or first thing in the morning. The pain may feel worst when you lie on your affected hip. Gentle hip range of motion exercises and stretching will help return the area to normal activity. Hip stabilization and core exercises to improve hip muscle control are vital to prevent reinjury. Recovery can vary between weeks and months, and in severe cases, surgical intervention may be required.

Concussion

Accidents and crashes at speed can result in head injury, and repeat head injuries can cause brain damage (even when wearing a helmet). Concussion is a head injury in which the brain is shaken about in the skull. The person can be conscious or unconscious when they suffer this injury. If conscious, the person will appear confused, disorientated, have unequal sized pupils, or memory loss. Symptoms may appear later on rather than immediately after the accident. Depression usually follows concussion, and thinking, memory, and attention deficiencies are seen.

If you suspect concussion after an accident or fall, refer the cyclist to a hospital or clinic. Do not allow them to cycle there. If the person is unconscious, phone for the emergency services immediately. Be prepared to attempt chest compressions and resuscitation breaths if the cyclist stops breathing.

D. Weather

There are two common weather-related situations that cyclists experience which require medical or first aid treatment.

Hypothermia

This is a condition in which the body temperature drops to extremely low levels, often seen in cyclists who ride in very cold weather. There are five stages of severity of hypothermia. If symptoms become worse, there is an increased risk of accidents. Symptoms of hypothermia are uncontrolled shivering for a long time; pale, cold skin; blue color around lips; and numbness in feet, hands, and face. In these early stages of hypothermia, treat by getting the cyclist out of wet weather and clothing. Put them in a dry, warm environment with lots of dry, warm clothes. Give them warm drinks, and after about an hour, they should have a more normal body temperature. If symptoms get worse (e.g., they become unconscious or their eyes glaze over), call emergency services and get them to hospital. Be prepared to attempt chest compressions and rescucitation breaths if the cyclist stops breathing.

Hyperthermia and Dehydration

Basic levels of dehydration are treated by replacing body fluids either by drinking more or in a medical facility with electrolyte infusions. Hyperthermia is a condition in which dehydration causes the body temperature to rise too much. There are three stages where sweating, headache, confusion, balance difficulties, shallow breathing, and weak pulse lead to more serious symptoms. The cyclist must get out of the hot environment, especially out of direct sun. If there is air conditioning in a building or a fan available, that will help cool them quickly. Loosen clothing, take off the helmet, and cool down by throwing lots of cold water on the skin, especially neck, back, and legs. Once they are cooler and more alert (may take around 30 minutes or longer), give them very small amounts to drink. They may not be able to keep the fluids down and may be sick if you give these to them too quickly or in too large of volume. If the symptoms get worse, then call emergency services and get them to the hospital. Be prepared to attempt chest compressions and resuscitation breaths if the cyclist stops breathing.

From the Amputees

Armin Köhli, Switzerland

I've experienced all-over body cramps twice so far. They were probably caused by a combination of riding too fast for too long in very hot weather, not drinking enough, and sweating too much without replacing the minerals. It was completely impossible to move any part of the body except my mouth and eyebrows. The treatment was complete rest for at least an hour and massage by a physiotherapist when it happened at an ultra-distance race.

Esneider Muñoz Marín, Columbia

My collarbone was broken, and I've had lots of injuries on my body. I've had blisters—injuries by the continuous rubbing—and calluses (rare). I've done some little adjustments to my prosthesis to improve my skin.

Habib Jan, Afghanistan

Once, I was going to the city to buy things for the family. On the way, I had an accident with a car. I injured my left leg as I fell, but the wounds were not serious, and I recovered in a day.

Joe Beimfohr, USA

Since I bear all of my weight on my one residual limb, I need to pad my knee so I can stay in that position for long rides. I wear a volleyball knee pad and use a custom seat cushion. I have a hip disarticulation on my right side. I don't sit level like most people, so I need to raise my right side.

Jon Pini, UK

You are more likely to get blistering and soft-tissue injuries on lower-limb than on upper-limb amputees. The upper limb is really just there for balance, steering, and a bit of support whereas the legs are doing a lot of the work in cycling. You can get bruising as well due to the repetitive motion if you are hitting the distal part of the tibia as you pedal.

With lower-limb amputees who cycle, they take things like that in their stride. They might go weeks or months without any problem, and then suddenly they might have an infection that causes swelling. With a lot of amputees, they will have a daily routine. They will do things such as have the limb on for certain amounts of the day, or they will do a certain amount of tasks in that time. If they go above and beyond those hours or above and beyond those tasks, that is when they tend to find issues can occur on the stump. It's almost like the stump gets used to a timeframe and a certain amount of pounding during the day, and if you have to go above and beyond that, it has to be slow and steady. This allows the residual limb to build up the extra tolerance to that stress or strain.

When cycling with friends and family, they are likely to go at your pace, whereas when taking part in a charity event or race, you will have to go at the pace set by others which can mean you disregard the damage to your stump and keep going at any cost. Determination takes over. It's human nature; even with marathon runners who get blisters, they still carry on running. It's the same with amputees. They've got blisters and bruising, but they will stick with it and do it. For a few days afterward, they might not be able to put the leg on or they might only be able to do very limited things on the leg, but that clears after a healing period.

The more intense the activity, the more likely you are going to have issues with the stump. Weather can be a big thing as well. If you have hot, humid weather, it can be a nightmare just doing daily tasks, let alone doing something above and beyond like cycling long distances. Build up activity levels gradually so tolerance improves. If things do happen, get it sorted and get back on the bike, and away you go again.

Kiera Roche, UK

We reached a road which had more potholes than a lawn at a moles' picnic. Cathy and Mike were riding in front of me on an uphill stretch when Cathy stopped suddenly to take a photograph. Mike pulled across my path to join Cathy which left me no option than to go head first into a pothole the size of a swimming pool. Shame it wasn't full of water to cushion the blow. I knew before I hit it that I was coming off because my road bike has a rigid frame and my artificial foot is attached to the pedal with SPD clips, so I can't unclip my foot to get out of danger. A small inconvenience—unless you are crashing headfirst into a pothole the size of a pool.

Mike said he saw it in slow motion but couldn't get to me on time. I landed on my elbow, which has a metal pin in the humorous shaft which was a tad painful, to say the least; however, I was more concerned with my beautiful new bike, and my immediate reaction was to check her for scratches. It wasn't until Doc pointed out that I was bleeding quite heavily from a puncture wound in my arm that I noticed I had a bruise, which looked more like a plum, from an internal bleed. It actually looked a lot worse than it was, and once Doc had patched me up and given me some painkillers, I was ready to go. Doc suggested that I take a rest, but I knew that if I didn't get straight back on, I might not get back on at all, and I had done a lot of training and come a long way to complete this challenge.

Mark Inglis, New Zealand

I recently went over the handlebars of the mountain bike on a downhill, knocked myself out momentarily, and broke my shoulder in several places. But the big problem was one of the legs had come off. (It was a very hot day, so sweat in the socket allowed the leg to come off.) I had to call a friend on my cell—not for an ambulance for my shoulder, but to help me put my leg back on. I could then walk out to get help for my shoulder!

Another time just 10 days before the Paralympics, while training, I had a major road crash and ended up sitting in the middle of the road with no legs on (they were still attached to the bike), lots of skin missing, and my bike hanging up in a fence 20 meters (66 feet) away!

Mark Ormrod, UK

For the first week of handcycling around the UK, I had to keep taking my arm off and pop pus-filled blisters, fill them with cream, put plasters all over them, and just keep going. There was lots of sweating and blistering for the first week, and then it stopped. My skin became tougher, and the scar line became tougher, and I didn't get any after that. I did get soreness, obviously, and very dirty. When mud goes down your shirt, it rubs as you're cycling and creates chafing and rashes, but nothing else major happened en route.

Mirsad Tokić, Croatia

In the beginning, I used an everyday prosthesis for cycling. It was good enough for the easy rides. But when I tried to push harder and longer, it hurt me in the back of the knee. The sweaty liner was pushed by the high edge of the prosthesis into my skin, causing an unusual wound— a horizontal line of red skin like a whiplash. Also, any kind of sudden jump from the bike caused spasms and pain in my left leg. Otherwise, no real trauma, just the usual scratches on the hands and legs.

Mona Krayem, Germany

In the very beginning, after cycling for a few days, I had little sore spots in the hollows of my knees, but quite soon I figured out that I just needed my prosthetics to be shortened in the back so I would have more mobility. I guess every amputee has to see in which way their prosthetics have to be adapted. Besides that, I didn't have any problems with my stumps because of cycling, yet I would say I still have quite sensitive stumps.

Nezir Lupcevic, Bosnia and Herzogovina

In 1973, Nezir got a prosthesis for his amputated right arm, but he is not using it as it causes problems (e.g., blisters) while cycling. On several occasions, he has fallen down, but he has learned to not fall on his stump, but rather on his left-hand side. He injured his stump on several occasions while working but without any major consequences. Once injured, he does not put unnecessary pressure on his stump and does not cycle at all until it is cleared up.

Nathan Smith, New Zealand

I used to get a lot of blisters around the top of my stump, but I got the socket adjusted, so that minimized them. When I have a big training week, I often develop a blister at the rear of the base of my stump which is from pushing on the pedal. Over time, the build-up of sweat causes some slippage in the silicon liner. To minimize this, I try and use the tightest liner I can tolerate and apply aluminium-based antiperspirant. This site is also prone to fungal and bacterial infections to which I apply appropriate creams. If I need to ride and a blister is bothering me, I find a gauze padding with a good covering of strapping tape (remember to shave first) will prevent further rubbing. Usually the pain is gone by the end of the warm-up.

Rajesh Durbal, USA

I have sweating issues, and those are overcome by wearing a sheath inside my liner. I also use high vacuum, which helps vacuum the sweat out the socket, and diaper rash ointment to help protect and prevent skin breakdown.

Robert Bailey, USA

Louisiana is Deep South. A normal afternoon reaches 97 °F (36 °C) and is very, very humid. The only reason Louisiana doesn't stay over 100°F (38 °C) is it is too humid to allow it. It would take too much heat to raise the temperature that high. One of the joys of living on the Gulf of Mexico!

One thing about exercising in prosthetics is your legs sweat. In the first years of riding a trike, I would have to stop and empty a cup of sweat from each liner. At 2010 RAGBRAI, I tore blisters all over my legs, but I kept going. In 2011, I suffered severe heat rash. I made sure I kept riding in the heat. My normal training was two hours plus just after noon. It worked. Soon I could take on anything. In my mind, I thought of the hills of Iowa. It made me push harder. You can use antiperspirant; I use Mitchum Solid Unscented on my stump. Put it on after you shower and the legs are still damp. You do have to be careful. Real heat can produce a heat rash if all your pores are blocked.

Srdjan Jeremic, Bosnia and Herzogovina

Srdjan has no major problems while cycling caused by the disability. These problems are not long term and usually go away during breaks he makes throughout the year. He enjoys cycling, but sometimes he has blisters and small callosities on his right fist and left elbow when cycling for a long time. When that happens, Srdjan must take a break until blisters and callosities heal. Over the years, Srdjan had several falls, but fortunately without any major injuries of his stump. As it was mainly small cuts and bruises, it healed very quickly (within 2 weeks maximum), but he had to take a break from cycling to fully recover.

Victor Walther, Canada

Most of the riding skills and techniques are the same for amputees, as are the consequences. While I was in training and racing I had 3 AC joint separations (where the collarbone meets the highest point of the shoulder blade), I tore my right deltoid (shoulder) muscle twice, cracked ribs several times, and ruptured my stomach liner. During one race, I crashed so hard I cracked ribs, had my prosthetic arm come halfway off, and twisted my seat and handlebar, and I still managed to straighten things out and finish the race (in last place). The following year, I won the race! As for twisting the prosthetic arm or stump, the only time that happens is when you crash.

Funny Things Happen on Bikes!

In August 2006, I had just started to ride a bike again after the accident. It was typical weather here, 95 °F (35 °C) and very humid. I had a package to mail, so I thought I would ride to a store a short way up the road that had mailboxes and was a drop-off for packages. I strapped the package to my rack, and off I went. A mile later, I reached the main road. It was very busy, and I waited 10 minutes or more in the heat to get my opening to cross the road. Finally I pushed off—and left my right leg on the road! It had been so full of sweat that it slid right off. I then had one of those horrible moments when I knew I was going down and nothing could stop it (including a particularly strong curse). Fortunately, I went down in a spot that was not in traffic. A nurse and her son saw me go down and helped gather me up.

Robert Bailey, USA

Further Reading

1. *First Aid Manual, 10th Edition* by St John Ambulance, St Andrew's First Aid and British Red Cross (Dorling Kindersley, 2014)
2. First aid books: giftshop.redcross.org.uk/category/first-aid-books
3. Avoiding injury: totalwomenscycling.com/fitness/avoiding-injury-strength-training-for-cyclists-18744/2/#Z1vIRJQU3B3OwP7C.97
4. How to solve saddle sores: www.roadbikerider.com/injuries/how-solve-saddle-sores
5. Overuse injury for upper limb amputees: www.oandp.org/JPO/library/2008_03_126.asp

Did You Know?

1. The Red Cross was created to treat sick and wounded soldiers in the field following the First International Convention in Geneva in the mid-19th century.
2. Arms are the most commonly broken bones in adults.
3. Collarbones are the most commonly broken bones in children.
4. Broken bones take around 12 weeks to heal.
5. Skin problems are experienced by nearly 75 percent of lower-limb amputees.
6. Before 1929, deaths occurred at velodromes during track racing.
7. *Healthy Living* (healthyliving.azcentral.com/cycle-high-altitude-2495.html) has an article on how to prepare for cycling at high altitude.
8. Male bees cannot sting.
9. A fear of bees is known as apiphobia.
10. The term anaphalaxis (severe allergic reaction) was coined by Nobel Prize winners Portier and Richet in 1902.

Things to Try for Yourself

1. Attend a first aid course near where you live.
2. Try bandaging and basic first aid skills on your partner, children, or friends (even if they haven't been hurt).
3. Attend a cycling competition or major sports event and make a note of the types of injuries and accidents that occurred there.
4. Warm up your muscles before each bike ride and stretch those muscles after each bike ride to reduce injury risk.
5. Discuss injuries and accidents and laugh about falls with other cyclists.

Armin Köhli, Switzerland

Cycling 4,805 kilometers (3,000 miles) in 48 days would not be an easy challenge for anyone. However, double below-knee amputee extreme sportsman Armin Köhli undertook the grueling challenge to cycle from Geneva to the Dead Sea to raise awareness about the fight against landmines.

Köhli set off on October 1 and travelled from Switzerland through Italy, Slovenia, Croatia, Bosnia-Herzegovina, Serbia, Bulgaria, Greece, Turkey, Lebanon, and Syria to Jordan.

He struggled with fever and flu over the Swiss mountain passes in the Alps, fought against hurricane winds in Slovenia, froze in snowfalls in Bulgaria, coughed his way through 70 kilometers (44 miles) of state motorway in Istanbul, and fell down in the deluge of torrential rain in Beirut.

He even managed to cross the bridge over the Bosporus on the saddle—thanks to two well-meaning Turkish policemen—a connection between Europe and Asia that has been closed for many years to walkers and cyclists. The mild winter sun of Syria and Jordan saw Köhli arriving at the Dead Sea in time for the international conference to mark the 10-year anniversary of the Mine Ban Treaty.

A translated excerpt from Geneva-Dead Sea 2007.

Photographs courtesy of the Swiss Campaign to Ban Landmines. This 2007 tour was organized by **www.stopmines.ch**.

Another useful website to consult is www.icbl.org, The International Campaign to Ban Landmines.

Funny Things Happen on Bikes!!

One of the last races before the Paralympics. A time trial. I had the ideal racing position, head down, fully aerodynamic, the arms on the aerobars. Last lap, I felt stronger than ever. I knew the circuit by now, so I just watched the ground in front of me to keep the ideal position. Another 300 meters, 200 meters, 150 meters before a sharp 90-degree turn. Booom! I was faster than I thought, and the turn had already come. With a speed of above 40 kilometers per hour, I hit the metal barrier in that turn and fell over it. The barrier was broken, my helmet was broken, and one prosthetic was broken. But I just had a few grazes.

Armin Köhli, Switzerland

Chapter 13

Expert Stuff, Part I

So, having done lots of cycling at beginner level, are you ready to take a look at what expert cyclists do? Are you feeling adventurous? This chapter provides a brief tour of the following complex cycling done by amputees who put their minds to it.

- Spin cycling and indoor cycling
- Spin cycling in water
- Cycling on water
- Conquering mountains
- Mountain biking
- Cyclocross
- BMX and stunt cycling

Designated cycling areas are the best places to try out some of the previous cycling if you are a total novice. There will be plenty of help, advice, and fun along the way. There is also the option of setting up and running your own cycling trails, cycling shop and repair center, cycling vacation company, cycling charity, group cycling event or race, or cycling newsletter or magazine. These will be discussed in chapter 14. They are all incredibly fun, but you have to work at them to be confident enough of succeeding.

Indoor Cycling, or Spinning–Written by Gemma Trotter

Lots of different names are given to this type of studio-based cycling fitness class. The most attended group exercise class all over the world makes this a great choice for a low-impact workout that enhances your cardiovascular health and is easy on the knees and other joints. Indoor cycling also improves strength, controls diabetes, reduces blood pressure, and helps with weight loss. Many start their indoor cycling journey to lose weight. Indoor cycling participants may experience a rush of endorphins that can aid in mental health. Benefits include better sleep, lower stress levels, and deeper relaxation. The indoor cycling workout I teach is where you ride to the rhythm of powerful music. Take on the terrain with me, your coach, who leads the pack through hills, flats, mountain peaks, time trials, and interval training.

Benefits to training on a spin bike are

- building up your cardiovascular fitness,
- not risking riding too far and being too tired to get home, and
- building up slowly and going at your own pace and intensity until you feel strong enough to push harder and challenge yourself.

Spin bikes have a weighted flywheel which simulates the effects of inertia and momentum when riding a real bicycle. The pedals are equipped with toe clips (cages) as on normal bikes to allow one foot to pull up when the other is pushing down. They may have clipless receptacles to be used with cleated cycling shoes. These are an absolute must for leg amputees so the foot stays in place.

Setup

Indoor bikes have a wide range of adjustment, and it is essential to obtain the correct setup for an amputee. Set the bike up from the perspective of the prosthetic side. Adjust the seat height to be level with the top of your hip bone when standing next to the cycle. It's all about the millimeters! The knee should be slightly bent at an angle between 15 and 20 degrees when the leg is extended with the foot resting flat at the bottom of the pedal stroke. If you cannot reach the pedal without losing your hip alignment, then the seat is too high. Handlebars should be level with the saddle or slightly lower to encourage correct tilting from the hips, effective muscle recruitment, and maximum power output. Beginners may want it slightly higher than saddle height until they get used to it. Check that you can reach the handlebars and still have a 90-degree angle between your upper arm and your torso in racing position.

For above-knee amputees, a cycling-specific socket is generally required to remove a lot of the bulk at the top and the rim. You need to be sitting square on the saddle and not be lifted off by a socket. Consider the knee. Whether it's polycentric (simple mechanical, friction), hydraulic (fluid, mechanical), or electronic (microprocessor, fluid, mechanical) doesn't really matter; what needs to be established is how it behaves on a bike. On a road bike, a very simple hydraulic knee is all that's needed. Standing up on a spin bike you need a small amount of resistance to balance you out. If the knee is too free, the action can be somewhat violent and unpredictable. Riding without a prosthetic leg is an option, although you wouldn't be able to stand up.

Push

Proper management of resistance is the key to a good indoor cycling workout. It provides control, safety, the feel of the terrain, and the results. The amount of resistance used throughout the class changes all the time and depends on the training track objectives, the pace of the music in some cases, and the choreography. In some tracks, it is light to moderate resistance with faster pace to train leg speed or to help recover the legs. In other tracks, the resistance is heavier with slower pace for strength training. Changing resistance throughout the class to work at different intensities uses different energy systems (aerobic and anaerobic) and recruits different muscle fibers.

For amputees, the amount of energy and oxygen needed is substantially higher than an able-bodied participant, especially in the beginning. Sweat can be a problem as studios are designed such that the sound system plays a bigger part than air conditioning. Liners may come loose with a tiny bit of sweat and potentially cause an accident as the prosthesis might come off. A seated position with or without prosthesis remains the safest way to spin as a total beginner. It takes quite a bit of time to build enough muscle power in your good leg to be able to stand, and I would recommend dozens of classes under your belt to gain the strength and endurance needed for standing out of the saddle. Transitions can also be hazardous (from seated to standing), and making sure the resistance is enough to stabilize you once standing is crucial. If working anaerobically at 85 to 92 percent maximum heart rate, then you will start to fatigue quickly. After three to six months of regular spin classes, you will find higher intensities easier to sustain.

For upper-limb amputees, the level of amputation and comfort with arm prosthetics will very much decide how you stabilize on the bike. Resting the stump on the handlebars is sometimes preferred if the amputation is below elbow, but each amputee will find his way to stay safe and be effective. Bespoke prosthetics can be made with different attachments. These must be safe, secure, and easily attachable. Through a period of adaptation your core stability will improve to be able to stand up and climb hills, but the emphasis over time will be to take more weight on your legs. Generally, an arm prosthetic is sufficient when positioned on the handlebars to give the right amount of balance. One thing to watch out for is too much leaning on the forearms can cause back pain. Chafing and rubbing mixed with sweat can create soreness.

You can train within your own limits to improve endurance, strength, interval, race day, and recovery. Training in a race day situation would be like a time trial—a max heart rate effort of 80 to 92 percent held for 30 to 40 minutes. This is a considerable test for your stamina and a great tool for monitoring improvement.

Gemma Trotter, UK

I had a road traffic accident at the age of 14 as a backseat passenger in Belgium. I spent two years and 24 failed operations to save my leg to no success. At 16, I elected for an above-knee amputation. I walked well for two years and then stopped walking for four years due to ill-fitting sockets and problems. I was then taken onto a research program called Osseointegration (Branemark) and had a pin inserted into my bone which sticks out of my baby leg. I now bolt a leg onto the pin. I can teach spin (and other classes) like an able-bodied instructor and can work as hard, too. I am a personal trainer but prefer to work with amputees as this is my specialist area I am more keenly interested in. I gained my qualification at the beginning of 2012 and have permanent classes now. Unfortunately, all my participants are able-bodied, but my goal is to see more amputees in indoor cycling classes to reap the rewards that I have. I've been spinning four to five times a week for 11 years now with only a few breaks (pregnancy and the odd operation).

Spin Cycling in Water

If the thought of loud music and a fast-paced workout sounds unappealing, an alternative is water-based (aqua) spin cycling. This is an exercise class in swimming pools with a fully submerged waterproofed bike and the cyclist in water up to chest level. There are no gear adjustments to be made to the stationary bike. Prosthetics for spin cycling in water require waterproofing. The materials used tend to cause the prosthesis to float. It is advisable to take some time to master controlling the prosthetic in water first so it will do what you need it to during the exercise class. Amputees can join in existing classes, and it is a personal choice whether to use prosthetics or not.

Lighting and mood are more relaxed and ideal for those who want to look after older, tired joints or simply prefer exercising in water. Aqua spin cycling proponents claim an hour's workout will burn around 800 calories without the sweating. Cycling maneuvers, such as pedaling while sitting, pedaling while standing, handlebar jumps, and other variations, are performed to appropriate music. In an ordinary spin class, you will sweat profusely and be out of breath; however, in water, you simply feel warm and weightless. Take a look around. Is there an aqua spin cycling class in your area? If there is, get in touch with the instructor and explain you are an amputee and want to try it. Work closely with them, on a one-to-one basis if necessary, before joining a class of regular attendees so you are confident you can do the maneuvers as well as others. If there isn't currently a class in your area, why not ask your local swimming pool about setting one up? It would be fun and new and could help others with or without disabilities, too.

Aqua Cycling on Water

While on the theme of cycling and water, did the prospect of cycling across the Channel (like Yvon Le Caer in chapter 1) cross your mind? Don't forget, Yvon is an elite-level cyclist, so it's not something you will be able to do straight away from novice level. In fact, it is not for the faint hearted at all! The bike and prosthetics equipment have to be made especially for the purpose of cycling on top of the water. A major factor to consider is the cost. Having a good chat with the local yacht club or boat builder in your area will be invaluable if considering this activity. It may even be possible to discuss setting up some aqua cycling clubs at swimming pools or small lakes around your area as a way to start the process. A lot of experimentation will be necessary as well as advice and support from those involved in water-based sports, such as waterskiing and windsurfing. The way the cycling equipment and your prosthetics behave in a swimming pool, on a lake, or in the sea will vary tremendously. It is important that people involved in attempting such cycling activities are strong swimmers and have excellent life-saving skills as water-based activities come with their own inherent risks. Life vests and wet suits should be worn throughout, even if practicing in a swimming pool, to get accustomed to manipulating prosthetics within such materials. The higher levels of expertise required for sea-based aqua cycling, aside from simply the fitness aspect, include an excellent mastery of tidal movements, currents, radio communications, and lifeguard and coastguard duties. If you have background knowledge of such areas before your amputation, it may not seem so daunting to consider this as an activity to aim toward to help you after amputation. If you are a poor swimmer and a non-cyclist, especially since your amputation, then there is a lot out there for you simply waiting to be discovered. Don't set your sights on the sea-based activities just yet; build up to them gradually in the swimming pool first.

Conquering Mountains

As a beginner, you will become quite accustomed to getting off your bike and walking with it uphill—especially on the steep ones! Eventually, if you keep at it, you will be able to cycle all the way up. When that happens, give yourself a pat on the back, celebrate, but don't stop there because the mountains will beckon.

There isn't really any consensus on what constitutes a mountain or when a hill is not a hill. It's all very subjective and open to debate. Hills can have steep, rolling, or gentle gradients whereas mountains tend to have steep, moderately steep, or very steep slope gradients. Hills are rounded; mountains are usually rugged. In general, if the peak is around 610 meters (2,000 feet) above sea level, it is considered to be a mountain. Some hills may previously have been mountains, but the effects of land erosion over centuries have reduced their size. There are various types of hills:

*   Drumlin—an elongated, whale-shaped hill formed by glacial action.
*   Butte—an isolated hill with steep sides and a small flat top formed by weathering.
*   Tor—a rock formation found on a hilltop; also used to refer to the hill, especially in Southwest England.
*   Puy—used especially in the Auvergne, France, to describe a conical volcanic hill.
*   Pingo—a mound of earth-covered ice found in the Arctic and Antarctica.

Cycling steep hills and eventually mountains is all about pedaling technique, using the right (low) gears, and fitness. Mountains may be steepest nearer the bottom, the top, or a combination of the two, depending on the height and the number of layers it is made of. Road engineering affects how you cycle mountains. Roads that go straight up a mountain are much harder to cycle compared to those that follow its natural curve.

Small, steep hills require the cyclist to pedal hard and shift down the gears before getting to the steep part. The legs (or arms, if handcycling) have to move faster to generate enough momentum. Timing is crucial as pedaling hard too early will be tiring, and you may not reach the top. Not pedaling hard enough at the right time makes the hill harder to climb. Very steep hills may require you to stand up in the pedals on an ordinary cycle or raise yourself slightly off the seat of a handcycle to get enough momentum and power. This should be practiced often on lower gradient hills before attempting a steep hill.

Once a single steep hill is mastered, look around for a series of hills to prepare for cycling mountains. A series of hills allow you to coast— not pedal—on the downhill phase until you reach a point where you need to start pedaling again to get ready for the next uphill. The speed and stability of the bike on the downhill part should be controlled, especially if the road is curved or winding on the way down. Traveling very fast on a bike down steep hills or mountains should only be attempted on very roadworthy bikes (especially tires and brakes) when you are used to cycling fast down smaller hills. Going downhill at high speeds can make the bike unstable, and it will take longer to stop. The biggest dangers at speed on a mountain downhill are from other vehicles, tight corners, and potholes or loose gravel. Use gears to control your speed.

If cycling up and down a series of steep hills is easy, then you are ready to try a mountain. Remember to pace yourself. You will probably have to stop on the way up to have a rest, cool off, and give your heart and breathing a chance to normalize. Walking a little with the bike if it is not too steep will help with this process. Reenergizing with food and drink is also important as the amount of energy consumed during cycling up steep hills or mountains is very high and will need to be replaced. Add to that the difficulty of cycling uphill in windy conditions (it might be a headwind or crosswind or, if you are lucky, a tailwind). and you really will be working hard to get anywhere at all, let alone fast.

A useful site for planning to cycle on mountains is www.cyclingcols.com. It prepares you with information on height, distance, and gradient. If there is more than one level of steepness (there usually is!), it provides a rough guide to the percentage of distance that is very steep (e.g., 10% as compared to steep 5%). Here are examples of mountain passes that double below-knee amputee Armin Köhli cycles.

The Albula in Switzerland is 2,319 meters (1.5 miles) in height and approximately 31 kilometers (19 miles) in distance. Nearly 15 kilometers (9 miles) of this are at a gradient of 5 percent, and 2 kilometers (1 mile) is at a gradient of more than 10 percent.

The Stelvio Pass in Italy also has formidable statistics for cyclists. It is 2,758 meters (2 miles) in height and 16.4 kilometers (10 miles) long. 15.5 kilometers (9.6 miles) is at a gradient of 5 percent, and nearly 4 kilometers (2.5 miles) is at a gradient of 10 percent.

So how does this compare to the mountains that are the center of the Tour de France? Well, one of the more difficult mountains that is often cycled during this incredible race is the Tourmalet. This mountain is 2,115 meters (1.3 miles) high and 18.8 kilometers (12 miles) long. Over 16 kilometers (10 miles) is at a gradient of 5 percent, and nearly 4 kilometers (2.5 miles) is at a gradient of 10 percent.

Still think you can't cycle hills or mountains just because you are an amputee? Continue to be amazed at what amputee cyclists are capable of doing on bicycles and mountains and keep reading.

The Countryside Code

Some cycling activities aren't particularly good for the environment if done indiscriminately or unchecked, so follow the countryside codes of conduct at all times. The countryside code varies among countries and among national parks. It is basically a set of common sense rules for visitors. Applying these will help maintain the environment for future generations. Always check for changes in these rules.

There are some very specific rules for countryside settings:

- Guard against risk of fire.
- Fasten all gates.
- Keep to public paths.
- Keep water sources clean.
- Protect wildlife, plants, and trees.
- Take your litter home.

There are also general sensible rules to help your day outdoors go well:

- Plan ahead and be prepared.
- Follow advice and local signs.
- Keep to existing trails (creating your own trails damages vegetation and causes erosion).
- Take enough food, water, and clothing.
- Always take a first aid kit, spare tube, bicycle pump, and tire levers.
- Always wear a helmet and ride at a safe speed, according to your experience, the conditions, and the terrain.

Importantly, the countryside code addresses courtesy to others (horse riders and walkers) and safety issues to ensure enjoyment of the beauty and serenity of outdoor life without incident or accident. For example:

- Consider other users—walkers should give way to cyclists, and both give way to horse riders.
- Approach with care and do not startle other trail users. Reduce speed to pass safely.
- Avoid areas where tree felling or machinery is in use.
- If you come upon an injured rider (horse or bicycle), get help immediately. If you come upon a riderless horse, seek help before approaching it. Only approach if you are experienced in dealing with horses.

Unless cycling in a highly urban area, you will come across all manner of wildlife, fauna, flora, birds, and insects along the way. If you do, the following set of rules will help you to fully enjoy the experience:

- Do not approach an animal that is stressed from your presence.
- Do not uproot plants or break branches.
- Respect the habitat of wildlife by leaving things as you found them. Minimize plant disturbances when photographing plants, animals, or landscapes.
- Do not take souvenirs, such as stones, plants, seeds, feathers, bones, antlers, or archaeological artifacts.
- When photographing wildlife, use your longest lens.
- Take only pictures and leave only footprints.

More detailed advice can be found on websites and notice boards at the entrance of national parks in most countries. The countryside code is especially important for specific types of cycling, such as mountain biking, BMX, and cyclocross, which place a heavy emphasis on cycling over particular terrain that leads to churning of soil, displacement of rocks, stones, or gravel, and fast-paced cycling in dangerous situations.

Mountain Biking and Cyclocross for Beginners

This section features the valuable advice and expertise of some of the best amputee mountain bikers and racers around the world—the excellent work of Victor Walther, Will Craig, Scott McDonald, and other amputees can be found at mtb-amputee.com. The site is developed and maintained by Victor who is from Canada and is a valuable resource for any amputee interested in this form of cycling.

To succeed in developing more advanced mountain biking skills, it is advisable that amputees fully master the absolute basics of general cycling to a highly proficient level first as this sport places greater stress on the use of brakes, gears, and balance. It is also important to be able to mount, dismount, and carry the bike several times during a ride without difficulty. The skills and fitness requirements for this sport are markedly different to a leisure ride around your local park.

The sport of mountain biking is perfect for those amputees who want to experience the F factor, the E factor, the A factor, the T factor, and, above all, the O...O...O factor! *(Fear, Exhilaration, Adrenaline, Thrills, and Oh, O-Wow, Ouch!)* It is the ultimate hair-raising, adrenaline-pumping challenge against nature where one wrong turn or mistake can cause serious bodily injury.

The type of bike and safety equipment you need depends on the type of riding you want to do. If you want to do technical free-riding or downhill racing, you will need a special heavy duty bike and helmet along with body armor padding. Always remember to take plenty of advice from the bike shop along the way.

Mountain biking is a universal sport that can be done virtually anywhere. There are many unofficial bike parks and trails all over the world. The more commercial bike parks and race venues generally double as ski resorts, and trails are marked accordingly.

Deciding on the appropriateness or level of technical difficulty of the trail is down to individual preference and experience. If you are an absolute beginner, then the starting point will be a cross-country type of trail until your mountain biking skills progress. Trail length and elevation change are factors to bear in mind as a beginner. While attempts are made to standardize trail information in different countries, it is worth checking trail and route information before setting off, especially following episodes of bad weather. A ratings system to consider is the Trail Difficulty Rating System developed by the International Mountain Biking Association. It is designed around the system used by ski resorts to help trail users choose the correct trails for their skills, with a particular aim to avoid injuries. Trails are rated in comparison with others in the area. This may not easily translate in different countries but should be sufficient to start you off. In fact, a trail in Australia will have different features to trails in the USA or Canada even though they have the same rating. In general, easy trails are usually wide and relatively smooth without large obstacles and a steepness gradient between 5 and 10 percent.

Difficult trails may have a steepness gradient of 15 percent or more and unavoidable natural large obstacles, such as rocks and logs, narrow bridges, and variable loose surfaces. There will always be an element of subjectivity surrounding the ratings of trails. Discussing trail features and ratings with other mountain bikers on forums such as those found on www.mtb-amputee.com will help you choose the appropriate trail for your skill level. As much as possible, as a beginner, choose trails that are wider and farther inland rather than at the edge of sheer mountain drops. Work on getting to know how to handle your bike safely before working on increasing speed as it increases the risk of falling off or losing control.

Build up to steeper trails as you progress. Many trails are in wooded or forest areas which grow dark very quickly once the sun sets. Always make sure you have a strong set of lights with enough battery power to take you around the trail. The front light should be white with a wide angle of visibility, and the rear light should be red or amber, showing clearly from a distance of at least 500 feet. Unless you have enough light capacity, don't start a trail in dark or poor weather conditions.

Be mindful of other regular users on the trail. They might be faster and will be looking for more challenging areas to practice their skills. All trails have engineering or design limits, and the more expertise you develop, the more challenging the trail you will want to use. If you come across a section of trail that you can't ride, get off your bike and walk it. As mountains are higher up, it tends to be naturally cooler, so take enough spare layers of clothing.

If you are not sure whether you are ready to try cycling challenging trails, why not simply learn more about such parks by offering to help out at them? Volunteers are always welcome, especially during the busy times. The more time you spend around those who do mountain biking regularly, the easier it will be for you to decide. It's also a good way of learning how trails are designed and maintained. Topics such as trail erosion, injuries, bike maintenance, and environment conservation feature highly among trail users, too, so the learning opportunities really are endless, whether you actually pluck up the courage to ride any of the trails or not.

Mountain bike skills courses at designated centers will help to initially provide you with the basic skills of overcoming an obstacle while riding as opposed to getting off the bike to maneuver around it. The aim is to be able to control your bike through different terrains, ride on narrow tracks without fear, and learn the advanced skills of how to jump over parts of the course safely. These are all skills navigated at speed or in motion. A statement you will hear often in this cycling environment is: Remember, momentum is your friend, and you have more control than you think. Always book in advance; let them know you are an amputee and the amount of cycling you have done so far. They may not have a suitable bike available to rent or may not have the adaptations you require, so these will need discussion and planning before you attend a course.

Some will be able to source the equipment you need, but be prepared to take along your existing bike, helmet, and other gear before attending the course, and check with them whether it will be suitable.

A good way to practice mountain biking skills is by trying them on a grassy area or field. Start off by choosing small obstacles, such as sticks or stones, and then choose bigger logs or bricks. As a general rule, if you look at the obstacle you want to avoid, you will hit it. Look instead at the line you want your front wheel to take to steer away from such obstacles. Look as far along the ground in front of you as you can for rocks, puddles, and bumps. First try avoiding them, and then try going over them. Keep increasing the size of the obstacle until you get to the point where you are ready to learn how to lift the front wheel over it without touching it. Expert mountain bikers can ride fast over ditches, tree stumps, and piles of earth or gravel. Further advanced skills taught at such courses are uphill restarts in loose terrain, how to go over large obstacles while standing in the saddle, bunny hops, and wheelies.

For those on handcycles or recumbent bikes, adaptations to these skills will be required, but there should be no reason not to attempt them, whatever type of cycle you use. Mountain biking is physically demanding but is a good way to develop a knowledge of how to overcome complicated environments.

While some amputees can ride, and choose to ride, without a prosthetic limb or device, others can't. It depends on the individual and type of riding. While it is possible to ride moderate cross-country trails with one hand or arm, it is impossible to race or ride technical downhill with one arm. An excellent interview and video of arm amputee Will Craig is available at www.bike198.com/insanely-cool-riding-shore-prosthetic. This will certainly take you on an amazing journey where you'll be wondering why you haven't tried it yet.

Mountain biking is as safe and fun as you make it. Some people do it for exercise, some for the love of nature, and others do it for an adrenaline rush. It's guaranteed that at some point you will fall or crash. It may be as simple as not putting your foot (or hand) down in time while coming to a stop or sliding out on a slippery corner. Minor bumps, bruises, and scrapes are part of the learning curve, and being mindful of the risks, listening to the advice of more experienced mountain bikers, and using the techniques shown to you in the courses will help reduce the incidence of more major injuries.

Safety is relevant to risk. The faster and more technical you ride, the greater the risk. If you ride technical trails, you should always ride with others or at the very least let someone know where you are going and when you'll be back.

Besides online resources, the best place to find information on mountain biking is your local bike shops. You can find examples of bikes and products as well as information on local clubs, trails, and events. If you are interested in organizing a group ride with other amputees, a good place to start is meeting with your local prosthetists and rehabilitation centers, as well as your local bike shops and clubs. Currently, mountain biking is not a Paralympic sport as there are not enough qualified competitors. However, with growing interest, it could be included in the future. The current difficulties for inclusion in the Paralympics are due to a combination of logistics, demographics, and politics. The majority of elite competitive amputee mountain bikers are of a standard equivalent to professional elite able-bodied racers.

Cyclocross

Do you remember those initial attempts at riding in the dark, in sand, and through water as a beginner? Why not get better at them as well as try snow and ice with your bike through a tougher form of cycling known as cyclocross? It really is the most adrenaline pumping activity for an amputee! The bike that is used for cyclocross is a race bike made to withstand more heavy duty cycling, especially the frame and the forks.

Cyclocross requires the rider to cross all sorts of different terrain, such as mud, grass, streams, ice, gravel, snow, and other fun stuff in all sorts of weather conditions. They don't cancel because of rain, leaves on the trail, too much sun, or any other reason. The rider should attempt to stay on the bike throughout the course. More often than not, the reality involves falling off and running or wading beside the bike. To make it even more exciting (as it is a race), cyclists are allowed to do whatever is faster: walking, carrying the bike, or cycling. Just expect to end up crashing a lot, feeling very cold, tired, sore, wet and muddy, and thoroughly enjoying feeling like that! It requires a lot of stamina, willpower, and a tremendous sense of humor to be a cyclocross racer. The best example of an arm amputee who is amazing at cyclocross is American Charles McDonald . He is featured in many magazines and on many Internet videos, such as:

→ www.courier-journal.com/article/20130202/BILLBOARD/130202008/Cyclo-cross-Amputee-cyclist-not-afraid-fail-video-

It's certainly inspirational, and it may make those initial concerns you have about cycling fade away. If you want to learn more about cyclocross or attend a race to get a better idea of what is involved, check out www.cxmagazine.com. There will be other magazines more applicable to your country or region, but it is a good starting point.

BMX and Stunt Cycling

This is a form of cycling that developed because young children attending adult cycling races would mess around on their bikes, attempting to try some of the tricks that they saw at the event. They would find obstacles to jump and attempt twists, turns, and other stunts on BMX bikes (see chapter 4, Bike Choices). This eventually became a recognized form of cycling that is divided into different disciplines: dirt, flatland, freestyle, street, park, and race. So what sorts of things do you learn to do on a BMX? The technical skills depend on the discipline. Dirt jumping involves riding a BMX bike over a jump and landing on the other side. The jump may be made out of dirt, wood, or cement. The easiest form of jump for new riders is the tabletop. One end is for take-off and the other for landing with a flat area at the top. Other jumps may be a single mound or a double with a gap in between. They can also be in step-up or step-down format. More difficult forms of jumps are the whoops or rhythms, which are a series of ramps close together; spine jump, which makes you go higher in the air; and berms, which is a curved wall ride.

The aim is to perform as many tricks and acrobatics on the way around in the best style. These include the tire grab, the X-up, the barspin, the table top, the whip, front flip, and back flip. The more expert BMX riders can combine tricks so that more than one trick is performed while in the air.

Flatland is a form of artistic cycling that originated in the 1980s. It does not require ramps or jumps, just a smooth flat surface. The riders perform spinning and balancing tricks on the bikes, manipulating these into various positions.

Flatland bikes have pegs on each wheel axle for the rider to balance on. The aim is to maintain coordination, balance, and style. Riders become very aware of the balance and counterbalance positions of the bike and how to control very small movements. The feet should not touch the ground, and the more stylish, original, or difficult the trick, the more points are awarded. Expert riders can perform consecutive tricks and moves in sequence without putting their feet back on the pedals or on the ground. Typical tricks include the endo, the Miami hopper, pogo, cherry picker, boomerang, and many others. These take dedication and many years to perfect.

Street BMX riding involves riders using railings, steps, curbs, ledges, banks, curved walls, and other manmade town and city obstacles to perform tricks. Tricks include a series of different grinds, handlebar turns, and bunny hops onto pegs.

Park riders use skate parks made from wood, concrete, or metal that are used by skateboarders and inline skaters.

Vert riders use two small pipes facing each other to form a ramp. Some are 2 to 3 meters (6-10 feet) high, but can be as big as 8 meters (26 feet) in competitions. Riders go from one pipe to another and, on the way, perform acrobatics and tricks. Different BMX bikes suitable for each of these disciplines are available, and some mountain bikers  try BMX biking as a way of increasing the element of danger and thrill. This type of cycling is definitely one in which safety gear is important. The helmet has to be approved and full face; body areas should be fully protected with padded safety gear; and gloves should completely cover the fingers. BMX stunt riding is considered a highly aggressive form of cycling, and riders should be made aware of the risks of injury and death. This is mainly one for those who have a very good mastery of cycling despite their age and are not put off by the possibility of increasing their existing levels of injury. Assuming you have taken to cycling like you were born to do it and are not put off by the risks, make sure you take lessons from a recognized or approved instructor first. BMX cycling centers, if you have any in your area, are good sources of information about choosing instructors. They should start you off with easy drills and skills and then move you on to more difficult levels involving stunts and jumps if they can see you and your bike are ready for it. The bike must be well maintained at all times, and manufacturer warranties may not cover such cycling. The types of tricks and skills shown to you as a beginner are best practiced in designated areas, such as bike parks, where there is enough support and supervision in case of injury.

Amputees known for this type of cycling are people like American Kurt Yaeger, an above-knee amputee who returned to BMX cycling after amputation. Some adjustments had to be made to the bike, pedals, and limb, but his successful tours and continuing acting and stunt work are real evidence of how you can do it if you don't let the amputation get in your way. Visit his website at kurtyaeger.com for plenty of interview material about his amazing work. Take a look and be inspired! Obviously, cycling tricks are not a new concept. Cyclists have been trying all sorts of tricks on their bikes. They were often seen at circuses doing balancing tricks, jumping on or off, and cycling seated backward. Some would ride a unicycle along a tightrope in midair. Here is a difficult balance trick you might want to try one day: the superman. It involves cycling steadily on a relatively straight downhill, then moving your bottom toward the back of the bike until your chest is on the seat. Support your weight on your chest and lift your legs out behind you. This aerodynamic position will mean you pick up speed, so be careful when trying to return your legs to the pedals. Rather than sitting back on the bike, it is easier to stand on the pedals, brake carefully, and bring your feet to the ground. It is not certain if many amputees have tried this, but choose somewhere very soft to fall if you do!

Unicycling and Sports

There are probably extremely few amputees who are unicyclists, so this section is a bit of wishful thinking for the future. Unicycling is possible as an amputee, especially if you have already unicycled before your amputation. The balance requirements are quite high, and the more severe the amputation, the more difficult it can be. To get some idea of what it involves, take a look at American leg amputee, Joe Savala. Read more at www. adventureunicyclist.com/tag/amputee.

(He also has a YouTube video of him roller blading!) Able-bodied unicyclists take part in competitions and sporting events, such as hockey and handball, and a good source of advice and information is the International Unicycling Federation based in the US. If you are very good at ordinary cycling and want to set yourself a new challenge, take a look at unicycling.

From the Amputees

Gemma Trotter, UK

As an above-knee amputee without prosthesis, I took to a spin bike some 11 years ago. So I have experienced four years of spinning with no leg and the rest with a leg. I use an electronic microprocessor knee (C-leg) which allows me to alter the resistance for what I want in and out of the saddle. For my setup, my good leg is more like 35 degrees from bottom center. This is purely to keep the leg from locking out straight on my prosthetic side. I then move the seat forward to gain more height, and because I have a small frame, I find this easier for the handlebar reach.

Victor Walther, Canada

When I first started to ride, and during most of my racing and training, there where no maps or GPS or cell phones; we got around by trial and error. Now I usually bring a cell phone just in case, and if I can't get a signal, it's usually a short hike to a good spot.

When it comes to marked trails, it really depends on where you live. The best place to get info on trails is through local bike clubs and bike shops. Basically, almost every community in British Columbia has a mountain bike club, and almost every bike shop does group rides, and usually they have maps of local trails. When it comes to actual signs on the trails, it depends on how involved your local mountain bike shops and clubs are.

In my case, the Nanaimo Mountain Bike Club is affiliated with IMBA (International Mountain Bike Associatino) and heavily involved in trail building and land access. They put up signs and provide maps to local bike shops and recently created the first dedicated mountain bike trail in our area (other than ski resorts) with insurance.

Excerpt from Mountain Biking by Alexis Gendron, of Biddeford, Maine, USA

(Published in dirtragmag.com/mountain-bike-poetry, January 16, 2013)

I know the surrounding woods like a life long friend, the squawking birds and wind rushing through the trees.

The bright leaves that litter the trail are like a collage of autumn colors, they are beautiful.

I start out on the trail, riding hard.

All I can see is the trail in front of me, all I can hear is the pounding of my heart, all I know is this moment, right now.

Here I come! Screaming down the other side, exhilarated, terrified, gaining speed, sure to crash.

Flying over the winding path, I let off the brakes and just float.

I feel light as a feather, it was worth the climb.

I feel like there should be nothing more to the world than this.

Just ride

Reproduced with kind permission from Alexis Gendron; Dirt Rag Mag; **www.portlandwheelers.org**; Trips for Kids, **www.tripsforkids.org**; and **www.communitybike.net**.

Further Reading

1. Spin cycling: http://www.spinning.com/en
2. Yvon Le Caer: http://www.yvonlecaer.com/
3. Mountain biking books: http://mountainbikefaq.com/2010/01/5-best-mountain-biking-books
4. *World of BMX* by J.P. Partland (MBI Publishing Company, 2003)

Did You Know?

1. The world's highest Trans Himalayan Mountain Bike Race is held in the Tibetan part of Mount Everest (17,160 feet).
2. The longest mountain bike race ran from Canada to Mexico over 2,700 miles and was last organized in 2010.
3. "Granny Gear" is the mountain biking term used to describe the lowest gear on a bike.
4. 40 minutes of spin cycling can help burn 400 to 600 calories.
5. The International Mountain Biking Association (www.imba.org.uk) is a good resource for mountain bikers.
6. The English Channel is around 560-kilometers long. At its widest, it is 240 kilometers long, and its narrowest point at Dover is 33.1 kilometers.
7. Handcycling has been part of the IPC cycling program since 1998.
8. Handcycling was including as a race in the Paralympics in 2004.
9. Challenge Alaska added handcycling to the Sadler's Ultra Challenge race in 1999.
10. The Sadler's Ultra Challenge is a six-day, eight stage 430-kilometer wheelchair and handcycling race that takes place between Fairbanks and Anchorage in Alaska (www.challengealaska.org).

Things to Try for Yourself

1. Get in touch with the nearest mountain bike park.
2. Arrange a visit or book a lesson.
3. Practice some of the skills they show you.
4. Visit some cyclocross racing events near you.
5. Try it all! Spin cycling, aqua cycling, or even cycling on water through recration centers or sailing clubs.

Mark Inglis, New Zealand—An excerpt from his book Off the Front Foot

The Rainbow Rage, a 106-kilometer mountain bike event in the mountains of New Zealand's South Island—a year previously I had a terrible experience, a "ride from hell"—this year I have come back in a better frame of mind, stronger in every way!

1,000 people on the start line, and I sure didn't want to start the race at the back, might end up there at the end but please, not start there. So why sit on the start line for 40 minutes when you are going to ride for 5-plus hours? I got there, watched the hordes milling around, and decided to be a hard-nosed bugger like others. I took my bike up to about 50 meters back from then start, an area already full of keen, hyped bikers. I just stood the bike up and said "I'll be back soon, just have to work on the legs." Worked a treat. I went back and sat in the back of the truck until 10 minutes before the start. I wandered across, picked up the bike, and shouldered my way into the queue, a few apologies and a few dirty looks, but tough, I am just taking disabled parking privileges to a new level. The start gun as usual means 5 kilometers of neutralized cruising, avoiding the less than experienced riders, lots of them freaking out in the crush, falling over everywhere, this seems somewhat repetitive I think. It's a bit like slalom ski racing really, dodging the fallen riders, the slow weaving ones just like I was attacking a steep run. Weight on the outside ski (pedal), carve around them, flick the weight to the other side, and carve around another. I had a big grin plastered on my face; this is fun. The difference, I was racing myself, no one else, nothing to prove to anyone other than myself. There was no one in that whole race that was my competitor other than me. Once again, I'm with over 1,000 riders, heading over that same 106 kilometers of rocky trail and big hills. As usual hundreds power past me. I chat, say hi, good luck, what a fantastic day, nice bike, nice legs, you know just the usual cyclist chatter. Cruising at 80% heart rate through the beech forest, only a few are passing me, mostly as they power along the flat, I catch up on the hills, either up or down. There are probably 10 of us riding at a similar pace but different styles, a few women, a few old men, some just out cruising. After two hours of weaving through the lower valley, we enter the beautiful and dramatic gorges before the first big hill takes us up to the high open alpine valleys and the big hill.

I can't believe it, I'm powering along, brisk pace, nothing earth shattering of course, but all the body parts seem to be working well. In fact I'm constantly singing, just a little ditty,

"I feel great, da de da de da, I feel great," and I did, every turn of the pedals. I was hydrating well, carrying the minimum in my hydration pack on my back, with two "bidons" (water bottles to you non-cyclists) in the cages on the bike, but no fluid in

them. Getting smarter in my old age, I just put the dry drink mixture in, no sense in powering that weight up hills for 50 or 60 kilometers before drinking it, now, is there? As the hydration pack emptied, just before the climb up to the pass I filled one from a fast flowing stream as I crossed it, drank it on the way up. The climb was as long as always; still people walking their bikes up, though. All I can think is, "hey people, it's a bike, it's for riding that's why it has wheels and pedals." Cresting the top, no stopping, it's all down hill from here, good tailwind, too. I filled the other bidon at the bottom of the pass, enough to get me the 40 odd kilometers home. I was flying, thanks to that helpful wind. The legs were working pretty well, full suspension bikes were still powering past me over the ruts, but instead of anger and frustration, I worked out how to nail it for next time— no movement in the ankles, in the legs at all, perhaps a light rigid alloy set of legs and go get a full suspension bike, done. The kilometers flew by; soon the smooth road that signaled the last climb was close. I hardly noticed the climb, just kept up a nice tempo and cruised up, still singing away, scaring the natives. That last downhill was a buzz, but a careful one, no sense ruining a great day by losing most of your skin to save that last couple of minutes. The cheering crowd was exactly what I needed. I had earned it and said thanks in my mind. I wasn't any fitter before this ride compared to the previous one, not any fitter physically, that is, but fitter mentally. By having everything sorted (on all levels, daily and the future) at work, by having the right expectation of myself, I went into the epic ride in the right headspace. My heart rate, my physiological performance differed by only a few percent, the difference being after one race I just about gave the bike away, after the other I wanted to celebrate the bike.

Chapter 14

Expert Stuff, Part II

There are lots more complex cycling skills to be amazed and enthralled at. This chapter looks into racing and other aspects of cycling:

- Road racing
- Track racing
- Ironman and triathlon
- Ultramarathon
- Mountain bike and cyclocross races
- Paralympics
- Cycling in heavy traffic
- Becoming a cycling instructor
- Running your own cycling business, cycling group or club, or charity

Racing

This is probably the most well-known form of cycling. There are various forms and disciplines. More detail is available on cycling websites, such as the UCI (Union Cycliste Internationale), British Cycling, and the Paralympic websites in all countries. It is possibly the one thing that people think of doing when they first learn to ride a bike.

The thrill of riding at speed and beating others is something that everyone has within them. Some will have the competitive spirit more than others and will become world renowned sports people whereas others may be quite happy taking part in local races and small events organized by their cycling clubs. If you are interested in competing, enter as many different races as possible. The more competitions you take part in, the more experience you will gain, and the more confidence you will have in your prosthetics and your cycling ability.

Introductory level racing (known as fun categories) provide enough opportunity for beginners to race. A race license is not needed for such events. They are either free to enter or the entrance fee includes food and drink stops, a T-shirt, water bottle, and other goodies. They are known in the UK as cyclosportives (for road cycling) and skyrides. Cyclosportives aim to attract all levels of fitness, and routes are often well marked. Skyrides are more about fun and mass participation than cycling performance. They are more of a family or group day out. If you try these and decide to start racing competitively, you will need to get a racing license, learn the categories of races, rules of entry, rules of competition, as well as the points score systems. There will be lots of information on these aspects provided by race organizers and on official racing websites. Once you know what is allowed and not allowed as well as what is expected and not expected from competitors and organizers, you will enjoy the event tremendously.

The Science and Art of Racing

Successful racing is a combination of art and science. The art of tactics, will power, quick thinking, focus, and determination are key to racing. Cycling skills invaluable in races with mass starts are paceline, drafting, slipstreaming, peleton, and the echelon. A paceline is a line of cyclists who alternate with each other to help set and keep the pace. Drafting and slipstreaming involves riding close to other cyclists to make use of the reduced wind resistance created by them. A peleton is the pack of riders in a bike race. Riding in a pack reduces the atmospheric resistance and saves riders energy. An echelon is the formation riders take in a group to help them ride through a crosswind. The peleton and echelon can only be as wide as the actual road surface they are cycling on. It takes a lot of team work to cycle in races.

Working out where to get the points and put in the effort is often half the fun of the race. It might appear easy as you watch others compete. If you want to race in the big leagues— mountain biking, triathlon, Ironman, Tour de France, Paralympics—you will have to put in the time and the training. Those pedals have to churn mile after mile all year round. Maximum effort will have to go into developing speed, power, agility, and flexibility. It requires a commitment and passion that you have to be prepared to be consumed by if you are going to succeed. A lot of this is based on science, but the art of keeping yourself motivated over such long periods of heavy training is one you have to develop within your brain. Eating to win and training to win will be vital facets in your race plan. Managing your hydration and energy levels is crucial for racing success. During endurance events, glucose in the body may only last around two hours. Water can be used not only to drink, but also as a way to cool you down in hot temperatures. Water showered on the skin while cycling evaporates heat, allowing blood to return to the work of fueling the muscles.

Some of the science of winning a cycling race can be found in physics. You need to produce a particular number of watts of power for every kilogram you weigh within a particular time or on a particular course. If you can accompany that amount of power with endurance, stamina, and technique as well as the correct amount of mental toughness, you'll be cycling alongside the professionals in no time. Most professional athletes start at an early age, either as young children or teenagers, and build up their capacity to race and train over time. It takes many years to develop such training abilities. Amputees in military or fitness settings tend to be more able to transition to high-level competition due to their pre-existing physical fitness. Amputees may be a lot older than able-bodied competitors as they acquire amputation in later life and have to learn to cope with the condition first. For everyone else of general health status and certainly for those who sit on the sedentary side of life, it is worth having a go at racing in one of the local races or charity events to see how you compare to the rest of the field. If you do well, go for bigger events. Even if you don't win but enjoy taking part in racing, keep at it, and over time you will get more proficient. Most countries will have some form of road race, track race, and short- or long-distance time trial events aimed at different levels of expertise. Local races are worth exploring to get a feel for the competition standard. Here is a brief overview.

Road Racing

Road racing takes place outdoors on normal everyday roads, and the bikes used are incredibly lightweight with very thin tires or solid wheels. They are usually single-day events which may involve cycling a circuit around a town or city center. This is known as a criterium. But road racing is most well known for its stage races,

the most famous and successful of which is the Tour de France—a combination of all the different forms of road racing condensed into four short, tense, and exciting weeks. The stages take place on consecutive days, and the winner is the person with the lowest cumulative time overall. The concept of the tour has now grown to include many other countries and cities. If you can't make it to France or Britain, how about a Tour du Rwanda, Tour du Cameroun, Tour de Taiwan, Qatar, Oman, or a Japanese or Chinese city? There are also cycling grand prix, vuelta, cycling world championships, and much more to enjoy learning about when you start thinking about the competitive side of the sport as it is today.

Track Racing

Track racing involves racing competitors in various events either directly against each other or simply against the clock in an indoor or outdoor arena known as a velodrome. This is a sloped, round series of tracks, and the bikes used by the cyclists are known as track bikes. These do not have brakes and have only one fixed gear. Track events tend to be a mixture of short, fast races and team races. They are commonly known as sprint, team sprint,

time trial, individual, and team pursuit. There are also others known as the Keirin, points race, and omnium. The Keirin is a racing event in which cyclists ride several laps around a track behind a motorized pacesetter before sprinting to the finish. A points race involves many laps of the track. Every tenth lap a sprint is held, and points are awarded to the first four. An additional way to get points is to gain a lap on the others.

The winner is the one with the most points. Races are designed to provide spectators with maximum amounts of tension and excitement as individuals cycle hard against each other or against the clock. The combination of these different track races is known as the omnium in which consistency over two days of competing are rewarded. The winner of the omnium is the rider with the lowest points overall.

Ironman and Other Triathlons

The Ironman is the name of a triathlon which is a commercial series of long-distance races organized by the World Triathlon Corporation. The original Ironman races were started in Hawaii in the late 1970s to resolve the question of which sport form was better at making people fitter. The Ironman World Championship is still held in Hawaii. It involves the disciplines of swimming, cycling, and running in tough, grueling conditions without a break. While the swim may be a "short" distance (2.4 miles or 3.86 kilometers), the bike ride is the longest element at 112 miles (180.25 kilometers). Running a distance of 26.2 miles (42.2 kilometers)—the equivalent of running a marathon—after all that takes a tremendous amount of willpower! There are start times and expected

final finish times, and if you come in within that timeframe, you are considered an Ironman or Ironwoman. Thousands compete in Ironman competitions around the world every year. Races take place in Australia, Canada, and many European countries, including Switzerland, France, UK, Denmark, Sweden, and Spain. In the US alone there are at least 11 official Ironman competitions. These events are also organized in countries such as Brazil, Mexico, South Africa, and New Zealand. Only the very elite athletes qualify using a points system to compete in the finals in Hawaii. The increasing popularity of triathlon has meant its inclusion in the Summer Olympics since 2000. The distances involved are much shorter than the Ironman challenge, but the stamina and endurance of the athletes that take part in such events is in no doubt.

Maybe you think it's impossible for amputees to compete a triathlon or Ironman event? There are already examples of amputees who have successfully competed in both triathlons and in the Ironman challenge. Take a look at Rajesh Durbal (rajeshdurbal. com), a triple amputee who has competed in triathlons and set race records at the Ironman championships in Hawaii—**twice**.

Or, if you are looking for an inspirational female triathlete, Paralympian, and Ironwoman, what about above-knee amputee Sarah Reinertsen (www.alwaystri.com). As the first female leg amputee to complete the Ironman World Championship in Hawaii, she is busy preparing for the triathlete event in the Paralympics in 2016—the first time the triathlon will be a Paralympic event.

Ultramarathons

These are endurance events against the clock. Riders can choose when they require a break from continuous cycling, and the first one across the finishing line is the winner. There are a couple of long-distance marathon rides, such as the Race Across America (RAAM) and the RAGBAI (Register's Annual Great Bicycle Ride Across Iowa). The RAAM is a coast-to-coast single-stage race of 3,000 miles. Riders take around a week to complete it. Thousands take part in these events, and many competitors use them as a way of fundraising for particular charities, such as amputee or war veteran charities.

From the Amputees

Robert Bailey, USA

In December 2005, I lost both legs below the knees. I was cutting a pasture on a tractor with a bush hog. A grassfire broke out on the bush hog (a pasture cutter designed to cut bushes with two swinging blades attached to a bar between them). I turned the tractor off and jumped off to put the fire out. The tractor lurched forward, and I was caught under it. I spent the next three months in the hospital and three months at home before I was fitted with prosthetics.

I have been cycling for as long as I can remember. In high school and college, it was my favorite transportation. After graduation from Louisiana State University, usually referred to as LSU, I rode a tour bike from Boston, Massachusetts, to Tuscaloosa, Alabama—about 1,200 miles. I was never a great athlete, but I was a good cyclist.

Gradually I got away from cycling. I didn't have as much time when I was in the U.S. Navy. I married. I became a father. I gained weight. I became diabetic, like most in my family. I had bought a racing cycle when I earned my Navy commission, but I didn't use it much. Finally, I knew I had to do something. I bought a Raleigh Sport Bike and a Twenty Folder. They were good, solid three-speeds. I started pedaling again. About a week before my accident, I bought a Rivendell tour bike off eBay. It had a 62-centimeter frame and long wheel base. It was beautiful. It arrived while I was in the hospital. My sister suggested I sell it. No way!

The Rivendell became my mountain. I was determined to ride it. I assembled it from a wheelchair. But the next few years were frustrating. Every time I tried to ride, I would develop blisters. Each time this happened, it took a month to heal from a wheelchair. I weighed 275 pounds. It was a dark time. Finally, in the fall of 2009, I noticed a cycle online. It was a recumbent tricycle. Something told me this was the answer. Operation Rebound of Challenged Athletes Foundation became my sponsor in 2008. In April 2010, an ICE Adventure trike arrived.

I had first heard of RAGBRAI in the 80s—these crazy people who ride across Iowa and drink beer. In 2008, I found out they still did both. Register's Annual Great Bicycle Ride Across Iowa had become a rite of passage in Iowa—15,000 cyclists crossing the cornfields of Iowa for seven days. That became my passion. I missed 2008 and 2009 because of blisters, but I kept that goal in front of me. CAF sent me to RAGBRAI first in 2010. I honestly did not know what I was in for; I was nowhere near any shape to ride that tour.

My oath climbing up that first hill cannot be repeated. But I loved the ride and completed about 350 miles of 450 miles. 2011 was much the same thing, but better. I had lost 225 pounds.

In 2012, I made my third trip to Iowa. Again, I rode with Spoke Folk of Ottumwa, Iowa. This time I was going to ride every mile. I was ready. Trikes, especially the Adventure, are not fast. You accept that you will pedal at around 10 to 12 mph. Each of the first four days reached over 100 °F (38 °C). It was brutal. I soon learned that I had to ride defensively. Between noon and 3 p.m. you rode 5 or 10 miles and found shade. You made sure your clothes stayed wet.

Being from south Louisiana, I fared better than most, but the radiant heat was a killer. I just kept moving. I had a tortoise mentality. Finally, the heat broke with a memorable frontal passage. It made for a pleasant couple of days.

Finally, the last day of the 2012 RAGBRAI. I had to ride the last 69 miles before 2 p.m. There was a bus scheduled to leave, and I knew my team had doubts. I declared that I would make it. I left the overnight camp at 5:30 a.m. It was a wonder to watch the bikes stretched out in front of me. Red blinkies flashing for miles. I put the trike in high gear and pushed hard. I was averaging 15 mph. I covered 30 miles by breakfast. I remember throwing my fists in the air. I knew I would win. Up and down the rolling hills of Iowa I went. Heading for Clinton, I never let up. I arrived by 12:30 and dipped my front wheels in the Mississippi River, a traditional finish.

If you haven't noticed, RAGBRAI has been the highlight of my year. I will try to ride it on two wheels this year, if the V.A. doesn't provide me with an ICE Vortex racing trike. I am very involved in amputee support. I am also starting an adaptive cycling program in Baton Rouge, Louisiana. You do not recover from losing a limb alone. It does take a couple, a family, or a village. You need people who understand what you have been through. You need people who know you can thrive as an amputee. For some, losing a limb is a burden whereas for others it becomes a catalyst. Strength that was always there is magnified and unleashed.

Cycling saved my life. It allowed my body, mind, and spirit to heal. Without it, I would be sitting in a wheelchair. I doubt I would have survived. I'm not finished yet. A news spot you might find interesting:

→ www.wafb.com/Category/240200/video-landing-page?clipId=8637841&autostart=true.

Register's Annual Great Bicycle Ride Across Iowa, commonly known as RAGBRAI, is big. It is a not a race. Over 15,000 riders traveling from the Missouri River to the Mississippi River over seven days. The average length is 450 miles. The route each year changes. It is considered to be an honor and a windfall to be named an overnight stop. RAGBRAI is always held during the last full week of July. It is best that you join one of the hundreds of established teams. After the teams finish registering, the remaining entries go into a lottery for the remaining weekly and daily wristbands. There are a total of 10,000 weekly and 5,000 daily. Several thousand riders just show up.

Iowa is NOT flat. That is a common misconception. It is made up of never-ending rolling hills covered in corn. I describe Iowa as corn, soybeans, corn, pigs, corn, windmills...and corn. Iowa has more land in crops then any other state in the U.S. The tree cover is about 3 percent. Iowa is a place of small, friendly towns. They believe in the concept of "Iowa Nice."

The average every day is about 80 miles passing through little towns. Overnight stops are in bigger towns. Every hotel is filled. Most riders sleep in tent cities. Teams carry luggage from overnight to overnight stops. Some teams have buses that meet riders along the way—with beer. The overnight towns usually have bands, vendors, and an incredible amount of food. I highly recommend the pork chops on a stick. No kidding. They are the best you will ever have. The weather varies. Iowa usually has temps in the upper 80s and cool nights. The last few years have been much hotter. The first four days of 2012 were each above 100. There are usually a few amputees every year. It is not a beginner's ride. There is a very active adaptive group called Adaptive Sports of Iowa. They are very well supported with air mattresses, showers, support riders, and mechanics.

Mountain Bike Races

These started in the 70s and 80s in southern California. The very first mountain bikes were beach cruisers with mud guards removed to make room for bigger tires. Bikers would transport their bikes to the top of the hill on pickup trucks and cycle all the way back down the hill or down dirt trails as fast as they dared. The most famous of these is known as the "Repack" because it required cyclists to repack their brakes with grease to keep them from overheating. This eventually developed into the sport of mountain bike racing which is popular in different formats in many parts of the world. The UCI recognized mountain biking in 1990, and races were organized in North America and Europe. The races can be divided into a number of events, and this can be anything from 6 to 10 stages over a period of several days.

With regard to mountain biking, cross-country is the most common race category in which riders have to cycle 5 to 9 kilometers (3-6 miles) over obstacles and rocky paths, single tracks, or forest trails in different categories of difficulty. The cross-country marathon is a longer version of this and can require a cyclist to cover a distance of 60 to 120 kilometers (37-75 miles). All riders of all abilities start together. Downhill racing is a race against time down a mountain side. It requires the ability to make sharp turns and jumps while balancing at high speeds. Bike trials involve the skill of balance in that the rider must slowly overcome obstacles without setting a foot down off the pedals. Dirt jumping involves the rider jumping off high mounds of dirt and performing tricks, twirls, and other stunts. An alternative to these types of races is mountain bike orienteering in which route choice and navigation are tested alongside bike skills. The International Orienteering Federation is a good source of information on this type of racing which involves endurance and skill as it is done over some very long routes. Stage races involve combining different events together either on one day or over several days. There are stage winners and an overall winner. Mountain biking sportives are conducted on very challenging trails. You have to travel to the remotest parts of a country to enter these. Similarly, Audax routes are races that are totally unsupported with food, drink, or other such facilities. These are extreme events and certainly not for the fainthearted!

Cyclocross

The first recognized cyclocross races were conducted in the UK. These require a high level of physical fitness and bike-handling skills. There are various categories. The easiest category is the cross-country race or the short track cross-country race. These involve a mass start of all riders, so collisions are to be expected. The downhill race is a timed stage event. Cyclocross racing mixes both elements of cross-country and downhill racing into an event known as the Super D. This involves racing on sections of both downhill and uphill trails. Freeride competitions test cyclists' ability over cliffs, drops, obstacles, and ramps. Time and technique are tested in this type of competition. There are also a number of endurance or ultra-endurance mountain biking events that take place annually.

Miscellaneous Races

Time trials can be individual or team events. An individual time trial involves the cyclist racing against the clock similar to the track event. Night races are sometimes organized in a similar manner to single-day events. They are known as the nocturne or twilight races. There are other races organized by cyclist messenger organizations such as Alleycat. Cyclist messengers organize their own competitions in urban areas.

The previous information refers to races that able-bodied cyclists do, but there is no reason not to attempt them. If you are lucky enough to live somewhere near an active paracycling organization, then the points and eligibility systems are quite different. Athletes are classified according to their functional class profiles based on the extent of activity limitation rather than simply on their disability. This is seen as a more enabling system of classification. Classification of athletes is attempted to ensure fairness in competition and to miminize the effect of the impairment on the ability of the athlete to succeed.

Theoretically, with the correct classification, an athlete should only concern themselves with their overall race preparation and physical readiness to compete as opposed to the obstacles posed by the disability. In practice, there is often no "correct" classification as every disability is different. Classification also enables race organizers to group riders in appropriate races. The assessment is undertaken by a medical doctor, a physiotherapist, and a sports technician. It may involve physical and technical elements in the appraisal. The person undergoing the assessment should attend in race clothing with their racing equipment—bike, helmet, and all adaptations.

The main classifications are handcycle (H1, H2, and H3), tricycle (T1 and T2), cycling (C1, C2, C3, C4, and C5), and tandem (Class B). The race formats are similar to able-bodied formats in that there are time trials, individual, and team pursuits in track or road competitions. As far as amputees with no other impairments are concerned, they may be eligible to race in handcylce class H4 and cycling classes C1, C2, C3, C4, and C5. This means that the race may involve competing against not only other amputees, but also people with more severe or not so obvious disabilities. There is no provision for amputees to cycle in tricycle races as yet, but that may change in the future if there is enough demand from amputees to compete in such events.

The issues of classification become more complicated when there are multiple conditions to deal with. There may be physical and neurological impairments together in one person. Younger disabled people may be generally a lot healthier than older disabled people due to extensive efforts to change attitudes toward inclusion of disabled people within society. While there is competition, there will always be controversy as to the fairness of the classification system. The assessment process is confidential, and the athlete has the right to challenge classification panel decisions should they be concerned with the outcome. Essentially, every athlete is going to want to be put in the classification group that provides them with the best chance of winning.

Paralympics

The classification debate is as valid in paracycling as it is in the wider sports of the Paralympics. The athletes that compete at such levels put in some incredible hours of training on a daily basis, often juggling this alongside work and family commitments. A significant barrier to participation in sport at such high levels on a consistent basis is funding provision. Most athletes seek a combination of business sponsorship and sports bursaries, or some even use their personal income to fund their participation in competitions. Those that receive such support are few and far between, and it is worth contacting the Paralympic bodies and paracycling bodies in your country for advice on funding applications for competitions, equipment, or coaching if you decide you seriously want to aim that high. It takes many years to get to the top, but if you decide to make a career out of professional cycling, then it is worth developing links with those who have spent considerable time in such professional circuits. Their experience, advice, and encouragement will be invaluable to your development, not only with regard to funding, but also for organizing training partners and competitors.

Winning Fairly

The topic of competing at any level and the issues of cheating or doping are never far apart from each other. Drug use goes as far back as the sport of cycling itself. In the Tour de France, name after name is associated with different drugs. Some lead to disqualification from an event; others end up with long-term cycling bans or acquittals. The whole process of clearing your name following an allegation of drug taking is a lengthy, frustrating one, especially if you were actually guilty of the offence in the first place but wanted to see what you could get away with!

Competition bodies such as the IOC (International Olympic Committee), paracycling, and Paralympics organizations provide common lists of acceptable and banned substances while training and competing. These organizations work closely with the World Anti-Doping Agency (WADA) to agree on testing methods and issue guidance on newer, unevaluated substances that come onto the market from time to time. Those who compete in high level sports competitions are subject to drug testing; however, there are flaws with even the most scientific of methods. Blood and urine tests are the common forms of drug test. Steroids and blood-enriching products or transfusions are most used by athletes who want quick results in their training or who want to win at any cost.

If ultra fast *(blink and you miss it!)* or endurance *(how many months?!)* racing is simply not your style, how about trying a different type of race altogether? In a s-l-o-w cycling race, the winner is the person who is the *s-l-o-w-e-s-t* to cross the finishing line.

It takes place in many countries around Europe and is probably the easiest form of racing to organize for small groups of non-athletes. The slower you pedal the bicycle, especially if it is a two-wheeler, the harder it is to balance. Why not think about it? Arrange a small session in a parking lot first with riders of two-wheelers, handcycles, tricycles, and tandems and see how you all get on with it. It will be hard work not to sprint to the finish line first, and most of all, it will be really enjoyable as you will hardly be out of breath!

Cycling in Heavy Traffic

This forms part of the expert cyclist chapter as commuting to work and other areas on traffic-free paths or tracks is the ideal place for cyclists, especially beginners, until they are able to keep up with traffic flows safely. Cycling in mainstream traffic with cars, buses, trucks, vans, motorbikes, and pedestrians is a recipe for stress, even for experienced cyclists. As towns and cities become more populated and congested, this leads naturally to impatience and frustration during peak travel times. Some cities, such as London, are moving toward encouraging more cycling. Further political pressure for cycling

will hopefully achieve more positive results globally. Before venturing out regularly on heavily used roads, get some road safety skills. These show you how to manuever around roundabouts, start and stop at traffic lights, overtake, and turn safely. Other techniques to be proficient in are lane positioning, looking back regularly, and making eye contact with drivers.

Practice these on quiet traffic days, but if there aren't any in your busy city, look for a quieter environment to try out your road sense. When starting with cycling, it will be natural to pedal slowly, but to cycle with traffic, it is important to pedal at a suitable speed for the road. When out on the roads in all weather conditions on a bicycle, it is important to wear high visibility clothing and a good safety helmet at all times. Being easily visible to other road users will help reduce the risk of accident. Most crashes with motor vehicles occur at driveways and junctions. Aim to ride predictably and follow the rules of the road. Road safety courses are available in many countries for both adults and children. Do take the time to attend one, especially if you are going to be cycling a low recumbent, a handcycle, or a two-wheeler in heavy traffic conditions.

Road Rules

Bikes are classed as vehicles. A safe cyclist observes the following rules:

1. Keep at least one hand on your handlebars.
2. Both feet should be on the pedals.
3. (These first two rules may be worth clarifying in your own country for arm and leg amputees who prefer to ride without prosthetics.)
4. Either cycle in the center of the lane or toward the left, but keep a meter (or foot) between you and the edge of the road or parked cars.
5. Don't ride too close to the vehicle in front. Stopping safely is your responsibility.
6. It is illegal to hold onto a moving vehicle or trailer.
7. Don't stop on the inside of a vehicle in a line of traffic. This is a blind spot for the driver of vehicles that want to turn into a side road in their direction of travel.
8. Cycling on sidewalks is illegal.

In some countries, roads are marked with separate cycling lanes. These come in a number of versions. The safest version is that of the cycle and pedestrian path being separated from the main traffic by a curb or railing in traffic-free lanes. However, this tends to not be applied on many established roads (especially in older cities where roads are narrower), so some countries use lane markings along existing lanes in an attempt to separate the cyclist from heavy traffic.

The problem with this is that the cycling lane is usually obstructed by parked vehicles or is narrow and next to the curb, guttering and other obstacles, making the cycling experience more unpleasant than it needs to be. Cycling conditions in winter are also not always pleasant.

Cycling alongside motorized vehicles will expose you to the exhaust fumes, dust, and smog of commuting. This can also reduce the overall enjoyment of rediscovering the open air commute to your place of work. This is especially the case when cycling uphill. The lower speed and chances of wobbling make it more frustrating when cars speed past you and then stop in front of you at a traffic light, making it harder to keep your momentum. Often the safest thing to do is to get off your bike and push it up the hill, even though you know you could cycle up given the space and time. Look for alternative routes with less traffic, if possible, even if they are slightly longer. It will be much more fun!

Take a look at the phenomenon known as streak cycling. This is the term used to describe those who decide to ride their bikes every day for long periods of time. Proponents of this type of cycling keep cycling for many, many years. It may be a good way to train for that round the world cycling journey you've been dreaming about.

Becoming a Cycling Instructor

This is where the amputee list grows as those amputees who have been cycling for many years have taken up the challenge of training others. Being taught by a cyclist who understands from experience about the effects and issues of amputation is a more powerful way of learning about cycling. Expert cyclists can take a course usually organized by a national cycling organization to become cycling instructors. It is worthwhile as the opportunity to show off to others on a regular basis what you can do is immense. Cycling instructors often work from charities or from fitness centers, like Gemma Trotter, Jim Bush, and John Thraves. Most will be self-employed and, therefore, running a small business.

Running a Cycling Business or Charity

For those who are very taken with cycling as a business, there is no need to stop at becoming an instructor. Why not consider opening your own bike shop with a maintenance area or a bike rental center or a cycling charity, even? It will involve negotiating with suppliers and finding enough customers to keep you going, but with the renaissance in cycling that is being experienced currently, it might just be a fun thing to try. There will be business rules to take into account, and these will be specific to the country that you live in as well as health and safety rules and much more, but the satisfaction that you get from running your own business will no doubt make up for all that beaurocracy and red tape.

Running a Cycling Vacation Company

If being in one location does not sound appealing, how about arranging group cycling rides and vacations? It may be that as you look for your own cycling trip, the existing providers may not cater enough for disabled people, and this is where you could have an input. If you have a good group of friends, you might want to experiment with them to work out the pros and cons of running a cycling vacation business together. Take the plunge and organize a small cycling break for beginner amputee cyclists or other disabled beginner cyclists. Testing out suitable trails for others and checking the quality of accommodation in different parts of your own country or other countries may be just what you enjoy doing.

Running a Cycling Group or Club

If branching out on your own seems too risky, getting involved in helping to organize competitions, events, and other such activities for existing cycling clubs and organizations may provide you with enough insight and confidence to eventually start out on your own. As many of these examples are of two-wheeler cyclists, perhaps if you have advanced skills in handcycling, recumbent, or tricycle, you might like to try to set up some classes, such as spin cycling, events, or arrange general cycling lessons for such forms of cycling.

Becoming a Cycling Reporter

If you have good writing skills, then negotiating a reporting contract for disabled magazines for cycling reports from various events may be an interesting way to help pay the entrance fees. Of course, you could take it all one step further and decide to set up your own global amputee cycling publication—there really isn't one out there yet. The world of online publishing makes it easier and cheaper to produce good quality articles for global audiences and is possibly something to consider if cycling takes off among sufficient numbers of amputees.

From the Amputees

Armin Köhli, Switzerland

Ask any champion, in whatever discipline—Tour de France, RAAM, track, time trials. They will tell you what made the difference on the day was their brain and mind. Who can maintain motivation for longer, who believes they are the strongest and unbeatable, and who can suffer and endure the pain, the weather conditions, and overcome the environment?

Joe Beimfohr, USA

I recently completed the Sadler's Alaska Challenge. It was a six-stage 228-mile race over five days. The last day we climbed Hatcher Pass, which topped out at 3,400 feet. We started at sea level and went to the top over the 22-mile course. That was the hardest day on the bike that I've ever had, but I felt such a sense of achievement after I had finished. I guess that's why so many of us race competitively; we want to push ourselves and see what we can achieve.

Esneider Muñoz Marín, Columbia

My greatest achievements have been: Para-Panamerican Champion on men's track (individual pursuit) and race. Gold medal in Germany's Euro Cup, champion in national games of track and race, and national champion for four4 consecutive years. In the last months, I earned the seventh place in men's road time trail (CRI) on Canada's World Championship Track, fifth place in men's road race, and eighth place in men's road time trial in Canada's World Cup. My advice for people interested in this sport is you just have to be dedicated and courageous. Attend your local or national league.

Stumps and Cranks Book Interview with Jim Bush, UK, 2014

I'm a right-leg above-knee amputee since I fell off a mountain in New Zealand in 1994. I work three days a week (Monday, Wednesday, and Thursday) for the London Cycling Campaign (LCC) as their bookkeeper (the easy finance stuff), although I am actually a qualified accountant. I sometimes cycle from Croydon to work in Bermondsey (near London Bridge), which is 11.5 miles, but if I cycle back to the swimming pool on the way home (14.5 miles) and the 2 miles home after that, it's nearly 30 miles a day.

If I don't cycle all the way in, I ride my folding bike to East Croydon station, get a train to London Bridge station, and cycle the rest. In the evening, I cycle back to London Bridge, get a train to East Croydon, take my folding bike on a tram up to near the swimming pool, cycle to the pool, swim, cycle back to the tram stop, get a tram back down the hill, and finally cycle home from the tram stop. That's six separate journeys during the day, totaling a massive 3.5 miles!

On Tuesdays, I'm a volunteer at Cycling for All, a disabled cycling charity which runs cycling sessions for the disabled (mainly adults with learning difficulties) at Croydon

Sports Arena (an athletics track—a flat, 8-lane traffic-free venue). I cycle to the arena (2.1 miles) and home again afterward, usually doing some food shopping on the way. Then I ride up to the swimming pool in the evening again (5 miles round trip).

On Fridays, I do a cycle courier job for an environmental charity in Carshalton, delivering council papers to their councillors for Sutton Council. By the time I've also been food shopping and swimming at lunchtime before the cycle courier round in the late afternoon, Friday is usually a 30-mile day.

Cycle mileage is a bit variable on Saturdays, but I have also pedalled 30 miles going nowhere much. On Sundays, I often go out cycling with Pollards Hill Cyclists, where we spend all day cycling 30 miles. All in all, that adds up to approximately 6,000 miles of cycling per year, and often when I get my car MOT tested, I have only driven approximately 200 to 300 miles per year!

Describe a typical commute

The direct route for my current commute is to go over the hill at Crystal Palace, but that's an unnecessary hill to go over, so I go around it on the A23 (main road through Streatham and Brixton). That means the route is flatter but carries a lot of traffic (at least the main roads get more green time at traffic light junctions!), so I tend to commute early (leaving home at 7 a.m. and getting to work at 8 a.m.) to avoid the worst of the traffic. It is a bit stressful because it is faster than I normally cycle (the 12-mile journey takes just under an hour in total), but I have always cycled in London (for approximately 35 years), so I can cope with the traffic. Pollution is not a problem in the early morning commute on the way to work, but it is notably worse in the late afternoon on the way home (especially going up Brixton Hill and along the pothole-strewn Streatham High Road). We do not have shower facilities at work, and I usually carry some spare clothes (especially spare, dry stump socks), but I don't generally change when I get there because, arriving at 8 a.m., I have to unlock the office and have an hour before anyone else arrives, so I can cool off in that time. Also, it is generally cooler in the mornings, so I don't tend to get that hot on the way in to work. On the way home, it is hotter, and I usually go uphill for two miles when I get back to Croydon to go swimming, so I am very hot when I get to the pool.

Why do you cycle?

Reasons for cycling include it is cheaper, it gets me some exercise (as an above-knee leg amputee, I can't run at all!), and cycling is much faster than walking. I did spend most the winter commuting by taking a folding bike on the train into London, because it is quicker and safer, especially in the dark.

How long after amputation before you cycled?

I think I was in hospital for six weeks after amputation, then two months in a rehabilitation unit, before being discharged and spending most of my time going to a whole succession of outpatient appointments at the hospital. I started trying to cycle again on Sundays in school playgrounds and car parks, just to get used to starting off and stopping (and having to remember to only try to put the good foot on the ground!). I did try hopping on crutches at the hospital (before I got even a basic "training prosthesis"), and I walked quite a bit at the rehabilitation unit.

Did you cycle before amputation?

Yes, I have always cycled. There are even a few color slides of me riding a trike in our garden (aged 3 onward).

Advice to new amputees and new cyclists to help them commute as an amputee on a bike?

Remember that cycling is non-weight-bearing exercise, so it is much easier than walking or running! Practice makes perfect, so make sure you know how to start off on a bike, how to pedal to keep going, how to stop, and where to stop so that it is easy to get a foot securely onto the ground. Practice your commuting route at a quiet time of day or the week and find out if there is public transit assistance available if it is raining or snowing. Consider taking a change of clothes to change into at work, ensure there is secure cycle parking at work, and try to persuade your employer to provide showers and changing facilities. Once you've got the basic commuting technique and route settled, you can try adapting and varying it (e.g., by going [food] shopping on the way home, or going direct to a swimming pool or evening meetings on the way home, as I do).

Nathan Smith, New Zealand

My best ever cycling experience was my first race on the London Velodrome in the 2012 Paralympics. It was the kilo, a race in which I had no chance in medaling, but the plan was to go out there, soak it up, and get ready for my main event (3-kilometer pursuit) the next day. The crowd was unbelievable—6,000, mostly Brits, cheering you on no matter which country you came from. And when they were cheering their own countrymen, it was truly deafening. I was so pumped up, and when I get that way, I start clapping to myself. I didn't hear it, but the announcer had just told the crowd it was my birthday the day before, and there I was giving myself a clap. Ha, ha! Anyway, I managed to smash my personal best over the 4 laps. I finished well down the leader board, but I was choked to have finished one of the fastest above-knee amputees and to have experienced such an arena. Most of the race is a blur, but that moment of climbing onto my bike and getting out from the start gates with the roar of that crowd will be one I'll never forget.

Sara Tretola, Switzerland – The Story of Athens

My biggest successes were the bronze medal in the time trial at the Paralympics in Athens, 2004. I was European champion in the time trial in 2005 and won the silver medal at the road race in the European Championships in 2005.

In the summer of 2004, I dreamed of taking part in the Paralympics in Athens. But because I had to prioritize revising for my final exams in order to gain my work qualifications, I couldn't take part in all the races organized by the Swiss Paralympic Cycling Team program. I decided with the team coach to only race in those that were compulsory in order to qualify. With each race, I improved my performance and my results. Despite the improvement in performance, my results were just short of the qualification criteria for the Paralympics. At the beginning of June, the only chance I had left was the track race in Augsburg, Germany. Because of exams, I could only travel to the competition the day before the race.

My parents and I drove off on Friday afternoon from Switzerland in the direction of Germany. We had an approximate five-hour car journey before us. We were supposed to arrive at our hotel around 6 p.m. so that we could enjoy a relaxing meal and go early to bed in order to recover well from the journey. Unfortunately, it didn't work out that way. It was about 5 p.m. as my father asked me to take a look at the map. We were approaching the motorway exit, and my father wanted to make sure he was going in the right direction. Before the exit came we had to go over a motorway junction. A few kilometers later, as the Augsburg exit still hadn't come, my father became uncertain that he had taken the correct road at the junction. Around 50 kilometers farther and still no exit. By this time, my father was certain that we were on the wrong road. The plan was now to leave the motorway at the next junction and find the correct road. We drove and drove and still no exit came. At around 9 p.m., my father started to worry about me and my race the next day. He told me I should try to sleep and not worry. In that time, we had informed that hotel that we would be coming later than planned. A hotel employee was very nice and left a room key for us in a box outside the hotel, so it didn't matter what time we got there.

Finally, we came to an exit. My father took it and stopped at the nearest opportunity to study the map. He saw that after the motorway junction he had taken the wrong motorway. It was around 9:30 p.m. by this time. My father studied the map intently. He saw that we not only had to travel around 100 kilometers back the way we came, but around another 100 kilometers farther. That meant that we would arrive at the hotel around midnight. He and my mother decided that I should sleep in the back so that I was well rested for the race that had become so important to me. I slept quite well in the car. I was sure my father would find the right road.

At exactly midnight, we arrived at the hotel. Without eating, all three of us went to sleep. I don't think my parents slept well that night for worrying that my dream would fall apart during the race the next day. In the morning, we all went early to breakfast in order to go straight to the racing track. My qualification race was to be at 12 p.m. At 10:30 a.m., I was gently cycling on the hometrainer. I started warming up properly at around 11 a.m. That meant that I had one hour of intensive warm-up so that my muscles and heart were at their optimal in preparation for the exertion during the race. 15 minutes before the race, I finished my warm-up and got ready to start. At the starting line, I was very nervous. In my head, I had only one thought: "This is the last chance, all or nothing, I wanted only one thing: to take part in the Paralympics in Athens."

5, 4, 3, 2, 1—the start gate opened, and I pedaled as hard as I possibly could. The race was 3 kilometers long, and I had to cover that distance in at least 4 minutes 20 seconds in order to reach the required time. On the 200-meter stretch of track, I had to complete 15 rounds. I cycled round and round to the point of exhaustion. The only thing that I was conscious of was the support of my parents. My father always stood at the first curve after the starting line. He always screamed "Go Sara" and "di più, di più, di più." He knew that I needed his support more than anything else. Now the last meters, and the race was over. After 15 rounds, the stop clock showed 4 minutes 17 seconds. Yes, I made it! I was a step closer to my Paralympic dream. I heard the joy of my parents. The Selection Committee still had to decide whether my times and the rest of my race results would be enough to qualify for the Paralympics. But I was happy. I knew that I had done everything I could in order to qualify. Despite the long stressful journey, I gave my best. I was chosen for the Paralympics in 2004 in Athens and could go on to fulfill even more dreams, such as winning a Paralympic medal. On September 24, 2004, I won the bronze medal in the individual time trials. On this important day, my parents and three sisters were there to support me.

Qaher Hazrat, Afghanistan

I was 15 when I started competing. It was an AABRAR competition. I have attended eight of these. They are national, mainly for road cyclists, and arranged one to two times a year. I have won them all. I have also competed in a friendly competition in Germany in connection with a land mine conference. Winning at the National Trials is my greatest achievement. But I am also proud I practically won a cycling competition meant for able-bodied only! The Ministry of Health arranged a bicycle competition. I asked if I could join. At first they refused, saying it was only allowed for able-bodied. But I didn't give up. I really wanted to join. With AABRAR to help speak my case, they finally let me compete as well. They had provided 57 old Chinese cycles and three professional athletic cycles. I won among the 57 who had the heavy amateur cycles. People at AABRAR have been of great help and inspiration. But I am also inspired by rivals at competition. They drive me to perform even better. With a good organization behind you, it is good to become an athlete, otherwise it is very difficult. For Athens, I did a lot of cycling and general physical training. I also try to eat healthy; I eat fruit.

Nezir Lupcevic, Bosnia and Herzogovina

In 1976, Nezir began some amateur sports cycling which resulted in his participation in many sport events in the region—Athletic Championship in Split, Croatia, in 1990; Open Championship in Belgium in 1997 (where he got his first Certificates for Accomplishments and medals for participation in a 100-, 200-, and 400-meter run and shotput); World Championships in Germany in 2002. Along with these competitions, Nezir participated to the 2004 Paralympics Games in Athens Greece, as member of the BiH national team.

Nezir usually uses mountain bikes with Shimano XT equipment specialized for hill- or plain-riding. All commands are on his left-hand side and have no problems due to his amputation.

Victor Walther, Canada

The only reason I started racing was I couldn't afford all the new high-end parts and bikes, and people were always taking my picture or stopping me to ask questions about my arm or bike. I have put some basic jump, drop, and wheelie pictures on the website, www.mtb-amputee.com, (bike riding tips page) for demonstration purposes.

Promoting the Sport to a Wider Audience

Amputees who cycle are happy to promote the sport whenever they can, especially the mountain biking set! Both William Craig and Brian Bartlet (leg amputees) have featured in videos, magazine articles, and on YouTube. William was featured on a couple of the original "North Shore" videos. Victor Walther has featured numerous times on TV and in newspaper and magazine articles of the mid 1990s for his racing achievements:

Mountain Bike Action magazine in 2009
Dirt Rag Magazine in 2002-2003 with Will Craig
Pedal magazine, 1996 summer edition
Mountain Bike magazine, 1995 fall (autumn) edition
Coast magazine, 1995 summer edition

TV news channels interviewed him in the 1995 Spokane Norba and the 1996 Canada Cup in Barrie (Toronto). While competing at the 1996 USA nationals on Mammoth Mountain, Victor was interviewed by several UK and Asian cycling publications and was featured on an *Outdoor Life Network* program.

So, that was a brief tour of what the experts are capable of and some ideas to consider if you want to get more involved in cycling. This book is not a comprehensive guide; it is simply an introduction to cycling for amputees. Hopefully it has brought together some visions of cycling for you to attempt. There is plenty more information, advice, and support available from not only the many amputees featured in this book on their websites and social media pages, but also cycling organizations around the world that currently support amputees and disabilities in general, including charities and business groups.

In the words of Victor Walther:

"Once you get the right prosthetics and bike, you are no longer an amputee, you're a cyclist! Ride on!"

→ **www.mtb-amputee.com**

Further Reading

1. Paracycling: http://www.uci.ch/para-cycling/
2. Classification system: http://www.paralympic.org/classification
3. Commonwealth Games: http://www.thecgf.com/
4. Asian Games 2014: http://www.korea.net/Government/Current-Affairs/International-Events?affairId=84

5. All Africa Games: http://www.aag.org.za/games/index.shtml
6. Para Pan American Games: http://www.toronto2015.org/
7. *World's Ultimate Cycling Races* by Ellis Bacon (Harper Collins, 2012)

Did You Know?

1. Beny Furrer (arm amputee) has completed the Race Across America (RAAM) *twice*—in 2003 and in 2014.
2. Gottfried Müller (leg amputee) has been active in the Paralympics since 1996, competing successfully at Atlanta, Sydney, and Athens.
3. Tomislav Zadro, Croatia, and Alfred Kaiblinger, Austria, (both leg amputees) tied in the LC2 Mens 63.9-kilometer race at the EPC Open European Disabled Championships in the Czech Republic in 2003.
4. Ibrahim Wahfula (leg amputee) is a paracyclist from Kenya who rides one-legged without prosthetics. He started his racing career in 1995 and 1996.
5. The slow cycling record was set by Tsugunobu Mitsuishi of Japan in 1965.
6. American Dory Selinger (leg amputee) set the world record in track cycling for flying and 1 kilometer and the US record for the 4-kilometer pursuit during his competitive career.
7. Mark Inglis, New Zealand, (leg amputee) won the silver medal in track cycling at the Sydney Paralympics in 2000.
8. In 2013, Ameican Hector Pickard (double arm amputee) cycled 3,200 miles across America in five weeks to raise money for a young American boy born with no arms.
9. Nezir Lupzevic, Bosnia and Herzogovina, (arm amputee) scored 30 points in the LC1 road race at the 2004 Summer Paralympics held at Vouliagmeni. He was ranked overall 14th.
10. In 2012, Italian ex-Formula 1 driver Alex Zanardi (45-year-old double lower-limb amputee) won Paralympic gold in the H4 handcycling time trial at Brands Hatch, UK.

Things to Try for Yourself

1. Attend a local cycling race to get a feel of the atmosphere.
2. Try timing cycling sessions. Are you getting faster over the same distances?
3. When you feel fast enough, enter a local race—just for the fun of it!
4. Discuss racing tactics and issues with other cycling racers.
5. Investigate the possibilities of setting up disabled cycling clubs and racing events in your area.

Paul Jesson, New Zealand

Jesson recalls: "I was in the New Zealand national squad; we were really just there for training for the Milk Race in Britain. We went with no expectations, but I ended up winning overall and my teammate Blair Stockwell took the last stage. I used to race the New Zealand road season then go to work to get money together so I could come back to Europe to race in the northern hemisphere summer. I'd ride a full program in Belgium, from stage races down to the kermises."

The prologue for the 1980 Dauphine Libere—the traditional 10-day "warm-up" race for the Tour de France—was held in Evian les Bains on May 26, over 7 kilometers, and was won by Raleigh's Dutch ace Joop Zoetemelk. That date was to be the low point of Jesson's life, the English Cycling Weekly magazine of the time reported it briefly: "Paul Jesson had the misfortune to hit a stationary car in the opening prologue time trial. He cracked his knee and it is feared he may not ride again." Jesson remembers little of the day which would change his life forever: "I was round the circuit three times before the start to familiarize myself with the parcours, but that's about it. I hit a parked car during the race—a Lancia, apparently—with my knee and was unconscious for a couple of weeks after. I learned later that I was unlucky with the medical care: I was admitted as the shifts changed, and there was no proper control of my circulation. You have to make sure that the blood keeps moving—if there's no blood circulation for a period of six hours, then that's a real problem. I was operated on by a specialist in Belgium who operated on the likes of Michel Pollentier and top motocross riders, but eventually the leg had to be removed; it was black, dead."

When he did return home, he worked as a frame builder, and it was a chance encounter that steered him back into competition. "I came home, worked as a mechanic for eight years, got married, and raised a family—my two boys. The late Graham Condon, a famous New Zealand Paralympian, used to visit the shop to get the wheels for his wheelchair built. One day, he said to me, "Why don't you get back into cycling?" I said that I didn't realize I could! After that, I went on a trip to Europe to see the Tour de France, and the Swart brothers arranged for me to do a circuit of the Champs Elysees in the Motorola team car on the last stage. That so inspired me that when I got home I bought a new bike and decided that I was going to try to reach the Paralympics. It took a lot of work, but I won the 1998 World Championships for my class in the pursuit and individual time trial. I got to the Olympics in Sydney in 2000 but only finished fourth, which was a disappointment. But I trained hard for Athens 2004 and won bronze in the road competition, which was a combined event—road race and time trial. I was second and sixth, respectively and that got me the medal.

This abridged article, written by Edmond Hood, was published in PEZ (www.pezcyclingnews.com) on September 25, 2012. Reproduced here with the kind permission of Edmond Hood and Richard Pestes of PEZCycling News. This book is dedicated to inspirational amputees such as Paul Jesson.

Appendix

List of Contributors

Contact directly through their websites:

Abdul Qahir, Afghanistan	www.aabrar.org.af
Abdul Qahir Hazrat, Afghanistan	www.aabrar.org.af
Alfred Kaiblinger, Austria	1a1b1r.com
Armin Köhli, Switzerland	www.tourdarmin.ch/en/index.html
Arnold Boldt, Canada	paralympic.ca
Beny Furrer, Switzerland	www.furybeny.ch
Dory Selinger, USA	www.doryselinger.com
Esneider Muñoz Marín, Columbia	arcangeles.org
Gemma Trotter, UK	www.douglasbaderfoundation.com
Gottfried Müller, Germany	www.gotty-mueller.de
Habib Jan, Afghanistan	www.aabrar.org.af
Hoang Thi Lan, Vietnam	www.aepd-vn.org
Jim Bush, UK	www.wheelsforwellbeing.org.uk
Joe Beimfohr, USA	www.darrellparks.com
Joe Sapere, USA	www.amputeesacrossamerica.com
John Thraves, UK	www.dcn.org.uk
Kiera Roche, UK	www.limbpower.com/contact-us

Kurt Yaeger	www.kurtyaeger.com
Margaret Biggs and Wyn Jenkins UK	www.douglasbaderfoundation.com
Mark Inglis, New Zealand	www.markinglis.co.nz
Mark Ormrod, UK	www.markormrod.com
Michael Caines, UK	www.michaelcaines.com
Nezir Lupcevic, Bosnia/Herzogovina	www.ipm-lsi.org
Rajesh Durbal, USA	www.rajeshdurbal.com and www.live-free.net
Sara Tretola, Switzerland	www.theodora.ch
Shafiqulla Samim, Afghanistan	www.aabrar.org.af
Srdjan Jeremic, Bosnia/Herzogovina	www.ipm-lsi.org
Steve and Anne Middleton, Canada	www.morethanmobility.ca/index.html
Tran Duy Khanh, Vietnam	www.aepd-vn.org
Tran Thi Ngoc Linh, Vietnam	www.aepd-vn.org
Victor Walther, Canada	www.mtb-amputee.com
Will Craig, Canada	prostheticarm.com
Yvon Le Caer, USA	www.yvonlecaer.com

Contact by emailing info@stumpsandcranks.co.uk

Dan Sheret, USA

Jon Pini, UK

Mirsad Tokić, Croatia

Mona Krayem, Germany

Nathan Smith, New Zealand

Robert Bailey, USA

Sonia Sanghani, UK

Tomislav Zadro, Croatia

Apologies to amputee cyclists we couldn't reach while putting this book together. If you have cycled previously or still enjoy cycling wherever in the world you are, please email us at info@stumpsandcranks.co.uk or through www.stumpsandcranks.co.uk.

Appendix

Acknowledgments

As with any project, this book would not have come together without a lot of help from an absolute Tour de Amputee Cycling-size peleton of sources and experts. With that in mind, we would like to thank the following for their enthusiastic provision of material, such as photographs, their patience, valuable advice, and support during the writing, editing, and publishing process.

AABRAR	www.aabrar.org.af
American Orthotic and Prosthetic Association	www.aopanet.org
Association for Empowerment for Persons with Disability (Nguyen Thi Thanh Hong)	www.aepd-vn.org
British Cycling	www.britishcycling.org.uk
Canadian Paralympic Committee	paralympic.ca
Commonwealth Games	www.thecgf.com
Handcycling UK (Matthew Lindley)	www.handcycling.org.uk
UCI (Yuko Sato)	www.uci.ch
Adam Rous	www.ukbikestore.co.uk

Alfred Kaiblinger	www.1a1b1r.com
Andrea White	www.rockinoggins.com
Armin Köhli	www.tourdarmin.ch
Atob magazine (David Henshaw)	www.atob.org.uk
Batribike	www.batribike.com
Bike It	www.bikeit.co.uk
Butterworth-Spengler Insurance Group	www.cyclesure.co.uk
Darrell Parks	www.darrellparks.com
DBF	www.douglasbaderfoundation.com
Debbie Gillespie	www.dillglove.co.uk
Draisin (Michael Denu)	www.draisin.com
Esther Banz	www.buerobanz.ch and www.velojournal.ch
Excellent Books (Richard Peace)	www.excellentbooks.co.uk
Garmin	www.garmin.co.uk
H7 Engineering	www.h7engineering.co.uk
Handicap International (Elke Hottentot)	www.handicap-international.org
Halfords	www.halfords.com
Help for Heroes	www.helpforheroes.org.uk
High 5 Nutrition	www.highfive.co.uk
Invacare	www.invacare.co.uk
Juan Salazar/Stevens Ruiz	arcangeles.org
Landmine Survivor Initiative (Ramiz Becirovic and Amir Mujanovic)	www.ipm-lsi.org
Limbpower (Kiera Roche)	www.limbpower.com
Limbs4all	www.limbs4all.co.nz
New Zealand Herald	www.nzherald.co.nz
Mark Ormrod	www.markormrod.com
Mtb-amputee (Victor Walther)	www.mtb-amputee.com
Mike Thurogood Össur UK	www.ossur.co.uk,
Momentum Electric Bikes	www.momentumelectric.co.uk
Odoni-Elwell(Callam Mccabe)	www.Odoni-Elwell.com
Peter Lago	www.elite-it.com
PEZ (Ed Hood and Richard Pestas)	www.pezcyclingnews.com
Ralph Coulson	www.batribike.com
Raphael Deinhart	www.highfive.co.uk
Roofbox	www.roofbox.co.uk

Rouleur (Ian Cleverly)   www.rouleur.cc
Team Hybrid   www.teamhybrid.co.uk
Firoz Ali Alizada   www.icblcmc.org
Helaine Boyd   www.stumpsandcranks.co.uk
Andrew Chamings   www.stumpsandcranks.co.uk

Many of those listed can also be contacted on Facebook and Twitter.

Poetry and paintings credited to:
Philip Sheridan: www.philip-sheridan.com
Steve Stevens: www.goldenoldy.org

We would also like to thank all authors and publishers who gave permission to use any material from their existing sources. Thanks to public and university libraries and professionals working at Limb Centres in South Wales, UK. Plus the many others that made this *Tour* a brilliant and exciting endeavor. Sorry we were unable to list you all, but you know who you are. Thanks to all of you!

Conversion Table

As the stories within this book are told by amputees in different parts of the world, the following conversion table may come in useful to help understand their measurement systems for weight, distance, currency, or temperature.

For weights, measures and temperatures:

1 pound = 0.45 kilogram
1 stone = 6.35 kilograms
1 miles = 1.61 kilometers
1 inch = 2.54 centimeters
1 foot = 0.31 meter
1 degree Centigrade = 33.8 degrees Fahrenheit

For recipes:

500 g = 2 cups
100 g = ½ cup
50 g= ¼ cup

Currency values for US Dollar ($), UK Pound (£), Euro (€), and Swiss Francs (CHF) as well as other currencies tend to fluctuate on a daily basis. For up-to-date values, refer to currency converters such as www.xe.com/currencyconverter or reputable ones in your own country.

Credits

Edited:	Armin Köhli, Switzerland, and Helaine Boyd, Canada.
Cover design:	Marc Locatelli, Switzerland. http://www.marclocatelli.ch/html/
Layout:	Eva Feldmann
Typesetting:	www.satzstudio-hilger.de
Cartoons:	Marc Locatelli, Switzerland. http://www.marclocatelli.ch/html/and Martin Proctor, MPD Associates Ltd, UK
Copyediting:	Elizabeth Evans

Credits for Photos and Images

p. 6: Watercolour courtesy of www.goldenoldy.org

p. 9: Cartoon courtesy of Marc Locatelli www.marclocatelli.ch

p. 11: Map of amputations courtesy of www.clker.com

p. 11: Photo of Abdul Qahir courtesy of www.aabraar.org.af

p. 12: Photo of Armin Köhli courtesy of www.tourdarmin.ch

p. 17: Photo of Dory Selinger courtesy of www.doryselinger.com

p. 20: Photo of Esneider Muñoz Marín courtesy of www.arcangeles.org

p. 21: Photo of zen garden courtesy of イーアン正モール https://commons.wikimedia.org/wiki/File:Zen_garden_horizontal.jpg

p. 24: Photo of Joe Beimfohr courtesy of www.darrellparks.com

p. 25: Photo of mountain biker courtesy of Getty Images/Stockphoto

p. 27: Photo of Habib Jan courtesy of www.aabraar.org.af

p. 28: Photo of Hoang Thi Lan courtesy of www.aepd-vn.org

p. 29: Photo of prosthetic limbs courtesy of www.tourdarmin.ch

p. 31: Photo of female amputee with bike courtesy of www.muktiindia.org

p. 31: Photo of Mono limb courtesy of www.muktiindia.org

p. 31: Photo of different types of liners courtesy of www.willowwoodco.com, www.ottobock.co.uk and www.ossur.co.uk

p. 32: Photo of Glide Wear Patch courtesy of www.amputeesupplies.com

p. 32: Photo of liner courtesy of www.tourdarmin.ch

p. 32: Photo of Esneider Muñoz Marín www.arcangeles.org

p. 34: Two photos of different stumps commonly seen in Africa courtesy of www.genevacall.org

p. 36: Photo of different hand systems courtesy of G. Smit et al. "Efficiency of voluntary opening hand and hook prosthetic devices, 24 years of development?," JRRD, vol.49, 2012 www.rehab.research.va.gov

p. 37: Photo of knee unit courtesy of www.ossur.co.uk

p. 38: Photo of prosthetic socks courtesy of www.prosindiana.com

p. 38: Photo of prosthetic sleeves courtesy of www.silipos.com

p. 39: Photos of joints and leg courtesy of
www.ottobock.co.uk and www.ossur.co.uk

p. 40: Photo of various feet courtesy of
www.willowwoodco.com

p. 41: Photo of arm and cable courtesy of
Motion Control

p. 42: Photo of Mark Omrod courtesy of
www.markormrod.com

p. 43: Photo of Robert Bailey courtesy of himself

p. 45: Two photos of legs and liners courtesy of Mirsad
Tokić

p. 46: Photo of female arm amputee cyclist courtesy of
Victor Walther www.mtb-amputee.com

p. 46: Two photos of arm adaptations courtesy of
www.1a1b1r.com

p. 46: Two photos of arm and liner courtesy of Sara
Tretola

p. 47: Photo of arm courtesy of Will Craig
www.prostheticarm.com/page 3.html

p. 48: Photo of Wisi courtesy of Esther Banz
www.velojournal.ch

p. 48: Photo of arm adaptation courtesy of
www.1a1b1r.com

p. 49: Photo of leg courtesy of www.ossur.co.uk

p. 49: X-ray courtesy of Denver Clinic www.pslmc.com

p. 50: Photo of Dan Sheret courtesy of himself

p. 51: Photo of Mark Inglis courtesy of
www.markinglis.co.uk

p. 52: Photo of Nathan Smith courtesy of himself

p. 52: Photo of Robert Bailey courtesy of himself

p. 53: Photo of Steve Middleton courtesy of
www.morethanmobility.ca

p. 54: Courtesy of Motion Control

p. 56: Photo of amputee cyclist courtesy of Siniša
Mazulović

p. 57: Photo of John Thraves courtesy of himself

p. 59: Photo of Ajiro Bamboo Bike courtesy of Australian
Design Awards

p. 60: Photo of saddles courtesy of www.dillglove.co.uk

p. 61: Photo of bike pedal courtesy of Mona Krayem

p. 62: Photo of above knee adaptation courtesy of
www.1a1b1r.com

p. 63: Photo of bike wheels courtesy of Halfords
www.halfords.com

p. 64: Photo of Kiera Roche courtesy of
www.limbpower.com

p. 66: Photo of gears and wheel courtesy of
www.halfords.com

p. 67: Photo of mountain bike wheel and gearing
courtesy of www.halfords.com

58. Page 67: Photo of triathlon bike and gearing
courtesy of www.rajeshdurbal.com

p. 67: Photo of gearing mechanism courtesy of
www.halfords.com

p. 68: Photo of Mark Inglis courtesy of
www.nzherald.co.nz

p. 69: Photo of handlebar courtesy of www.1a1b1r.com

p. 69: Photo of triathlon handlebar courtesy of
www.rajeshdurbal.com

p. 69: Six photos of handlebars, tape and grips courtesy
of www.bikeit.co.uk

p. 70: Photo of handcycling amputee courtesy of
www.darrellparks.com

p. 70: Photo of banana seat courtesy of John Thraves

p. 71: Two photos of adapter and steering courtesy of
Sara Tretola

p. 73: Photo of gear/brake adaptation courtesy of
www.1a1b1r.com

p. 73: Photo of Wisi Zgraggen courtesy of Esther Banz
www.velojournal.ch

p. 73: Photo of Jaye Milley courtesy of Canadian
Paralympic Committee www.paralympic.ca

p. 75: Photo of Srdjan Jeremic courtesy of
www.ipm-lsi.org

p. 77: Photo of Mirsad Tokić courtesy of himself

p. 78: Courtesy of Motion Control

p. 79: Photo of amputee cyclist courtesy of Getty Images / Stockphoto

p. 83: Two photos illustrating bike fit courtesy of Robert Bailey

p. 83: Photo of hand cyclist courtesy of www.darrellparks.com

p. 84 : Photo of Robert Bailey courtesy of himself

p. 86: Photo of Steve Middleton courtesy of www.morethanmobility.ca

p. 87: Photo of Gemma Trotter courtesy of herself

p. 89: Photo of handbike adaptation for wheelchairs courtesy of www.riomobility.com

p. 90: Two Photos of handcyclists courtesy of www.handcycling.org.uk and Andrew Chamings

p. 91: Photo of handcyclist in snow courtesy of www.handcycling.org.uk and Andrew Chamings

p. 91: Photo of Joe Beimfohr courtesy of www.darrellparks.com

p. 92: Photo of adult tricycle courtesy of www.missioncycles.co.uk

p. 93: Photo courtesy of www.missioncycles.co.uk

p. 96: Photo of Mirsad Tokić courtesy of himself

p. 99: Photo of handcyclists and Armin Köhli courtesy of www.tourdarmin.ch

p. 100: Photo of Dan Sheret courtesy of himself

p. 100: Photo of Esneider's bike courtesy of www.arcangeles.org

p. 100: Photo of Nathan Smith courtesy of himself

p. 102-105: Four photos of electric bikes courtesy of David Henshaw and Richard Peace, authors of Electric Bicycles: The Complete Guide (Excellent Books, 2010)

p. 107: Photo of electric bike courtesy of John Thraves

p. 110: Photo of Nezir Lupzevic courtesy of www.ipm-lsi.org

p. 111: Photo of Nathan Smith courtesy of himself

p. 111: Photo of Arnold Boldt courtesy of Phil MacCullum, Canadian Paralympic Committee

p. 113/5/6: Four product photos courtesy of www.bikeit.co.uk

p. 116/7: Photo of helmet cover courtesy of www.rockinoggins.com

p. 117/8: Four photos of products courtesy of www.bikeit.co.uk

p. 120: Four photos of products courtesy of www.bikeit.co.uk

p. 121: Photo of product courtesy of www.bikeit.co.uk

p. 122: Photo of Judi Bachmann courtesy of herself

p. 122: Photo of cycling clothing courtesy of www.reversegearinc.com

p. 123-125: Photos of products courtesy of www.bikeit.co.uk

p. 125: Photo of Abdul Qahir Hazrat courtesy of www.aabraar.org.af

p. 126: Photo of Habib Jan courtesy of www.aabraar.org.af

p. 127/8: Four product photos courtesy of www.bikeit.co.uk

p. 129: Photo of leg and shoe – courtesy of Steve Middleton

p. 131: Two photos of Sara Tretola – courtesy of herself

p. 135: Two photos from Wikimedia commons open use licence

p. 136: Two photos from Wikimedia commons open use licence

p. 141: Photo of Rajesh Durbal courtesy of www.rajeshdurbal.com

p. 142: Photo of Nathan Smith courtesy of himself

p. 142: Photo of bike courtesy of John Thraves

p. 145: Photo of Mona Krayem courtesy of herself

p. 148: Photo of Esneider on grass courtesy of www.arcangeles.org

p. 148: Photo of handcyclist on grass courtesy of www.handcycling.org.uk and Andrew Chamings

p. 151: Photo of Robert Bailey courtesy of himself

p. 152: Photo of Jim Bush courtesy of himself

p. 153: Photo of handcycling courtesy of www.handcycling.org.uk and Andrew Chamings

p. 154: Photo of Dory courtesy of www.doryselinger.com

p. 156: Photo of cyclists courtesy of Jim Bush

p. 157: Photo of bicycle courtesy of Robert Bailey

p. 158: Three photos courtesy of Mona Krayem

p. 159: Photo of Tran Duy Khanh courtesy of www.aepd-vn.org

p. 160: Photo of tandem cyclists courtesy of www.douglasbaderfoundation.com

p. 161: Photo of tandem cyclists courtesy of www.douglasbaderfoundation.com

p. 165: Photo of Tran Thi Ngoc Linh courtesy of www.aepd-vn.org

p. 167: Photo of Gemma Trotter courtesy of herself

p. 167: Photo from TEMA, Nezahat Gökyiğit Park, Istanbul 2008 courtesy of Nevit Dilmen, commons. wikimedia.org/wiki/File:Tema_Nezahat_Gokyigit_ Park_1060601_20080513125056.JPG

p. 168: Photo of Armin courtesy of www.tourdarmin.ch

p. 169: Photo of Armin courtesy of www.tourdarmin.ch

p. 171: Photo of Parque Mirador de los Nevados, Colombia/Bogota/Suba 2007, courtesy of Archivo Imagenes Javonauta www. commons.wikimedia.org/ wiki/File:PMN1.jpg

p. 172: Photo of cyclist courtesy of Mona Krayem

p. 173: Photo of cyclists courtesy of www.limbpower.com

p. 179: Photo of Armin Köhli courtesy of www.tourdarmin.ch

p. 182: Two photos courtesy of Mirsad Tokić

p. 186-188: Three photos courtesy of www.markomrod.com

p. 189: Cartoon courtesy of Martin Proctor

p. 192: Rubbish on footpath Path no 500 passes behind a caravan site, Blackmore Park, 2009 courtesy of Bob Embleton, geograph.org.uk and https://commons. wikimedia.org/wiki/File:Rubbish_on_footpath_-_ geograph.org.uk_-_1153627.jpg

p. 192: Photo of Koeln Lindenthal Park, 2005, courtesy of Pixie, originally on he.wikipedia.org/wiki/%D7% A7%D7%95%D7%91%D7%A5:Koeln_Lindenthal_ Park.jpg

p. 193: žuolyno parkas Žaliakalnyje, Kaunas, 2006 courtesy of Creative originally found at lt.wikipedia. org/wiki/Vaizdas:Azuolynas_2006_06_18.jpg

p. 193: Photo of Parque Brasil en la 39 con Cra 17. Barrio La Magdalena de la localidad de Teusaquillo. Bogotá 2010, courtesy of Pedro Felipe https:// commons.wikimedia.org/wiki/File:BOG_Parque_ Brasil.JPG

p. 197: Two photos of navigation instruments courtesy of www.garmin.com

p. 201: Photo of Armin Köhli courtesy of www.tourdarmin.ch

p. 202: Photo of hand cyclist in snow courtesy of www.handcycling.org.uk and Andrew Chamings

p. 202: Photo of Armin Köhli courtesy of www.tourdarmin.ch

p. 205: Two photos courtesy of www.bikeit.co.uk

p. 210: Photo of Dan Sheret courtesy of himself

p. 211-213: Three photos of Kiera Roche courtesy of www.limbpower.com

p. 216: Photo of Shafiqulla Samim courtesy of www.aabraar.org.af

p. 220: Photo of cyclists courtesy of www.limbpower.com

p. 221: Photo of product courtesy of www.bulkpowders.co.uk

p. 222: Photo of product courtesy of www.karrimor.com

p. 228: 2015 Dietary Reference Intakes for Koreans courtesy of www.kns.or.kr

p. 230: Photo of product courtesy of www.build-muscle-101.com

p. 239 Courtesy of Motion Control

p. 241: Photo of recipe – courtesy of Michael Caines www.michaelcaines.com

p. 242: Photo of recipe – courtesy of Michael Caines www.michaelcaines.com

p. 244/5: Two photos of Wisi Zgraggen – courtesy of Esther Banz www.velojournal.ch

p. 247: Photo of Srdjan Jeremic courtesy of www.ipm-lsi.org

p. 255: Photo of Alfred Kaiblinger courtesy of www.1a1b1r.com

p. 260-262: Three photos of Gemma Trotter courtesy of herself

p. 262: Photo of personal trainer monitoring movement during a fitball exercise courtesy of www.localfitness. com.au and https://commons.wikimedia.org/wiki/File:Personal_trainer_monitoring_a_client%27s_movement_during_a_fitball_exercise.JPG

p. 269: Photo of Alfred Kaiblinger courtesy of www.1a1b1r.com

p. 276: Photos of products courtesy of Halfords www.halfords.co.uk

p. 278-282: Photos of bike maintenance courtesy of Mirsad Tokić

p. 284: Photo of Shafiqulla Samim courtesy of www.aabraar.org.af

p. 285: Two photos of bike maintenance courtesy of Mirsad Tokić

p. 286: Photo of Habib Jan courtesy of www.aabraar.org.af

p. 287/8: Two photos of bike maintenance courtesy of Mirsad Tokić

p. 288: Photo of Shafiqulla Samim courtesy of www.aabraar.org.af

p. 292: Photo of tent and prosthetic legs courtesy of www.tourdarmin.ch

p. 314: Photo of cyclist courtesy of Siniša Mazulović

p. 316: Photo of Armin Köhli courtesy of www.stopmines.ch

p. 317: Photo of Arnold Boldt courtesy of Phil MacCullum, Canadian Paralympic Committee www.paralympic.ca

p. 319: Photo of Gemma Trotter courtesy of herself

p. 325: Photo of Armin Köhli courtesy of www.tourdarmin.ch

p. 327/8: Photo of hand cyclists courtesy of www.handcycling.org.uk and Andrew Chamings

p. 329-331: Three photos of mountain bikers courtesy of Victor Walther www.mtb-amputee.com

p. 333: Photo of Kurt Yaeger during a stunt courtesy of www.kurtyaeger.com

p. 335: Photo of Gemma Trotter courtesy of herself

p. 341/3: Two photos of racing courtesy of Yuko Sato www.uci.ch

p. 343: Photo of Dory Selinger courtesy of www.doryselinger.com

p. 344: Photo of Rajesh Durbal courtesy of www.rajeshdurbal.com

p. 345: Two photos of racing courtesy of Yuko Sato www.uci.ch

p. 352: Photo of Armin Köhli courtesy of www.tourdarmin.ch

p. 364: Photo of Paul Jesson courtesy of Edmund Hood and Richard Pestas of www.pezcyclingnews.com

p. 370: Courtesy of Motion Control